RECLAIMING ADAT

Khoo Gaik Cheng

RECLAIMING ADAT

Contemporary Malaysian Film and Literature

UBC Press · Vancouver · Toronto

SINGAPORE

15 14 13 12 11 10 09 08 07 06 5 4 3 2 1

Printed in Canada on ancient-forest-free paper (100% post-consumer recycled) that is processed chlorine- and acid-free, with vegetable-based inks.

Library and Archives Canada Cataloguing in Publication Data

Khoo, Gaik Cheng, 1969-
Reclaiming Adat : contemporary Malaysian film and literature / Khoo Gaik Cheng.

Includes bibliographical references and index.
ISBN-13: 978-0-7748-1172-9 (bound); 978-0-7748-1173-6 (pbk.)
ISBN-10: 0-7748-1172-2 (bound); 0-7748-1173-0 (pbk.)

1. Motion pictures – Malaysia – History. 2. Malaysian literature (English) – History and criticism. 3. Adat law – Malaysia. 4. Malaysia – Civilization – 20th century. 5. Malaysia – Social life and customs – 20th century. 6. Islam and state – Malaysia. I. Title.

DS594.K56 2005 306'.09595 C2005-905682-7

Canada

UBC Press gratefully acknowledges the financial support for our publishing program of the Government of Canada through the Book Publishing Industry Development Program (BPIDP), and of the Canada Council for the Arts and the British Columbia Arts Council.

This book has been published with the help of a grant from the Canadian Federation for the Humanities and Social Sciences, through the Aid to Scholarly Publications Programme, using funds provided by the Social Sciences and Humanities Research Council of Canada.

UBC Press
The University of British Columbia
2029 West Mall
Vancouver, BC V6T 1Z2
604-822-5959 / Fax: 604-822-6083
www.ubcpress.ca

Published in Singapore for distribution in Asia, Australia, and New Zealand by:

Singapore University Press
NUS Publishing
AS3-01-02, 3 Arts Link
Singapore 117569
Fax: (65) 6774-0652
E-mail: nusbooks@nus.edu.sg
Website: http://www.nus.edu.sg/npu

ISBN 9971-69-338-0

Contents

Illustrations

Acknowledgments

I thank the Asia Research Institute for making it possible for me to produce this book. Also crucial to the enterprise is the Ford grant that I received from the Northwest Regional Consortium for Southeast Asian Studies, which enabled me to carry out field research in 1998. My utmost gratitude goes to Mr. Poh Sim Gark, Ms. Chew Siew Bee, and family for their kind generosity and hospitality as hosts during my numerous research trips to Kuala Lumpur. This book would also not be complete without the goodwill, friendliness, warmth, and support of my fellow Malaysians: academics at Universiti Sains Malaysia, Universiti Kebangsaan Malaysia, and University of Malaya who generously shared their knowledge and interests with me; Nor Faridah Manaf, who took me under her wing; Pak Hamzahat FINAS for his experience and enthusiasm about film; Gordon Gray and Amir Muhammad for stimulating e-mail discussions on Malay cinema; Hassan Muthalib, Noritah Omar, and Washima Chedan for their friendship and support; and the numerous other Malaysian writers and filmmakers I have had the good fortune of meeting.

In Singapore, I thank colleagues who had chapters thrust at them and kindly provided feedback, discussion, and friendship: Goh Beng Lan, Eric Thompson, Matilda Gabrielpillai, David Lim, Daniel Goh, Dayaneetha De Silva, and Vatthana Pholsena. Special thanks go to my UBC committee members: Sneja Gunew, Margery Fee, Jacqueline Levitin, and Tineke Hellwig; to my external examiner Maila Stivens for taking my work seriously; and to my parents and sisters for their unfailing support and love.

Early versions of some material from this book have been published as essays in *Risking Malaysia* (ed. Maznah Mohamad and Wong Soak Koon, 2001), *Women Filmmakers: Refocusing* (ed. Judith Plessis, Jacqueline Levitin, and Valerie Raoul, 2003), *West Coast Line* journal (2000), and *Asian Media Studies,* ed. Chua Siew Keng and John Nguyet Erni (Blackwell Publishing, 2004).

Abbreviations

ABIM	Angkatan Belia Islam Malaysia, Malaysian Muslim Youth organization, originally headed by Anwar Ibrahim
BA	Barisan Alternatif, Alternative Coalition, opposition coalition
BM	Bahasa Malaysia, or Malay as the national official language
BN	Barisan Nasional, the National Front
bumiputera	Sanskrit for "sons of the soil," a political status implying autochthonous rights for Malays and other "indigenous" peoples of Malaysia
dakwah	Muslim missionary or proselytizing movement
DBP	Dewan Bahasa dan Pustaka, National Language and Literature Board
ISA	Internal Security Act
MSC	Multimedia Super Corridor
NDP	National Development Plan (1990-2000)
NEP	National Economic Policy (1971-90)
PAS	Parti Islam SeMalaysia or the Pan Malaysian Islamic Party (opposition party)
Sejarah Melayu	The Malay Annals
SIS	Sisters in Islam
UMNO	United Malays National Organisation

RECLAIMING ADAT

1

Reclaiming Adat

The Malaysian cultural and literary scene during the heady economic boom of the early to mid-1990s held much promise for a graduate student of postcolonial literature and film returning from Vancouver, Canada. The overall economic well-being of the country supported confidence in the publishing sector. Small local English-language presses like Skoob Books (particularly its Pacifica series) and Rhino Press (the Black and White series) had started up, and together with Times Books International, Heinemann Asia Press, and other smaller presses, they began to publish the works of established Malaysian writers such as K.S. Maniam and Shirley Lim as well as works by emerging writers like Dina Zaman and Karim Raslan. Moreover, self-financed publications like Rehman Rashid's *A Malaysian Journey* or Che Husna Azhari's *The Rambutan Orchard* became available on the shelves of local commercial and university bookstores. As a sometime writer of local fiction myself, I was keen to find out what other Malaysians were writing about. What was it about being Malaysian in the 1980s and 1990s that preoccupied middle-class writers and filmmakers? What were the issues they chose and what was at stake? How do these writers and filmmakers speak through their work and how does their work speak about them as part of a larger epistemological framework? Having been away for studies abroad since 1990, I was hoping to catch up and learn something about Malaysian politics and culture. I was not disappointed. More middle-class Malaysians were writing in English by the 1990s, and these included the bumigeois or new Malay middle class. The genres included fiction, poetry, plays, and compilations of cultural essays culled from newspaper columns and journalistic writing. In this book I have chosen to focus predominantly on these non-canonical writers.

Things were also exciting in the Malaysian film industry. Newspapers heralded a new wave of filmmakers who were suddenly able to attract audiences back to the cinemas, despite the video boom of the previous decade. Not only were some of the films box-office hits, they also had something to say about Malay identity and culture, speaking with artistic integrity within a largely commercial medium. In my focus on some of the works from this wave of filmmakers, which include Shuhaimi Baba, U-Wei Haji Saari, Adman Salleh, and Erma Fatima, I began to notice similar themes in the works of writers like Karim Raslan, Dina Zaman, and Salleh Ben Joned.

Socio-economic forces, state-initiated, and the cultural development of the NEP years (National Economic Policy 1971-90) had produced a burgeoning discourse about subjectivity among the children of the NEP themselves: what is it like for urban Malay women and men to be both modern and Muslim (e.g., Anwar Ibrahim 1996; Sloane 1999)? More crucially, what did it mean to be "Malay" as it is defined in the constitution, via language, *adat*/custom, and the practice of Islam? How is Malayness performed? Some cultural producers and intellectuals went further in their inquiry into identity by actually engaging with Prime Minister Mahathir Mohamad's Vision 2020 speech, which raised the question of what it meant to be a "bangsa Malaysia" rather than a "bangsa Melayu."[1] Because the word *bangsa* conflates meanings like "race" and "nationality," the most optimistic reading of "bangsa Malaysia" suggests a Malaysian race, a nation able to imagine itself as a hybrid whole rather than one permeated by ethnic divisions. Many people chose to read this as moving beyond Malay ethnic nationalism, a concept alienated from UMNO (United Malays National Organization, the main political party) mentality and its raison d'être since its formation in 1946. Re-evaluating the goals and weaknesses of the NEP, these writers/filmmakers struggled with questions about how modernity in its myriad forms had an impact on readings of Islam and its concatenations with adat which, in turn, play out in gender and gender relationships.

Based on the 1990s films and literature analyzed here, I make the case that modernity facilitates the conscious and unconscious recuperation of adat, usually through a focus on sexuality or a return to forms of the archaic such as magic or traditional healing. This reclamation of adat is simultaneously a postcolonial or anti-imperialist strategy and a subversion of more restrictive notions of Islamic discourse that emerged since the 1980s. Middle-class Malay cultural producers struggle to reconcile their adat with resurgent forms of

Islam and to enunciate their place and identity in global modernity, whether in literature or cinema. They discuss adat, try to reclaim, reconstruct, and reconstitute it in its various forms. This is evident in the popular retelling of the myth of Hang Tuah and Hang Jebat, and in the reconceptualization of Jebat's sensuality. Adat also appears in the discourse and rituals around female sexuality (the straddled rice or *nasi kangkang*) and bawdy language used by Salleh Ben Joned, Dina Zaman, Karim Raslan, and illustrated in U-Wei and Adman Salleh's films. Then there are the rather touristy references to adat that appear in Shuhaimi Baba's films as mysticism, magical healing, and music and dance forms, which are now regarded as somehow unIslamic. Adat is also manifest in the authentic male characters who embody it in their *silat* rituals and knowledge or by their running amok, and who arm themselves with their phallic traditional weapons, ever ready to defend race and nation (*bangsa dan negara*) in the face of great socio-cultural upheaval, rendered so by modernity and changing gender configurations.

ADAT AND ISLAM

Adat and Islam are integral to Malay identity and exist in a complementary fashion with each other (Wazir 1992; Sharifah Zaleha 2000). Originally an Arab word, adat is used to describe the local customs or customary laws that existed before the advent of Islam. It acts like the "residue" of all customs that are considered Malay but not Islamic (Nagata 1986, 42). Among such customs are bilateralism in gender relations, an openness about sexuality and sensuality, belief in magical healing, and mysticism. Many aspects of Malay adat are regarded as traditionally tolerant (though still patriarchal) and more open to sensual or sexual matters than resurgent Islam is – this feature of adat is also aligned with secularism, a product of modernization. Because adat encourages women's power and autonomy, it continues to function in Malaysia as "a system of 'checks and balances' between incompatible or conflicting ideological systems [resurgent Islam and Westernization] which culturally determine the distribution of power and responsibility between the sexes" (Wazir 1992, 230). While anthropologists study state-led Islam and how it serves to further a patriarchal agenda that contravenes the more egalitarian practices and beliefs of adat, one should be aware that adat in itself delineates gendered spaces (see Peletz 1995). What needs to be challenged is the notion that adat and modernity are mutually exclusive and represent opposing spheres of East versus West. While Wazir Jahan Karim may argue that there are differences between adat and Islam, one advocating gender bilaterality and the other emphasizing its patriarchal aspects as promulgated by state discourse, I argue that, in the modern constructions of culture by Malaysian writers and filmmakers, adat is not impermeable to patriarchal interpretations; in fact, patriarchy responds through various channels: through the secular discourse of nationalism and the nation-state, through the conservative interpretations of Islam promulgated by PAS (Pan Malaysian Islamic Party, the Islamic opposition party), certain fringe *dakwah* (Muslim proselytizing) groups such as Darul Arqam and Jemaah Tabligh, and perhaps more subtly, through the more moderate *dakwah* group ABIM populated by Malay urban professionals.

While the general tendency is to perceive adat and Islam as binary yet complementary forces in some situations, it becomes difficult to tell them apart since Islam has become such an integral part of Malay adat and vice versa.[2] The types of Islam to have made an impact on Malaysia also alter the status of adat in Malay society. At their cultural historical base, the indigenous peoples of the Malay archipelago were animists, who believed that the universe was populated by spirits (*jinn, roh, hantu*) and that all animate and inanimate objects held a spiritual essence (*semangat*). Later, when Hinduism-Buddhism came to the region, it was adapted to fit with this existing system of beliefs. At the same time, elements of Hindu culture such as the *Ramayana* and *Mahabharata* were retained through oral transmission and performative art forms like *wayang kulit* (shadow puppetry). In 1414, Megat Iskandar Shah, the son of the founder of the Malay empire Melaka (1400-1511), became the first Malay ruler to convert to Islam thereby ensuring, among other things, Melaka's viability as a trading centre. Sufi Islamic mystical teachings (brought by Indian Muslims and/or religious teachers from Aceh) helped cement existing beliefs with Islamic monotheism and subsequently produced a syncretic Islamic tradition. Thus, adat, as symbolized by the ruler, feudal society, the *bomoh* (traditional healer) and life-cycle rituals, was retained and regarded as a living tradition that complemented Islam (Sharifah Zaleha 2000, 23).

But beginning in the late nineteenth century, religious scholars who relied on scripture began to question the compatibility of certain adat practices and beliefs with Islamic teachings. As a result of "scripturalist Islam" (ibid.), which relied on Wahabbi reform ideas and *syariah*-mindedness, Malays were to have the correct religious focus, view Islam as a total way of life, and regard piety and salvation as the outcome of lawful and ritually correct behaviour, rather than blind obedience to adat (ibid., 30). Unlike syncretic Islam, which embraced adat without reservations, scripturalist Islam was more ambivalent towards adat and ranked it lower. Adat was relegated to the realm of the local, mundane, tangible, and private while Islam reflected humankind's more abstract preoccupation with salvation, the hereafter, unity, and justice (ibid.; Nagata 1986).

The dynamics between scripturalist Islam and syncretic Islam regarding adat persisted into 1990s Malaysia and became manifest in the contest for Malay votes between the more orthodox PAS (Pan Islamic Malaysian Party) and the modern, more liberal UMNO. Such tension is played out in literary and cinematic discourse, for example, in Erma Fatima's film *Perempuan Melayu Terakhir* (The Last Malay Woman) where the female protagonist Mustika is caught between having to choose between her religious fundamentalist fiancé, Engku Leh, and a Westernized Malay theatre director, Haikal/John, who is newly returned from London. This film captures the crux of my argument about the gendered representation of adat (essentialized as "the last Malay woman," Mustika) that is caught between Westernized modernity and resurgent Islam (Figures 1, 2, 3).

I'm interested in a contemporary version of scripturalist Islam for its effects on Malaysian writers and filmmakers. This newer wave of radical Islam culminated in the fall of the Shah of Iran in 1979. It influenced Malay

Figure 1 Mustika (Vanida Imran) personifies adat as a makyong dancer, from *Perempuan Melayu Terakhir* (The Last Malay Woman), with permission from Grand Brilliance, Sdn Bhd.

students who had been sent abroad to study under the auspices of the NEP; they experienced the call of Muslim solidarity while overseas and returned to proselytize (Nagata 1997, 83-84). This *dakwah* or proselytizing movement began as early as 1969 when, in the aftermath of the race riots, the National Association of Muslim Students set up a youth organization named Angkatan Belia Islam Malaysia (ABIM), headed by a young Anwar Ibrahim (Shamsul 1995, 113). From the mid-1970s until 1990, radicalized students began to spread their ideas in universities, educational retreats, and even to villages (Nagata 1986). Thus the UMNO government, fearful of the presence of PAS in the coalition government and external pressure emerging from the revivalist movement, increased its involvement in Islamic affairs. This included the establishment of the Islamic Research Centre in 1971 and, in 1974, the Institute of Islamic Mission and Training; the co-opting of Anwar Ibrahim into UMNO (1982); setting up of the International Islamic University (1983), Islamic banking systems, etc. (Syed Ahmad 2002; Nagata 1997; Hussin 1990, 134). During the 1990s, the federal government adopted a liberal Muslim

Figure 2 Mustika and her religious fundamentalist fiancé, Engku Leh, from *Perempuan Melayu Terakhir* (The Last Malay Woman), with permission from Grand Brilliance, Sdn Bhd.

position to reassure non-Muslim Malaysians and non-Malaysians that its Islamic policies were not a barrier to trade and investment. Moreover, the state, through the Institute of Islamic Understanding (IKIM), tried to reach out to leaders of other faiths to reassure them of their common values, doubtless in the spirit and rhetoric of the so-called Asian values discourse that was synonymous then with the burgeoning economy of the Asian tigers (Nagata 1997).

By the late 1980s and into the 1990s, the majority of female Muslim students in secondary schools and universities were wearing the *tudung* (head scarf). Unsurprisingly, the most noticeable elements of the new Islam in the 1990s were scripturalist and Arabic-influenced as opposed to the more syncretic indigenous Islam that had co-existed with and even co-opted other spiritual practices in Malaysia for centuries. In fact, the Malaysian government succeeded so well in selling Malaysia as a Muslim tourist location to Saudi nationals that, during the 1990s boom, *jellaba*-clad tourists began to be a visible part of the urban Malaysian landscape. (One such Arabic-speaking

Figure 3 Mustika's fantasy of being seduced by the westernized Haikal, from *Perempuan Melayu Terakhir* (The Last Malay Woman), with permission from Grand Brilliance, Sdn Bhd.

tourist appears in Amir Muhammad's irreverent English-language film, *Lips to Lips,* telling a stranger in a bookstore in Arabic that her personal philosophy has always been "to screw anything that moves" and that in fact she was late for a threesome right then! At least, this was what she said according to its English subtitles.)

If modernity, reflexive modernity, and tradition can be said to play out on the garbed bodies of Malay and Arab women, and the female body becomes the obligatory performance site of collective national-traditional identity (Yuval-Davis 1997, 45-46), the reclamation of adat by male filmmakers follows the same course. As a response perhaps to the pressure for Muslim women to cover up, male filmmakers portray the Malay woman wearing only a sarong around her midriff (*berkemban*), hearkening back to a pastoral image of Malay women more common in 1950s and 1960s Malay cinema (Khoo G.C. 2000). So an indigenous strategy like the reclamation of adat can still have a sexist or misogynist slant. After all, such recuperative efforts might be in danger of complicity with capitalist forces that only seem progressive because they are new or modern, as is the liberal atmosphere that encourages a more open discourse of sexuality.[3] In other words, in my concept of reclaiming adat I do not regard the adat that is sometimes nostalgically represented as a fixed, unchanging body of customs and beliefs. Instead, the process of reclamation put forward here also involves a degree of reconstructing, recreating, reconstituting, and recombining (Stivens 1996). Such "recuperation" allows room for fantasy (the unconscious processes at work) and imagination (the conscious processes at work) in the act of regaining or recovering one's health/strength or, in this case, culture. This recovery will inevitably affect the result of the modern representations of adat, which are as much a counter-response to the surrounding uneven forms of capitalist modernity as they are evoked from within such complex modernity. In this endeavour, there are obvious parallel perspectives to be drawn between the reconstitution of matriliny (*adat perpatih*) in Rembau (Stivens 1996), the "reinvention" of Malaysian Islam (Nagata 1997; Malhi 2003), and the reclamation of adat in the works of Malaysian writers and filmmakers in the 1990s.[4]

QUESTIONS OF MODERNITY

Much was written about the Malaysian discourse of modernity in the 1990s (Gomes 1994; Kahn and Loh 1992) – about its intersections with gender, Islam, Malay identity (Shaharuddin 1992), and politics, with the discourse of democracy and civil society, and even pop culture (Kahn 2003). But there is a need to bring these analyses into contact with 1990s literary and cinematic textual analysis.[5] When dealing with issues of modernity in Malaysia, it's useful to be armed with postmodern consciousness, especially Homi Bhabha's psychoanalytical and semiotic sense of the "belatedness" of modernity, its "time-lag" and disjunctures, and Habermas's idea of the counterdiscourse of modernity (Bhabha 1995; Habermas 1997).

In this book, I use the term *modernity* to indicate something more than modernization, to suggest the more dynamic and positive aspects of inhabiting the contemporary global world. Definitions of modernity range from that which is current or new to an equation with Westernization, reason, industrial development, rapid urbanization, the rise of individualism or individual freedoms, the idea of a civil society, materialism and consumer culture, and the latest manifestation of modernity – the development of information technology (IT).[6] On one hand, a modernity aligned with Western liberal notions of gender equality can serve to undermine or erode Islamic patriarchy, specifically when the welfare of female spouses comes under the laws of the secular nation-state instead of the Islamic *syariah* court, as with the controversial passing of the Malaysian Domestic Violence Act in 1994. But on the other hand, as Aihwa Ong has so clearly and consistently demonstrated in her work, late-twentieth-century modernity in the form of state and transnational capital also relies on patriarchal structures already in place in villages in order to recruit young Malay women into the industrial workforce where newer forms of gender hierarchy prevail (Ong 1987, 1990, 1995). A global modernity does not only imply a one-way effect – it is neither a benign Westernization nor a more malignant "Westoxification."

Historically, the Malay Peninsula's geographical location has made it the centre of trade and religious-cultural exchange between eastern and western Asia. Today, one has only to turn on Malaysian cable or local television in order to realize that popular cultural influences on Malaysian audiences come from multiple directions and locations: Taiwan, Hong Kong, the United States, Canada, Australia, Britain, India, Japan, Korea, Lebanon, Mexico, and Egypt, to name only a few. Hence, it would be inaccurate to equate modernity and globalization with homogeneous Westernization. For example, the mainstreaming of Islamic revivalism can be regarded as a modern phenomenon that began to influence Malaysian society only in the 1970s, suggesting that Islam participates in modernity as a globalizing force as well. (I discuss this in Chapter 5.)

One of the main threads of modernity is its connection to the nation. This link is often conveyed in phrases such as "the modern nation-state" and in the general belief that nationalism is a relatively new or modern phenomenon. For example, in postcolonial Malaysia under the leadership of Prime Minister Dr. Mahathir, the project of modernity is constructed as the way to fulfill certain nationalist ambitions. Mahathir's plan to transform Malaysia into a fully developed industrial nation by the year 2020 includes making Malaysia the technological "Multimedia Super Corridor" (MSC) of the region: fully armed with a large skilled labour force and supporting infrastructure, Malaysia hopes to attract foreign capital investment and computer technology. The MSC is just one of the many symbols of modernity and nationalism in Malaysia today. Others include the new Kuala Lumpur International Airport (KLIA), which boasts that it is the most modern in Asia, and of course, the Petronas or Kuala Lumpur Twin Towers, the world's tallest buildings at the time they were built.[7] Hosting the Commonwealth Games in September 1998 was another nation-building event, coming at a time when confidence in the capability of the government to boost the local economy was much needed.[8]

RACE/ETHNICITY, NATION, LANGUAGE, AND HISTORY

In *Imagined Communities,* one of the foundational texts on nationalism, Benedict Anderson suggests that the idea of the nation is formed in the minds of its citizens, who imagine an affinity with each other through reading the daily newspapers in the vernacular simultaneously and in different parts of the nation (1983). When he turns to the cultural roots of nationalism, however, it is only to refer to religious communities and dynastic lineages rather than ethnic homogeneity. More problematically, as the modal narrative of the imagined community, his espousal of a "simultaneity across homogeneous empty time" – this imagined connection that occurs among the readers of the nation – obscures the issue of race/nation, giving rise to the idea of race an "an archaic ahistorical moment outside the 'modernity' of the imagined community" (Bhabha 1995, 248-49). In other words, race, with its connotations of an inability to transcend primordial ties, is outmoded and out of place within the Andersonian concept of nationalism. It is this inability to recognise the importance of the ethnic origins of nationalism (Smith 1991) that makes racial difference and racism such a surprising anomaly to modern Western societies.

Bhabha, in focusing on contemporary metropolitan racism in the West, insists that "It is in that 'weld' of the colonial site as, contradictorily, both 'dynastic and national,' that the modernity of Western national society is confronted by its colonial double" (249). But, while the concept and discourse of multiculturalism did not get underway in Europe and the West until after the fall of European colonialisms (and American imperialism), which then included migration from former colonies to metropolitan centres, the postcolonial Malaysian nation was multi-ethnic at its very inception. The high influx of immigrants from China and India during the British colonial era meant that 40 percent of the post-independence populace was not indigenous Malays. Hence, ethnicity is integral to the construction of the nation, always present in the minds of all Malaysians and therefore, hardly "an archaic ahistorical moment" (1995, 248).[9]

That "race" is an inescapable category hinges on the one traumatic national point in Malaysian history: the race riots of May 13, 1969. Like the Malayan Union proposal in 1946, which allocated equal Malayan citizenship to all immigrants, May 13 galvanized Malay nationalist sentiments, resulting in the creation of *bumiputera* (literally "sons of the soil," *bumi* for short) under the aegis of the NEP to reassert Malay dominance and privilege over the Chinese, Indians, and other minorities in all arenas.[10] Economic parity was the key motivation behind the NEP for Malay nationalists. Prior to the NEP and during the colonial period, there had already been a general consensus among factions within the Malay nationalist movement that the three pillars of "Malayness" would constitute "bahasa, agama dan raja" (language/Malay, religion/Islam, and royalty/ sultan-chiefs; Shamsul 1999, 94). The ethnic chauvinist sentiments behind the NEP again narrowed the criteria for Malaysian nationalism to a specific homogeneous cultural identity: identifiably bumiputera, Muslim, and Malay speaking. While Shamsul correctly refers to "loyalty to the sultan" as being one of the traditional three pillars of Malayness enshrined in the Malaysian constitution, it was the least important for the Malays during the economic-driven climate of the 1980s and 1990s when feudal loyalties, while still present, were being challenged by modernity (in the form of economic progress and material desire), higher education (i.e., university students/graduates played a major role in street demonstrations protesting against the authoritarian Mahathir government), and the constitutional erosion of the rights of the monarchy in 1983-84 and 1993.[11] Generally, although another of the NEP's goals was to wipe out poverty across all ethnicities, this did not occur and the Tamils have become the most underprivileged non-bumi minority today (Jayasankaran 1995).[12] In short, any discussion of gender, modernity, and nationalism has to address the question of ethnicity.

During its implementation, the NEP catapulted the country into full-scale industrialization (for example, by introducing the manufacturing of semi-conductors) and vastly improved the economic status of the Malay or bumiputera compared with that of the Chinese. The term *bumiputera* generally refers to the Malays but it includes several other indigenous groups as well.[13] Urbanization and modernization had occurred under British rule during the late nineteenth and early twentieth centuries, but the majority of Malays remained peasants and fishermen located in the rural areas, far from the major towns whose economies were being monopolized by Chinese tradesmen. The NEP sought, once and for all, to throw off the colonial practice of divide and conquer by removing the identification of ethnicity with economic function for purposes of classification (i.e., Malay farmer and fisherman, Chinese middleman or tin miner, Indian rubber tapper). Recognizing that Malay socio-economic discontent and Chinese political and economic arrogance had led to the 1969 riots, the NEP aimed to alleviate the plight of the Malays by modernizing them. In the 1970s and '80s, many rural Malays migrated to the urban areas to seek jobs in the industrial sector. As a result of twenty years of modernization and pro-Malay economic policies under the NEP, a noticeable number of Malays with kampung (village) roots settled in urban and suburban areas and became part of the new urban Malay middle class. The rural/urban dichotomy still exists, though, and is evident in the settings of Malay films and in both English-language and Malay novels and other literary works (Hooker 2000; Khoo G.C. 2002b). For Malay writers and filmmakers alike, the portrayal or invocation of the pastoral is one way to assert their non-Western difference, a way of taking pride in their ethnic identity – which is tied to the village community, even though they now live in the suburbs, work in the city, participate in everyday urban modernity, and even regard themselves as modern Malays. (This is not to deny the fact that some non-Malays continue to inhabit rural areas and participate in agricultural production. For example, the majority of rubber estate workers continue to be Tamil Malaysians.) More importantly, the urban-rural dichotomy does not necessarily overshadow obvious class differences, nor does it fit smoothly into the "urban middle class versus rural poor" binary. For example, many new urban middle-class Malays originate from the rural middle class that includes local officials, schoolteachers, the police, and small entrepreneurs (Stivens 1998, 98; Embong 2001, 61).

In the field of literature, the NEP's move to homogenize and nationalize Malaysian culture meant elevating writings in Bahasa Malaysia to the level of "national" literature and relegating writings in other languages by Malaysians to "sectional literatures" or, at most, "Malaysian" literatures. The disjuncture here between "national" and "Malaysian" gives the lie to Anderson's notion of nationalism as a binding rationale that transcends ethnicity. Even though the motto "Art for Society" has come and gone with the 1950s Malay literary movement (*ASAS 50*), the government's wide support for Malay literature keenly demonstrates the linkage between politics and "national" literature. Government support for Malay writing comes in the form of state- and federal-level literary competitions organized by the Language and Literature Board (Dewan Bahasa Dan Pustaka or DBP), a body activated during the early 1970s as a consequence of the NEP.[14] This agency publishes award-winning Malay literature as well as monthly literary and cultural journals that provide an avenue for creative expression. Fictional writing in English, however, is left to the private sector (corporations, banks) to support in the form of organized competitions.[15]

In the post-NEP 1990s (a similar plan known as the National Development Policy or NDP has replaced the NEP since 1991), class and language use have become noticeable identity markers as the Malay literati complains that the Malay middle-class and elites are more at home speaking English than Bahasa Malaysia (BM). Meanwhile, BM is reduced to being the language of bureaucracy (Mandal 1998). Malaysian historian Sumit Mandal argues that, while state policy advocates and encourages the use of Malay as the official language, political leaders send their children abroad to be educated in English. He claims that the use of English has never really faded out among the political elite, who even publish their books in English.[16] Thus we should not underestimate the unofficial importance and influence of English in Malaysia (ibid.). English continues to perform the role that the state needs it to perform: it gives the impression that Malaysia is a modern, progressive, and liberal nation that is part of the globalized world. In fact, in recognition of English as the language of global trade, English began to be used as the medium of instruction for certain subjects in the local universities in the early 1990s. In 1996, new laws allowed English to be the medium of instruction in private tertiary institutions (Loh 2002, 29). And since 2003, mathematics and science education is conducted in English.

For Malaysians writing in English, identity becomes more fluid. They can choose to identify themselves with others outside the nation who write in English and become "Commonwealth" or "Third World" writers, or, within the nation, they can identify with Malaysians of all ethnicities whose daily discourse may be conducted mostly or partly in English. Yet because this middle class makes up a minority of the total population, and the state persists in asserting what Bhabha terms "the pedagogical" for purposes of consolidating and gaining power, these writers continue to struggle with their marginalization, engaging directly or indirectly with the hegemonic, whether it is on issues of national policy, language, culture, or religion.

SCOPE OF THE BOOK

Reclaiming Adat is an interdisciplinary study that brings postcolonial, gender, psychoanalytical, and anthropological/sociological perspectives to bear on contemporary Malaysian writing and film. The work of feminist anthropologists such as Aihwa Ong, Maila Stivens, Wazir Jahan Karim, Norani

Othman, Sharifah Zaleha, and even Patricia Sloane in studying the position of women in Malaysian Islam and, in particular, how women fit into the national agenda of contemporary modernity, has informed my analysis. Of foremost importance is the collection of essays on Malaysia entitled *Fragmented Vision: Culture and Politics in Contemporary Malaysia* (Kahn and Loh 1992) whose premise is that Malaysian socio-political and artistic culture is fragmented along ethnic, class, and religious lines. The essays in the collection contribute a diversity of views, though none address gender issues specifically.

While my involvement began first with Malaysian postcolonial literature in English, my goal here is more narrowly focused on presenting a postcolonial gender critique of works by a few bumigeois writers writing in English.[17] I will deal primarily with English-language writing and Malay-language films while referring to a few works written in Malay.[18] The following chapters examine the ways some writers and filmmakers have found to subvert state-constructed ideological positions for women within the nation and to reclaim agency. The cracks that have appeared within the nation (in Islam and within UMNO, the main Malay-dominated political party) have and will ultimately provide routes for escaping state ideology and the dominant discourse.

Less focus has been given to the academic study of Malaysian cinema. A few books about its general history have been published, some in more detail than others (Baharudin 1983; Naim 1995; Hatta 1997; Hamzah 1997; Van der Heide 2002), as well as articles (Lent 1990; Fuziah Kartini and Raja Ahmad 1995) and dissertations (Kueh 1997; Gray 2002). In the new millennium, several articles emerged to offer a more sociological perspective of Malaysian cinema and Malay identity (Hassan and Wong 2002; Khoo G.C. 2002a, 2002b; Zawawi 2003). And more academic work on Malay cinema of the 1950s and '60s is emerging. (I will examine Hatta's and Hamzah's books in more depth in Chapter 4.) Van der Heide's book, *Malaysian Cinema, Asian Film,* is problematic because, although his attempt to place Malaysian films within the rubric of other global influences is laudable, the book deals only very superficially with Malay culture and identity. In fact, Van der Heide's reading of older and more contemporary Malay films gives the impression that Malay cinema might as well be Hindu cinema. In that sense, the book fails to marry film studies with an in-depth understanding of Malaysian culture and politics of identity.

My own reading of the literature and films is deeply political insofar as I regard the study of material culture as embedded within larger conscious and unconscious ideological structures and processes. To teach and study postcolonial theory in Malaysian literature departments requires more than just talking back to the West; it requires moving away from the safe strategy of anticolonialist discourse (which rings all too familiar in Mahathir's speeches) to deconstructing the racism inherent in ethnic nationalist texts. Frederic Jameson's claim that all Third World literatures are national allegories, while totalizing, nevertheless applies to the works I have selected in both literature and cinema.[19] Writers like Rehman Rashid explore the personal meanings and significance of state policies for individuals, and 1990s nostalgic or period films like *Sayang Salmah,* which purportedly focuses on the relationship between two brothers, can be read as an allegory of contemporary Malay politics. Aligned with this notion, Malaysian cinema can be defined as the Cinema of Denial, implying a larger politics of the symbolic order (what Renata Salecl in *The Spoils of Freedom* [1994] calls the Lacanian big Other) at work.

In Lacanian psychoanalysis, the symbolic order or the big Other is predominantly language, and secondarily, the whole social network of laws, ideologies, and linguistic communication that socializes individuals. In the political context I'm describing, the social symbolic order would refer to living in Malaysia under policies put into place since Mahathir came to power, as well as relying on the very language that conveys and supports the fantasy structure meant to neutralize and incorporate the impossible trauma of May 13, 1969. If a strain of Lacanian psychoanalysis runs through the book in discussions of the subject in the nation, or producers of culture who are living and working within the structures of hegemonic ideology, it is because psychoanalytical theory helps us to understand inconsistencies in human behaviour. I am not the first to apply particular Lacanian or Žižekian concepts to an analysis of the modern Singaporean and Malaysian national contexts (see Gabrielpillai 1997; Lim 2005; Yao 2000).[20] Set in the socio-historical framework of culture at large, the theory of repression can at least account for the ways we deal with national traumas, whether in the East, West, or in Eastern Europe (Salecl 1994).[21] Cultural products from the Malaysian middle class demonstrate an ironic awareness of and engagement with such repressions, implying simultaneous resistance and limited agency. The critical acts of subversion can be read in Lacanian terms as overt expressions of disbelief in the big Other, in the authorities. In fact, writers employ forms and genres that support and reflect such cynicism. One of the most blatant expressions of cynicism that displays the oblique ways wherein the big Other can be questioned and critiqued is the reliance on modernist genres and philosophies such as absurdism and existentialism in the reconstructions of the Hang Tuah/Hang Jebat conflict.

If this discussion focuses mainly on the thoughts, opinions, and psyches of the Malaysian middle class, it is because this class has the greatest potential to fulfill the Malaysian dream of a real multicultural society by overcoming ethnic barriers. Members of the middle class are creating a civil society through their involvement in non-governmental organizations that work on issues of human rights, feminism, workers' rights, heritage conservation, and the environment. When former deputy prime minister Anwar Ibrahim was arrested under the Internal Security Act and beaten while in custody in late 1998, these activist groups and common people proved their power as a broad-ranging class by gathering in the streets to voice their protest about the injustice towards Anwar.[22] Those who took to peaceful (albeit illegal) street marches and demonstrations were not just Malays, and ethnic and multi-ethnic opposition groups rallied to Anwar's calls for reformation. As for the artistic and discursive ways of reflecting a multi-ethnic national identity, many would agree that there is more hope of achieving this in English-language writing and the theatre arts than in Malay cinema.[23]

Because Chapters 2 and 3 deal with the very modern discourse of national loyalty and national identity, they inevitably touch on Malay classical myth – the story of Hang Tuah and Hang Jebat. I begin with the Hang Tuah/Hang Jebat debate to situate the Malay myth as a base for the linkages between adat, Islam, and Malaysian modernity. Benedict Anderson's and Partha Chatterjee's theories of nationalism, especially Chatterjee's model of anticolonial nationalism that combines the material and spiritual elements under difference, can explain how a feudal hero such as Hang Tuah can figure as a national hero in postcolonial Malaysia. While examining the changing attitudes towards nationalism or the political leadership, one recognizes that the Hang Tuah/Hang Jebat myth has been a constant discourse for and by men among men. So hoping to provide the much-missed, much-needed dimension and expression of Malay nationalism through the female voice, I include and discuss Fatimah Busu's short story, "Al-Isra," together with the male versions.[24] Fatimah Busu brings a philosophical modernist dimension that is tinged with Islamic faith and Camusian existentialism to the legend. To complicate things even further, her short story lends itself to a reading of homosocial and homoerotic relations between the king and his subordinates, Hang Tuah and Hang Jebat, nudging the critical reader in the direction of Eve Kosofsky Sedgewick's theory of homosocial desire but also reworking the theory in the Malay context. In examining the many contemporary reinscriptions of the Tuah-Jebat question, Chapter 2 argues that modern Malaysian nationalism in its imaginary schema has not changed significantly since feudal times, and the presence of parliamentary elections and a constitutional monarchy has not crushed the feudal notion of "followership."

Chapter 3 explores nationalism in Malaysian writings. Using Bhabha's theory of the performative versus the pedagogical, I demonstrate the complexity, if not the paradox, of talking about "a Malaysian national literature." The works and self-representations of four English-educated bumiputera male writers – Salleh Ben Joned, Rehman Rashid, Karim Raslan, and Amir Muhammad, who write in English and are liberal Muslims – defy and challenge the hegemonic pedagogical notions of the nation. However brave and frank these writers' critiques are, they're also anchored in a gendered position of privilege. Social pressure from adat, Islam, and patriarchy dictates that female challengers of the hegemonic employ less confrontational modes of discourse, thereby causing them to defend their actions in the rhetoric of postcoloniality as non-Western cultural difference. These very same women would assert that avoidance of conflict and confrontation defines Malay culture, and that therefore, one's directness may be regarded as unrefined or coarse behaviour (there's an analysis of "effective" feminisms in the film *Femina* in Chapter 6). This is not to say that there are no Malay women writers who write as boldly as Salleh Ben Joned. Marina Mahathir comes to mind for her strong feminist statements in the newspapers, except that her status as the daughter of the prime minister connotes another type of privilege.

Chapter 4 lays out the general background of Malaysian cinema, briefly tracing its history from the studio days of the 1950s right through the nationalization of Malay cinema in the 1970s until the 1990s. Malay film history accounts for the present state of its film industry where earnest filmmakers juggle commercial factors with artistic expression. They also have to be in line with state policies because all film scripts have to be approved by a government body, FINAS, and filmmakers are restricted in terms of subject matter by various government-decreed "sensitive" issues such as race, the special position of the Malays, and religion. Other more arbitrary forms of censorship are carried out by the censorship board, separate from FINAS. With this in mind, Chapter 4, called "Malay/sian Films: Cinema of Denial," critiques Malay film critic Hatta Azad Khan's theories about Malay cinema as national cinema and whether it can be considered Third Cinema. Hatta, like many critics writing about films from the developing world, refers to Teshome Gabriel's theory of Third Cinema, which relies on Fanon's three phases in the evolution of national culture. Gabriel's account has been critiqued by filmmaker Jacqueline Levitin for misrepresenting and obfuscating Argentinian film theorists and guerrilla filmmakers Fernando Solanas and Octavio Getino's original coinage of the term "Third Cinema," so I will turn directly to Fanon's three phases.[25] Fanon's background as a psychiatrist and his analysis of the native intellectual's conflicted psyche are actually more compatible with Salecl's theory. If Salecl applies Lacan's theory of the individual subject to culture at large, Gabriel and I are similarly applying Fanon's psychoanalytical theory of the individual native subject living in a colonial culture to the broader structures of post-independence/national culture or national cinema. The chapter also considers the current popular subjects treated by Malaysian filmmakers today: gender and sexuality, whether as incest, uncontrolled female desire, or homosexuality.

Chapter 5 explores secular visions of the modern Malay woman by filmmaker Shuhaimi Baba and writers Karim Raslan and Dina Zaman. As a contrast to their liberal perspectives, I briefly discuss conservative Malay-language poet laureate Shahnon Ahmad's works. This chapter broaches the issue of sexuality and adat. Theoretically, it begins by referring to current debates and ideas on women, nationalism, and modernity put forward by various feminists and sociologists, and then considers Maila Stivens's questions about polygamy, resurgent Islam, modernity, postmodernity, or neo-modernity with regards to the new Malay middle classes of the 1990s. There is a widespread misconception of what feminism is in Malaysian society. Many feel it is a Western import that is irrelevant for Malaysian society. Western feminists are often demonized and portrayed as aggressive, confrontational, morally loose, and responsible for social decay in the institution of the family and marriage (Lai 2002, 48). Writer and FINAS officer Hamzah Hussin, for instance, regards feminism as a militant movement that threatens to reverse the present gender power structure to women's advantage.[26] Such a limited notion of feminism can all too easily lead to the backlash against women that we see in the hypermasculinity of Malay films.

Chapter 6 looks at how modernity and its effects redefine constructs of ideal masculinity in Malay films, resulting in hypermasculine (i.e., violent) behaviour. Violence as visual spectacle is becoming very noticeable in Malay cinema because the success of foreign action films featuring Jean-Claude van Damme, Jet Li, and Jackie Chan has spurred local filmmakers to imitate these models of cinematic masculinity known as the "hard body" (Jeffords 1994). I posit four physical types of masculinity, including the "hard body" in contemporary Malay cinema, though I focus on the one I call "authentic masculinity." Arguing that male violence or hypermasculinity derives from the discursive authentic male's inability to cope with modern changes to gender roles and relationships, I claim that hypermasculinity is the overacting or highly dramatic performance of authentic masculinity in crisis, a disavowal of male inadequacy or lack in the face of male-depicted uncontrolled and uncontrollable feminine desires. In contrast to the excesses associated with feminine desires, male lack is typically constructed within a gendered framework as "feminine," "effeminate," or even "emasculated," and therefore has to be compensated via hypermasculine actions. The representations of women who display uncontrolled and uncontrollable feminine desires are also important, since these women pose such a colossal threat to the authentic male stereotype. They are women with active libidos who evoke the same kind of fear and ambivalence in male characters as they do in the collective imagination of male writers and filmmakers. In this chapter, reclaiming adat seems an ambivalent gesture. The fictional characters deploy hypermasculine practices of adat to stave off the perceived corrupting influences of modernity, exemplified by the uncontrollable woman's libidinal desires. Yet on the part of the filmmakers, modernity facilitates the recuperation of adat – the portrayal of the woman in a sarong (*perempuan berkemban*) – to counter resurgent Islam.

2

Malay Myth and Changing Attitudes towards Nationalism: The Hang Tuah/Hang Jebat Debate

> Perhaps the Malay political consciousness also recognizes something enduringly compelling in the idea of the rebel ... I am not, and never have been, "Malay" enough to fully understand the complexities of Malay heroism. A few years after the episode of which I'm writing now, the director of the Police Special Branch, while interviewing me for possible subversive tendencies, would pose me the conundrum: "Who do you think was right? Hang Tuah or Hang Jebat?" It was a question that seemed to strike to the very heart of matters; the true "Malay Dilemma."
>
> — REHMAN RASHID, *A Malaysian Journey,* 1993

National myths continue to hold a strong currency in Malaysian popular consciousness. Perhaps the most renowned among them involves Hang Tuah and Hang Jebat and the question of which is the greater hero. These two were warriors and childhood friends during the reign of Sultan Mansur Shah of Melaka in the fifteenth century. Their exploits, specifically Hang Tuah's, were recorded in the seventeenth and eighteenth centuries in the *Sejarah Melayu* (*The Malay Annals*) and *Hikayat Hang Tuah* (Epic of Hang Tuah), two semi-historical classical Malay literary texts that are seminal for encapsulating Malay identity. The central story in the *Hikayat Hang Tuah (HHT)* goes something like this: the sultan made Hang Tuah his *Laksamana* (admiral) after he proved his bravery by defeating a man who had run amok in the kingdom.[1] Hang Tuah's four childhood friends also served the king but Hang Tuah was his majesty's favourite.

However, due to court jealousy, Hang Tuah was accused of socializing with a palace courtesan, an act of high treason. Without investigating Hang Tuah's "crime," the king hastily ordered his execution, but the cautious *Bendahara* (prime minister) hid the admiral in a village instead of carrying out the king's orders. The sultan's unjust ruling provoked the anger and rebellion of Tuah's childhood friend, Hang Jebat, who ran amok and took over the palace after receiving Hang Tuah's magic *keris* (a Malay dagger with a ridged serpentine blade) – and symbolically, his position as the king's favourite. Hang Jebat refused to duel with his three childhood friends Hang Kasturi, Hang Lekir, and Hang Lekiu, whom the king sent to kill him. Moreover, no one was worthy of defeating him except Hang Tuah, for it had been predicted that Hang Jebat would die at the hands of his best friend. When the king discovered that Hang Tuah was still alive, he ordered him to kill the traitor, Hang Jebat, which Hang Tuah dutifully did.

The Tuah-Jebat conflict has been reinscribed in many ways. It captures the tension between loyalty to the state as represented by Hang Tuah and loyalty to friendship (*setiakawan*) as represented by Hang Jebat. These two characters symbolize the contrast between the feudal hero and the modern hero, and replicate the Muslim debate over the *hadith* (sayings and traditions of the Prophet) about blind loyalty (*taqlid*) and individual judgment (*ijtihad*).[2] Because Hang Tuah and Hang Jebat signify and reflect Malay concepts of politics and custom (adat) as well as Islamic debates about *taqlid* and *ijtihad,* it appears that adat and Islam may not be mutually exclusive or opposing categories. In fact, there is significant overlap between the two, and the same goes for adat and modernity. What may seem like "modern" ideas of individuality may already be embedded within adat, in the figure of the Malay rebel, Hang Jebat. (In fact, under the leadership of Prime Minister Mahathir Mohamad, who began the "Look East" policy in the early 1980s, the Tuah-Jebat dichotomy also projects "Asian values" of group rights versus Western individual rights.)[3] Finally, Hang Tuah and Hang Jebat may stand as opposites in the Malay psyche, representing the rational ego that is always in control and the emotional, sensual, excessive id.

The Hang Tuah/Hang Jebat antagonism resurfaced in real Malaysian politics in the late 1990s when the tension between Mahathir and the former deputy prime minister and heir apparent, Anwar Ibrahim, became an outright power struggle.[4] These men differ in personality and political vision. Mahathir is a shrewd, authoritarian leader known for his anti-imperialist rhetoric and ambitious nationalist projects. Anwar, a charismatic former student radical and leader of the Islamic Youth Movement (ABIM), which was popular in the 1970s and 1980s, was imprisoned in 1974 for his involvement during the farmers' revolt. Characterized as an intellectual and idealist, he appealed to the principles of social justice within Islam (as did his image as a staunch Muslim) and to Western liberal values of civil society and democracy as highlighted in his book, *The Asian Renaissance.* In contrast, Mahathir's Asian dictatorial leadership, along with his adoption of the discourse of "Asian values," associated him with the loyal courtier Hang Tuah, whereas Anwar, with his criticisms of Mahathir's patronage system, emerged as the wronged modern-day Jebat. Allegations of Anwar's being a national traitor (an agent selling secrets to the United States!) would further support this image of him as the Jebat who commits *durhaka* (treason).[5]

In late 1998, among the many "alternative" websites and internet news stories that suddenly appeared after Anwar's arrest, there was a domain named after Jebat. Internet discourse drawing parallels between Mahathir/Anwar and the Hang Tuah/Hang Jebat debate abounded. Many regarded Anwar as Jebat (Hang Nadim 1998; Tan C.K. 1998; Sabri 1998), and some as both Tuah and Jebat (Jihad Siber, n.d.). Those who did not believe that such connections could be made nevertheless felt compelled to join the discussion about the analogy (Mohd. Raman Daud n.d.). Anwar's case also spurred Ahmad Faiz to write a revisionist version, "Rethinking Jebat" (1998), and encouraged Malays to rethink Malaysia's postcolonial social contract while drawing parallels to its mythical feudal past (Hassan Karim 2000; Sabri 1998).

In terms of literary critical responses, Muhammad Haji Salleh charts Malay intellectuals' emulation of Hang Tuah and later Hang Jebat in his essays, "Central Values of the Malay Hero: Hang Tuah" and "The Traditional and Contemporary Malay Literary Hero" (1991). His central point is that for many modern Malays, Hang Jebat has become their real protector and defender because he exercised individual discretion and was critical of the corrupt practices in his society. Muhammad Haji Salleh posits Hang Tuah and Hang Jebat as classical Malay literary heroes who influence "committed young people, the writers and the intellectuals" (1991, 165). To carry further the parallel between Anwar and Hang Jebat: Anwar's sudden arrest under the draconian Internal Security Act (ISA), his beatings while in prison, and the general heavy-handed treatment he received from his "mentor" Mahathir mobilized Malaysians around issues of injustice and reform, especially university students, writers, and intellectuals. Such contemporary reinscriptions of the Tuah-Jebat dilemma in 1980s and 1990s discourse show that the dynamics of nationalism and betrayal between men have seeped into the popular unconscious, even though the actual plays about Tuah and Jebat were being staged less and less frequently. (To understand how the Tuah/Jebat debate has evolved, see Appendix A.)

My study considers the Hang Tuah/Hang Jebat discourse in non-fictional texts that deal with Malaysian culture and politics, texts such as Rehman Rashid's *A Malaysian Journey* (1993), Karim Raslan's essays in *Ceritalah* (1996a), Salleh Ben Joned's collection of essays *As I Please* (1994), and Kit Leee's review of Kee Thuan Chye's play, a political satire entitled *1984 Here and Now* (1987). In these texts, Hang Tuah and Hang Jebat represent intrinsic values such as loyalty and betrayal that are associated with Malay ethnicity and politics, as when Rehman Rashid was asked who the greater hero was by a police interrogator after he wrote a *New Straits Times* editorial that criticized the Malaysian government's mass arrests of the opposition in Operation Lallang, 1987; or when Kit Leee hailed Kee Thuan Chye as a Hang Jebat for criticizing self-censorship in Kee's Orwellian play, *1984 Here and Now*.[6] In fiction, two of the various works that feature Hang Jebat as the defender of truth are Usman Awang's 1961 play *Death of a Warrior, Jebat* (published 1992) Johan Jaafar's *Kotaku Oh Kotaku* (*My City Oh My City*) (1975, published in 1992). I include Karim Raslan's short story "Heroes" (1996b) because its Mahathirist ideology (pro-Hang Tuah in its conception of the modern Malay hero) reflects the yuppie psyche of the heady economic boom that preceded the currency crisis and the economic downturn in 1997. Its characters subscribe to the ideology that the trampling of some democratic rights is acceptable, even justifiable, as long as the national economy is thriving.

Particularly striking in the Hang Tuah and Hang Jebat debate is its predominantly masculinist character in public discourse. Its discussants are mostly male journalists, playwrights, filmmakers, and critics, though there are still women writers interested in the myth's two male heroes. Fatimah Busu's version, a short story entitled "Dark Night of the Soul," first published in 1985 and translated by Harry Aveling into English in 1991, is the only reconstruction by a woman writer, yet it is not mentioned by critics examining the various Tuah and Jebat narratives.[7] If Fatimah's version of the Tuah/Jebat debate has been excluded before by scholars such as Abdul Rahman Napiah (1994), it is only because its Arabic title, "Al-Isra," does not refer to Tuah or Jebat but instead points to Prophet Muhammad's night journey to Jerusalem. Another possible reason could be that these critics are interested in analyzing only plays and films rather than short stories that feature Hang Tuah or Hang Jebat. Fatimah Busu brings to her retelling her experience as a Malay woman who recognizes the limitations placed on women in a patriarchal system.

The national Islamic ideology constructs women as wives and mothers above all other roles, thereby restricting them from fulfilling larger functions in the public political realm. This is not to neglect the presence of a few women politicians but to explain that they are nevertheless appointed to positions considered closer to their traditional gender roles.[8] Indeed, the story of two male warriors battling over the question of personal or national loyalty leaves little room for any female characters to have substantial roles. In this regard, Fatimah Busu's story does not diverge from the original. However, she portrays this masculine public/national realm as fraught with internal problems of personal homosocial loyalty and homoerotic desire.

The relationships between the king and Hang Tuah, and between the king and Hang Jebat, are represented in symbolic ways that raise questions about power and homosocial and national relations. Thus, Fatimah Busu's text provides a strategic feminist intervention not by pointing out the exclusion of the gendered other (women) but by focusing instead on the categories of inclusion that bind the men together in the discourse of the nation. Fatimah Busu's short story also combines Albert Camus' essay, "The Myth of Sisyphus," with Malay myth, positing Hang Jebat as a martyr whose spirit is doomed to wander the land with a perpetually bleeding wound caused by Hang Tuah. Its eclectic weaving of sometimes contradictory philosophies (such as absurdism and Islam) and literary cultures resonates strongly with the complex condition that is Malaysian modernity. This is assuming that by "absurdism" one means an anti-religious philosophy that "conceive[s] the universe as possessing no inherent human truth, value, or meaning, and [that] represent[s] human life, as it moves from the nothingness whence it came toward the nothingness where it must end, as an existence which is both anguished and absurd" (Abrams 1988, 1).

In the many ways the Tuah-Jebat question has been reinscribed in contemporary cultural texts, modern Malaysian nationalism, in its imaginary schema, has not changed significantly since feudal times, even though we now have parliamentary elections and a constitutional monarchy. The example of Hang Tuah, or the notion of "followership" or loyalty towards the king, has merely been transferred to the ruling coalition, which has been in power since independence in 1957 (Kessler 1992, 147, 159; Chandra 1979, 144-45). A long history of feudalism, of loyalty to authority, has a far stronger grip on ideas about cultural identity and unity than does the more recent notion of nationalism that came in the wake of anticolonialism (Alatas 1972; Chandra 1979; Shaharuddin 1984). Hence, the period touting Hang Jebat as the greater hero followed shortly after independence with the publication of Kassim Ahmad's thesis in 1959 (which portrays Hang Jebat as an anti-feudal hero) only to peter out in the economic boom of the immediate post-NEP era. Evidence for Hang Tuah's hegemony as the more enduring hero would take into consideration the results of government policies such as the NEP (i.e., the consequent burgeoning Malay middle class) and in particular, the leadership style and vision of Prime Minister Mahathir. Fatimah Busu's rewriting of this masculinist national discourse can shed light on Malaysian nationalism as a practical form of nationalism, especially as theorized by Partha Chatterjee (1996).

Chatterjee refines Benedict Anderson's theory of imagined communities by assuming that anticolonial nationalism divides the world of social institutions and practices into the material and the spiritual domains (Chatterjee 1996, 217). He formulates this division to account for a more nuanced indigenous anticolonial nationalism that would not necessarily end up replicating the history of the modern state in Europe. Dividing the material and the spiritual is a way for "anti-colonial nationalism [to create] its own domain of sovereignty within colonial society well before it begins its political battle with the imperial power." This material domain is "the domain of the 'outside,' of the economy and of statecraft, of science and technology, a domain where the West had proved its superiority and the East had succumbed." But the spiritual, "an 'inner' domain bearing the 'essential' marks of cultural identity" is declared "sovereign territory" that refuses any colonial intervention (ibid., 217). Chatterjee submits that this sovereign domain, acting as cultural resistance to British colonialism in Bengal during the period of social reform, was already in place before the apparatus of the material domain, such as actual anticolonial nationalist politics, emerged.

In colonial Malaya, the spiritual domain included Islam and the Malay royalty as symbols of religion and culture, a domain where the British supposedly maintained a hands-off policy. Today, the Malay vision of modernity is reconfigured differently – here by Joel Kahn and Francis Loh from the so-called three pillars of Malay identity: Islam as the key to Malay identity; attachment to a leader or patriarch; and/or a tradition of egalitarianism and democracy (Kahn and Loh 1992, 5-6).[9] According to these views, Islam would be at odds with "attachment to a leader" as it is represented in the Tuah-Jebat conflict in Fatimah Busu's short story where the conflict is between loyalty to Allah and loyalty to one's corrupt king. However, it would be too simplistic to assume that Islam and followership come under the spiritual domain, and egalitarianism and democracy under the material realm, just because "the dominant elements of [the outer domain's] self-definition [are] drawn from the ideology of the modern liberal democratic state" (Chatterjee 1996, 221). In fact, the rebellious figure of Hang Jebat in Malay classical literature suggests that the desire for egalitarianism and the display of anti-authoritarianism existed in Malay culture, and therefore, Hang Jebat and the seeds of democracy are part of the Malay spiritual domain.

For example, if democracy involves the common people constituting political authority, Kassim Ahmad (1971) uses Hang Jebat, the figure of feudal rebellion, to symbolize modern-day socialist rebellion. In Kassim Ahmad's poem "Dialog" (1967), Hang Jebat proves to be a "model leader of the peasantry." In this poem, a young farmer vows, "I will go / with a thousand Jebats of the peasantry / so long we have died in loyalty / now we live in rebellion" (Muhammad 1991, 164). If Jebat represents the seeds of democracy, then the *reformasi* movement can be regarded as evidence of democracy having taken root in Malaysian civil society (Loh and Khoo 2002). An echo of Kassim Ahmad's poem resonates in a letter from C.K. Tan to the on-line *Detik Daily* where he claims that Datuk Seri Anwar Ibrahim once said that if an Anwar falls, ten Anwars will arise; if ten Anwars fall, thousands of Anwars will arise (September 2000). Democracy in Malaysia is also often defined as the freedom to criticize or express dissent, as Hang Jebat does, but without being censored or punished.[10] The spiritual and material domains are thus inextricably linked by the symbolic power of Hang Jebat.

While Chatterjee begins by proposing two domains to anticolonial nationalism, he ends up explaining that now "the task is to trace in their mutually conditioned historicities the specific forms that have appeared, on the one hand, in the domain defined by the hegemonic project of nationalist modernity, and on the other, in the numerous fragmented resistances to that normalizing project" (Chatterjee 1996, 224). This is because the domain of subaltern politics (i.e., the spiritual) has adapted itself to the institutional forms characteristic of the elite domain (i.e., material), thereby blurring the two domains. (Joel Kahn and Francis Loh, the editors of *Fragmented Vision: Culture and Politics in Contemporary Malaysia,* have to a certain extent fulfilled Chatterjee's call to carry out this task.) Hang Tuah and Hang Jebat fit into Chatterjee's theoretical configuration if we think of Hang Tuah as representing "attachment to a leader" within the spiritual and inner realm. However, Hang Jebat's position is debatable, especially once the mythical figures are replaced by real political figures such as Mahathir and Anwar, and the demarcating lines between material and spiritual get even further blurred. For example, Mahathir blends a mixture of secular modernity with feudal authoritarianism in his anticolonial nationalism, whereas Anwar represents an Islamic democratic notion of civil society as his ideal nationalism. In fact, just as a dialectical relationship and function characterizes the Hang Tuah/ Hang Jebat debate, the same dialectical tension exists between the spiritual and material: "Each domain has not only acted in opposition to and as a limit upon the other but, through this process of struggle, has also shaped the emergent form of the other" (Chatterjee 1996, 223-24). Using Chatterjee's theory to frame these two national literary figures is not a futile exercise despite the resulting ambivalences. Rather, as he suggests, it is a move towards theorizing "new forms of the modern community" and "new forms of the modern state" outside the "Western universalism" versus "Oriental exceptionalism" argument (ibid., 224).[11]

NATIONALISM AND FEUDALISM

Critics generally regarded Hang Tuah as the ideal Malay hero from the fifteenth century until 1959, when socialist Kassim Ahmad established Hang Jebat as the modern Malay hero rebelling against colonialism and feudalism. Thus, Hang Tuah was relegated to the role of the "traditional" or "feudal hero" in Malay literature (Muhammad 1991, 148). He was at one time also considered the Malay "national" hero (ibid., 144), as the popularity of the film *Hang Tuah* (based on the *bangsawan* Malay theatre version) demonstrated during its first big screen appearance in 1956.[12] Later in the 1970s, the film was made accessible to a multi-ethnic television viewership. The *bangsawan* or Malay urban theatre version, which dates back to the turn of the twentieth century, portrays Hang Tuah as the traditional hero. The film's popularity is divided between its legendary content and its star, P. Ramlee, who is equally popular with non-Malay audiences. While the story of Hang Tuah as the ideal hero was popularized on television to a mass national audience, other means of mustering nationalism via print culture and ideological state apparatuses such as school history textbooks continued. For example, Muhammad Haji Salleh hints at Hang Tuah's status as the traditional hero when he argues that "in Tuah's values and actions we see clear shades of *traditional nationalism*, which were important then as well as in modern times when Malaysians are trying to redefine themselves, especially in terms of contemporary identity and culture" (1991, 134, emphasis mine). Muhammad's comparison of feudal Melaka society then and the multi-ethnic post-1963 contemporary nation meriting the name Malaysia instead of Malaya supports the idea that both feudal and modern nationalism demand loyalty to the nation as represented by the king or ruling government (cf. Sharifah Maznah 1993).

According to Anthony D. Smith's "ethnic" concept of the nation, a nation shares not only historic territory, a common economy, and common legal rights and duties for all members but also "common myths and historical memories, a mass, public culture" (Smith 1991, 14). Muhammad Haji Salleh's linkage of traditional and modern nationalism can be furthered by Smith's theory that educator-intellectuals are "intent on purifying and mobilizing 'the people' through an appeal to the community's alleged ethnic past" (Smith 1991, 68). Thus, the story of Hang Tuah and Hang Jebat becomes the "cognitive map" that is "drawn from the poetic spaces and golden ages of the communal past" (ibid., 69). If we believe that nationalism was conceived in Europe only two centuries ago, then Muhammad Haji Salleh's labelling of feudal Melaka as "traditional nationalism" is the kind of wishful projection that prompts Anderson to ask why nations celebrate their hoariness and not their astonishing youth (summarized in Bhabha 1994, 293). In other words, for the educator-intellectual, establishing a link with a nation's antique past gives the modern nation a sense of genealogical validity and nationalist, anti-imperialist pride. A manifestation of this is Prime Minister Mahathir's project, Vision 2020, which he has likened to the golden age of Melaka (Hooker 2003, 58). "In this way, [the educator-intellectuals] hope to transform a backward traditional [feudal] ethnic community into a dynamic, but vernacular, political nation" (Smith 1991, 69).

What makes the idea of a feudal hero as national hero seem odd is that "feudal" implies a relationship/loyalty to hierarchical authority whereas "national" suggests a relationship/loyalty between equals, as implied in Benedict Anderson's concept of nationalism as "a deep, horizontal comradeship" (Anderson 1991, 7). Inherent in this notion of modern nationalism that involves "the people" and embodies revolutionist ideals of fraternity and equality is the unstated idea of democracy, if not socialism. Yet Anderson also acknowledges that in the case of official nationalisms, it is "leaderships, not people, who inherit old switchboards and palaces" (ibid., 161), thereby demonstrating that both forms of loyalty continue to operate in modern nationalism (whether it is within the framework of capitalist democracy or socialism).[13] Thus, and even better, Chatterjee's model of anticolonial nationalism, which combines the material and spiritual elements, permits a feudal hero like Hang Tuah to be considered a national hero in postcolonial Malaysia.

Consistent with Muhammad Haji Salleh's conflation of the feudal hero with the anticolonial nationalist hero, a slippage appears in his quotation of the *Hikayat Hang Tuah (HHT)* that belies a tendency to occasionally blur loyalty to authority with loyalty to friendship.[14] The misquotation of the *HHT* reads: "Ini Hikayat Hang Tuah yang amat *setiakawan* pada tuannya dan terlalu berbuat kebaktian kepada tuannya" (Muhammad 1991, 135, emphasis mine). The slippage occurs when the word *setiakawan* is substituted for *setiawan. Setiakawan* literally means "loyalty to friends" but *setiawan* means "most loyal." Translated, the sentence in Muhammad's version of the opening of *HHT* states, "This is the epic of Hang Tuah, who was greatly loyal to his master and has performed numerous great services to this master" (Muhammad 1991, 135). This unconscious blurring of horizontal and feudal loyalties perhaps exemplifies the inherent paradox of nationalism and bears closer examination. It reinforces Anderson's notion of nationalism as a fraternity that condones killing and dying for one's nation. Along similar lines, Anderson notes that "the family has traditionally been conceived as the domain of disinterested [i.e., natural, unchosen] love and solidarity" (Anderson 1991, 144). If I am conflating friend and family, it is because *setiakawan* seems to imply this melding in Hang Tuah's friendship with his four childhood companions: "Hang Tuah was full of love for his four friends, and all of them for each other. If they went anywhere to play they went together. Even when they ate, they did it together and played together, as though they were inseparable family members" (Muhammad 1991, 130). Seen in the light of the mixture of friendship and brotherhood between Hang Tuah and his friends, perhaps Hang Tuah's deep loyalty to the king (*setiawan*) has to be justified in these fraternal terms (*setiakawan*), especially when His Highness turns out to be vain, weak, and rash in his judgments.

Liberal nationalist ideology distinguished the public domain from the private domain (Chatterjee 1996, 221), separating loyalty to the state from loyalty to personal friendship. However, the Tuah-Jebat conflict is based on the impossibility of separating the public from the private spheres, pointing to a rather different discourse of nationalism. Judith Nagata, too, alludes to the blurring of one's personal/public ties to the king: "In the 'pre-modern' era the legitimacy of states did not derive from a particular people. Thus ancient empires encompassed multiple 'nations' within their boundaries, in a free-floating pluralism, ultimately held together by the strength of a ruler, *based on personal/feudal loyalty*, coercive military force or myth of divinity" (Nagata 1994, 86, emphasis mine; see also Sharifah Maznah 1993, 62, 100; Hooker 2003, 30-31). Indeed, Syed Hussein Alatas also illustrates the continuities of what he calls "psychological feudalism" in Malaysian society in the 1970s (1972, 111). He points out "the lack of a clear and consciously upheld distinction between what is private and what is official" in the fusion between the interest of the individual and that of the state (106). Also implicit in the use of *setiakawan* to characterize the relationship between the king and his beloved admiral, Hang Tuah, is a strong homoerotic strain that emerges most clearly in Fatimah Busu's short story. But I will save for last my analysis of her text and its tracing of the intricate relationship between nationalism and homoeroticism.

THE HEGEMONY OF MALAY CULTURAL IDENTITY

Transforming a feudal ideal into a nationalist one is problematic only outside of the Malay chauvinist psyche. In other words, Malays are bumiputera, who trace their nationalist roots back to the Melaka empire, the seat of Malay civilization. This golden age embodies a modern nationalist fantasy of Malay hegemonic power over a homogeneous population. In a pre-colonial period sheathed more in myth and legend than factual history, it is recorded in the various literary epics or *hikayat* and *Sejarah Melayu* (*The Malay Annals*). But in reality, the population of Melaka in the fifteenth century was probably more heterogeneous than some Malay chauvinists would like to think – Melaka being a trading centre where people from India and the Arab countries came to trade with merchants from China. Negotiating his way around this multi-ethnic, cosmopolitan arena, Hang Tuah could have been well-versed in as many as twelve languages. However, the narrowly defined modern nationalist fantasy naturally occluded the later waves of immigrants from India and China who arrived during British colonial rule in the nineteenth century and are now citizens of the modern nation-state, Malaysia. This nationalist fantasy of a Malay golden age is important in view of over four hundred years of colonialism and later economic oppression of, and competition from, "the hardy immigrant races, Chinese and Indians" (Muhammad 1991, 159). Although Muhammad Haji Salleh does not note it, one can conclude that the Tuah-Jebat conflict rarely appears in the writing of non-Malay Malaysians who have been marginalized by the quota system and the overall privileging of the bumiputeras since the introduction of the NEP in 1971. Nevertheless, their silence regarding Hang Tuah and Hang Jebat is hardly an indication of the strength of their national loyalties. Furthermore, a National Cultural Policy (1971) that defines the regional culture as the official one and calls for cultural assimilation and adaptation of the immigrant races to the region's culture guarantees the preservation and hegemony of the Malay language, the Malay religion, Islam, and the monarchy as head of adat in modern-day Malaysia. The hegemony of Malay cultural identity therefore enables Muhammad Haji Salleh to make the easy slippage, when discussing Hang Tuah's values and actions, from Melaka's feudal order into Malaysia's pluralist democracy in which "Malaysians are trying to redefine themselves, especially in terms of contemporary identity and culture" (Muhammad 1991, 135). One might venture to ask whether "Malaysians" here include non-bumiputera as well.

In the past, Malay feudal cultural identity called for absolute loyalty to the sultan because he was said to have descended from the heavens. He was the representative of God – "the shadow of Allah on earth" believed to exude *daulat*, a supernatural or mystical power to punish those daring to act against the customs and beliefs traditionally associated with Malay life and institutions (Tham 1981, 254; Hooker 2003, 30). This accounts for Hang Tuah's loyalty to the king since to defy the *daulat* is to commit *durhaka* (treason) (Salleh 1994, 128; Sharifah Maznah 1993, 47-53). One critic has even speculated on an etymological comparison between two Malay cognates, *menderhaka* (to commit treason) and *merdeka* or *merdaheka* (independence), to demonstrate the strong connection between ruler and subject, and to claim that to seek one's independence was to be a traitor (Kessler 1992, 148).

Today, urbanization, Western education, and globalization have gradually worn away belief in divine kingship. More importantly, the institution of a constitutional monarchy and parliamentary rule after independence meant that political power resided with the ruling coalition, the Barisan Nasional, headed by UMNO. While during the Melaka Empire the subjects derived their social, cultural, and religious identity from the king, in the postcolonial present of the nation-state, it is to UMNO that the people look for political guidance and protection of their socio-economic and cultural rights. The monarchy retains its ceremonial position as the head of adat and Islam, thus becoming more important as a symbol of tradition than as a power-wielding institution. In 1983, Prime Minister Mahathir attempted to curb the powers of the monarchy, precipitating a constitutional crisis (Rehman 1993, 189). The fact that the sultanate "provided the Malays a fount of their identity and a focus for their loyalty" meant that the Malays were kept "in thrall to a hereditary sovereignty, and this flew in the face of everything a democracy was supposed to achieve" (ibid., 191). Mahathir wanted to prevent the king from the one crucial power he had over Parliament, the right of signing/approving legislation into law. As a result of the constitutional crisis, a bill to which the king fails to give assent would nevertheless automatically become law after a delay of thirty days. A decade later, in 1993, the power of the monarchy was further reduced in another constitutional crisis that limited the legal immunity of the nine hereditary Malay rulers (Sloane 1999, 82).

UMNO originated from the unexpected Malay grass-roots resistance to the formation of the Malayan Union proposed by the British in 1946, which would have accorded the non-Malays equal rights to citizenship, taken away the Malays' special privileges, and transferred the sovereignty of the rulers to the British Crown. UMNO clearly regarded the Malayan Union proposal as a colonial violation of Malay sovereignty and British intervention in the Malay spiritual domain. Through its organizing and influence, the party came to symbolize the hold that Malay elite groups continued to have on their rural masses through the traditional institutions of government in rural areas such as the village headman (*ketua kampung*) and the sub-district chief (*penghulu*) (Banks 1987, 17). In the 1970s, UMNO once again sought ostensibly to protect the rights of Malays by introducing the NEP and bumiputera policy.[15] The strong reliance and dependence on the UMNO leadership has inspired Kit Leee to coin the term "Umnoputraism." Umnoputraism, according to Leee, claims that "the *bumis* do not form the inner party at all, having been supplanted by the Party's Deep Throaters or the UMNOputra, i.e., the oligarchs" (in Kee 1987, xxi). The transfer of loyalties from a feudal leadership to a national political party is facilitated by the concept of what Chandra Muzaffar and Shaharuddin Maaruf call "followership" (Kessler 1992, 147).

FOLLOWERSHIP

According to Clive Kessler, the problem between Malay political leaders and their followers lies with the followers rather than the leadership: "All the conventional concern (in Malay literary, cultural, and sociological studies) with leaders, protectors, and heroes in this view may well be a displaced or disguised recognition of what is uneasily central to Malay politics and culture: not leadership, which is not conceptually or socially problematic, but followership, which is" (1992, 147). In this view, the refusal of followership is like rebellion and impermissible in Malay popular consciousness. "Fully to be a Malay, this understanding again emphasizes [that] one must have a ruler [and] be ruled as a follower" (ibid., 149). Presumably then, because followership defines Malay identity in such a crucial way, Hang Tuah rather than Hang Jebat is regarded as "the champion of his country and his race" (Muhammad 1991, 116).

The value of followership is evident in Johan Jaafar's play, *My City Oh My City* (first Malay version in 1981). His Jebat claims to be "the new Jebat. Jebat the Realist! Jebat the agitator! Jebat of the twentieth century!" as he announces upon his stage entry to the subalterns he sees there: the Night Soil Collector, the Sweeper, and the Prostitute (Johan 1992, 90). Carrying a book in one hand, this Jebat is the organic intellectual who defends the weak and champions their cause. He reads the subalterns their rights from the constitution (the book he carries) and provokes them to go on strike when the government threatens to destroy their village slum in order to build something luxurious for the rich. However, when their strike leads to his death, they are quick to blame themselves, unable to see the larger framework in which ideology functions:

> *Sweeper:* (Begins to cry). I'm a murderer! All the rubbish has polluted the air! And Jebat is dead from breathing in that air!
>
> *Night Soil Collector:* (He cries too). I too am a murderer! Excrement is full of germs. The germs have gone into Jebat's body. And Jebat is now dead!
>
> *Prostitute:* (Bursts out crying too). I too am a murderer! People's Leader needs

me to sooth and calm him. But I'm on strike! And People's Leader lost his senses. And he imprisoned Jebat! Jebat suffered! And died! (Johan 1992, 123-24)

They then decide to end the strike and happily begin cleaning up the city. The Night Soil Collector's resigned statement "I too want to work again" (ibid., 124) echoes strangely the placard "Shut Up And Work" described in *A Malaysian Journey*, the attitude being that focusing on work would keep the masses so busy that they would not have time to think about the violation of their basic individual rights (Rehman 1993, 267). Although one critic, Abdul Rahman Napiah, attributes Jebat's death to air pollution caused by the striking garbage workers and road sweepers it's equally plausible that Jebat died from worse conditions in prison (such as torture).

Focusing on the formal aspects of playwriting, Abdul Rahman Napiah repeatedly stresses that while Johan Jaafar's play is absurdist, the language and message of the play are not abstract. But in terms of the play's bigger political implications, Abdul Rahman Napiah has little to say. He does not critique Johan Jaafar's rather narrow and simplistic view of what or who causes the most environmental pollution, that is, factories and land developers instead of striking garbage workers. He fails to point out that the play ultimately blames the victims or subalterns for their own oppression. Despite Johan Jaafar's attempt to demonstrate the poverty and despair of the squatters through the character of Hang Jebat, the play's conservatism prevails: the playwright's glib portrayal of what a strike is all about illustrates the futility of rebelling. More than that, the subalterns, as much as the doctor, city planner, and office boy who kowtow to the People's Leader, represent impotent followership. During the strike, instead of negotiating for their rights, all they do is chant "Serve you right! Right! Right!" – even when the rich urban dwellers are pleading for mercy. Their lack of initiative, the failure of the strike because it never occurred to the subalterns to use it as leverage to improve their lives, and their immediate recanting after Jebat's death belittle Jebat's efforts. He does not even die a martyr because the class struggle dies with him. Instead, he is portrayed as an instigator and troublemaker who succeeds merely in temporarily stalling the city's daily activities.

Kessler views followership not necessarily as a culture of absolutism or domination but as a culture of deference. As in the saying "Tak Melayu Hilang Di Dunia" (commonly translated as "the Malays shall not perish from the world"), in order to survive, one must at times be dissimulatingly deferential (Kessler 1992, 148). If we extend Kessler's theory about Malay political culture to Malay mythological and literary characters, Hang Tuah can be read for this role of follower, the "total servant, completely subjected to the desires of his king, his moods, gifts and honours." His diplomacy and meticulous decorum require "usually burying his real intentions and thoughts under pretty words" (Muhammad 1991, 160-61). And for his loyal service and deference, he was paid handsomely by the king (ibid., 143; Sharifah Maznah 1993).

This form of political patronage or cronyism continues to dog Malaysian politics today (Khoo Kay Jin 1992, 57) as politicians compete over whose cronies or close business associates will receive the most lucrative privatization opportunities awarded by the government to the corporate sector. Thus, in addition to Kessler's belief that followership is based on *hormat* (respect or honour) or the deference owed to a social position, I would argue that followership is also motivated by gains made through political patronage and cronyism.[16] This can be seen in the events following UMNO's internal division in April 1987. Supporters who chose the losing side, Semangat '46, eventually returned to the UMNO fold when faced with economic exclusion (Khoo Kay Jin 1992, 73; Hooker 2003, 258-59). Their actions reinforce the links I am making between followership and political patronage or, more precisely, Umnoputraism. Compared to bumiputraism, which privileges all bumiputeras, Umnoputraism benefits only those who are UMNO party members. The followers do not merely "attain a fully Malay identity by acknowledging [the ruler]" (Kessler 1992, 148) but they also attain financial benefits by prudently acknowledging the leader best able to serve them.[17]

Such a perspective admits that followers do possess agency. After all, just as it is believed that "Malays do not and shall not rebel against their rulers," another often forgotten but equally entrenched conviction in Malay oral culture is that "Malays shall remain loyal to their rulers *so long as their rulers rule over them with justice*" (Kessler 1992, 147, emphasis mine; Sharifah Maznah 1993). Ultimately, the followers with their electoral votes wield some power over the politicians who, in turn, are obliged to serve them through the allocation of privileges.[18] In the case of the 1994 tension between Deputy Prime Minister Anwar Ibrahim and Finance Minister Daim Zainuddin over whose close business associates were getting the contract for the Bakun Dam project, this "justice" can be narrowly interpreted as the ability to provide one's followers with financial deals (Gomez 1995, 6). Of course, the logical conclusion from this is that followership adversely fosters political patronage, cronyism, nepotism, and corruption.

However, agency for change exists not only for followers but also for those who believe in democracy in postcolonial Malaysia. For example, voters for the opposition PAS, despite threats of economic exclusion and lack of federal assistance in developing their state, are exercising their democratic rights.[19] More likely, PAS voters' non-conformity shows their contempt for the notion that UMNO's kind of followership, which promises corrupt patronage, is central to UMNO's ethnic agenda. Indeed, PAS capitalized on UMNO's reputed corruption and dirty tactics during the Anwar *reformasi* period and won over many UMNO supporters, subsequently winning the state elections in Terengganu in 1999. For PAS supporters, Islam plays the more definitive role in the ethnic make-up (Jomo and Shabery 1992, 101-2). Anwar's calls for a more genuine democracy and the end to corruption and patronage show a political contempt for the extreme results of followership. Under the urgent cry of *reformasi*, Anwar called for a broad reformation of government and financial structures, and for Mahathir himself to step down. As if to reaffirm his image as a model of religious faith, his supporters constantly chanted *Allahu Akhbar!* (God Is Great) outside the court where he was being tried. For once, former UMNO members (Anwar supporters) and PAS party members shared a similar discourse in their appeal to Islamic ideals of social justice and equality to counter corruption, cronyism, and nepotism. The fact that Anwar was completely ousted from UMNO – sacked from his positions as finance minister and deputy prime minister, and forced to step down as leader of UMNO during the general assembly of UMNO members – and his supporters purged from UMNO ranks in 1998 demonstrates the lasting dominance of Umnoputraism under Mahathir's leadership.

As the symbol of fraternal loyalty and independent thinking, Hang Jebat poses a challenge to a corrupt feudal system: "I was defending truth, justice and the fundamental human freedoms God gives us at the time of our birth" (Fatimah 1991, 273). To support the idea of Hang Jebat as hero, we may then read his mass murder during his amok as a retaliation against everyone who directly or indirectly collaborated with the system. This includes the cowardly villagers who want to dip their daggers in his blood when he is down (Fatimah 1991, 269), the soldiers who carried out the king's orders, and all who are unaware that in his rebellion lay the seeds of democracy. Indeed, Hatta Azad Khan's 1984 play portrays Hang Jebat as a modern-day Robin Hood who evicts the king from the palace and turns it over to the masses. More importantly, this Hang Jebat "exposes the malpractices of those in power" (Solehah Ishak in Usman Awang 1992, 54), just as Anwar exposed the malpractices of the finance minister who replaced him, Daim Zainuddin, in his epistle from prison (Anwar 1998a).

ISLAM, MALAYSIAN STYLE

The Tuah-Jebat conflict highlights the incompatibility of the hybrid elements of pre-Muslim Malay animism, Hinduism, and Mahayana Buddhism in Malaysian Islam. The Malay Muslim is an orthodox Sunni of the school of Shafi'e but in the Islam that Malays adopted from Indian Muslims there were Shi'ite elements, such as "a crude pantheism, a Gnostic concern with mystic names and formulae and the worship of innumerable saints" (Winstedt 1961, 37). The coexistence between Hinduism and Islam is evident in *The Malay Annals*, which records a social covenant between the representative of the people, Demang Lebar Daun, and the representative of the divine king, Sri Tri Buana, in which the people must accord total loyalty to the king. However, Demang Lebar Daun acceded only if the king's descendants kept to the terms of the pact. The two representatives discuss the contract in terms of Muslim law. For example, the people's representative states that if the subjects' offence is grave, they will have to be put to death, if that is in accordance with Islamic law.

Fatimah Busu's Hang Jebat tries to separate out the Hindu elements that existed in Islam during the Melaka Islamic empire: "In [Melaka] we bow down before the king as though he were a stone idol, and treat his ministers like wooden images!" (Fatimah 1991, 258). By suggesting that divine kingship and idol worship are part of feudal loyalty and incongruous with (the true) Islam, Hang Jebat becomes the voice of a more genuine, democratic Islam that stipulates everyone is equal in the eyes of God. In response to Hang Lekir, who reminds him of the seriousness of disobeying the sultan, Jebat says: "God made man to live on this earth for a short while. No man deserves our worship, only God" (ibid., 257).[20] The mindset behind Hang Lekir's words demonstrates that "obeisance and homage were the essential signs of submission and inferiority that subjects displayed before their rulers" (Tham 1981, 254). By contrast, Fatimah's Hang Jebat, if only for one significant moment, poses the idea of a horizontal comradeship under the nationalist flag of Islam. The Islamic rhetoric this Hang Jebat employs recalls resurgent Islamic forces in Malaysia in the 1970s and 1980s, which may not necessarily refer only to the negative notion of fundamentalist or radical Islam (Hooker 2003, 252). In this instance, resurgent Islam becomes the impetus for democratic change.

Fatimah Busu's Hang Jebat irreverently targets Hang Tuah's blind loyalty to the king before he and Hang Tuah begin duelling: "It is time you learned that your loyalty to the sultan is about as important as a frog's concern for a piece of cat-shit" (1991, 266). And she is not alone in her reading of Hang Jebat. Muhammad Haji Salleh describes him as "very much more independent both in action and thought" than Hang Tuah (1991, 160). An analogy of the different views of Hang Tuah and Hang Jebat can be summed up in the borrowed Islamic language of jurisprudence: *taqlid* versus *ijtihad*. Salleh Ben Joned explains that *taqlid*, translated as imitation or blind acceptance of authority, has "immobilised the minds of Malaysian Muslims for far too long" presumably because followership is entrenched in Malay culture. *Ijtihad*, on the other hand, means individual judgment. The right to *ijtihad* is rooted in the Quran to use one's God-given mind, conceived here by Salleh as "the right for every Muslim in possession of a sound mind and a sound education" (Salleh 1994, 32). The important point here is that by enshrining both *taqlid* and *ijtihad*, Islam can be read as allowing room for individual subjectivity. This is important because individual subjectivity is too often perceived as a Western construct by Westerners and non-Westerners alike, who are keen to use this perception for their own ends.

ASIAN VALUES, ASIAN-STYLE NATIONALISM

The dichotomy of blind loyalty versus individual judgment overlaps with the opposition between Asian values and Western values. Summing up the shift from social group values to individual rights in Malaysia, Muhammad Haji Salleh evidently subscribes to this overlap:

> Over the centuries, the individual and his rights have slowly taken centre stage. The Western education system which lays a great value on the person has given him a new confidence and a sense of himself ... In the meantime, social values have changed. Even in the close-knit Malay society that puts the interest of the community over that of the individual, the latter has been slowly recognized and applauded in his success. Literature plays a big role in foregrounding the new individual. He may appear as a leader of his people, a nationalist, a fighter against the colonialist, but also a rebel in the tradition of Hang Jebat. (1991, 162)

According to this perception, Hang Jebat epitomizes the modern, Westernized Malay hero. Similarly, Prime Minister Mahathir Mohamad, regarded as "quite untraditional and even anti-traditionalistic" (Kessler 1992, 149), took on what some consider a pseudo-Jebat role in 1983 when he challenged the powers of the sultans (Rehman Rashid 1993, 189-91), even though his own leadership is often criticized as authoritarian (Crouch 1992; Mauzy 1993).

In 1987, Mahathir's government cracked down on 115 social activists, environmentalists, Chinese educationists, opposition politicians, and various radicals; it also banned three newspapers. Journalist Rehman Rashid made a stand for democracy in his editorial comment in the *New Straits Times* but was called in for questioning by the Special Branch, a police arm vested with the powers of the ISA. During the interrogation, the ISA director said, "What are a hundred people compared with 16.4 million? Nothing. A sacrifice" (Rehman 1993, 237). Clearly, this statement made under Mahathir's leadership shows how little Mahathir's government thought of individual rights in the formation of an economically strong nation. The Special Branch director then posed this problematic question to Rehman, "Who was the greater hero? Hang Tuah or Hang Jebat?" Unable to give an honest answer without expecting punishment, Rehman replied, "I don't know." In the situation, the correct answer would, of course, be Hang Tuah, who, in the words of the director, "was very faithful to the sultan" and "carried out the order [to kill the rebel Jebat] even though Hang Jebat was his closest friend" (ibid., 237). This episode, taken together with Mahathir's Vision 2020, which invokes Melaka's golden age by promising a "second golden age" (Van der Heide 1996, 109), points to the political conviction that the era of Hang Jebat as the modern Malay hero came and went (between 1959 and the 1980s) and that under Mahathir's authoritarian government, especially during the economic boom (1987-96), the feudal hero Hang Tuah reigned supreme once more.[21] Mahathir's admission in his book *The Malay Dilemma* that "feudalism can be beneficial if it facilitates changes" serves to substantiate this idea (1970, 173).

A similarly conservative view emerges from Western-educated Malay writer, Karim Raslan. Writing about the ability of the South African party, the ANC, to impose their Reconstruction and Development Programme (RDP), he says that it "*lacks the iron hand*, authority and commitment to development of Malaysia's ruling party, UMNO. As a result, it's hard to see the RDP being put into effect by *dangerous populists* such as Winnie Mandela" (1996a, 95, emphasis mine). Karim Raslan strives to redefine democracy, to tailor it for Malaysia:

> What we have to do ... is start to see the whole process – and not just the elections – outside the prism of what a Western liberal democracy would call a democracy. Our elections are our own. This may sound nonsensical. Surely all elections are *sui generis* – true to themselves, the people, their culture and their community.
>
> We in Malaysia are creating a different political language, and a whole new set of political reference points. We are inventing the wheel in terms of race relations and religious integration, as well as the democratic structure that holds the whole apparatus together. I might sound like a Government apologist but there's no doubt in my mind that the harsh realities of race, religion and culture require equally harsh politics. (1996a, 166)

Karim Raslan's statement here does portray him as a government apologist, and in fact, he was an "ambassador of the NEP" in South Africa in the early 1990s. He abides by the Old Testament notion that man is inherently evil, and that the race riots of May 13, 1969 have proven this; therefore, man needs to be controlled via the iron will of the state (1996b, 33; 1996a, 164). His justification for accepting the feel-good ideology advanced by the government contrasts with Rehman's nuanced, more cautious and ironic outlook regarding Mahathirism.[22] Here is Rehman's more sarcastic reminiscence: "And so the years passed, and Malaysia moved buoyantly onward and upward, and there was less and less ambiguity over the true nature and seat of authority in the nation. The Malaysian model of nationhood was seen to be using all the many tools at its disposal. If and when necessary, even the blunt instruments. No one really relished the thought of using them, but they were there, and Malaysia had shown how they, too, could be useful in nation-building. It all hinged, as always, on the sort of nation being built" (1993, 263).

Karim Raslan's views of Asian-style modernity are echoed in C.J. Wan-Ling Wee's questions: "What is the feasibility of modernity in the context of the post-colonial world?" and "is the issue that of an *Asianized* or an *Asian* modernity?" (1996, 220). Wee is distinguishing between a modernity that originates from the West but which has been transformed by its new setting ("Asianized modernity") and an alternative modernity found in Asia today ("Asian modernity"). As a firm believer in equal rights, I am suspicious of the resurgence of anticolonialism dressed up in the rhetoric of Asian modernity and cultural difference in such debates, for its emphasis on "communitarian values" is often an excuse for the oligarchy to trample on individual rights. Chatterjee talks about an anticolonial nationalism keen to distinguish itself from the European and American models by its differences: "The greater one's success in imitating Western skills in the material domain, therefore, the greater the need to preserve the distinctness of one's spiritual culture" (1996, 217). But this argument can be problematic. For example, when delegates of a peaceful closed-door conference held in Kuala Lumpur (the second Asia Pacific Conference on East Timor or APCET II, held in November 1996) were detained after a violent government-linked mob disrupted the conference, the detainees were not allowed to inform their families about their whereabouts. As an anonymous detainee said, "the right to a lawyer and a phone call belongs only in Hollywood movies, we were told."[23] In this climate, those who speak up against self-censorship, institutionalized racism, and the violation of human rights under the Internal Security Act in Malaysia are considered bold like Hang Jebat. For example, Kit Leee's rave review of Kee Thuan Chye's play says: "Am I suggesting, then, that Kee Thuan Chye's name be submitted to the Committee that hands out the annual award for bravery (what is it called, the *Pingat Hang Jebat*?)" (quoted in Kee 1987, 118).

The dedication of Karim Raslan's collection of short stories *Heroes and Other Stories* is telling: "For 'Tuah.'" Does he believe that Hang Tuah is the greater hero, and is the book dedicated to the ideals Tuah embodied? This is assuming that Karim Raslan is referring to the legendary figure from the *Hikayat Hang Tuah.* On the other hand, *tuah* also means "luck," though this is less likely to be what the author intended by spelling it with an uppercase *T.* In the story "Heroes," the protagonist uses Tuah's blind loyalty to cover up his personal cowardice. When violence erupts and his deputy, Nazrin, is attacked by a group of Chinese villagers, the protagonist, fearful for his own life, leaves without helping Nazrin: "I stopped for no man. I had to press on. Hang Tuah would have approved of me. I never questioned. I acted on instructions whatever the consequence" (1996b, 34). The male protagonist is a government civil servant who had an important mission in the aftermath of the race riots in May 1969: "'69 might have been a terrible year for some, a scar on the nation and all that, but for me it was a high point of sorts, a moment of rare harmony, a time when I was vigorous, capable, important and, if only to my daughter, even heroic" (ibid., 24). By the end of the narrative, he is no longer a hero to his daughter or to us. Making his situation analogous to Hang Tuah's disguises his lack of personal integrity, for he had considered working with Nazrin to be "rather like having an intelligent, charming son on hand" (ibid., 39).

"Heroes" suggests that followership stems from a lack of personal integrity: the protagonist is no Hang Jebat loyal to his "brothers," but neither is he Hang Tuah because of his cowardice. The dedication, read with the painting by Wong Hoy Cheong entitled "The Discreet Charm of the Bourgeoisie" that's used on the book cover, yields a possible explanation, though it does not make Karim's perspective on Tuah less naïve or simplistic. The stories are indeed, as the book jacket describes, "morality tales" that highlight the spiritual hollowness and materialism of the bumigeois. As in Luis Buñuel's film of the same name, the characters are selfish, morally deficient, and shallow. Collectively, the stories sum up the nostalgic desire in the jaded 1990s for an ideal, traditional hero as embodied by Hang Tuah. Hence, Karim's dedication can be read as a plea for the real Hang Tuah to stand up. If his dedication is not ironic or subversive, his invocation of Hang Tuah and not Hang Jebat, whose loyalty to friendship and kinship we want to see in the protagonist's own relationship with his daughter and Nazrin, says something about the deep-rooted quasi-feudal values that prevail even with the modern, urban, Malay middle class.[24] These values remain deep rooted because they help preserve the interests and privileges of the bumigeois.

THE MALAY PSYCHE

Hang Tuah and Hang Jebat symbolize opposite modes of Malay masculine behaviour: *merendah diri* and *amok* (the feminine "equivalent" of amok is *latah*). Hang Tuah has been described as self-effacing, *merendah diri*, a trait traditionally regarded as positive but which Mahathir suggests contributed to the "Malay dilemma" (economic lagging behind the Chinese). In his controversial book *The Malay Dilemma*, Mahathir theorizes that running amok is a symptom of Malay repression: "*Amok* represents the external physical expression of the conflict within the Malay which his perpetual observance of the rules and regulations of his life causes in him. It is a spilling over, an overflowing of his inner bitterness. It is a rupture of the bonds which bind him ... a final and complete escape from reason and training. The strain and the restraint on him is lifted ... His timid, self-effacing self is displaced. He is now a Mr. Hyde – cruel, callous and bent on destruction" (Mahathir 1970, 118). Mahathir's rather essentialist reasoning about Malay behaviour deduces that Hang Jebat is to Hang Tuah what Mr. Hyde is to Dr. Jekyll: both represent opposite extremes of the same Malay psyche. So in a society that emphasizes group loyalty, strong individual or personal loyalties will either have to be repressed or, alternatively, sacrificed. This was the major conflict facing Malay subjects during the Melaka Sultanate (1400-1511), as well as listeners and readers of the *Hikayat Hang Tuah* in the following centuries; it remained the central conflict in 1990s Malaysia.

Hang Tuah's rationality, his great exercise of self-control, patience (*kesabaran*), and general caution (he would investigate/*periksa* before acting) contrast strongly with Hang Jebat's emotional, sensual excess and lawlessness – or what Salleh Ben Joned considers Hang Jebat's hedonism and anarchism. For example, when Tun Teja, the Pahang princess meant for the sultan, fell in love with Hang Tuah, "there was not even a flicker of doubt, of desire, or a moment of weakness that crossed his mind or person. She was meant for his master and he treated her as his future queen, whatever her feelings were towards him at the moment." Hang Tuah's deeds and virtues make him "superhuman" and we know nothing about his private life and emotions (Muhammad 1991, 124-25).[25]

On the contrary, Hang Jebat embodies extreme sensualism. Usman Awang's play focuses on his tender relationship with Dang Wangi, the sultan's favourite concubine (Salleh 1994, 128). He equates her singing voice with the melodious lovelorn bamboo or *buluh perindu* before asking her to dance as if they shall never die (Usman 1992, 67). And Fatimah Busu alludes to an intimate gesture of Hang Jebat with two maidens where "he shared the same quids of betel-nut with Dang New and Dang Flower" (1991, 260). Salleh Ben Joned also discovers that Hang Jebat's name has to do with smell – *jebat* is the strong musky perfume of civet, and Salleh invests musk with the universal association of passion and sexuality "because of its reputed power as an aphrodisiac" (1994, 127). He points to the scene that precedes Jebat's famous amok, in which Jebat is reading a romance to the sultan, surrounded by the court ladies and concubines who are attracted by his seductive voice: "Jebat's reading is followed by singing, his voice becoming more enchanting, so enchanting that the sultan actually lays his head in the warrior's lap and falls to sensuous sleep. In the light of the blood bath to come, there is an undercurrent of the sinister in the uncanny sensuality of this scene. Sensuality and violent death – the juxtaposition is suggestive" (ibid., 153-54).

Hang Jebat's zest for life runs counter to Hang Tuah's cautiousness: "Always looking before you leap can be dangerous for the spirit. Jebat knew that" (ibid., 160). More pertinently, Salleh believes that Hang Jebat's amok is a result of his *sakit hati*; literally "sickness of the liver," the organ that is the seat of all passion: "Never listening to your *hati* when it's *sakit* (sick), always ignoring the complaints of the liver, can be fatal for the liver. Jebat knew that too. *Sakit hati* is always associated with the amok and the lover blighted in love" (ibid., 160). Salleh also speculates that hedonism might be part of the essential nature of the Malays, a repressed id "lurking in the subconscious" (ibid., 161) that surfaces in Hang Jebat's "highly individual gesture of friendship" – his amok (ibid., 127). Salleh's project of recovering the passion and hedonism supposedly inherent in Malayness as opposed to Islam (especially with the Islamicization that began twenty years ago) is in line with his own maverick identity, evident in his earthy and sensuous poetry and non-conformist attitude.[26] One might declare that he is a Hang Jebat in his own right.

Salleh's interpretation of Jebat supports the idea that neither Tuah nor Jebat make unflawed heroes, lending the *Hikayat Hang Tuah* the qualities of a Greek tragedy whose complexity may account for the legend's sustaining power down through history. If Hang Jebat represents the uncontrollable id, the rational ego and symbol of social and moral order, Hang Tuah, is required to curb his moral and social excesses and to rein in his anarchy. At the same time, perhaps Hang Jebat's excesses can be read as the much-needed human folly, the supplement if you like, to the "perfect" Hang Tuah, whom Muhammad Haji Salleh also describes as "a superman of sorts" (1991, 149). To say that Hang Jebat provides a supplementarity to Hang Tuah is to add *setiakawan* or fraternal loyalty to authority, to keep alive the democratic element in a postcolonial nation with strong feudal roots.

NATIONALISM AND HOMOEROTICISM: A FEMINIST INTERVENTION

Briefly, Fatimah Busu's short story, "Dark Night of the Soul," begins with the spirit of Hang Jebat in a kind of limbo. He has a perpetually bleeding wound that will heal only if Hang Tuah apologizes to him. In this version of the legend, Hang Jebat's past unfolds, and Fatimah Busu portrays scenes of his rebellion until his death at Hang Tuah's hands. After this, she attempts to link Hang Jebat's story with the tale of Sisyphus. That is, Hang Jebat witnesses several masochistic scenes representative of hell. Every time he asks the perpetrator why he continues hurting himself, he is told "ask Sisyphus." Finally, when he meets Sisyphus and asks him to account for his futile act, Sisyphus replies, "Ask God." Hang Jebat does not receive an answer but continues to be stranded in limbo in the company of a chorus of sympathetic skulls.

Before moving into a discussion of the short story, the links between homoeroticism, male friendship, and nationalism or state power (signified by a king in this case) need further explication. George Mosse, although he is discussing middle-class morality and sexual norms under modern European nationalism, could just as easily be speaking about Hang Jebat's relationship with the king when he claims that "male friendship faced ... homo-eroticism always close to the surface of nationalism ... Eroticism was difficult to banish from the ideal of friendship" (1989, 67). However, to be intimate with the king, whether homo-erotically or through friendship, suggests a power component not evident so much in the relationship between Hang Tuah and Hang Jebat as much as between the king and his two hamba.[27] The king's homoeroticism functions most obviously as a sign of feudal decadence and consummate power.[28] It is not so much leadership but power that is eroticized, and this consummate power is portrayed as potentially corruptible. For example, Hang Jebat's sexual attractiveness is highlighted at the height of his megalomania. By "homoeroticism" I mean a homosocial relationship (male bonding) infused with melodramatic sentiment, and a physical though not sexual intimacy that may or may not contain sublimated sexual desires – all mostly on the part of the king. Hang Tuah is the passive recipient of the king's show of affection, which stops short of homosexuality.

Eroticizing the king's relationship with his warriors to the point of categorizing it as homosexual instead of metaphorically homosocial or homoerotic has to be purely conjecture, for even though the *Hikayat Hang Tuah* contains highly suggestive imagery its language and rhetoric of courtly Malay is filled with polite expressions and hierarchical forms of address that should not be read literally. For example, Jerry W. Wright Jr. talks about how Abbasid poets "create satire and parody in which faithful submission [to Islam] means pursuing illicit homoerotic activities" (1997, 10). In other words, the homoerotic content is less a reflection of the social reality of the times than it was a motif to subvert and parody religion. According to Wright, "it is not unusual for homoerotic allusions that create political and social satire to be mistaken as evidence of 'sexual culture of the Muslim societies' or as 'dimensions of gay religious history'" (Ibid., 2). This is a useful caveat because a reading that eroticizes the relationship (informed by the work of Eve Kosofsky Sedgwick) risks looking at Malay traditional literature through the lenses of a twentieth-century American queer theorist.

But with this in mind, if Sedgwick's theory applies to patriarchal societies in general rather than strictly to Western societies, it might still be validly employed here, especially if we remember that there are variances such as gender complementarity that make some patriarchies less gender-hierarchical than others. Anthropologist Michael Peletz notes that in Southeast Asian societies, where complementarity has long existed and men and women complement each other and their roles are given equal value, people are traditionally more tolerant of deviance than Westerners and that homosexuals are treated with kindness and an amused tolerance (1995, 123). This may be because the social hierarchy is structured in terms of descent, age, birth order, and, in recent times, social class rather than gender, or, I would hazard, sexual orientation (ibid., 130).

If the king's relationship with Hang Tuah "stops short" of homosexuality, it is not out of homophobia but out of an understanding of Muslim culture that does not immediately associate physical intimacy between men with homosexuality. For example, the frequency of physical intimacy among Muslim men is a cultural difference duly noted by Denny in his chapter "Patterns of Islamic Personal and Communal Life": "[In Cairo] I soon learned that friends like to be physically close to each other, that it is a sign of trust and mutual regard" (1985, 330). However, there's a crucial difference between physical closeness and a sexual act: official Islamic rhetoric regards homosexuality as illegal, so to think of the king, the representative of God on earth who embodies *daulat* (power), as homosexual would be quite blasphemous. It is this complex juxtaposition of adat, official Islamic rhetoric (i.e., what Homi Bhabha would call the "pedagogical"), and Muslim daily social practices (Bhabha's "performative") that makes any use of Sedgwick's theory of homosocial desire quite slippery. Because Sedgwick means by "homosocial desire" "the potential unbrokenness of a continuum between homosocial and homosexual" (1985, 1), it is perhaps more useful to analyze the continuum between homosocial and homosexual as "a strategy for making generalizations about, and marking historical differences in, the *structure* of men's relations with other men" (ibid., 2).

I take from Sedgwick not so much her theory of a male-to-male relationship triangulated and displaced by two men's pursuit of the same woman (i.e., homosexual desire displaced or subverted by heterosexual desire due to *strong* homophobia), nor her idea that such a homosocial relationship is characterized by male paranoia (though this may be said to emerge in the king's dream) but rather, her suggestion about analyzing the power structure of the male relationships. Homophobia stemming from Islamic doctrine exists in the Malay psyche insofar as ethnic Malay identity is heavily intertwined with being Muslim. (For instance, it is such official homophobia that outlaws homosexuality and sodomy in Malaysia. As for the accusations of homosexuality levelled at Anwar Ibrahim by the Mahathir government, the issue of homosexuality between Anwar and his friends is strategically used to complicate or mask the tense homosocial relations of power between the prime minister and his deputy.) Remnants of a pre-Islamic tolerance of sexual and gender deviance continue to exist in Southeast Asia, and hence, in applying Sedgwick's theory to Fatimah Busu's text, I emphasize the relativity or strength of the homophobia that underlies homosociality, and theorize it as weaker in the Malay context.

In the king's and Hang Tuah's relationship, the power imbalance is foremost: the king is *raja* (or king) to Hang Tuah, who is his *hamba* or slave. Because the king's position is unquestionable, the *hamba* has little choice but to offer his fullest loyalty to his feudal lord. In this way, Hang Tuah's passivity resembles that of the young boy in the relationship with his older lover and mentor in ancient Greece (as in Plato's *Symposium*). Just as the Athenian boy finds it befitting "to perform any service for one who improves him in mind and character [i.e., his mentor]," the *hamba* of the Melaka king finds it equally suitable in his culture to perform any service for his king as a test of his loyalty (Plato 1989, 18). Of course, there are material and political benefits to being the king's favourite, though there are no guarantees of any stability in this subordinate position.

Fatimah Busu mentions twice that the king called Tuah his "beloved" (1991, 257, 263). The monarch confesses his homosocial desire when moaning in despair, "My beloved admiral ... Oh Laksamana, ... Oh Laksamana ... I do love you" (263). His relationship here differs from Western homoeroticism because it is not conceived as a danger or a challenge to social norms by the queen or the prime minister, who "were aware of the sultan's lovesong" (ibid., 263). Indeed, the queen had nothing to worry about because "the relationship between hamba [slave] and raja [king] is acceptable and rational [as in feudal society], [so] emotions may be confused with the show of loyalty" (Noriah Taslim, e-mail 28 May 1997). A specialist in Malay classical literature, Noriah Taslim feels that the king's professed love for his admiral was selfish: Hang Tuah "was useful to the king," an ever-faithful reminder that the power balance favours the ruler, never the subject (ibid.). Unlike the homosocial desire Sedgwick discusses, the sultan's feelings for Hang Tuah are not in conflict with his feelings for the queen.

Another example of the clear expression of Hang Tuah's loyalty to his king and the centrality of the male-to-male relationship appears in the *Hikayat Hang Tuah* when Hang Tuah tries to regain the sultan's trust by abducting Princess Tun Teja for him (she had rejected the king once before). Even though she falls in love with Hang Tuah instead, he steadfastly rejects her, his main concern being to return to the king's good graces. To this end, I would agree with Gayle Rubin's theory that "patriarchal heterosexuality can best be discussed in terms of one or another form of the traffic in women: it is the use of women as exchangeable, perhaps symbolic, property for the primary purpose of cementing the bonds of men with men" (in Sedgwick 1985, 25-26).

Not only are women used as symbolic exchange to strengthen homosocial bonds among men, but within this patriarchal system a man's prestige is also enhanced by his sexual prowess. (The more women he has, the more powerful he is thought to be.) For example, the polygamous sultan has sole access to the palace maidens. And it is rumoured that Hang Tuah was consorting with one of his favourite concubines, which led to the sultan's order for Tuah's execution in the first place; indeed, it is the king's loss of face due to sexual betrayal that triggers the series of events affecting the whole state and leading to Jebat's tragic death.[29] When Hang Jebat takes over the palace, and the maidens, deeply attracted to him, refuse to leave with the sultan's entourage, the sultan's male ego suffers another blow. In short, Fatimah Busu highlights moments of tension in the *HHT* where personal sexual rivalry among the male ruling class blurs the arenas of public and personal in the nation. The exclusion of women (and their relegated status to sexual, commodified objects) emerges strongly from the dynamics of homoerotic male friendship that define the national ideology.

Fatimah Busu's short story highlights and expands on the potentially homoerotic elements evident in the *Hikayat Hang Tuah* to which Salleh Ben Joned has alluded. By making the king dream of cannibalizing Hang Tuah, Fatimah Busu seems to explore what Sedgwick would call a potential continuum between homosocial and homosexual. She plays with the value of *setiakawan*, showing how Hang Tuah "would even die at a royal feast to amuse the king should that be his majesty's will" (1991, 257). In the dream, with his two hands tied behind his back, "firmly displaying his eternal and unyielding loyalty, even to the point of death, to a sultan who regarded him as nothing more than a snack to be consumed with a simple fern-bud sauce," Hang Tuah lay "gracefully on his back and stretched out beside the golden tray and bowl of sauce" whereupon the king ate him (ibid., 262). The fact that the maid who served the king was a naked "beautiful concubine with long ornamented curling hair reaching down to her waist," suggests sexual tension, though it's not heterosexual, as the king ignores her and concentrates on eating Hang Tuah instead. This scenario goes against Sedgwick's argument, which would have the king subvert his desire for Hang Tuah by displacing it with his desire for the maid.[30] Instead, his eating symbolizes incorporation and appropriation of power.[31] While the sultan (due to his birthright and his being the consumer) exercises power over Hang Tuah, he lacks the many virtues associated with his admiral, something that might have worried his unconscious. In fact, Muhammad Haji Salleh claims that it is Hang Tuah's diplomacy, wisdom, courage, and fame that made Melaka a great empire and that "the fate of Melaka was intertwined with Hang Tuah's personal fate" (1991, 138-39). Hang Tuah's passivity and extreme sacrifice in the king's dream reflects the idea that male friendship is somehow deeper and more meaningful than any relationship with a woman. The sacrifice men are willing to make for other men is presumably larger than the sacrifice found within heterosexual relationships, a notion that prevails in an unrelated modern cultural text like the 1996 film *Jimi Asmara* (set in the 1950s and '60s).[32] The film concludes that purity of love can exist only between men. Unfortunately, the friendship between Hang Tuah and Hang Jebat is not strong enough to overcome loyalty to authority, which is sometimes disguised in more appealing forms such as friendship and kinship, demanded of Hang Tuah by the king. Thus, followership outweighs fraternal bonds in importance.

As for the king's homoerotic relations with Hang Jebat, there is a scene in the *Hikayat Hang Tuah* (also represented in Fatimah Busu's updated version) where he rests his head on Jebat's lap while Jebat sings lullabies to him. Noriah Taslim reads this episode as demonstrating the king's trust in Hang Jebat – it's not uncommon for the sultan to lie in the laps of his concubines – and Hang Jebat's violation of that trust when later he takes over the palace and runs amok: "The author [of the *HHT*] wants to juxtapose Jebat's character to that of Hang Tuah, who given such privileges will never react in the way Jebat does. It then qualifies him as *penderhaka* [traitor] and thus justifies all subsequent actions, including his execution in Tuah's hands" (e-mail, 16 June 1997).

Both Fatimah Busu and Salleh Ben Joned view Hang Jebat as hedonistic. Indeed, Fatimah Busu's story is infused with a sense of *jouissance:* the sensual (visual, olfactory, auditory) and erotic aspects of the story highlight Hang Jebat's powers of attraction. When the sultan and his entourage leave the palace, the environment comes alive with sensual imagery. The flowers in the royal garden bloomed and "gave off a lovely fragrance," the clouds "looked like shining pieces of kapok" or "dazzling pieces of silver" and are further personified into "passionate yet shy nymphs leaving Jannatul-Naim heaven dressed in blouses of sea-green silk" (Fatimah 1991, 260).[33] Moreover, the smell from the flowers causes Hang Jebat and "those serving maidens loyal to him [to become] even more intoxicated in their games of love." When he takes over the palace, it is described as shining "radiantly": "every pillar seemed to have been bathed in resin. Candles gleamed on silver and brass trays sending their beams through the palace windows as far out into the black night as their rays could reach" (260-61). By daybreak, the people of Melaka can hear "the sweet and sometimes plaintive sound of the serving maids still reciting *pantun* verses to each other and chatting happily, to a background of Arabian flutes and Persian flutes" (261). This display of sensuality is meant to show that Hang Jebat, as the protagonist and hero of Fatimah's story, is a tremendously virile and sensual character, gifted with an expressive singing voice that can attract women as well as charm the king. In relation to Hang Jebat, every object is gendered; even the clouds are eroticized as shy nymphs. The palace, "now the palace of Immortal Jebat," becomes a metonym of his sexual power. The objects in the palace singled out for reference are phallic: pillars, candles, beams, rays, black and light stripes, flutes (ibid., 206-61).

However, the danger in Hang Jebat's form of *jouissance* and hedonism is that it is limitless, out of control, and adversely affects his social and physical environment. Fatimah Busu's metaphors for such chaos and violence derive from natural disasters that are beyond human control: the people's curses of Jebat spread "angrily like lava from a burning volcano," the fields dry up, a thick cloud of dust "spread[s] like a fearsome plague," the sky turns into "a dark red glow," and the birds and animals flee into the forest (ibid., 254). Unlike other writers' representations of the myth, Fatimah Busu's makes reference to Jebat's killing of the palace maids only once, and even then, it's almost incidental when the narrative focuses on the sorrow of the nymphs for him: "Some of their tears landed on the naked bodies of the serving maidens, stretched out with wounds on their breasts, bellies and thighs, anywhere Taming Sari [Hang Tuah's special *keris*] had been able to touch before Hang Tuah entered the audience hall" (ibid., 267). Instead, the violence in the palace is portrayed in metaphorical terms: "The royal residential palace was coloured a thick dark red. The floors of the audience chamber were a damp dark red and were steadily becoming blacker. The walls, the pillars ... everything, was covered by a vivid red skin which dripped from the ceiling, the crossbars, the trellises, slowly stretching out like the glowing red legs of a cockroach, slowly, silently blazing" (ibid., 255). Obviously the colour red symbolizes Jebat's violence motivated by his passionate anger and *sakit hati* (lit. sickness of the liver) against the king for unjustly ordering his best friend Hang Tuah's execution.

The excess of sensuality in the palace after Hang Jebat moves in affects the king, and is described in hyperbolic prose: "The sultan's tears fell on his pillow in the royal chambers. The sultan's tears fell on his rice in the royal dining quarters. The sultan's tears fell into his drinking mug. The sultan's tears fell into the royal bathing tank. Eventually everything connected with the royal personage was wet, thoroughly dampened by the sultan's own endless weeping" (ibid., 261). In a later scene, "his tears were like a sad gentle rain, or the earth moaning because of all the human suffering it bore" (ibid., 264). Although the mythic proportions and heavy sentimentalism are Fatimah Busu's attempts to recapture an archaic style of storytelling akin to the tall tales in the *Hikayat Hang Tuah*, this sentimentality also reveals the king's utter helplessness without Hang Tuah; his weak leadership provokes the reader once more to question his ability to rule.

His emotional vulnerability or weakness is feminized with a metaphor of maternity, when Fatimah Busu compares His Highness to a "mother cat" or "mother tiger kissing her long-lost cub" – the "long-lost cub" here being the prime minister. In this scene, the prime minister has just confessed that he had disobeyed the king's orders to have Hang Tuah executed and that Tuah is still alive. In the *HHT* the king does cry in despair, but he is not compared to a mother cat nor is he maternalized, as he is here by Fatimah Busu. The kitten or long-lost cub outwardly refers to the prime minister (*Bendahara*), but the king's excessive love indirectly reflects his feelings for Hang Tuah, whom he thought he had lost: "The sultan's *ardent* embrace sent the Bendahara's turban and keris flying across the floor, *so eager was his longing* for the face of Laksamana Hang Tuah" (ibid., 265, emphasis mine). The king-as-mother thus signifies what Benedict Anderson calls the trope of "the family-as-articulated-power-structure," the family as nation (1991, 143). But while the nation is a masculine construct and, in most figurative language, "manliness symbolize[s] the nation's spiritual and material vitality" (Mosse 1996, 23), in Fatimah's text it is the maternal instead of paternal that marks the sultan's relationship to and reign over his subjects. There are a few reasons for this.

In "Dark Night of the Soul", the representation of the ruler as mother reveals the repressed matriarchal base underlying the patriarchy of that time, a patriarchal Islamic system that was grafted onto a combination of local matrifocal, animist, and Hindu roots (Windstedt 1961, 63).[34] This maternal symbol may be a form of dressing up patriarchal feudalism or traditional nationalism as more benign (in a gender-stereotyped fashion) than modern nationalism.[35]

It could also symbolize the intimacy of the primary mother-child relationship that cannot be replicated in the secondary identification the child has with his/her father. Thus, in the discourse of Malay traditional nationalism, the-king-as-mother becomes a deft and concise method of ensuring loyalties from subjects by invoking the primary relationship. The feudal king, like the all-powerful mother who can either reject or love the helpless child, has the power to care for his passive *hamba* or to abuse them. Or this trope of family-as-nation can be read as a sublimation of homoerotic desires, which Fatimah Busu's passage ("the sultan's *ardent* embrace ... *so eager was his longing*") and my emphasis suggests.

What makes Fatimah Busu's representation of Hang Jebat unique is that it is open to many readings. The emphasis on Jebat's sensualism is akin to the project of reclaiming adat that other Malay writers such as Salleh Ben Joned are engaged in. However, in trying to avoid or resist a prescribed Muslim patriarchy in this recuperation of Malay custom, there is a danger of sliding into another kind of misogyny or patriarchy. Such a return to misogyny is suggested by the resexualizing of the Malay woman, evident in the works of some male writers and filmmakers. By contrast, women writers like Fatimah Busu and filmmakers like Shuhaimi Baba focus on aspects of adat such as male sensuality or passion that continue to subvert patriarchy or male reason. For instance, in the process of recovering a sensualist Jebat as the fighter for "truth, human dignity and justice," Fatimah Busu has abandoned the megalomaniac Hang Jebat of the *HHT*, who kills for the sake of being famous, "supaya namaku masyhur pada segala negeri" (so my name will be known throughout the state) (A. Bakar Hamid 1979, 110). But Fatimah Busu's Hang Jebat is not let off scot-free from his crimes. Perhaps the term "hedonist" suits him best because his irresponsible sensuality and passion implicate him as someone governed by emotions rather than reason. Despite his being the champion of truth, his hands are also stained with the blood of the innocent. Towards the end of the story, he explains to his audience of skulls that he belongs to a mixture of two groups of people who keep their physical bodies but live in the world of the dead: the group that is cursed and the group that is honoured (Fatimah 1991, 274). The fact that he exists at this in-between stage or limbo (simultaneously cursed and honoured), rather than being an immaterial soul in heaven (merely honoured) points to the general ambivalence his actions and misdemeanours provoke in us.

Although Jebat's hedonism figures large in the story, at times he also functions as the martyred voice of truth. Harry Aveling, who translated Fatimah Busu's story into English has retitled her "Al-Isra" as "Dark Night of the Soul," based on the Christian treatise "Dark Night of the Soul" by the Spanish mystic St. John of the Cross. According to Frederick Denny, al-Isra refers to the Prophet Mohammad's night journey to Jerusalem. As for "dark night of the soul," it describes the period when the contact with Prophet Mohammad's divine source did not occur or when contact was not established. It's a time when he felt abandoned and depressed. This, explains Denny, is the common experience of other visionaries and mystics who have been plunged into grave doubt and distress after having reached an exalted state of spiritual awareness (Denny 1985, 70). Ironically, Aveling's (mis)translation of Fatimah Busu's title does in some way clarify the absurdist framework of Fatimah Busu's reconstruction of the Tuah/Jebat conflict. Hang Jebat is portrayed allegorically as a visionary. His inability to physically disintegrate suggests his own crucial status as a rebellious, contestatory voice in Malaysian politics and culture today, a voice most vociferously projected by Anwar Ibrahim and his supporters during the height of *reformasi*.[36] Indeed, the Anwar and *reformasi* rhetoric is aligned with that espoused by Fatimah Busu's Hang Jebat: a defence of truth, justice, and the fundamental human freedoms God gives us at the time of our birth (Fatimah 1991, 273). At the same time, Jebat's perpetual vigil for Hang Tuah to come and apologize for killing him reflects the condition best exemplified by Sisyphus's futile action of repetitively pushing a boulder up the hill only to let it roll down again.[37] In an absurd world, Sisyphus can offer no explanation when Hang Jebat asks when he will stop, except to refer it to God: "I can't give you an answer to that question ... Go and ask God!" (ibid., 281). Moreover, Fatimah Busu specifically notes, in the vein of Camus' Sisyphus, that the man is contented to carry out his job into perpetuity: "Sisyphus *contentedly* allowed the boulder to roll back down the hill again ... Then [he] ran down the hill to his beloved boulder and once again started pushing it to the top of the mountain" (ibid., 281, emphasis mine). The derivation of contentment from the purposelessness of the job seems to be Camus' main point, that within the framework of that endless task, we can at least exert control over that one certainty: "The struggle itself towards the heights is enough to fill a man's heart. One must imagine Sisyphus happy" (Camus 1955, 99). The muscular Sisyphus in Fatimah Busu's story is a "champion sportsman" (ibid., 280) who treats his endless task as a method of exerting control over his physical environment. Moreover, there is a sense of pleasure to be gained in pain as the condemned victims tell Hang Jebat: "Painful? In our world pain is the greatest form of pleasure imaginable!" (ibid., 277). Likewise, Hang Jebat's perpetually endless vigil in limbo, his absurdist condition wherein he is dead but continues to have a body, speaks of the human persistence and exercise of will over the forces of physical decay and even moral corruption.

CONTINUITIES

Hang Jebat's classic Malay literary roots as a rebel place him as a crucial contestatory foil and challenge to the powers that preserve the existing social system. In any social or national order, his amok and killing of innocent people is unacceptable, even if the blood he spills during his mad rampage to purge the populace of feudal corruption and blind loyalty is considered "sacrificial blood" (Salleh 1994, 128). Hang Tuah tells Hang Jebat in the course of their duel that anything is pardonable except Jebat's amok, which took the lives of innocent people (A. Bakar 1979, 116). It therefore seems ironic that Hang Jebat is more popularly remembered as a defender of the oppressed. For example, Usman Awang's and Kassim Ahmad's Hang Jebat reigned as Malay hero during a period of anti-neocolonialism (after independence) when Malay rural poverty was at its height (leading up to the student-supported farmers' revolts in 1974). The NEP, the rise of Umnoputraism, and top-level bureaucratic corruption provide the impetus behind plays that deploy Hang Jebat as a champion of the underprivileged and the voice of truth in the 1970s and 1980s. Resurgent Islam, too, plays a role in judging Malaysian political leadership; hence, Fatimah Busu's story uses Hang Jebat as the voice of Islam to critique the moral corruption of the feudal leadership, even though, in turn, Hang Jebat's sins place him in limbo. The overriding powers of the state that thrive on feudal values of followership would suggest that Hang Tuah is the ideal national Malay hero, as Karim Raslan's short story makes evident, and as the fate of Anwar Ibrahim proves.[38]

That some Malay critics and government officials from the Dewan Bahasa Dan Pustaka (National Language and Literature Board) such as Muhammad Haji Salleh lauded Hang Jebat as the modern Malay ideal hero in the early 1990s neither contradicts nor displaces the hegemony of Hang Tuah the hero. Hang Jebat supporters, by their advocacy of freedom of expression and thought, actually give the impression that true liberal democracy exists in Malaysia, an illusion that the conservative government was keen to project both nationally and internationally during the economic boom years. During the period of economic success (1987-96), a success that was in part fostered by an authoritarian state of politics that discouraged trade union activism and individual freedom (Khoo K.J. 1992, 61), Malaysians had to be diligent in preserving their democratic rights from both transnational corporations and the government, which, in the interest of industrial progress and "national development," demanded the sacrifice of such freedoms. When the currency crisis then turned into a full-blown economic recession in Southeast Asia in 1997, that illusion of democratic well-being was openly questioned by Anwar, the *reformasi* movement, and various other non-governmental organizations (new and old) that coalesced around social and civil liberty issues to dismantle the Internal Security Act and to demand more accountability to the people. No matter how nominal his role is in the eyes of the ruling hegemony, when it comes to political power, the figure of Hang Jebat is therefore still quite crucial. He symbolizes the protest vote, the voice of dissent, nonconformity, truth and justice, the moral and religious opposition, and the non-governmental organizations that act as watchdog over abuses in the ruling government. In this sense, he belongs in the material domain, "act[ing] in opposition to and as limit upon the other but, through this process of struggle, [shaping] the emergent form of the other" (Chatterjee 1996, 224). At the same time, his role as perpetual rebel during feudal times as well as in the modern postcolonial nation means that he embodies the maverick spirit of Malayness, which also places him within the spiritual domain of nationalism.

The *reformasi* days may be over – many Web articles on *reformasi* have yielded dead links – and the political martyr Anwar Ibrahim was freed from prison in September 2004, but the Hang Tuah/Hang Jebat metaphor is so deeply embedded in the Malay conscience that it only remains to be seen what new socio-political conflict will bring this comparison to the fore again in future.

3

DissemiNation of Malay/sia

"It's a curse, I know, but I've always felt the need to bite the hand that fed me."

—AMIR MUHAMMAD, 2003[1]

This chapter further examines the factors of language, ethnicity, and Islam in Malaysia by focusing on the works of four Malay male writers: Salleh Ben Joned, Rehman Rashid, Karim Raslan, and Amir Muhammad, who is also a filmmaker.[2] I read their works that deal with issues of identity through postcolonial scholar Homi Bhabha's theory of the pedagogical and the performative, largely because Bhabha's reliance on Lacanian psychoanalysis provides a more complex picture of Benedict Anderson's theory of the dissemination of nationalism through novels and print capitalism. Bhabha explores the slippery crack between "the people" as historical social beings and the way they are constructed and deployed rhetorically through language and discourse. This recognition of unconscious processes functioning as metaphor and as strategies of cultural identity validates those who do not conform to a national type. In this case, just how "Malay" are these four writers, based on their writings that address the nation? Do they fit into the constitutional definition of Malay? That is, are they Muslims? And do they habitually speak Malay and practise Malay custom?

Bhabha's influential essay, "DissemiNation: Time, Narrative, and the Margins of the Modern Nation," discusses the contradictions within the modern liberal nation by situating them within the symbolic structure of signifier and signified and Lacan's mirror stage. In Lacan's visual metaphor, the child with its uncoordinated body parts misrecognizes itself as whole and perfect in the mirror, signalling a disjunction or splitting between the signified (the child) and the signifier (the mirror image). This parallels the split between the performative and the pedagogical, which Bhabha uses to describe the nation: "The borders of the nation are ... constantly faced with a double temporality: the process of identity constituted by historical sedimentation (the pedagogical); and the loss of identity in the signifying process of cultural identification (the performative)" (Bhabha 1994, 304). Simply summarized, the pedagogical stands for the theoretical and ideological meaning of nation while the performative refers to the practical "perplexity of living" (ibid., 307). Using the comparative model of the mirror image, one can also think of the pedagogical as the one perfect whole and the performative as representing the nation/subject's many uncoordinated parts. The pedagogical can never reflect the entirety of the subject as s/he is, but can only ever be a misrecognition of the self as whole or complete. "In the production of the nation as narration, there is a split between the continuist, accumulative temporality of the pedagogical, and the repetitious, recursive strategy of the performative. It is through this process of splitting that the conceptual ambivalence of modern society becomes the site of *writing the nation*" (ibid., 297). And it is this splitting and ambivalence that give shape to double-writing or dissemi-*nation*.

A similar process of splitting is inherent in the concept of Malay/sia as nation. There are sufficient contradictions in and between the (pedagogical) constitution and (performative) government policies to suggest this psychic tension. Although Malaysia is officially a democracy whose constitution recognizes the multi-ethnic character of the populace enough to permit minorities to freely practise their religions and cultures, the indigenous Malays or bumiputeras have special privileges and their religion and language are granted official or national status above the religions and languages of other ethnic groups. There is even a National Cultural Policy, although it's fortunately not strictly enforced, which states that non-bumiputeras have to assimilate to the culture of the region. Thus, the first contradiction presents itself: the name change from *Persekutuan Tanah Melayu* or "Malaya," meaning "the land of the Malays," to "Malaysia" occurred in 1963 to reflect the less homogeneous population of the nation when Sabah, Sarawak, and Singapore became part of Malaysia.[3] However, this "50:50 split" between the indigenous peoples and immigrants that had marked Malaya's independence since 1957 (Rehman 1993, 14) changed with the separation of Chinese-dominated Singapore from Malaysia in 1965. It changed again in 1971, with the introduction of the National Economic Policy and the National Language Policy, which made Bahasa Melayu

Bahasa Malaysia, the national language, and therefore, the medium of instruction and communication for all ethnicities.

Rehman regards the late 1950s, when the population of ethnic Malays and non-Malays was balanced, to be a special time because "being in balance they resisted each other's defences, and each was compelled to recognize the other as an inescapable, ineradicable element of his own reality" (1993, 14). He nostalgically sees the pre-NEP era, 1957-70, as a time when the disjunction between Malay and Malaysian (of many ethnicities), between the pedagogical and the performative, was not quite so clear. Indeed, the policies instituted after the race riots of May 13, 1969 operated and continue to operate as the pedagogical, proclaiming that Malayness represents the nation. For example, when the Chinese lobby group Suqiu presented a petition to Mahathir in 1999 asking for parity rights and the phase-out of special Malay rights, he was said to have viewed the claim with disdain and "likened it to the claims made by the communist [sic] during the Malayan Emergency" (Shome 2002, 191). Most of the policies were inspired by the suggestions in Mahathir's book, *The Malay Dilemma* (1970), which detailed what he thought had led to the race riots and what should be done to alleviate the plight of the Malays who had gradually become the dispossessed of their land (the book was banned at the time). Yet the performative – the existence of the non-Malays who lived within the boundaries of the nation – defies the pedagogical.

Reading Rehman's words, "something in Malaysia resisted too pat an imposition of a postcolonial New Order, insistently making of it something more," brings to mind Bhabha's notion of the incommensurability found in the disjunctive temporalities of the nation (14). Something escapes in the process of signification between the pedagogical and the performative. The Chinese, Indians, and the *Lain-lain* or Others such as the Eurasians not classified as bumiputera, collectively represent the multi-ethnic character of the performative that challenges the pedagogical reliance on Malay homogeneity and cultural purity. These people are Malaysian not Malay; they are the supplement that adds "the many" to the nation "as one," that makes it Malaysia rather than Malaya.

This chapter focuses on a specific group of Malay writers and aims to challenge and test the present borders of the pedagogical ideas of nation, which are meant to ultimately produce "the discourses of emergent cultural identities within a non-pluralistic politics of difference" (Bhabha 1994, 305).[4] The heterogeneity of ethnicity is one aspect of the performative. However, ethnicity in Malaysia is not only a question of skin colour but usually includes language and religion as well. Loyalty to the king or *raja* is also considered one of the three pillars of Malayness but is downplayed because the Agung (the elected leader of the sultans from the various ex-federated states) retains only symbolic powers since the constitutional crises of 1983 and 1993. As a consequence of these constitutional amendments, the urban Malay business and middle classes no longer view the traditional rulers as an important emblem of Malay identity (Loh 2002; Sloane 1999). The pedagogical idea of the nation could be categorized as Malay by ethnicity and language and Muslim by religion, while the performative in terms of languages and religions would generally also include Mandarin and other Chinese dialects, South Asian languages, and English (the religions being Taoism, Buddhism, Hinduism, Christianity, etc.). However, for the purposes of this discussion, I want to focus solely on four writers of the dominant group, the bumiputera, to discuss the split in the 1990s – not between Malay and non-Malay but within the Malay identity and collective psyche itself.

These writers' works demonstrate that their positions of authority as bumiputera are a part of a process that Homi Bhabha has called ambivalent identification (Bhabha 1994, 296). Even though they are considered part of the majority, they function as the "supplementary space of cultural signification that opens up and holds together the performative and the pedagogical," that "provides a narrative structure characteristic of modern political rationality: the marginal integration of individuals in a repetitious movement between the antinomies of law and order" (ibid., 305). Their liminality is reinforced by the fact that they write in English (to a limited audience) and disrupt notions of cultural purity, authenticity, and homogeneity in other ways. Early in his essay, Bhabha asks, "What might be the cultural and political effects of the liminality of the nation, the margins of modernity, which cannot be signified without the narrative temporalities of splitting, ambivalence and vacillation?" (ibid., 298). This chapter will attempt to address Bhabha's question.

Taken together, the writers reflect the attitudes and mentality of four "generations" of male intellectual Malays writing in English in the 1990s: Salleh Ben Joned (b. Melaka, 1941) sees himself as a symbol of the Old Malay; Rehman Rashid (b. Taiping, 1955) represents the Merdeka generation and provides a transition between colonial and postcolonial Malaysia; Karim Raslan (b. Petaling Jaya, 1963) is emblematic of the New Malay, a child of the NEP; and finally, the youngest, Amir Muhammad (b. Kuala Lumpur, 1972), has artful essays that provide a marked contrast with the work of other young Malay/sian anglophone writers of his NEP generation.[5] All are liberal thinkers who were educated abroad – Salleh Ben Joned in Australia and the other three in England. Salleh Ben Joned is a poet and an academic, Rehman Rashid has a degree in marine biology but gravitated to journalism and writing, Karim Raslan is both a writer and practising lawyer, and Amir Muhammad trained as a lawyer but works as a writer, critic, and filmmaker. They have also, at one time or another, written for English-language Malaysian newspapers. I will be referring to Salleh's book of essays, *As I Please*, Rehman's autobiographical novel, *A Malaysian Journey*, Karim Raslan's essays in *Ceritalah* and short stories in the collection *Heroes*, and Amir Muhammad's essays in *Generation: A Collection of Contemporary Malaysian Ideas* and his essay-films in *6horts* (2002). Many would regard this group of writers as part of the bumi elite and somewhat privileged in relation to other Malaysians. Recognizing that they are part of the bumigeois anglophone intelligentsia, I won't argue that their status marginalizes them or that they are oppressed. I do however find that the ideas, beliefs, and values they represent in their narration of the nation, and their ability to broach sensitive issues that are usually outside the bounds of public discourse, certainly contest, intervene in, and disrupt the ideal and static image of hegemonic Malay/sianness. Moreover, in a climate where state and self-censorship is rife, their works are like "a liminal, uncertain state of cultural belief when the archaic emerges in the midst or margins of modernity as a result of some psychic ambivalence or intellectual uncertainty" (Bhabha 1994, 295).

RELATIONSHIP TO LANGUAGE

The language issue troubles the "pedagogical" notions of Malaysian nationhood. The split within Malay identity is not only brought into effect by colonialism but is further complicated by the NEP and the language policy introduced by those who uphold Anthony D. Smith's notion of the genealogical "ethnic nation." The National Language Act and National Educational Policy meant the progressive introduction of Malay language as the sole medium of instruction in secondary schools and universities beginning from 1971. Yet by the end of the NEP era and into the era of the National Development Policy (NDP), some ethnic nationalists remained dissatisfied. On the pedagogical side, these are purists who regarded the implementation of Bahasa Malaysia as an anticolonial and nationalist move against the English language. This mentality is evident in the booklet *Wawasan 2020 dan Pembinaan Bangsa Malaysia*, published by the Department of Anthropology and Sociology at Universiti Kebangsaan Malaysia (UKM). This document is the result of a dialogue held by a group of UKM academics in 1991 about Mahathir's Vision 2020 and its construction of a Malaysian nation/race. Salleh tells us that the academics involved in the dialogue more or less agreed that two main reasons for the failure of the emergence of "a true Malaysian nation" were: "the unwillingness of the majority of non-bumis and a section of the bumi elite to show a genuine and full commitment to the national language" and "the persistence of cultural pluralism despite demands by the bumi literati for a full implementation of the National Cultural Policy" (1994, 55). Further, Salleh reports that they were "particularly concerned about the continuing presence of the language of our former colonial masters." Salleh, Rehman, Karim, and Amir would presumably be targets of this group for belonging to that "section of the bumi elite" regarded as unwilling to commit to Bahasa Malaysia (ibid.).[6]

For Salleh, English is "part of our colonial inheritance" (ibid., 63) and "it's *our* English; along with BM it expresses our 'soul,' with all its contradictions and confusions, as much as our social and material needs" (ibid., 65). Clearly miscast as an anglophile, he defines himself in this passage not only as a postcolonial subject but also as a hybrid national subject for whom two languages play equally important roles in self-expression. Here and in another article in the collection, "Be Sophisticated and Silly All the Way" (12 January 1994), where he discusses the reactions of Malay nationalists to the deputy prime minister's statement about the policy of returning to a greater emphasis on English and the problems of translating textbooks from English into Malay, Salleh echoes Ngugi Wa Thiong'o's calls for a two-way flow between the colonial and the indigenous languages. If Ngugi's point is that Africans who go West to study should return to their home countries, bringing their newly acquired knowledge of the West with them to share and disseminate to their own people in their own languages, then Salleh's statement, "I believe we can be bilingual and at the same time committed to the modernisation of BM" (1994, 69), demonstrates his willingness to "move the centre." During his lecture on "Moving the Centre: Struggle for Cultural Freedom" at the University of British Columbia in November 1996, Ngugi talked about how he used his knowledge of English literature to create and build up Kikuyu literature and theatre (Ngugi 1993). Similar national projects have occurred in the Malay literary world: Shahnon Ahmad's exposure to Western literature when he was in an Australian university signalled the introduction of stream-of-consciousness technique into Malay writings in the early 1970s. Another prominent Malay literary figure educated in the West is Professor Muhammad Haji Salleh; like Ngugi, he began writing in English but chose later to return to writing in his mother tongue, Malay. As for form, Salleh Ben Joned admits that modern Malay literature is largely influenced by the West and that Western-style literary criticism is applied freely to Malay works (1994, 181). Yet somehow, these adoptions and adaptations do not seem to bother the cultural purists.

Salleh points out further the ambivalent nature of purists' relationship to the English language in his parody of their fascination with Western literary jargon. Contrary to what we would assume, those who borrow indiscriminately from English are not the English-educated but "the Malay-educated, especially those who make a lot of noise about the sanctity of the National

Language" (1994, 71). He quotes an example of this absurd transformation: "dalam hubungan konteks pada proses exteriorization dan interiorization lahir perilaku-perilaku osilasi dan stasis organisme" (in the context of the process of exteriorization and interiorization emerge features of oscillation and organic stasis) (ibid., 72). Note that for the purists, this process is not even marked with the ironic subversion and play of Bhabha's notion of mimicry. Instead, Salleh views the Malay-educated nationals' indiscriminate borrowing from English as a desperate attempt at "ego-boosting or something with which to dress up the poverty of their ideas" (ibid., 71).

Such ambivalence created out of simultaneous rejection and desire for the Other, English, possibly reflects the Malay nationalists' underlying inferiority complex or internalized colonial mentality. Ironically, their postcolonial pedagogy recalls the agenda of the so-called anti-imperialist Japanese army during their occupation of Malaya in the 1940s. For example, in Yeap Joo Kim's historical Peranakan romance *Of Comb, Powder and Rouge*, we are told that the Japanese "hated the British, yet they strove to ape them. They forbade any hint of British influence in our lives, yet eagerly and unashamedly broke their own rule" (1992, 171). In the case of Malay literature, the inferiority complex and "poverty of ideas" are understandable outcomes of a "national" culture "jealously guarded" via ethnocentric government policies that, according to Salleh, provide "protection to second and third rate writers against the competition of writers who write in languages that disqualify them from being part of this select band [called National Literature]" (1994, 61-62). In effect, Salleh's rather harsh statement reveals that the place of sanctuary has become a museum for those trapped by their own anticolonial, postcolonial, and homogeneous nationalist stance, those who too diligently police the borders of authenticity and whose culture remains frozen in time. The sense of xenophobia is especially keen when we adopt the Malay expression Salleh uses to describe these nationalists, *seperti katak di bawah tempurung,* which means "like the frog who lives under a coconut shell." Thus, Salleh's essay intervenes as "the present of the people's history," by which Homi Bhabha means "a practice that destroys the constant principles of the national culture that attempt to hark back to a 'true' national past" (Bhabha 1994, 303). Bhabha further adds that "continuist national narratives miss the 'zone of occult instability where the people dwell'" (Bhabha 1994, 303), the zone here representing the culture that is constantly in flux.

The pluralist Salleh explains that there is a role for English to play within the nation: because English is not identified with one race or another, it is a better medium for integration, especially among middle-class Malaysians (1994, 58). At the same time, the English language (and therefore English literature) provides an avenue out of the narrow confines of Salleh's identity as defined by the pedagogical: "Malaysia is my country and so is the world. Actually, my true country is not the world, but world literature" (ibid., 50). For Salleh, world literature is a borderless place of freedom and consciousness, while narration is seen as a desired ideal borne out of the contradictions and ambivalence of the nation space.[7] By gesturing towards a kind of literary or authors' universalism or cosmopolitanism, Salleh is attempting to avoid having to write through ethnicity, which is an admirable albeit impossible feat for a bumi in multi-ethnic Malaysia. As he explains, "If, like me, you happen to be a writer somewhat alienated by your education from the dominant values of your ethnic kind, a writer who stubbornly persists in trying to see through and beyond the inherited blinkers of race and religion, what you call 'loyalty to truth and beauty, justice and freedom' can be considered a betrayal. And for the Malays, this 'betrayal' is a form of apostasy. People like me, bilingual and untroubled by sentimental pieties, are particularly vulnerable" (ibid., 49).

Shades of such a "cosmopolitical" attitude also appear in Amir Muhammad's writing. While some discourse around cosmopolitanism seems to polarize loyalty to nation with the notion of global, Pheng Cheah and Bruce Robbins (1998) invest in a version of cosmopolitanism that neither abjures nationalism for the diaspora, nor for an abstract universal common morality, nor alternatively, a globalized market. Rather, their term "cosmopolitical" can be adapted to refer to those writers whose exposure to world literature and global issues nuances their perspectives on local culture without displacing or dislodging their very embeddedness in the local socio-economic and political realities. To quote the cosmopolitical Amir Muhammad himself: "You have a choice of opting out completely into a consumerist, materialist haven where all your reference points are Western, or you can try to engage with what's actually happening around you" (in Stephen Tan 2002). For example, in an article from 1 June 1996 entitled "The Malay/sian Dilemma," Amir dismisses the interest in the Malay diaspora as another ethnocentric move on the part of the political elite who are (intentionally) blind to the racialized situation in Malaysia: "Some of the political and language leaders seemed more interested in establishing solidarity with Malay South Africans rather than non-Malay Malaysians" (1998, 105). The answer to the question of when all citizens can achieve equal rights and justice and be known under the one name "Bangsa Malaysia" (Malaysian race/nationality), he asserts, "can be found right here. Not in South Africa" (ibid.).

Lest it seem as if these Malay language purists make easy targets for sharp wits like Salleh, Amir Muhammad (who is multilingual) is also concerned about the health and survival of the Malay language. Malay, he claims, is threatened first by "the very real reluctance of people to utilise the language in all situations" and second, by "the very real reluctance of the guardians and policymakers of the language to embrace non-Malay Malaysians as part of their audience" (1998, 104). Amir then affirms that this is a problem beyond mere semantics and is "crucial if we ever want Malay to be a *truly* national language" (ibid.). He then points to state-supported Malay-language magazines like *Dewan Masyarakat*, which assume their readership to be Malay (with phrases like "Sebagai orang Melayu, kita harus") and which concentrate on issues that pertain only to Malays (1998, 103).[8] Clearly, his concern for Bahasa Malaysia arises not from an ethnic-nationalist pedagogical perspective but from an ethnically inclusive performative one. And his emphasis on "*truly* national" exposes the patriotic feeling behind the cosmopolitical gesture/strategy.

THE BUMI DILEMMA

Salleh, Rehman, and Karim face what the oldest among them calls the "Bumi dilemma," which "afflicts only a tiny minority among the Bumiputeras": whether "to be or not to be part of a 'protected species': that is the question. Whether it is nobler in the mind to 'opt out' for the sake of necessary pride and independence and fidelity to ideals that transcend barriers of ethnicity – that, or to commit some kind of moral suicide by accepting unquestioningly those convenient pieties about ethnic survival and dominance" (Salleh 1994, 47). The bumi dilemma is especially acute and stressful for the Malay/sian writer, who is forced to confront questions of fidelity or loyalty (ibid., 47). To whom does a "Malaysian writer of Malay origin" owe his loyalty? Malay readers or Malaysian readers of all ethnicities? As a product of his generation whose education abroad, for example, was supported by the Colombo Plan rather than a MARA government scholarship, Salleh is less constricted by ethnic debt to the NEP. However, this is not the case for someone like Karim Raslan, who attributes his journalistic political conservatism to the debt he, as a wealthy, educated Malay, owes his nation: "The assistance (moral, political and financial) that I have received over the years makes me both indebted and perhaps more importantly, somehow responsible" (1996a, 66). This experience of indebtedness is complex; he admits that "*as a writer*, I'm forced to tussle both with this responsibility and a changing world, a world where the verities I grew up with – those democratic, liberal ones – are no longer valid" (ibid., emphasis mine). Despite this admission, Karim's writing in *Ceritalah* reveals his caution and anxiety to please everyone rather than to do as Salleh does, which is to please himself. Instead, it is in the area of short fiction that Karim's cynicism projects itself in a scathing critique of the bumigeois of the 1990s.

Although wary about being the token Malay, writers like Rehman realise that "the Bumi thing" allows them to "take on subjects that no non Bumi commentator would have been allowed to treat with as much impunity" (Rehman 1993, 200). Indeed, it is by testing the limits of journalism in the government-controlled media that Malay/sian writers like Salleh, Rehman, Amir and, to a limited extent, Karim, attempt to cope with the bumi dilemma.[9] Using humour to cloak pertinent political commentary, Rehman says: "I began to take it as a personal challenge to test the limits, to write about as many of the things that were happening to Malaysia as possible: the political hot potatoes, the 'sensitive issues'" (1993, 201). His self-published book, *A Malaysian Journey,* is a testament to this idea, for all four publishers to whom he showed his manuscript liked it but could not accept it, based on their lawyers' advice. This constitutes the kind of self-censorship that Malaysian publishers and writers practise all too often (Salleh 1994, 51-54; Amir 1998, 90-93; Stothard in Amir M. et al. 1998, 49-52). Amir Muhammad, too, tested the boundaries in his fortnightly literary column "Perforated Sheets" (1996-December 1999) in the government-run *New Straits Times* but less through the confessional self-as-nation mode than through style, timing of issues, veiled allusions to Malaysian local politics, satire, irony, and irreverent wit (see Khoo Boo Teik 2002). Amir had written for the print media since he was fourteen years old, but his literary and film column was terminated on 7 December 1999 (Ng 1999), after it began to be regarded as "anti-establishment" for making connections between Western literature and the treatment of Anwar Ibrahim in 1998.

Rehman's hope for a final rest to the bumi dilemma (which arose from the Malay dilemma of economic backwardness culminating in the 1969 race riots) lies in Mahathir's Vision 2020 policy. The policy is a plan for Malaysia to attain the status of a fully developed nation by that year. It means "a self-sustaining economy, serving a populace that considered itself Malaysian first, anything else second. [It meant] the elimination of race as a function of the Malaysian reality" (Rehman 1993, 267-68). Because the bumiputeras rather than minority groups stand to gain from identity politics, the elimination of this category will benefit the non-bumis. And such an elimination can be achieved only through the dismantling of race-based policies. In Rehman's view, the day the NEP comes down will be the day the bumiputeras no longer need it. In his book, he explained to a group of sixth formers: "The NEP's ultimate success will only come when the emerging generation of Malaysians has no memory of it, no feeling for it, no knowledge of it other than what they learn in history class" (1993, 277). Hence, when he met a generation of hybrid Malays born in the early 1970s and educated abroad who were totally ignorant of what the NEP was, he was unduly optimistic about their innocence, unsuppressed ambitions and lack of what Karim Raslan calls "Melayu angst" (1996a, 14): "How innocent of the baggage of expectations imposed upon the Malays in the effort to exorcise their insecurities. And how effortlessly, even ignorantly, they exceeded these expectations!" (Rehman 1993, 277). He believed that a new Malaysian definition was emerging, that "it would be devised by the new generation of Malaysian for themselves, in all their blessed arrogance and freedom, and not be imposed upon them by the need to atone for the sins of their fathers" (ibid., 277).

Rehman's optimism stems from his failure to question the privileges and wealth of this young group of *bumiputeh* (what they call themselves, meaning Malays with Caucasian blood), one of whom is actually a member of the Kedah royalty. Because of their education abroad, their ignorance about racialized experiences or about the NEP is not so much a sign of their uninhibited creative ambitions as it is of their "sheltered" lives. In a way, Rehman envies them their lack of emotional baggage, their psyches uncomplicated by the neurosis of the bumi complex from which he perceived himself to suffer. A similar, younger sense of optimism can be found in Amir Muhammad's writing, which speaks from a distance, removed from such personal psychological tuggings about a bumi "complex." Instead, he assumes the confidence of his post-1969 generation in finding the thought of the New Malay being "prepared to deal with the other races on a level playing field, and to throw away his subsidised crutches while marching confidently to Vision 2020" to be "an encouraging sign" (Amir et al. 1998, 105).

Rehman Rashid's personal (yet public) tussle with this dilemma is probably a necessary step towards eliminating racial discrimination on the part of a conscientious bumi majority. Rehman Rashid's account of the future of the nation being Malaysia rather than Malay/sia is certainly more optimistic than Salleh's. And there is room for optimism because he seems to be moving only within the limited borders of those who speak and live in English. Here, I am not referring to the people he met during the journey he describes in the subtitled sections of his text but rather to the political and personal accounts in the numbered chapters of the book. Both Karim and Salleh acknowledge that English is largely the language of the elite (Salleh 1994, 58; Karim 1996a, 42). For example, the English-language newspapers attract only 10 percent of the reading population. Therefore, Rehman's membership in a group of like-minded English-educated bumi elites isolated him from the ethnocentric thinking of Malay nationalists, even as it simultaneously opened up communication with those racial others negotiating in English. However, if like Salleh he believed that political change and leadership would come from the middle class and the elite, then perhaps his optimism is not unrealistic.

ETHNICITY AND RELIGION

The treatment of ethnicity and religion by these writers further exemplifies the disjunction between the pedagogical and the performative. In Amir Muhammad's case, he seems to be less preoccupied with the bumi dilemma than the Malay/sian dilemma, which is also the title of one of his essays. In this essay, he opens with the line, "Not all Malaysians are Malays" and then follows it up with "But no matter how obvious said fact may be, there are Certain Quarters that still don't know how to play properly, and seem to insist that the two words are synonymous" (Amir et al. 1998, 103). Five years later, Amir explores in more depth the issue of racial division in Malaysian society in his short film *Pangyau,* in which the Malay author-narrator's musings about Cantonese lessons take him back to his teenage friendship with a Chinese schoolmate. The narrator talks about the normalization of racial segregation in the classroom where the Chinese students sat with the Chinese and the Malays sat with the Malays. Being only half-Malay, he did not feel he really belonged to either. When this racial segregation is pointed out by one of the boys in an essay, the teacher reprimands him, saying, "You shouldn't mention something like that. It's a sensitive issue." If, as Mandal suggests, Amir believes that there is a struggle underway between the pluralist tendencies in society and the institutions that have been ethnicized (Mandal 2001), it is because Amir is personally involved in the contestation. In *Friday,* a film essay about the practice of Islam and being Muslim in Malaysia, he writes that, according to the website of the National Mosque, the mosque symbolizes unity as well as racial and religious tolerance in Malaysia because many Indians and Chinese gave money to help build it. Amir then adds, "A true test of unity would be if Muslims gave money to the construction of non-Muslim houses of worship as well. After all, fair is fair." In such instances, the filmmaker shows how dialogue about ethnicity and religion is suppressed by ideological state apparatuses, the same Althusserian ideological state apparatuses that operate through ethnic chauvinist policies, which assume and target assimilation to the cultural hegemony in the guise of racial tolerance and support from the ethnic minority groups.

Generally, the four writers have a very liberal approach to Islam. Rehman informs us that his not knowing how to pray set him apart from the other boys in the Malay College at Kuala Kangsar (Rehman 1993, 82); Karim "hardly ever [goes] to the mosque" (Karim 1996a, 14); and Salleh probably enjoys drinking beer, as can be gleaned from this playful passage about a pub called The

Crescent: "Well, being a good Moslem, when I thought of the crescent, the Islamic paradise promised by the Prophet immediately came to mind. And I had a vision of paradisal rivers cascading with *aqua paradiso*. 'Know that paradise is beneath the shadow of the sword.' So goes one apocryphal prophetic tradition; and paradisal swords are always crescent-shaped – at least to my mind" (1994, 1). In an interview, Amir candidly remarks, "I stopped drinking alcohol in 1997 so I don't go to bars anymore" (Wira 2003) and in his film *Pangyau* the narrator mentions that he ate pork for the first time a few years later in another country. Amir also regards religion as a private matter, a personal relationship between the individual and God, which is why he chooses not to show the prayer scene in *Friday*.[10] This liberalism sets Amir in quite stark contrast with canonical Malay writers writing in Malay such as Shahnon Ahmad, who was one of the pioneers of the *dakwah* novel in the 1970s and 1980s.

Amir's short film *Friday*, also included in *6horts*, is a frank portrayal of mainstream Islam in Malaysia. The film begins with the Friday afternoon call to prayer and follows Muslims through the activities of eating, buying, and selling outside the mosque to performing the ablutions before prayer to their final dispersal. Here Amir points out how the Prophet's sayings are freely interpreted to suit some Malays' lax attitudes towards worship. His approach to Islam as the hegemonic religion of a multicultural Malaysia is to not regard it as separatist or repressively homogeneous – that is, a religion that bodes no tolerance for internal and external (interfaith, inter-ethnic) dialogue. The film text explains how the sermons have been tamed and the *khatib* of the mosque is not supposed to deviate from the text provided by the central religious authority. "The ostensible aim is to create unity. But it is also to curb dissent." As a result, the sermons in the National Mosque, which are broadcast nationally, are bland, moralistic, and uninteresting. It is no wonder then that the congregation is not listening: their minds are on work, food, and their toenails. Nevertheless, fiery independent sermons delivered from remote mosques accuse political leaders of secularism – "the rudest word of all," Amir adds in parenthesis. Obviously, secularism is regarded as the antithesis of religious belief.

It is no wonder then that Salleh and Karim are concerned that a Western liberal education may be necessarily detrimental to one's Asian ethnicity and religious beliefs. Karim poses the question of modernization's influence on his ethnic identity: "Could I be a modern Malay and still be a Malay? Or had I, in fact, betrayed my roots, my *adat* and my faith by being so modern?" (Karim 1996a, 15). Similarly, Salleh admits that he is quite Westernized and that he made a conscious attempt to recover his lost cultural self upon returning from Australia. Only half-succeeding in this cultural recovery, he claims, "Quite frankly, I didn't want to recover my original cultural identity in its fullness and purity. The idea of recovering something of the 'purity' of Malay language itself might appeal to the poet in me, but not those values whose 'purity' or 'Malayness' cannot be distinguished from atavism" (Salleh 1994, 49). Thus, the pedagogical, by reverting to a static homogeneous past, is in danger of being atavistic.

WRITING THE NATION/SELF

If the national newspaper articles that turned into book publications contribute to national and public discourse, so obviously do films (Dissanayake 1994). Yet what qualifies Amir Muhammad's short films as performative gestures to the pedagogical is the form they take, which subsequently defines the boundaries of their content and meaning. Formulated with low-budget digital video technology, and screened only in small public spaces/forums to avoid censorship, Amir Muhammad's essay-films blend the personal documentary with socio-political commentary about middle-class life in Kuala Lumpur. In fact, the headline on the VCD cover proudly announces, "Amir Muhammad *6horts:* sharing his thoughts in an *uncensored way.*" In his Director's Notes (http://6horts.tripod.com), Amir insists that if essays are necessarily about ego, then his essay-films are saying, "For God's sake, open up the universe a bit more!" In other words, as an independent filmmaker, he wants to be innovative ("not merely imitate the tropes of our monolithic and unadventurous big-budget peers") and yet be able to make a connection with his viewers (not make films that are "nothing more than mannerist artiness"). He also frequently maintains that these shorts are not really experimental but provide "fun for the whole family" (S. Tan 2002). The films are personal stories that not only constantly subvert the state ideology and deconstruct notions of pedagogical Malayness but also leave room for dialogue with an audience about the self/nation, as if to suggest that, through the dialectical interaction with the films, other more grassroots and flexible ideas about nation can emerge. Quoting a poem by Malay artist and poet Latiff Mohidin, "Siapakah yang kau cari? Kalau tak dirimu sendiri, tiap-tiap hari" (Who are you looking for? If not your own self, every single day) in his "Director's Notes," Amir asks his viewers/readers, "What am I looking for? You tell me and I bet you will feel really empowered." He seems to be suggesting here that telling about one's quest can serve to empower others. Non-bumi readers/viewers probably appreciate his statements in *Friday* that overturn bumi-centric assumptions such as, "A true test of unity would be if Muslims gave money to the construction of non-Muslim houses of worship as well. After all, fair is fair" (quoted from the film).

Of the three older writers, Salleh is more subversive and critical than Rehman Rashid and Karim Raslan. He is incisively honest and candid in providing his views on Islam and the Malay identity. And although he does not mention the precise details of his ethnic background the way Rehman and Karim do, it is probably because he is all-Malay. Salleh's unquestionable ethnicity perhaps gives him a kind of "autochthonous" right to be more outspoken than the other two, bearing in mind that the basis for autochthonous rights depends on how far back one is willing to go to trace one's genealogical ties to the land (Vickers 1997; Van der Heide 1996, 108). Instead of being explicitly subversive like Salleh, Rehman and Karim, neither of whom are "pure" Malay, are more involved in the legitimizing process of writing themselves as and into the heart of the nation.

Indeed Rehman's narrative about a physical Malaysian journey begins at the literal border of the nation, at the Padang Besar railway station near Thailand, and arrives or ends in the capital city of Kuala Lumpur only in the final subtitled section "The Journey Home." Both Rehman's and Karim's self-referential texts echo Rushdie's connections between the narrative of the self and that of the nation in *Midnight's Children.* Compare these three passages:

> I was born in the city of Bombay ... once upon a time. No, that won't do, there's no getting away from the date: I was born in Doctor Narlikar's Nursing Home on August 15th, 1947. And the time? The time matters, too. Well then: at night. No, it's important to be more ... On the stroke of midnight, as a matter of fact (Rushdie 1991, 3).

> I was born soon after midnight, soon after mid-year, soon after mid-century, in a town called Taiping, in the state of Perak, in the north of what was then known as British Malaya (Rehman 1993, 25).

> I was born in August 1963. I like to think it's an auspicious month because I share the month, if not the exact date, with the nation – one of those little coincidences that bring a smile to your face (Karim 1996a, 23).

While Rehman Rashid does not refer to the birth of the nation at this point, his novel, *A Malaysian Journey*, spans fifty years of Malaysian history, from the end of World War II to Independence in 1957 for Malaya, to the birth of Malay*sia* in 1963, the separation from Singapore two years later, the race riots in 1969, the NEP in 1971, and the resurgence of Islam until the 1990s. In the citation above, Karim Raslan identifies with Malaysia, whose name change from Malaya, that is, land of the Malays, reflects more accurately the multi-ethnic facet of the nation and his own identity. More pertinently, Karim Raslan explains, "I am, in my own way, a curious reflection of the whole. Because if we accept that Malaysia, the nation and its diverse people are the whole, then I, as a mix of Malay and English blood, am a combination of similar contrasts" (1996a, 24). Further, he points to the link between nation and narration: "I am just one of the many aspects of our nation, because Malaysia is the sum total of all these strange mixtures and all their stories" (ibid., 24). This linking of the self and the nation through narration is part of the performative aspect of nationalism for it is through repetitive narrating of difference that the multifaceted nation is constructed. Karim Raslan is aware of the absence of the master narrative; his is only one of many stories. And Malaysia, being "the sum total of all these strange mixtures and all their stories," reflects the nation or what Bhabha would term "the many as one" (1994, 294).

Karim Raslan's mixed heritage belies the ambivalence of his bumiputera status. A friend once asked him, "How can you call yourself a Malay? Firstly, you hardly ever go to the mosque. Secondly, your Malay is so bad you sound like a Bangladeshi. Thirdly, you look like a bloody *Mat Salleh*" (1996a, 14).[11] Rehman, too, is of mixed heritage. His father's family came to Malaya in the wake of the Indian Mutiny of 1857 and intermarried with the local Malays so that "in time, there grew to be no question but that they were Perak Malays [Perak being a state in Peninsula Malaysia], for all their Arab-Indian stock" (1993, 40). However, his mother is an Indian Christian (now a Muslim convert), and his parents' disparate ancestries "had become intertwined in a common language, which was English, and united by what their generation was convinced had to be a common future, which was Malayan" (ibid., 42). So it's no surprise that Rehman had "an English-speaking upbringing" (ibid., 81). His limited command of Malay and his un-Malay looks are in direct contradiction to his bumiputera status. In this, there is a sense that his position is as tenuous as that of the non-bumis: the Chinese, Indians, and other ethnicities sometimes still classified as *pendatang* – or immigrants (despite the fact that they might have already been the third or fourth generation to be born in Malaysia).

Perhaps it makes sense then that both Rehman and Karim are sympathetic to immigrants and subscribe to the idea of their nation as a land of immigrants: "Malaysia is nation that is built on the sweat, determination and ingenuity of its immigrants ... when I use the word 'immigrant,' I don't just mean those of us who came from China and India. Because, by using the word 'immigrants,' I am also referring to the many Malaysian Malays who came from Sumatra, Java and Sulawesi, the ones who bequeathed us the *Tuhfat al-Nafis* with its descriptions of the Bugis warriors who were to lay the foundations for many prominent Royal Houses in Malaysia today" (Karim 1996a, 43). Karim might have in mind his own father, who was a Bugis. Rehman's emphatic valuing of immigrants can be further seen in his account of Malaya at the time of Independence. He notes that the percentage of immigrants compared to that of the indigenous populations in Malaya was "literally a 50:50 split" which he understands as the reason that Malaysian multiracialism has been relatively successful (1993, 14). He adopts a Rushdian perspective that "the immigrant is the central figure of our time" and applies it to Malaysia:

> This had indeed been the anthem of the twentieth century: the sound of ships' horns and jet engines, the susurrus of arrival halls and departure lounges; the great discordant chorale of commingled humanity. Rivers of people, adventurers and refugees, flowing to and fro, rushing swollen with hope or shrunken in despair, breaking their banks and spilling over borders and boundaries, endlessly seeding new lands or inundating old ones, irrevocably reshaping their human geographies, raising again and again the conflict of old and new, "here" and "there," "us" and "them," imposing on ancient lands new realities, new social orders ... It had become a hybrid, grafted, cross-fertilized world, and diversity alone explained little. (Rehman 1993, 13-14)

The idea of "spilling over borders and boundaries" is worth consideration. In a way, by writing themselves into the nation and into Malayness, Rehman and Karim hope to work from within to break down stereotypes of Malay identity and to problematize borders that separate ethnicities and boundaries that keep orders pristine and pure. For example, Karim finds that he has to play conflicting roles in order to be considered Malay: he is between the traditional model that emphasized "loyalty, obedience and blind devotion to authority," and the NEP model – "a dynamic, cosmopolitan businessman, hunting down business opportunities in Yangon, Tashkent, Jo'burg and Santiago" (1996a, 15). These two images come into simultaneous contradictory play due to the opportunities of the NEP. Yet what each has done to the other is to disrupt notions of culture as static, homogeneous, and exclusionary; they challenge the idea that one has to be only one thing or the other, not simultaneously both. Furthermore, Karim recognizes that "a cultural identity is not fixed," but always in flux, constantly changing due to historical, geographical, environmental and socio-economic factors (1996a, 16). In fact, he embodies a perfectly cultivated cultural hybrid identity that a Malaysian journalist describes as "disarming candour and charm ... attractively packaged as it were in a British accent plus blend-in-with-the-locals-type *lahs* tacked onto words" (Sia 1996).

Rehman's ideal for Malaysian nationhood is summed up in an epiphany about hybridity:

> MIX THE BLOODS! Mix them in the most enjoyable way imaginable, which is on a molecular-genetic level, and we need never again fear they might mix in the gutters of our streets, streaming from the mortal wounds we might inflict on each other. Mix the bloods! Unlock the mighty hidden potential of Malaysian genetics; expand the gene pool! Create wonderful new generations of astonishingly beautiful children of indeterminate race, the property of no one culture, and therefore the owners of them all! (1993, 269)

Salleh shares this sentiment, though he expresses it in terms of cultural pluralism and in his reclamation of the derogatory term *kebudayaan rojak* (salad culture): "Anyway, what's wrong with *kebudayaan rojak?* Malaysians like *rojak.* It's good for them, and it helps nation-building" (1994, 57). Countering the UKM academics who wanted the National Culture Act to be enforced, he argues that "Unity in diversity is certainly better for the vitality of our cultural life than the imposition of an artificially conceived national culture through legislation. A living culture, as everyone knows, grows naturally; it cannot be programmed or legislated according to an abstract recipe" (ibid., 57). Salleh may not have read Homi Bhabha but his description of hybridity certainly coincides with Bhabha's. It is "the perplexity of the living as it interrupts the representation of the fullness of life" (Bhabha 1994, 314).

While Rehman and Karim write themselves into Malayness, altering or reconstructing Malayness in the process, Salleh writes himself out of Malayness. His methodology is post-structuralist while his general attitude towards society and humanity can be described as liberal humanist. Such an attitude forces him to break out of the narrow ethnocentric confines of what it means to fulfill the pedagogical ideas of bumi identity: his loyalties belong more to the broader space of world literature than to his nation's own literature. Meanwhile, his Derridean play with language across cultural meanings helps him deconstruct these cultural boundaries. For example, he gives multiple readings on his name Salleh: in English, to sully; and a trace of the French *sale* (dirty); it hearkens to the Malay nickname for a Britisher, Mat Salleh; but, finally, in Arabic, it means "pious" (1994, 37-38).

Despite his movement across languages, Salleh also writes out of a confident sense of being Malay. In fact, he seems to be on a one-man mission to recover or recuperate the abject in classical Malay literature. Julia Kristeva defines abjection as "what disturbs identity, system, order. What does not respect borders, positions, rules" (1982, 4). In Salleh's essays, the abject refers to the scatological (see "Kiss My Arse – In the Name of Common Humanity" 1994, 142); it defines the hedonism, the earthiness, the sexuality of Malay adat that are evident in the rhymed quatrains or *pantun* that the pedagogical notion of Malayness has sanitized/Islamicized, and repressed. Upon analyzing several *pantun*, he concludes that "anybody who claims that the Malay is a compulsory puritanical exile on earth must have a fantasy Malay in mind" (ibid., 156). With this puritanical or fantasy Malay, he is responding here to Frank Swettenham's Orientalist version of the "real" Malay. By contrast, Salleh's Malay "loves this world with all the pleasures it has to offer. And if he is a natural poet, he can – or at least he used to – celebrate it in a language that vibrates with sensuous openness, without any sense of shame or guilt" (ibid., 156). Not surprisingly, then, is his own collection of poems entitled *Sacred and Profane*. The poems demonstrate his intention to transport the sensuality found in classical Malay literature to modern Malay literature and, by doing so, to transform the modern. It has to be clarified that by "sensuality" Salleh is referring specifically to the "raw pleasures of the senses" (ibid., 154). Elsewhere however, his discussions of Classical Malay *pantun* and literature frequently include the word "erotic" to describe the sexual aspect of sensuality. As we saw in Chapter 2, perhaps Salleh's reclamation of Malay hedonism can best be seen in his "'deviant' image of the notorious rebel Hang Jebat," whom he presents as a hedonist, rather than as a hero (ibid., 153). While Salleh's musings seem to be veering on the edge of essentialism – "If it is true that hedonism was part of the essential nature of the race" (ibid., 161) – he is actually skeptical of essentialism per se, for he insists "that 'essential Malayness,' *whatever it is*, does not have to remain completely pure, if that is possible, for a Malay poet to remain Malay" (ibid., 42, emphasis mine). Perhaps his effort to recover the abject "lurking in the subconscious" may be regarded as a strategic essentialist manoeuvre to disrupt the "bigger alien force" (ibid., 161), which is the agent of pedagogical Malay/sianness.

Amir Muhammad's stance with regard to issues like ethnicity and immigration brings an interesting twist to this question. The identity problems that raised questions for Salleh, Rehman, and Karim no longer guide Amir in his work. Although not fully Malay, he is not preoccupied with the degree of his Malayness or limited by it in his criticisms that deal with sensitive issues like race, religion, and the power of the monarchy – all issues that emerge in his documentary-fiction *The Big Durian* (2003). Perhaps this has to do with having grown up in the post-May 13, 1969 era.[12] In *The Big Durian* for instance, Amir claims that the big thorny event for his generation was not so much May 13, 1969 but 1987, when a soldier by the name of Private Adam went amok with an M16 through KL's Chow Kit district. Although Amir is just as bold and sharp as Salleh Ben Joned, if not even more daring, in tackling the sensitive issues head on, neither the sale, distribution, or limited exhibition of *6horts* has been banned. And when Amir was asked about the possibility of its censorship, he answered tongue-in-cheek: "There have been no fatwas yet that I know of," referring of course, to the case of Salman Rushdie (Wira 2003).[13] Amir Muhammad's work follows from Salleh's in more ways than one. An admirer of Salleh's irreverent style, Amir frequently refers to Salleh's work. The synopsis for his short film *Friday,* found on the back cover of the VCD and on the website, makes reference to the title of Salleh's book of *Poems Sacred and Profane:* "An afternoon at the National Mosque encourages thoughts both sacred and profane."

Amir pushes the boundaries of social and political decorum by using sexual discourse to destabilize serious topics. Deliberately sounding as pedantic and moralistic as a Malaysian television *ustaz,* he explains, "The Lesson for Today has to do with the rarity of true individual thought and action, and the consequent threat it poses to those who want a monopoly on truth and power" (Amir et al. 1998, 18-19). But then he follows it up with this: "'Individualism' has, of late, been the new whipping boy, or whipping girl, in the increasingly sadomasochistic arena of Malaysian public discourse. You want to be an individual? Whack! Smack! Try on these chains for size. Let me gag you first. You like that? Yeah, you're begging for it, aren't you? Take it like the tart you are" (ibid., 18). This form of sexual discourse cannot be equated with Salleh's efforts to reclaim adat. Its reference points (sadomasochism) are very Western.

In fact, Amir Muhammad's writing belies his facility and familiarity with English and American idioms, lifestyle, films, and academic and intellectual language. For example, "It's a Queer World," an essay that appears in the magazine *Men's Review,* seems to be an ode to Oscar Wilde in its content, style, and ironic tone. He begins: "Heterosexuality, that quaint but mysteriously long-lived practice of fancying only people of the opposite sex, has passed its sell-by date. Good. The wonder of straightness is not that it is in decline but that it has lasted so long" (Amir et al. 1998, 69). In "The Case for Critics," he describes self-professed critics as "wankers," thereby pushing the boundaries of social propriety for a literary column in the government-controlled *New Straits Times.* But the first definition of the term *wanker* he offers is obscure except to the very literary: "In its strictest sense, it refers to one who indulges in the sin of Onan. But it is generally applicable to anyone who indulges in some sort of seemingly futile and po-faced activity" (ibid., 32). Speaking about his trip to New York City, and about New York as a postmodern, overquoted location, he writes: "I look at the fire hydrants and think:

You schmucks, you've got nothing on the hydrant in *Do The Right Thing*. Even when I write about this place, I think of Tom Wolfe, who did it a lot better. Intertextuality is inevitable when you're trying to capture New York" (ibid., 24). As for the 1980s blockbuster novel, he says that "she can also be described as the Bonk Bonanza, the Beautiful Bitch or the Ballsy Babe (The BB as a genre inspires nothing if not a certain earthiness of vocabulary)" (ibid., 57).

Yet at the same time, his writing shows he is well versed in the language of modern urban Malays, bumigeois lifestyle, Malay myths, and even Malay literary aesthetics. He examines four "trashy Malay entertainment magazines," claiming that he is not delivering a value judgment but "acknowledging trash as a valid genre of its own, with its artistic conventions and iconography" (ibid., 29). Bored with "the increasing 'bourgeoisification' and 'yuppification' of the Time Information Highway set," these magazines provide him with "refreshing respite" (ibid.). And he draws the readers' attention to the Malay myth of "The Attack of the Killer Swordfish" in Singapore to discuss "mould-breaking, singular, blazing" individualism but plays around with our sense of time/history and middle-class conformist values by speaking about it in anachronistic ways. Referring to the myth, he cannot resist making jibes at the authoritarian Singaporean PAP government of the present: "There was once a very bright Singaporean kid, but he never got a chance to go to the NUS [National University of Singapore] or even to join Mensa. He was killed before he became a man. He was killed by the State, in fact, because he was a threat to the established order. No, you won't find this tragic tale in the files of Amnesty International, and it never became an issue in the Singaporean elections" (ibid., 18). Amir Muhammad's position in these essays and films illustrates the complex parallels, tense connections, and contradictions in the relationship between modernity (its Western liberal discourse and developmentalist ideology) and Malay culture (though not solely limited to adat). While hearkening back to the Malay myth ostensibly to criticize middle-class conformism, his position offers also, perhaps, a subtle critique of the remains of something more feudal-like: followership.

As a columnist who critiques Malaysian immigration policies as racist, Amir shows he is no follower. He points out the racism inherent in the poor treatment of Bangladeshi migrant workers as opposed to the treatment of their fairer Muslim counterparts, the Bosnians. Then he makes linkages between this racism and the sudden proliferation of skin-whitening products to criticize Malaysians' hypocrisy with regard to their anti-imperialist rhetoric and class discrimination. While he finds that most heroes and heroines of the *Sejarah Melayu* or *Malay Annals* are "unusually pale" he notes the exceptions when "skins that are *hitam manis* and *putih kuning* are also thought to be comely" (ibid., 152).[14] But even after such attacks on hypocrisy, there is a glimpse of Amir's ideal Malaysia: "I interpret these exceptions as being victorious proletarian ruptures in the otherwise bourgeois fabric of today's life. They offer evidence of a teeming, throbbing world out there, a world that's boisterous and confident enough to accommodate all colours. This sounds like a very nice Malaysia indeed" (ibid.).

Amir gets away with his transgressive critiques partly because of a cunning style: subtle, ironic, and understated, at times he is playfully arrogant, self-knowingly moralistic, and campy. Such a style confuses the reader in its maze-like gallop through numerous cosmopolitan references, its carnivalesque strategies of bringing the high-brow desires of the new Malay middle class to the low via kitsch aesthetics, and elevating the low-brow to the heights of high culture. His cheeky use of apologies and qualifiers such as "or so I've heard" and "or so I've been told" commonly heard from seemingly pious gossips shames the reader for confusing the thoughts and experiences of the public writing persona, Amir Muhammad, with those of the private individual, Amir. In *The Big Durian,* which explores in more depth weighty issues such as race and the deployment of the Internal Security Act during 1987, Amir blurs the line between fact and fiction and makes the viewer "do some of the work." He mixes real and staged interviews about the events of that year, which include the mass arrest of Operation Lallang and Private Adam running amok. The difficulty in telling fact from fiction may have been, as Amir has stated, intented as a way to get viewers thinking, but this ambiguity also acts to protect the filmmaker.

LOOKING FOR HEROES

Jebat is worth recalling here again because the notion of heroes and national identity seems to be an important factor in the postcolonial world where emerging nations are coping with various transitions, whether from colonialism to nationalism or from feudalism to, ideally, socialism or capitalist democracy.[15] In young nations, the people continue to rely on leaders or heroes, having been too accustomed to the feudal order. In the transition from a feudal system (where leadership from the top is a given) to a democracy, leaders and heroes usually emerge from the ranks of nationalists. In the colonial situation, oppression sparks rebellion and nationalism, which spawns nationalist heroes. For example, India had Gandhi and Indonesia had Singgamarajah, Cut Nyak Dien, Ibu Kartini, and General Sudirman, all of whom "paid much blood for the ideal of nationalism" (Rehman 1993, 219). But the Malays have few heroes, "no grand benevolent monarchs, no shining religious saints, no nationalists untainted by controversy," and so, are forced to return to the feudal past (ibid.). This return to the past is problematic for a nation that must remove itself from its atavistic roots in order to fulfill its agenda as a progressive, modern, multi-ethnic, and democratic society.

However, looking backward can be positive if it grants a reinterpretation, as Rehman suggests for Tuah's famous words, *Tak Melayu Hilang Di Dunia*, usually taken to mean "the Malays shall not perish from the world." Aloysius Robless, the Eurasian whom Rehman meets in his travels through Melaka, offers an alternative reading. The Indonesian definition of *Melayu* is to flee, or, from *melayar*, to sail. So although Tuah's statement is traditionally construed as bold fortitude, it is actually "a pragmatic testament to the wisdom of strategic withdrawal" – not to flee is to perish (Rehman 1993, 219). After all, Parameswara, the founder of Melaka, fled from Srivijaya to Temasik (now Singapore) before fleeing yet again to found Melaka. It is significant that it takes a Eurasian Malaysian to point out the ambivalence of a Malay statement that is so entrenched in the Malaysian ethos. This ambivalence in Tuah's words about the Malay race, together with Salleh's and my own ambivalence about Malay heroism (seemingly embodied by Tuah and Jebat), are destabilizing to the pedagogical. They act, as Bhabha would say, as "the discourse of the minority [which] reveals the insurmountable ambivalence that structures the equivocal movement of historical time" (1994, 308).

Living in a time of destabilizing social transition and flux, caught between westernized capitalist modernity, Malay adat, and Islam, Karim Raslan articulates and reiterates contemporary Malaysia's need for heroes in a collection of short stories entitled *Heroes*. The title piece focuses on a civil servant who has told his daughter of his heroic deeds during the 1969 crisis. When he is pressed to reveal what he actually did, his narrative reveals his cowardice and selfish interest. His unheroic action destroys his relationship with his beloved daughter and brings him down in the eyes of his subordinate, the driver Omar, demonstrating that heroes are needed to preserve familial and social hierarchical order.

Many of the protagonists in the collection are shams of heroes and heroines: Shukor, the writer who backs out of a potentially fulfilling love relationship in "The Beloved"; Datin Sarina, who spies on her neighbours; and Mahmud Mokhtar, the son who is supposed to avenge his mother's cause against his father's mistress but who lets his mother down. Ultimately, the stories imply that there is a dearth of heroes in the 1990s among the middle- and upper-class bumiputeras. Those who claim this status turn out to be shams and those who are perhaps genuine heroes and role models are absent, just like Karim Raslan's father, who died in an accident when he was seven. Karim Raslan writes of his father with the nostalgic pride and reverence of a child for his national hero: "Finance was my father's chosen world and, in quick succession, he rose to become the first Malay accountant-general in the days when the Sultan Abdul Samad building had been the secretariat, sauntering across the Padang to the 'Spotted Dog' for his lunch. Later, he went on to found one of the country's largest banks at a time when the only Malays working in banks were the drivers and the *jagas*, as well as a now flourishing accountancy practice that still bears his name. He was 39 when he died" (1996b, 180). His early death not only signifies the cut-off of his potential but also makes him lost to his young son: "I tried to retrace in my mind at least the outline of my father's face, fitting into it all the stories and anecdotes that I listened to. But the man still eluded me and all that I was left with was a cipher, as thin and transient as the mist that continued to obscure my view" (ibid., 181). It is the search for the lost father (and hero) that brings him back to Kuala Kangsar: "Perhaps it was only by living out a life amongst the half-remembered memories of my past, by living a life just as he did, that I would learn about him and then myself" (ibid.). This journey home through the paternal "ethnos" becomes Karim's way of reclaiming his Malay roots.

Karim's short fiction offers a glimpse into bumigeois life. His characters live in the midst of national economic stability and increasing capitalism and self-interest; they are greedy and obsessed with wealth. If anything, his satirical portrait of the bumigeois is devastatingly bleak compared to Salleh's and Rehman's vision that the middle class, the children of the NEP, is where hope lies for the nation. For Rehman especially, the uncritical attitude of the bumigeois towards materialism and conspicuous consumption is facilitated by the nation's unaccountable economic success despite its problems in the early 1990s: "Something was saving this country; something so elusive and difficult to define. Dissected to its constituent parts, Malaysia was a hopeless mess of conflicting priorities, mutually unintelligible languages, contradictory cultures and blinkered religions. Malaysia's politics were divisive, its economy exploitative, its pillars of authority buttressed by an impenetrable scaffolding of draconian laws upheld by a parliament in which dominance seemed to matter far more than debate. There was no reason for Malaysia to have survived this far ... But Malaysia had (Rehman 1993, 273). Here Rehman is driving at the notion of incommensurability where "something greater than the sum of [these disparate constituents'] parts seem to emerge" (ibid.). Indeed, the idea of nation is always doubled and arbitrary, impossible to pin down. What Rehman Rashid has done can be summed up by Walter Benjamin: "To write a novel means to carry the incommensurable to extremes in the representation of human life. In the midst of life's fullness, and through the representation of this fullness, the novel gives evidence of the profound perplexity of the living" (1970, 87).

There's a glimpse of further idealistic "performativity" in the younger generation in which Rehman puts his faith. Amir Muhammad's move from writing in the government-controlled press to writing for the internet and then into making independent low-budget films reveals an important social-activist-like process: he is making while working through, creating and enacting the unspoken, and stimulating public discussion.[16] As an example of his process-oriented work, when he realized that *6horts* (filmed mostly in English) could reach only a limited audience, Amir decided to narrate in Malay for his next film *The Big Durian* (Yap 2003). The Malaysian premiere of *The Big Durian* was, in part, a fundraising project in aid of Malaysiakini, Malaysia's sole internet (and independent) news agency, which had been raided by the police in January 2003. His choice of projects imply that perhaps it is time we stop looking for heroes to define us or to help find our identity and future. Perhaps it's time we just plunge into finding our identity and making our future ourselves. Indeed, Amir admits that he "put [his] money where [his] loud, preachy mouth is" by making short films in order to demonstrate how digital video can democratize the film medium: "These shorts belong squarely in the 'any idiot also can do' school of filmmaking; I just happen to be the first, but I hope not the last, Malaysian idiot to try it" (S. Tan 2002). In another interview, he explains that there should be more variety and fewer restrictions in the local film industry and that, for this to occur, people who are interested in taking the plunge should just do it (Al-Attas 2002). As a member of the middle class who often strives to transcend the smug complacency and mindless conformism of the bourgeoisie, Amir writes optimistically and perhaps with personal relevance, that the "comforts of our Subang Jaya terrace houses, Proton Sagas and 2.2 children" are "not the only way of life; nor, conversely, are outward trappings of bourgeois comforts necessarily indicative of timid souls" (1998, 21).

Altogether, Salleh Ben Joned, Rehman Rashid, Karim Raslan, and Amir Muhammad produce a discourse of the minority-within-the-majority that intervenes from what Homi Bhabha calls "the liminality of the national culture" wherein "the figure of the people emerges in the narrative ambivalence of disjunctive times and meanings" (Bhabha 1994, 304). As for Bhabha's question "What might be the cultural and political effects of the liminality of the nation, the margins of modernity, which cannot be signified without the narrative temporalities of splitting, ambivalence and vacillation?" I have tried to show that "which cannot be signified" (ibid., 298): the languages other than Bahasa Malaysia that are continually being used, especially English; the multiethnic character of the nation; and within Malay identity itself: the bumi dilemma, hybridity, Westernization, and suppressed hedonism (also evident in Karim's fiction, which will be more fully explored in Chapter 5 as the reclamation of adat). Perhaps the political and social upheaval in the aftermath of the arrest and trial of former deputy prime minister Anwar Ibrahim (on charges of sodomy and corruption) best illustrated the cultural and political effects of the nation's liminality that Bhabha mentions, "which cannot be signified without ... splitting, ambivalence and vacillation" (1994, 298). The political fall-out between Mahathir and Anwar within UMNO ranks highlighted the fissures in the hegemonic ideology of nation. The opening of these fissures was accelerated by external and internal forces, which, in a nutshell, can be summed up as effects of a global, economic, and cultural modernity.

Of course, one crucial issue of modernity involves gender. If I have not touched on gender at all as one of the particular disjunctures between the pedagogical and performative, it is because the Lacanian substance of Bhabha's theory, the mirror stage that describes the child's subject-formation, precludes gender misrecognition. At this early stage the child neither identifies with the mother nor the father as a socially gendered subject.[17] Nevertheless, my focus on four male writers' disseminating the nation implicitly suggests that the writing of the nation is predominantly a masculinist preoccupation.[18] This is not to say that there are no women writers who address the question of being a Malaysian (see Stothard in Amir Muhammad et al. 1998).

For example, the first essay in Marina Mahathir's book *In Liberal Doses* amply illustrates her position on the issues that Rehman Rashid and Karim Raslan have broached. It employs the same Rushdian device of writing the self into the nation. She begins: "I was born in the same year as independence so I have a particular sense of my destiny being closely linked to that of our country's. I believe that our future lies in our multiculturalism and I have little patience for the chauvinists of whatever stripe among us" (1997, 15). Marina shares the liberal ideology of the four male writers I have discussed in that she is opposed to racism, religious intolerance, and closed-mindedness. However, her work differs from theirs in that a consciousness about gender difference figures predominantly in her self-representation: "Here I go trying to define myself again. Female, mother, wife, working woman, thirtysomething, speaks more or less four languages (English, Malay, French, Japanese). I have been educated and lived abroad. I married a foreigner. Am I Malaysian?" (ibid., 16). Four out of Marina Mahathir's eight categories of self-definition are gendered as female: two situate her positions within the nuclear family, and one speaks to her role outside the home as a career woman. This is in deep contrast to the way Karim Raslan sees the current image that is tailored for the new Malay male – "a dynamic, cosmopolitan businessman, hunting down business opportunities in Yangon, Tashkent, Jo'burg and Santiago"

(1996a, 15). In effect, this businessman's kinship ties need no articulation. He stands alone. Such unquestioned representations of modern Malay male (as opposed to modern Malay female) individuality frequently appear as visual images in Malay magazines and advertising.[19] Marina Mahathir's self-definition as an overseas-educated Malaysian reflects her status, not unlike those of Salleh Ben Joned, Rehman Rashid, Karim Raslan, and Amir Muhammad, as a privileged border-crosser participating in the global movement of people. But at the same time, what is noticeably missing is her need to define herself within the pedagogical categories of Malay and Muslim. Being the daughter of the prime minister and having the foreword of her book written by her father conveniently precludes her having to announce her ethnic and religious identity. But at the same time, her constant effort to make the hegemonic term "Malaysian" more inclusive exceeds the narrow confines of the pedagogical, as does her reference to her multilingualism (mentioning English first before Malay).

4

Malay/sian Films: Cinema of Denial

The title of this chapter refers to the frequent conflation of Malay cinema with national or Malaysian cinema. My goal is to discuss how Malay cinema's history, together with a post-1969 national ideology, helps to construct, shape, and dictate the desires of its audience even today. An outline of the problems Malay cinema confronted in the 1990s will also give the reader an idea of the kinds of stories Malay films tell and what issues preoccupy contemporary filmmakers. Denial in Malay cinema is facilitated by self-censorship and state censorship whereby suppressive state measures such as the Internal Security Act serve to maintain a general atmosphere of repression in which filmmakers avoid portraying current social realities that might be deemed sensitive to national unity or critical of the government.[1] However, some filmmakers have deployed irony and parody to question and destabilize the state ideology that the national cinema purports to convey. Even some films that seem to convey a "straightforward" message can be read subversively to yield a social critique of race, class, and gender in the 1980s and 1990s. In more than one instance, the readings here are indebted to the work of fellow Malaysian, Hatta Azad Khan, especially his book *The Malay Cinema*.[2] I take up the issues in his book about where Malay cinema fits into theories of national cinema or Third Cinema. His notion of a "middle cinema" – one that combines artistic and commercial motivations in filmmaking – aptly describes what the new wave of 1990s Malay filmmakers were doing. My focus is on films from the 1980s and 1990s, but I draw extensively on historical material from Hatta's

The Malay Cinema and Hamzah Hussin's memoir. Because Hatta's book does not encompass the cinema of the 1990s, the discussion here commences where his leaves off and concludes with a short analysis of Shuhaimi Baba's film *Layar Lara,* which addresses key points in this chapter.

Linked with issues of censorship, the project of reclaiming adat is underway in contemporary filmmaking, as it is in literary production. Recuperating adat in film takes the form of representations of Malay folk customs, some of which are deemed unIslamic, and the portrayal of female sexuality embedded in the image of the woman wearing a sarong tied around her midriff (*berkemban*). Such an image evokes an earthiness and raw sensuality that is rooted in the imagery of the kampung, or village, and suggests a kind of Malay essentialist femininity that preceded the advent of urban modernity, before the period of *dakwah* (i.e., proselytizing) activism.[3] This representation of native female sexuality results from recuperating an essential or essentialized Malayness that is cathected onto the body of the gendered Other. Often, this image of an original Malayness embodied by the woman is produced by male filmmakers. Thus, in the process of reclaiming ethnic roots while resisting a homogeneous global modernity and fundamentalist Islam, an elision or sleight-of-hand of another kind occurs, for privileging ethnicity in this case means sacrificing gender politics. That is the problem with male filmmakers who reclaim adat through the image of the woman in a sarong in contemporary Malay cinema.[4] In Chapter 6, I argue that male fears of the emancipated modern woman, who is beyond the control of male desires, underlie the representations of the sexualized woman in films such as *Amok* (directed by Adman Salleh) and *Perempuan, Isteri Dan ...?* (Woman, Wife and Whore, directed by U-Wei Haji Saari).

Using Renata Salecl's understanding of how a Lacanian psychoanalytical theory of subjectivity works on culture and ideology, it is possible to theorize Malaysian society based on the discourse of its cultural productions: "In Lacanian psychoanalysis, fantasy is linked to the way people organize enjoyment (*jouissance*), the way they structure their desire around some traumatic element that cannot be symbolized. Fantasy gives consistency to what we call 'reality.' Social reality is always traversed by some fundamental impossibility. It is fantasy that attempts to symbolize or otherwise fill out this empty place of social reality. Fantasy thus functions as a scenario that conceals the ultimate inconsistency of society" (Salecl 1994, 15).

The recuperation of adat, it would appear, provides this fantasy that is structured around censorship (manifested not only in what I call the Cinema of Denial but in the general post-NEP Malaysian society), around the repressed that cannot be symbolized. It might seem a far stretch to link the recuperation of adat to the race riots of May 13, 1969, but May 13 provided the impetus for the broad-ranging effects of the NEP, one of which is the influence of resurgent Islam on the Malay populace from the late 1970s onwards.[5] Since then, some Malays have begun to identify themselves as Muslims rather than Malays. The government's emphasis on Islam as the official national religion and the religion of the bumiputeras came to hold a hegemonic meaning for non-Muslims as, for example, the call to prayer began to be shown on television five times a day. Simultaneously, while Muslims were allowed by law to convert non-Muslims, other religious denominations were not allowed to convert Muslims. Islamic resurgence and some say, Arabicization, persuaded Malays to reconfigure their version of Islam – which has coexisted alongside adat for centuries – as non-Islamic. In that sense, the reclamation of adat is an unconscious attempt to restore the ethnic part of Malayness, which does not exclude some localized form of Islam, to the "empty place of social reality" (ibid.). However, while the recuperation of adat in the Cinema of Denial is a way of resisting Arabicization and asserting Malay indigenous identity, it problematically also denies or excludes the customs of non-Malays, due to the political sensitivity around portraying the cultures and religions of other ethnic groups.

But let me return to the unsymbolizable trauma. At the risk of oversimplification, the May 13, 1969 race riots represent an eruption of the Malaysian traumatic Real that cannot be symbolized. According to Salecl, the Lacanian Real is "a dimension which is always missing, but which at the same time always emerges; this elusive dimension, which society tries to incorporate in the symbolic order and thus neutralize, always exceeds society's grasp" (1994, 15). In the Malaysian case, the Real, or the violent return of the repressed that erupted through the race riots, is the "social antagonism" (Laclau and Mouffe 1985) between "Chinese" and "Malay" that traverses, constitutes, and simultaneously negates Malaysian society.[6] In the wake of the riots, the changes instituted by the NEP to privilege one ethnicity over the others form an attempt to incorporate the Real of May 13 into the symbolic order, an attempt to neutralize and avert the potential occurrence of racial violence and to ensure that May 13 will never resurface again in the history of the nation. For example, the new NEP constitution made it illegal to question Malay "special rights," which were a legacy from the British colonial "divide and rule" policy. However, we should take heed that "even though the social symbolic order is oriented towards a homeostatic equilibrium, it can never attain this state because of this alien, traumatic dimension at its core" (Salecl 1994, 15). Because the race-based NEP so quickly and monolithically pre-empted any other detailed, alternative analysis and open discussion of the trauma, the symbolic order cannot attain a homeostatic equilibrium. In fact, this "equilibrium" was tilted by oppositional forces and street demonstrations in Malaysia in 1997-98 that protested against the authoritarian, nepotistic, corrupt powers of the state. Instead of exploring and deconstructing the fantasies on which racist enjoyment feeds, the whole social symbolic order and its institutional networks simultaneously repress the discourse around May 13 by turning "race" – overdetermined by the symbolic date "May 13" – into a "sensitive" and, therefore, censored issue. By racist enjoyment, I am getting at the sadomasochism that underlies social behaviour and societal order. In opposing ways, both racists and anti-racists obsess over racialized identity. Holding onto racialized stereotypes gives them a perverse satisfaction and pleasure. An example of racist enjoyment is the normalization of racist jokes and how they circulate more widely in Malaysian society than in North America or Europe. Thus, we organize our enjoyment around the fantasy that the NEP will resolve the racial as well as class problems of May 13, and we accept censorship in support of this logic.[7] It becomes a "sensitive" matter for non-Malays to question the hegemony of bumiputera status/privilege in all arenas of Malaysian life: political, cultural, linguistic, economic, and religious. This is manifested, for example, in the *Rukunegara* (the term used for the five principles of the national ideology) and the National Cultural Policy, both of which promote ethnic assimilation.

The mere evocation of the May 13, 1969 date conjures up an amorphous notion of racial violence that many have now internalized ideologically to be a result of the economic disparity between the Chinese and Malays, which led to the dispossessed status of the indigenous Malays. However, what has gone largely unquestioned is the class disparity and the unequal distribution of wealth *within* ethnic groups before the riots. Refusing to look at class is a strategy perpetuated by the monolithic focus on inter-ethnic economic disparity in discourses around May 13. Hence, perhaps race as a sensitive subject is only a disguise for an even more sensitive issue, class. Under Mahathir's leadership during the second NEP decade, segments of the Malay peasant class, specifically women with small land holdings in Negri Sembilan, were further economically marginalized by statist capitalism (see Stivens, Ng, Jomo, and Jaharah 1994; Jomo 1986). Arguably then, even though the NEP with its aims to eradicate poverty has seen the emergence of a broad Malay middle class, it has also accentuated the disparity between the very poor and the very wealthy. So although Salecl isn't talking about Malaysia, her psychoanalytical insight about failed intentions can make sense for modern Malaysia, especially her point that what is excluded from the Symbolic returns as an unsymbolizable Real. She claims that "when we intend to achieve some definite aim and our intention fails, this very failure brings about another, unintended result which reveals itself to be the true aim of our activity" (1994, 57).

If May 13 is just a vague memory in the national un/conscious, its memory is also obscured in the sense that the public receives only two sanctioned versions of its causes and what took place: the official one written by the then-prime minister, Tunku Abdul Rahman, entitled *May 13 Before and After,* and Mahathir's *Malay Dilemma,* which critiqued the Tunku's government for not foreseeing the possibility that economic problems could lead to inter-ethnic violence.[8] Neither book mentions the specific atrocities committed on both ethnic groups (the Malays and Chinese) or those carried out by the national army on the citizens. This sort of discussion and description of what actually occurred is available only through oral accounts, and even then, these accounts may be first-, second-, or third-hand narratives that lose accuracy somewhere in the transition.[9] Although one may question the usefulness of reviewing the "gory details" of May 13 and what this would achieve for national unity, it is a necessary step in the process of confronting the systemic and internalized colonial racism that has become entrenched at all levels of government, especially since the government has so obviously tried to suppress this discourse. At least, this is also the surmise of a writer identified only with the initials "PKK." The writer responded to the words of Dato Dr. Lim Keng Yaik, the president of the Gerakan party, one of the parties in the Alliance, who warned of racial riots if the Malaysian People's Justice Movement (Gerak Keadilan) continued with its rallies in late 1998.[10] Dr. Lim had insisted, "We do not want a repeat of the racial riots of 1969 which was caused by agitations [sic] during such rallies. If these people want to have big rallies, others who support the government will want even bigger rallies and the consequences will be harmful to the country's racial and religious harmony" (PKK 1998). Dr. Lim's words constitute what Salecl calls "ideological meaning," the official and "spelled out" rhetoric that is one of two levels of political discourse. This ideological meaning is then intercepted by the addressee, PKK, who surmises or deciphers the hidden meaning of what was said. The surmise, which involves a level of fantasy on the part of the addressee, is the second level of political discourse. In the deciphering, the surmise "necessarily touches upon fantasy" in that it requires the addressee to ask herself why the speaker spoke that way and what the speaker's motivations really are (Salecl 1994, 35). PKK concludes from Dr. Lim's statement, "Is [Dr. Lim] implying that if the people reject the Barisan Nasional, the Barisan can create a racial riot? As far as Gerak (not Gerakan) Keadilan is concerned, the rallies have nothing to do with any racial politics and in fact for the first time in the history of Malaysia, Malaysians are rejecting the Barisan's institutionalised racism at every level of Malaysian society" (PKK 1998). In other words, communal politics function to prevent other kinds of alliances (i.e., class) from forming across racial boundaries and becoming a collective political threat to the ruling elite.

I would say that it is in the long-term interest of a multi-ethnic democratic nation keen on the establishment of a civil society to open up a (psycho)analytical discussion of May 13 that interrogates our enjoyment of racist fantasies such as "the Chinese are economic opportunists who will take over Malaysia if we don't protect Malay interests" or "the Chinese are not loyal to Malaysia." Salecl sums up what the ideal politics of a democratic, multi-ethnic nation should be when articulated through the language of Lacanian psychoanalysis:

> There is no politics without fantasy. As long as there is some hidden surmise which organizes enjoyment, the aim of democratic politics is not how to replace one type of fantasy with another, more democratic fantasy or how to prevent racist fantasies from being articulated. The goal of democratic politics should be to create a political space in which racist fantasies would not have any real effect. Only a society that "believes" in democratic institutions and has mechanisms of "self-binding" of power ... is able to stand having such fantasies articulated without fearing that the democratic order will consequently collapse (1994, 37).

One the one hand, a society with self-binding mechanisms such as the separation of powers into the judicial, legislative, and executive blocks would have no need for heavy state and self-censorship. But on the other hand, in authoritarian or totalitarian states, there is strong censorship, few if any self-binding mechanisms of power, and no distance between the ideological meaning of political discourse and surmise. In its need to repress criticism of its policies and to hold on to power, and having undermined many of these self-binding mechanisms of power in the nation already, the contemporary Malaysian political leadership veers between democracy and authoritarianism.[11]

Mahathirism, which describes the processes and measures taken to achieve the NEP under Prime Minister Mahathir, can be defined for the period under discussion as the Lacanian "big Other" in that it designates a set of society's institutions, the authorities and so on, and more generally the whole social symbolic network in which the subject is embedded (Salecl 1998, 4). Since language facilitates this symbolic structure, state and self-censorship exist because the belief in the power of the word (and visual imagery, in the case of cinema) can be seen as the belief in the big Other. The national censorship board is, therefore, an ideological state apparatus that sustains and preserves the hegemony of the big Other by filtering out any elements of disbelief that would be perceived to undermine the social order.

However, disbelief in the big Other crept into Malaysian politics and society in the late 1990s, as manifested in peaceful but unlawful street demonstrations protesting the use of the Internal Security Act against political dissidents and the political conspiracy against former deputy prime minister Anwar Ibrahim. To a certain extent, disbelief in the big Other had always been present, as expressed in Kee Thuan Chye's play, *1984: Here and Now*, and in some television viewers' skepticism about locally made productions due to what they consider to be their propagandist content. But it is only since September 1998 that widespread dissent has been publicly and openly expressed. Perhaps Malaysian society ironically became, to quote Salecl, "a society that 'believe[d]' in democratic institutions" (1994, 37) even as its mechanisms of "self-binding" of power had collapsed or were collapsing. Whether there is evidence that contemporary Malay cinema reflects a disbelief in the big Other is a question we should consider after reviewing the history of Malay cinema.

The title of this chapter stems from an interview I had with Malay filmmaker Hishamuddin Rais and writer/film critic (and since 2000, filmmaker) Amir Muhammad at old Bangsar, Kuala Lumpur, during research in June 1998.[12] At that time I was interested in the representations of the *pondan* (transvestite with connotations of homosexuality) in Malaysian film and literature. Both men agreed that transvestism and homosexuality were not issues that were dealt with realistically in Malay films or on television.[13] They thought that the lack of realism was mostly because transvestism and homosexuality are outlawed by Muslim law, whereas traditional Malay society is generally more tolerant of "deviant" behaviour. In the early 1990s, a popular locally produced television series *Two Plus One* (*Dua Campur Satu*) was banned because one of its characters was a *pondan*. Because the series had started in the mid-1980s, one might well ask why it took so long before the censors decided to ban the program. The ban is a manifestation of the constant struggle between the liberal forces of modernity and the conservative right to preserve "traditional identity," which is more and more perceived as Muslim rather than Malay. Hishamuddin explains that *pondans* are frequently represented as other and employed for "cheap laughs" or comic relief. He also objects to the portrayal of weepy women in Malay cinema, saying it is unrepresentative and uncharacteristic of the strong Malay women (his mother and sister) he knows in real life. He argues that weak female characters are male constructions of women that are formed in the aftermath of a resurgent/reformist Islam in a nation undergoing both rapid development and transforming gender roles. In short, he theorizes that because of the huge numbers of women dominant in the workplace today, there is an unconscious male desire to control the no-longer controllable women by manipulating female images on film (see Chapter 6). In the course of the conversation wherein we touched on politics, culture, and gender in contemporary Malay cinema, I then suggested that perhaps ours is a Cinema of Denial, which prompted agreement from both men.

A BRIEF HISTORY OF MALAY CINEMA

The first cinema in Malaya was opened in Singapore, 1908, by an Englishman named Willis (Hatta 1997, 52). The Malay film industry has its roots in Malay theatre or *bangsawan*, as many film actors were from *bangsawan* companies.[14] *Bangsawan* was based on Persian plays that encompassed songs and music. This explains in part the love of the Malay lower classes (including the peasant and working classes) for the cultural elements of India and West Asia, which had long influenced the development of Malay culture (Fuziah and Raja Ahmad 1995, 59). The first Malay film is commonly believed to be *Laila Majnun* (1933), directed by B.S. Rajhans and produced by S.M. Chisty. It was a remake of an Indian film originally derived from an Arabian tale (Hatta 1997, 62). Critics today question the "Malayness" of this film since its "economic, social and ideological aspects ... were Indian" (ibid., 63). Due to the influx of directors from India, the scripts of early Malay cinema were derived and adapted from Indian cinema and mythology. Altogether, thirteen films were produced, mostly by Indians and Chinese before the Japanese occupation of Malaya. After the war, Shaw Brothers reopened its studio for production.

Runme Shaw and Run Run Shaw originally came from Shanghai. Before the war, they imported Indian and Western films to be shown in their chain of cinemas (ibid., 64). The popularity of two Indonesian films, *Terang Boelan* and *Alang-Alang*, with Malay audiences in Singapore and Malaya around 1938 inspired the brothers to make their own films, so they set up their film production company Malay Film Productions at Ampas Road, Singapore, in the late 1930s (ibid.). The only other studio that could compete with Shaw Brothers in terms of production, distribution, and exhibition was Cathay-Keris Productions (1953-73), formed by the partnership of Loke Wan Tho and Ho Ah Loke.

The studio era lasted from the late 1940s until 1970, with 1955-65 being the golden era during which as many as 174 films were produced. The film industry was divided along ethnic lines in the various tiers of operation: Chinese capital ruled over Indian (and briefly, Filipino) directors, cinematographers, editors, scriptwriters, Malay actors, and over predominantly Chinese production and post-production crews from Hong Kong. The first successful Malay director was P. Ramlee, whose *Penarik Beca* (Trishaw Man) was "hailed by film reviewers as the best Malay film in 1955" (Hatta 1997, 88). He had written the screenplay himself (adapted from a work by Chinese writer Lu Xun) and he played the lead as a poor young trishaw pedaller who lives with his blind, aged mother and falls in love with the wealthy young woman he drives to school every day. P. Ramlee was extremely versatile, for he was not only famous as a talented actor and director, but also as a musician and composer whose talents were justly recognized by awards at the annual Asia Pacific Film Festival in various years. His composition for *Hang Tuah* won an award in the category of best musical score in 1956, and his film *Pendekar Bujang Lapok* won the best comedy award in 1959. Today, he has posthumously become an icon in Malaysian pop culture, loved by Malaysians of all ethnicities.

From the mid-1950s to the mid-1960s, the studios encountered labour problems in the form of union strikes, and from 1957 to 1967 the crisis between the management and the employees continued (Hatta 1997, 97). Other factors such as overworked and understaffed directors (who were also writing the screenplays themselves), Singapore's separation from Malaysia in 1965, an international slump in Malaysian commodity prices, competition from a new technology (television, introduced to Malaysia in 1963), and better-quality American television programs also contributed to the studios' closing down and to the collapse of the Malay film industry by 1973 (ibid., 100). Researchers of Malay cinema John Lent (1990) and Gordon Gray (2002) also attribute the end of the studio system to the loss of the Indonesian and non-Malay markets and to government apathy. Closure of the Singaporean studios encouraged film industry workers to move to Kuala Lumpur, the capital city of Malaysia, where studio bosses assumed there would be a larger audience for Malay films than in Chinese-populated Singapore. However, even though Merdeka Film Productions, an independent Kuala Lumpur studio that was eventually taken over by the Shaw Brothers, continued to make films until 1980 (Jamil et al. 1993), the films were substantially fewer and of a lower quality.

The Independent Era began in 1974 with the formation of independently owned Malay film companies by Malay film veterans such as P. Ramlee, Jins Shamsuddin, and Sarimah. Jins was the first Malay director to be sent to film school abroad. Subsequent Malay filmmakers who received formal training in filmmaking abroad were also directly or indirectly supported by the government through scholarships, grants, and sponsorship.[15] However, the film industry itself received no government support or incentives in the early 1970s despite the National Economic Policy being already in effect (Hatta 1997, 146). In 1974 a commission of inquiry on the local film industry was formed. It produced a report, published the following year, identifying the problems faced by the industry and proposing the formation of a National Film Development

Corporation (which eventually became FINAS). But it took seven years before FINAS was finally established in 1981, to be run first under the Ministry of Trade and Industry, and then in 1986 under the Ministry of Information.[16]

According to its homepage, FINAS's objective is to nurture, promote, and facilitate the development of the film industry in Malaysia. In line with this objective, the corporation provides training, assistance, facilities, amenities, and equipment to filmmakers as well as to students of the film academy (affiliated with FINAS). Further, it promotes research, marketing, a resource centre, publications, and licensing for and enforcement on members of Malaysia's film industry in order to promote locally made films and videos.[17] FINAS also organizes the Malaysian Film Festival. The effectiveness of FINAS has continually been challenged by filmmakers who feel that it should be run by industry people instead of bureaucratic administrators inexperienced with film. Beginning in 1998, there was talk of privatizing FINAS but by 2004, this had still not happened (Mohd. Yusman Awang 1998, 12-19). The establishment of the Ministry of Multimedia in the new millennium may further threaten the future of FINAS because this new ministry may be perceived as duplicating the services of FINAS.

During the 1970s, foreign films from Indonesia and Hong Kong flooded the market as the number of Malay films dwindled. In the 1980s, the introduction of video became one other obstacle among others that contributed to the local film industry's recession. Between 1977 and the end of 1986, 622 cinemas had closed down and about 10,000 people from various parts of the industry were out of work (Hatta 1997, 149). According to Hamzah Hussin, Malay films began to make a comeback in 1974 with the widescreen colour comedy *Keluarga Si Comat* (Comat's Family).[18] Hamzah surmises that the reason for the film's warm reception then was that it filled a vacuum, not because it was exceptionally well made (1997, 102).

The Malay film industry finally picked up again in the 1990s with the box-office success and critical acclaim of *Fenomena* (1990). It "grossed RM$1.8 million, making it the first Malay movie in this decade to achieve the unbelievable figure after a long slump in the film industry" (Al-Attas 1996, 15). Directed by the young Aziz M. Osman, an actor turned filmmaker, it was about a dying English woman who is also a graduate in Malay Studies, who comes to Malaysia to seek a cure for her strange disease. *Fenomena* heralded "a turning point" in Malay cinema and the emergence of a "new breed of filmmakers." Al-Attas points out a few notable Malay films from the 1980s but explains that they have been "too few and much, much too far between" (1996, 15). Of the few, she mentions Hafsham's *Mekanik* (1983), Nasir Jani's *Rozana Cinta '87* (1987), Jamil Sulong's *Ranjau Sepanjang Jalan* (1983), and

Jins Shamsuddin's big-budget historical film *Bukit Kepong* (1982).[19] Reviewing the advent of the studio-independent bumiputera films from the mid-1970s to the 1980s, and summing up the 154 films made during that period, one headline in the *New Straits Times* reads, "Mediocrity Rules the Day" (Ahmad 1999).

The 1990s generation of filmmakers includes Aziz M. Osman, Shuhaimi Baba, U-Wei Haji Saari, Adman Salleh, Mahadi J. Murat, and even the more mainstream Yusof Haslam, known as the "Six-Million-Dollar Man" for the box-office records he sets. Older generation filmmakers such as Z. Lokman and Ahmad Fauzee continued to make films of lesser quality, but the younger filmmakers produce critically acclaimed films and are establishing names for themselves in international film festivals outside of Malaysia. Among them, Shuhaimi Baba won Best Director award for *Layar Lara* at the Brussels International Film Festival 1997, and Mahadi J. Murat's film *Sayang Salmah* was selected for the ninth Singapore International Film Festival (1996), while its actor Sidi Oraza won the Best Supporting Actor award at the forty-first Asia-Pacific Film Festival held in Auckland in 1996. Another notable success for this generation was U-Wei's film *Kaki Bakar* (The Arsonist), which screened at the Cannes Film Festival in 1995 and was named Best International Film at the 1995 Brussels Film Festival. U-Wei's film *Jogho* (Champion) played in the 1998 Singapore Film Festival.

In 1994, Hishamuddin Rais, who was in exile in London after being involved in student protests in the early 1970s, returned to Malaysia to make *Dari Jemapoh ke Manchestee* (From Jemapoh to Manchester, 1998), a road movie about a group of rural young Malay men making their way to Manchester to see their favourite soccer team (Manchester United) in action. Although the reviews from people who watched his premiere were positive, a quick internet survey reveals more mixed results. The film was screened in Singapore, Munich, Stockholm, Berlin, and Jakarta in 1998-99, but was not shown in local cinemas until August 2001 because the filmmaker refused to make the cuts that were suggested by the censorship board. Even so, the screening in Kuala Lumpur was cut short (a month and a half at MidValley Golden Screen and KLCC cinemas) when the exhibitors came under pressure to pull it out because Hishamuddin Rais was by then imprisoned under the Internal Security Act, having been arrested in April that year for taking a supportive stance on mass demonstrations in his column. He was informed by friends on the outside that there was still a full house on the last days of the film's screening. There were indeed some cuts to the released version (profanity in one case) but having been in prison at that time, he could not confirm whether the other cuts were scenes that might be construed as homosexual, though the filmmaker considers sexuality in the film as simply "fluid" or polymorphously sexual.

Local filmmakers continued to face problems in the 1990s, including stiff competition from foreign box office favourites. For example, a critically acclaimed film such as *Layar Lara* could not compete with the simultaneous exhibition of a Jet Li movie. Despite improvements that FINAS had made (for full details, see Mohd. Yusman Awang 1998, 14), lack of enforcement meant that exhibitors did not always abide by the regulations and pirate video producers did not uphold copyright laws. Apart from video piracy, there was also the growing phenomenon of cineplexes, which opened only in the early 1990s and charge high admission rates (Wahab 1998, 29). Traditional big cinemas like Odeon and the Coliseum (with cheaper tickets) rake in more money in daily collections than the cineplexes, but many of these big cinemas have closed down. FINAS statistics showed that, throughout 1997 alone, as many as fifty-one big cinemas shut down while many new cineplexes were being constructed (ibid., 28).

Other potential major copyright problems stem from pirated CD-ROMs or video CDs frequently sold at night markets. In the late 1990s, a pirated VCD cost between RM$5.00 and RM$12.90 whereas there was a flat rate of RM$9.00 for the price of one admission at the cineplex. Ironically, the availability and popularity of CD-ROMs (pirated or not) among the middle classes, or at least among those who could afford to have a computer at home, is merely one consequence of national state policies such as the Multimedia Super Corridor that are geared towards propelling Malaysia into the information age and transforming the country into a developed nation. Conflicts between national policies such as these dishearten local filmmakers who feel that a national cinema needs more support from the government.[20] Because of a lack of film production work, filmmakers sustain themselves by working for television. With the emergence of Astro cablevision in 1998, at least four television channels featured Malay programming by the end of the 1990s: RTM 1, NTV7, TV3, and Astro Ria.[21]

Without being able to predict the economic downturn in 1997, the general impression that Malay films were making a comeback in the 1990s was nevertheless overly optimistic, given the fact that Malay films have a very limited market within Malaysia itself and in small neighbouring countries like Singapore and Brunei. Many industry insiders agree that the Indonesian market is virtually impenetrable, as the failed attempts through joint ventures between the two governments have proven in the past. Without even bringing up the subject of Malay cinema as national cinema, Adman Salleh questions the very notion of whether filmmaking in Malaysia can be considered an industry in the proper sense of the word: "We make very few movies here and it seems to be an extension of a hobby rather than a serious industry" (K.T. Chelvi 1996, 3). Within the discourse of the nation, Malaysia does have a film industry, albeit a small one. During the post-boom 1990s, it suffered from the economic recession that hit the whole region. Salaries in the film industry fell substantially and began to resemble salaries from ten years ago. The financial situation for film people got so precarious that a barter system of paying in kind emerged.[22] The film industry seems to be recovering, though, with sixteen films being made in 2003 and twenty-two in 2004.

It is difficult to separate a discussion of the aspects of the industry from an analysis of film as a socio-political and cultural allegory of the nation. Although the general discourse around Malay cinema in the media usually begins by focusing on filmmaking as an industry and gauging its effectiveness in terms of box-office successes and failures, sooner or later the talk turns to the role of film in dealing with issues of national unity, heritage, and culture. Hatta Azad Khan's book offers an analysis of the industry rather than analyzing films as cultural discursive documents. A close study of film as narrative text helps us to think about national identity, culture, and politics in more depth. We can also apply to film Frederic Jameson's notion of Third World literature as political allegory.[23] Moreover, I concur with Wimal Dissayanake that Benedict Anderson's notion of nations as "imagined communities" that are constructed through print media, specifically through novels, can be applied to film as well.[24] Nevertheless, I would not limit the idea of written and visual narrative as national allegory to the Third World alone. Like other national cinemas, an explicitly commercial and entertainment-oriented Hollywood also produces nationalist films: that they are not perceived as nationalist contributes to their imperializing ideological impact.

NATIONAL CINEMA IN THE MALAYSIAN CONTEXT

Malay cinema is a Cinema of Denial in numerous ways, provided we ask the following questions: 1. If what we have is supposed to be a national cinema, who and what are excluded from representing and representation? 2. Is the national cinema Malay or Malaysian? 3. What are the processes of exclusion and how do they function? 4. Who controls the representations of race, class, gender, and sexuality? While these questions are easily applicable to other cinema traditions such as Hollywood, the focus here is specifically on Malay cinema as a national cinema, where questions of race, class, and gender exclusions and biases are heightened in a postcolonial, post-NEP era when so few films are produced each year.

A general analysis of the Malay film industry reveals the complex nature of just this one ideological state apparatus existing within postcolonial Malaysian society. According to Louis Althusser, "All Ideological State Apparatuses, whatever they are, contribute to the same result: the reproduction of the relations of production, i.e., of capitalist relations of exploitation" (1994, 117). Each ideological state apparatus contributes in its own way towards this single result. For example, "the political apparatus [contributes] by subjecting individuals to the political State ideology," which, in the case of Malaysia, is "the indirect (parliamentary) 'democratic' ideology" (ibid.). In the case of film, "the communications apparatus [functions] by cramming every 'citizen' with daily doses of nationalism, chauvinism, liberalism, moralism, etc. by means of the press, the radio and television. The same goes for the cultural apparatus [censorship among other things]" (ibid.). Althusser's model of ideology enables a discussion of all Malaysian films as part of the capitalist "democratic" ideology of national cinema instead of dismissing some films as commercial entertainment and others as overtly "political" and artistic, as critical film theorists of Third World cinemas frequently tend to do. Connecting Althusser's idea about ideology with Salecl's psychoanalysis of the relationship between subjects and the state, one could then say that the ideological and cultural state apparatuses sustain the hegemony of the big Other. The subject of censorship, central to the Cinema of Denial, is explored later in this chapter.

When talking about films from developing countries, the discussion inevitably arrives at the formal and critical strategies a postcolonial cinema will employ to mark its difference from imperialist cinema, and more importantly, what its position is with regards to Third Cinema. The progenitors of "Third Cinema" were Argentinian filmmakers, Fernando Solanas and Octavio Getino, who conceived Third Cinema in opposition to First Cinema, that is, Hollywood and its imitations, "Bollywood" (Bombay Hindi cinema), and "Hollywood-on-the-Nile" (Egyptian commercial cinema). Such film industries follow the Hollywood-style structure, values, concept, and film language. There is also Second Cinema, which includes "author's cinema, expression cinema, *nouvelle vague* [New Wave, and] cinema novo" (Solanas and Getino 1970-71, 4). However, although Second Cinema is better than First Cinema because it demands that the filmmaker be free to express him/herself in non-standard language and makes an attempt at cultural decolonization, Solanas and Getino still consider it as entrenched in "the System," because it does not propose developing a distribution system separate from the current one that is dominated and monopolized by the network of current capitalist institutions (ibid.). Third Cinema, on the other hand, provides a real alternative to First Cinema because it is "making films that the System cannot assimilate and which are foreign to its needs, or making films that directly and explicitly set out to fight the System" (ibid.). These two filmmakers go on to explain that Third Cinema is "a cinema of liberation" (ibid., 5), "a revolutionary cinema [that] is inconceivable without the constant and methodical exercise of practice, search, and experimentation" (ibid., 7), or, in short, guerrilla cinema: "In this long war, with the camera as our rifle, we do in fact move into a guerrilla activity" (ibid.). In this sense, Third Cinema displays a consciousness that is anti-imperialist and socialist in ideology, and experimental in form.

Unlike Solanas and Getino, who do not lay down a set of aesthetic norms, Teshome Gabriel, writing ten years later, attempts to form a critical global theory and aesthetics of Third World films. He explains in his book *Third Cinema in the Third World:* "The principal characteristic of Third Cinema is really not so much where it is made, or even who makes it, but, rather, the ideology it espouses and the consciousness it displays. The Third Cinema is that cinema of the Third World which stands opposed to imperialism and class oppression in all their ramifications and manifestations" (1982, 2).[25] While he quotes a passage from Solanas and Getino (1970-71, 30), he mostly bases his notions of Third Cinema on Fanon's model of the three evolutionary phases that the native writer/intellectual undergoes before arriving at national culture. Gabriel's reformulation of Third Cinema using Fanon's theory confuses Solanas and Getino's categories of First, Second, and Third cinemas. Nevertheless, Gabriel is worth a mention because he is frequently referred to in discussions about cinemas in the developing world. But Gabriel also comes under attack from critics for attempting to describe, categorize, and differentiate in opposition Third (World) Cinema aesthetics from the aesthetics of Euro-American cinemas.[26] For example, Paul Willemen reminds us that various Latin American manifestos arguing for a Third Cinema did not reject all Western filmmaking styles but instead, fused Italian neorealism and Grierson's social documentary with various Marxist aesthetics (1989, 4-5). In fact, Solanas and Getino were influenced by Godard and the French New Wave. Malay Cinema is by no means Third Cinema, according to Solanas and Getino's criteria, for it generally tends to be depoliticized and fits loosely in the category of First Cinema because its structure, language, and commercial motivations are modelled after Bombay Hindi cinema.[27]

Fanon defines three phases in the process of liberation experienced by the native writer in colonial cultures: unqualified assimilation first, then remembrance, followed by the last and revolutionary step, the combative phase. In the first phase, the native intellectual or writer proves that he has assimilated the culture of the occupying power by employing European-inspired forms and trends (1963, 222). In the second phase, "the native is disturbed" and "decides to remember what he is" (ibid.). Hence, this period finds the native intellectual recalling the past events of his lost childhood, reinterpreting old legends "in the light of a borrowed estheticism" for "since the native is not a part of his people, since he only has exterior relations with his people, he is content to recall their life only" (ibid.). Fanon's third phase occurs when "the native, after having tried to lose himself in the people and with the people, will on the contrary shake the people" (ibid.). The literature of this phase is "a fighting literature, a revolutionary literature, and a national literature" whereby many people who have never thought of producing literature now find themselves under forced exceptional circumstances ready to express "the heart of the people, and to become the mouthpiece of a new reality in action" (ibid., 223).

Applying Fanon's three phases to the process and formation of revolutionary filmmaking and nationalist cinema in the Third World, Gabriel's phase one (i.e., unqualified assimilation) closely adheres to Fanon's first phase (and Solanas and Getino's model of First Cinema): phase one includes cinemas that identify with Hollywood in being entertainment oriented (Gabriel 1989, 31). Gabriel's phase three focuses on the "lives and struggles of Third World peoples" and "signals the maturity of the filmmaker and is distinguishable from either phase one or phase two by its insistence on viewing film in its ideological ramifications" (ibid., 33). More pertinent for these theories of contemporary Malay cinema is Solanas and Getino's definition of Second Cinema or Fanon's second phase (remembrance). The 1990s new wave Malaysian films, which reclaim adat in their attempt to reconcile the traditional and modern, highlight the conflicts faced by the rural classes when they come into contact with urban lifestyles and the consumer habits of late capitalism. They incorporate folk mythology and rituals that aptly capture the second phase or moment when "the native is disturbed" and "decides to remember what he is" (Fanon 1963, 222). Some Malay films also fit Gabriel's reformulation of Fanon's phase two in emphasizing "the clash between rural and urban life, traditional versus modern value systems, [and] folklore and mythology" (Gabriel 1989, 32). Like Fanon, Gabriel, too, issues a warning that the problem with this phase is "the uncritical acceptance or undue romanticisation of ways of the past" (ibid.).

With these definitions in mind, Malay cinema as a whole cannot be considered to be at phase three because this phase for Gabriel implies a very radical socialist ideology whereas the Malaysian nation-state is extremely anti-communist.[28] Any critique of class that shows up in the films is therefore an unconscious manifestation within the Cinema of Denial (see my analysis of *Lenjan* in Chapter 6). The long history of Malay cinema as entertainment and, indeed, the history of the anti-communist struggle in Malaya during the

Emergency (1948-60), supports the notion that Malay Cinema is, at best, Second Cinema (according to Solanas and Getino's definitions), or at phase two (according to Fanon's and Gabriel's models), and functions in the grey area between unqualified assimilation and remembrance. I doubt that Malay filmmakers and writers, especially those who reclaim adat, are as alienated as Fanon's colonial-educated native intellectuals were from their people and cultural roots. This is because, in the past, the British strove to preserve, enshrine, and sanctify adat as an important "tradition" of Malay society. Further, generally speaking, most urban middle-class Malays today are recent migrants from kampungs, having relatives still living in the rural areas with whom they maintain ties.

In his book, Hatta places Malay cinema in the context of other national cinemas, especially other Southeast Asian cinemas, most of which are modelled after Hollywood rather than Third Cinema. He claims that separate from commercial filmmaking, there is a small, artistic, new wave of filmmakers in these countries who employ social realism to reflect the truth of people's daily lives. These films gain recognition in film festivals abroad but do not make any impact on local audiences because they could be banned at home or because their focus on unglamourized truth (i.e., poverty) instead of entertainment appeal fails at the box office. Hatta has a pessimistic outlook on Malay films as national cinema compared to the cinemas of other Asian countries. Going by the few historical films he cites as examples of Malay "national" cinema, it seems he has a limited notion of the multi-ethnic nation that is the "many-as-one" (Bhabha 1994, 294), even though he claims that cinema has an important role to play in the construction of nationhood and that it "will have to give a true picture of the various ethnic groups" (Hatta 1997, 49). Ernest Renan mentions that it is the shared memory of past suffering that unites the nation, as well as "the possession in common of a rich legacy of memories" (Renan 1990, 19), so it is not surprising that Hatta refers to films set in Malaysian history around national crises: *Bukit Kepong* (Kepong Hill, 1982), *Sergeant Hassan* (1958), *Hang Jebat* (1961), and *Jasmin* (1984) (Hatta 1997, 199).

However, Hatta is aware of the limitations of some of these historical films for attracting non-Malay audiences: "Films based on the multi-racial historical facts about the country such as *Bukit Kepong* (Jins Shamsuddin) and *Yassin* (Kamarul Ariffin) were not patronized by the non-Malays because they were regarded as being pro-Malay and pro-Muslim" (ibid., 209). The films are indisputably pro-Malay in sentiment and ideology, and a brief glance at Hatta's summary of the film plot and motives behind the production of *Bukit Kepong* would support this view. That is, more than half of the film budget was subsidized by the Royal Malaysian Police, which originated the plan to make the film in the first place (ibid., 194-95). The facts of the plot centre on the Chinese-dominated Malayan Communist Party's attack on the Bukit Kepong police station in 1950, where eighteen Malay policemen fought against 180 communist insurgents in a five-hour battle (ibid., 193). The attack was considered by Malays to be "a national tragedy" and "regarded as a symbol of gritty courage of the Malays fighting against what they believed was an invasion of their own motherland" (ibid.). Hatta's academic attempt to be objective in his prose ("they were regarded as being pro-Malay and pro-Muslim") does not disguise the fact that the nationalism he perceives is really not so much the "many-as-one" variety but more a specific autochthonous Malay nationalism.

Since the strategy of basing national unity on narratives of historical crises like this has proven ineffective with local audiences, it may be preferable for filmmakers to represent the other half of what constitutes the nation, which deals with the present rather than with the past or what Renan describes as "present-day consent, the desire to live together, the will to perpetuate the value of heritage that one has received in an undivided form" (Renan 1990, 19). Renan's phrase here establishes the criterion of what "the nation" is when looking at these films. For example, the popular comedy *Mekanik* (1983) partly succeeds in portraying this present-day multi-ethnic consent to Malay hegemony by featuring Chinese and Indian Malaysians conversing in a mixture of English, Malay, and their own mother tongues.

Addressing the tension between art and commercial cinema, Hatta suggests that "a kind of middle cinema is necessary as a trademark for a local national cinema" (1997, 49). He defines "middle cinema" as "a marriage of art and commercial cinema; at its best it could certainly be regarded as national cinema" and he gives, as examples, the work of Hong Kong and Indian new wave filmmakers (ibid.). He claims that while young and new talented directors in Indonesia and Thailand strike a compromise between the aesthetic and the commercial in order to attract large crowds and to make some profit for their producers, "Malaysia has yet to experience this kind of situation" (ibid., 223). Hatta's statements must be contextualized, as they apply to the 1980s, which preceded the advent of a new 1990s generation of Malay filmmakers such as Shuhaimi Baba, U-Wei Haji Saari, Adman Salleh, and Mahadi J. Murat. To be fair, it should be noted that Hatta adds a footnote and mentions some of these directors (ibid., 231) but does not incorporate them into the real material of his essay. The 1990s younger filmmakers attempt to break down the binary of art versus commercial cinema, but only for pragmatic reasons of survival in the industry. For example, in order to attract moviegoers and music fans, Shuhaimi Baba employs popular singers in her films *Selubung* and *Layar Lara*, Mahadi J. Murat features the handsome but bland

Azhar Sulaiman in *Sayang Salmah*, and the leading roles go to beautiful actors like Deanna Yusoff, Ramona Rahman, Tiara Jacquelina, and Sofia Jane Hisham, all four of whose pan-Asian looks might presumably attract non-Malay viewers as well.

Hatta's notion of middle cinema points to some of the crucial problems facing the film industry in Malaysia. The tension between art/political and commercial cinema also appeared in my conversations with Hamzah Hussin, who, apart from being a film industry insider, is one of the foremost nationalist writers of the 1950s. Discussing a certain film, Pak Hamzah ("uncle" Hamzah, a form of address for one's elders) would inevitably bring up the question of the film's failure or success at the box office. As a film-industry insider, he valued commercial success, but for Pak Hamzah the nationalist, the box office is also an indicator of, among other things, the film's cultural authenticity in the viewers' lives. Hence, he would not consider a film such as *Femina* (1994), which deals with issues of feminism and focuses on two militant feminists, as a Malay film. Yet it is more than just the issue of feminism in the film that seems disjunctive and alien. Razlina Ramli, a young female scriptwriter I spoke with, also felt that *Femina* did not integrate local culture and that it was neither believable nor real (personal interview, 24 June 1998). From her words, I assumed she was referring to the actions of the characters.

Pak Hamzah also talks extensively about *ciplak* or copying in his memoir of his work for Cathay Keris Film Studio as its information officer. The memoir spans the period between the 1930s and the 1990s with a concentration on the golden era of Malay cinema (1955-65). Moreover, he has read so many books and watched so many films that he can identify the source of most Malay movies. For example, he claims that *Mawar Merah* (Red Rose, 1986) derives from Arthur Miller's *A View from the Bridge* and that *Bintang Malam* (Night Star, 1992) is adapted from a Michael Caine film. So the Malaysian search for authenticity is not defeatist, self-undermining, or nostalgic. It despairs at the lack of creative imagination and originality of locally written scripts: "Sejak 1963, pengusaha filem Melayu sudah kehabisan cerita" (By 1963, the Malay film industry had run out of story ideas) (Hamzah 1997, 37). Underlying the film industry's preoccupation with authenticity is an awareness of the colonized mindset that looks to Hollywood for ideas. For example, Aziz M. Osman's science fiction *XX Ray* (1992) has an opening scene of a Malay newspaper delivery boy on a bicycle more reminiscent of American small-town culture, as seen in *Back to the Future*, than of Malaysian reality where newspaper deliveries are usually conducted on motorbikes by Indian vendors.

Sensitive adaptations to the local culture are crucial, if we take for granted that adaptations will prevail in Malay cinema. In its history, Malay films have derived from Western, Indian, Chinese, and Japanese scripts, and even from Greek mythology with the adaptation of *Oedipus Rex* into *Kalong Kenangan* (Necklace of Memory, 1964).[29] The effective adaptations have been *purba* films, films set during the pre-colonial era. Thus, period films from Japan, such as *Cucu Datuk Merah* (1963) and *Istana Berdarah* (1964) (from Kurosawa's *Throne of Blood*), have been easily adapted into Malay cinema because they fit in with other Malay *purba* narratives that revolve around mytho-historical characters like Tun Fatimah, Hang Jebat, Hang Tuah, and Mahsuri.[30] Perhaps the most successful adaptation of the 1990s is U-Wei's *Kaki Bakar* (The Arsonist) which derives from Faulkner's short story "Barn Burning" (Zawawi 2003, 149).

MALAY OR MALAYSIAN CINEMA?

The best way of defining Malay cinema as national cinema is to discuss, paradoxically, the myriad ways in which the films are not "national." As if ignoring the multi-ethnic, linguistic, and cultural diversity of Malaysians, the films usually feature an all-Malay cast speaking mostly in Bahasa Malaysia and they cater predominantly to a Malay audience. Like the schism noted earlier on the "dissemiNation" of Malay/sia, even though the films locate the narratives in geographical Malaysia, they revolve around Malay society and Malay issues and customs rather than providing a multi-ethnic and therefore realistic perspective of Malaysian society. Because Malay/sian cinema is dominated on and off screen by Malays, it is more popularly known as Malay cinema. The films' Malay-centrism is compounded by their not being subtitled, unlike imported films from India, Hong Kong, Taiwan, and the United States, which may sometimes carry subtitles in three different languages. That is, the films aren't seen as requiring subtitles, because the general assumption since the NEP language policy came into effect (1971) is that all Malaysians should be able to understand Malay after having been educated in Bahasa Malaysia.

When asked how many Malay films can be considered Malaysian films, most people recall immediately Hafsham's *Mekanik* (1983).[31] This was a truly Malaysian film because it showed Chinese Malaysians speaking in a mixture of English and Chinese, and Tamil Malaysians speaking Tamil. For once, there was no erasure of other ethnicities visually and audibly, although such erasure has otherwise become a habit with Malay films (and television) in the hegemonic tradition of constructing the nation, whereby Malaysian Others are assimilated. An example of such assimilation occurs in the scene in *Tsu Feh Sofiah* (1986) where Tsu Feh, a Chinese woman who converts to Islam, converses with her Chinese father in Malay. Unlike the Chinese in Indonesia, Chinese Malaysians do not speak Malay at home or to each other unless they are Peranakan Chinese (which is not the case in the film). *Mekanik* by contrast not only featured non-Malay actors but it also incorporated a Bollywood musical sequence which, while parodying the stale format of Bombay cultural cinema, also satirized the desires of a Malay audience infatuated with Bollywood. Generally, in Malay cinema if and when non-Malay actors are featured, they are mostly caricatures or stereotypes with Indians appearing as comic figures or thugs, Chinese being mercenary shopkeepers or landlords, and Caucasian women behaving promiscuously.

Hatta mentions the important role of cinema in the construction of nationhood, especially in a multi-ethnic country like Malaysia, and asserts that "Cinema will have to give a true picture of the various ethnic groups, while at the same time maintaining a balance so as not to offend sensitivities about differing customs and religions. Sensitive issues will have to be examined in a positive manner in order to contribute towards national integrity and solidarity" (1997, 49). In this regard, his suggestion coincides with the motivation behind the formation of the censorship board in 1966, the LPFM, "to safeguard the harmony of Malaysia's multiracial society" (Fuziah and Raja Ahmad 1995, 71). However, although such a principle might aim for cultural integration and solidarity, it inadvertently continues to support the notion of a pluralist society that began during the British colonial period. The inherited perception of pluralism that Malaysians hold is not, as a dictionary definition would have it, "a state of society in which members of diverse ethnic, racial, religious, or social groups maintain an autonomous participation in and development of their traditional culture or special interest within the confines of a common civilization."[32] Instead, it also includes the idea that these distinct special cultures are fostered apart from each other and, at times, compete with each other for prominence.[33]

Later, Hatta gives as models of Malaysian national films (in the sense that they are racially inclusive of non-Malays) Hafsham's *Mekanik* and Kamarul Ariffin's *Yassin* (1988). *Yassin* "tells the story of a man who was tried by the Malayan People's Anti-Japanese Army, or the *Bintang Tiga*, for allegedly helping the Japanese during the Pacific War" (Hatta 1997, 213). It portrays "Malays and Chinese as they were during the last few days of the Japanese Occupation in Malaya. Even though the relationship between the two races was rather strained and vindictive, *Yassin* also gives us the *ésprit de corps* of the Malayan society of different races during that period" (ibid., 214). Hatta claims that Kamarul, the director of *Yassin*, is "by far the most nationalistic among the filmmakers in Malaysia" and that he "loves to make films on history" (1997, 213). Hatta gives him this title probably because Kamarul Ariffin insists that local films should be premised on the multi-ethnic make-up and cultural wealth of the country, and that the production of Malay and other ethnic films should be abandoned because it will keep the objective of multiracialism and national unity remote (ibid., 214).

Multi-ethnic diversity is not typically shown in Malay cinema because anything pertaining to race relations has been deemed a sensitive issue ever since the May 13, 1969 race riots. Touching on "sensitive" issues can lead to arrest under the Internal Security Act. However, the problem with labelling something "sensitive" is that it automatically shuts down any potential for critical analysis or intellectual debate. Some critics may even argue that to deem "race relations" sensitive leaves the way open for Malay cultural domination, and, in seeming to want to prevent ethnic conflict, the state actually sets up a Malay hegemony. Instead of dealing with the issue in a rational and public fashion, the state represses it and thereby increases its potential danger in the public psyche.[34] Consequently, the threat of state censorship and the Internal Security Act leads to self-censorship. However, this did not prevent a film producer from titling his domestic drama *May 13* (1984) in order to take advantage of the sensational aspects of the historical event. In fact, the film had nothing to do with the race riots at all, and the title merely signifies the day someone in the family will be in danger. To my knowledge, the film was not banned, precisely because it did not pose a threat to national unity (but neither was it a financial success). Although fear of censorship has led to the production of "safe" and uncontroversial films, filmmakers are not solely to be blamed. When the rare attempt to discuss race relations in a serious manner occurs, such as in Rahim Razali's films *Tsu Feh Sofiah* (1986) and *Anak Sarawak* (1989), the films fail to garner large Malay audiences who have been trained to treat film as pure entertainment. *Tsu Feh Sofiah* deals with the idea that a Chinese Muslim woman doctor could and should be accepted by the Muslims in the kampung where she settles, although a group of fundamentalist Muslims makes it impossible for her to stay. *Anak Sarawak* features an interracial romance between a Chinese female journalist and a Malay male civil servant in Sarawak.[35]

There is a historical precedent for the rejection of interracial romances between Malays and Chinese. In 1955, *Selamat Tinggal Kekasihku* (Farewell My Love), a tragic love story about a romance between a young Malay man and a Chinese girl, caused a furor when it was shown in Kota Bahru in Kelantan (an Islamic stronghold). The manager of the cinema received phone threats to burn the cinema down if the film continued to play there (Hamzah 1997, 61). Hamzah explains why some Kelantanese spectators could not accept the film: "First, the film was perceived as polluting the honor of the nation and religion when a young Malay Muslim man was portrayed as dying for the love of a Chinese girl. Secondly, the film showed a dog, considered defiling in Islam, following Roomai Noor and Molly Lim [the actors] to school when they were young. Although the scene explains that Molly's father was a professional dog trainer and does not show S. Roomai Noor at any point holding the dog, nevertheless the very presence of the dog in the film and in a Malay story was unacceptable among Kelantanese viewers" (ibid., 61-62, my translation). The same film, however, did well in the other states.

The issue of representing non-Malay ethnic diversity was not broached in the 1990s. Instead, 1990s Malay filmmakers like U-Wei turned away from portraying a mainstream, ethnically diverse, and middle-class Malaysia. U-Wei admits that his films deal with different forms of alienation and marginalization: *Kaki Bakar* (The Arsonist) revolves around a family of Javanese migrants in Malaysia; *Perempuan, Isteri, Dan ...?* deals with the displacement of an uninhibited woman in a misogynistic village setting; and *Jogho* focuses on a Muslim community in southern Thailand (U-Wei 1995, 15). The Javanese and Thai Muslims may be ethnic minorities but they are still considered Malays.[36] Mahadi J. Murat's films *Wanita Bertudung Hitam* (The Black Veiled Woman, 1992) and *Sayang Salmah* (For the Love of Salmah, 1995) are marked with a strong Malay identity that roots itself in Islamic and Malay communal values. *Sayang Salmah* in particular features the theme of Malay nationalism. Aziz M. Osman and Shuhaimi Baba's films, on the other hand, focus on the middle-class Malays who may have more in common with the Chinese and Indian middle class than with the rural Malays. Perhaps this is what prompts Aziz to say that his films attempt to "cater for audiences across the board" but that "it is difficult to attract non-Malay viewers" (K.T. Chelvi 1996, 4). As K.T. Chelvi further explains, "Perhaps a majority of non-Malays do not watch locally made films because they cannot relate to movies which confine themselves to depicting the Malay culture" (ibid.); the ethnocentric vision is seen to be so firmly entrenched in the tradition of Malay filmmaking that non-Malays would still keep away from "Malaysian" films (*Mekanik* being an exception). One local filmmaker believes that s/he would like to be able to see more Malay movies with a Malaysian sentiment and that overcoming ethnic barriers was the last problem. However, by making films too Malaysian, they also risk losing both the Malay and the non-Malay audiences. As for the lack of non-Malay actors in the industry, there is the problem with language because non-Malays feel their Malay is not adequate. Not only are non-Malay actors too few in numbers, there are not many directors willing to coach them and provide the necessary speech training.

In fact, it was Australian-trained Chinese Malaysian filmmaker Teck Tan's *Spinning Gasing* (2000) and Amir Muhammad's *Lips to Lips* (2000) that brought attention back to the representation of Malaysian ethnic diversity.

Even so, these films are more Malaysian than Malay because they are both in English. It took one of the New Wave directors, Adman Salleh, to rectify the racial representation with the FINAS-funded *Paloh* (2003), a historical film set towards the end of the Japanese occupation that revolves around an interracial relationship (Chinese-Malay) jeopardized by the national and ethnic politics of the time. *Paloh* was unlike other historical films in that it sought to provide historical and social accuracy: the Chinese characters spoke in Mandarin, Hokkien, and broken Malay and the whole film was subtitled in English.

CENSORSHIP

State and self-censorship are realities Malaysian filmmakers face. Self-censorship begins at the writing stage but carries into the editing process, and filmmakers are faced with constant pressure to censor or cut potentially controversial scenes. Some filmmakers feel they might as well censor by editing parts of their own work before the official censors get to the controversial bit and force them to destroy the rhythm and continuity of their film. Censorship functions as one of the processes of exclusion in the Cinema of Denial. But despite censorship, controversial issues are still aired. In fact, *The New Straits Times* noted that "controversy [seems to be] one of the yardsticks of success" of Malay films of the 1990s where taboo subjects such as lesbianism, prostitution, the seedy side of the modelling world, the supernatural pre-Islamic world of Malay culture, incest, and female sexuality are all included (Al-Attas 1996, 15). In Malaysia, controversy most likely arises when a film encounters problems with the censorship board. Some of the films that have suffered from the "scissor-happy" board include *Fantasia* (renamed *Fantasi*) (1991), *Amok* (1995), *Perempuan, Isteri Dan ...?* (1993), *Kaki Bakar* (1995), and *Panas* (Heat, 1998). In *Panas*, vigorous cutting by the censors results in an incoherent narrative.

In light of such difficulties, Hatta's failure to emphasize the importance of censorship seems quite problematic. Instead, he attributes the lack of good quality films only to the commercial interests of filmmakers and the inclination of the audience for entertainment-oriented films, whether locally made or foreign: "National crises like poverty, power abuse, corruption at the highest levels and national identity concerning attitudes, values and world views of the people are left untouched by filmmakers and producers who prefer the popular and trendy approach in order to gain recognition from the movie-going public" (1997, 200). He all too easily dismisses Malay films of the 1980s as non-political and uncritical of poverty, corruption, and money politics (ibid.). For example, although he mentions Patrick Yeoh's film *Kami* (1982), it is only with reference to the film production company during the

Independent Era, 1976-86 (ibid., 125). Later on when he talks about the denial of poverty in Malay cinema, and explains that it was discussed in the films of the 1950s and 1960s (ibid., 203), he does not include *Kami,* which is as close to socialist realism as any Malaysian film I have seen in its detailing of the friendship between two homeless boys trying to survive in an urban Malaysian landscape. As for money politics, Rahim Razali's *Matinya Seorang Patriot* (Death of a Patriot, 1984) actually confronts these very issues by showcasing a company whose board of directors misused the company funds for political purposes. There is a scene where one of the main characters walks towards a notice on the wall featuring the UMNO slogan of the 1982 elections, "Bersih Cekap dan Amanah" (Clean, Efficient, Trustworthy), suggesting a skepticism and loss of faith in party politics. Yet while Hatta refers to the BMF scandal that exploded in 1983 and 1984, wherein "the initial public calls for more 'information' intensified into a clamour for a 'full scale investigation' and crystallized into a demand for a 'Royal Commission of Inquiry'" (Khoo Boo Teik 1995, 212), he does not read the disillusionment or disbelief towards the political discourse (the big Other) that is present in Rahim Razali's film.[37]

By targeting filmmakers and viewers, Hatta misses the bigger picture: he fails to address the structural problems that make it impossible for "serious" films to be made and supported – problems such as self-censorship, state censorship, and repressive ideological apparatuses such as the Internal Security Act and the Official Secrets Act that make expressions of dissent and questioning of the status quo extremely difficult and risky for individuals. When he does mention censorship, it is again relegated to history and vague generalities: he explains its origins beginning as early as 1927 under the British colonial period and states that sixty years later, the Malaysian government continues to censor films using officers appointed by the king to sit on the censorship board (ibid., 217). Then he ends this discussion of censorship on an ostensibly objective note: "For the last sixty years little has changed" (ibid., 207). I disagree with this claim because although there are shared principles, colonial policies are substantively different from policies effected by the post-independence Malaysian government, and later during the NEP era. Actually, according to Fuziah and Raja Ahmad, the National Film Censorship Board or Lembaga Penapis Filem Malaysia (LPFM) was established in June 1966 under Section 3 of the Film Act (Censorship), 1952, and is situated in the Ministry of Home Affairs. The minister in charge of home affairs is Dr. Mahathir Mohamad himself (1995, 71).[38] Its objective is to regulate and censor local and imported films prior to distribution and viewing.

Hatta does not address what is being censored (which varies from time to time), nor the arbitrariness of the process (probably stemming from the vague guidelines of the censorship board), which could depend on the personal and individual quirks of the censor of the day. Neither does he query who has the final say on censorship. For example, the American film *Babe*, about the adventures of a talking pig, was nearly banned from Malaysian cinemas because its protagonist was an animal deemed dirty and non-*halal* by Muslims. It was the intervention of the then deputy prime minister, Anwar Ibrahim, that permitted the film to be shown. A ban on the film *Amok*, too, was lifted only after the "powers-that-be" (Al-Attas 1996, 15), the prime minister and minister of home affairs, Dr. Mahathir Mohamad, intervened (Fuziah and Raja Ahmad 1995, 72). In the Cinema of Denial, seemingly trivial decisions involving mass or pop culture are arbitrated by the topmost political leaders. Thus, if local cinema lacks credibility with the public, it is because "like all mass media in Malaysia, [it is] regarded as an arm of the government" and "function[s] in concordance with government policies and aspirations" (ibid., 71).

The censorship board perceives itself to be the moral and national guardian of Malaysian society. Apart from safeguarding the harmony of Malaysian multiracialism, its other guiding principles are:

> to protect society from the probability of being influenced to behave immorally and/or to sympathize with ideologies contravening the principles of the Rukun Negara [national ideology] as a result of film viewing; to protect Malaysia from the distribution of anti-government films and films that denigrate the government's image, ridicule Malaysia's allied countries and their leaders, especially Muslim and ASEAN countries; to avoid films that depict wrong and deviationist teachings, criticize and humiliate religions that are permissible according to the federal constitution; to become guidelines for the good conduct of society in conjunction with the national identity and aspirations; and to avoid the good name of an individual or association from being tarnished as a result of the showing of a movie. (ibid.)

In its attempt to foster national unity and pride, it has to constantly pre-empt any signs of defying Islam and reassure the religious authorities of Islam's pre-eminence in Malaysia. For example, the censorship board raised the issue that Muslim actors should not be put through a non-Muslim ritual in Shuhaimi Baba's film *Ringgit Kasorrga.*[39] The director fought to lift the ruling on the basis that the actress of Chinese-Burmese descent, Tiara Jacquelina, was still a non-Muslim playing the role of an Indian woman during the shooting of that scene because, at that point, she had not yet married a Muslim. As a result of the censorship, the whole scene had to be reshot for the sake of continuity. In its religious vigilance, the censors also target "anti-Islamic" elements. For instance, *Fantasia* was shelved for two years when it was deemed "anti-Islamic." The ban was lifted only after a reshoot and overhaul (Al-Attas 1996, 15; Fuziah and Raja Ahmad 1995, 72). Razlina Ramli informed me that the fuss centred on a charged remark made by a female character who told her rapist that she would defend her body beyond death (personal interview, 24 June 1998). The nitpicking censorship board took issue with the notion of the spiritual or ghostly realm in the statement. Anti-Islamic elements have become a popular target for censors ever since the *dakwah* movement began popularizing resurgent Islam in the country in the 1970s.

In the 1990s, filmmakers seemed even keener to test the blurry boundaries between adat and Islam. One of the challenges in the 1990s for Malay filmmakers was to find an identity that was a fine balance between Islam, adat, and modernity. Women filmmakers like Shuhaimi Baba (see Chapter 5) and Erma Fatima were certainly keen to explore this idea, especially in Erma's 1999 film, *Perempuan Melayu Terakhir* (The Last Malay Woman). As with writers Karim Raslan and Salleh Ben Joned, there was a strong attempt with these 1990s filmmakers to establish connections with Malay traditional roots (exemplified in U-Wei's works) and to define an Islamic identity that is localized in the Malay hybrid context. This continues to be problematic for Malays who regard themselves as Muslims first and who try to separate themselves from the cultural content of their identity, an identity whose founding Islamic history incorporated Hindu elements. While Salleh Ben Joned recuperates the "hedonism" within Malayness and restores the sensuality present in the *pantun* (Malay rhymed poem) that he sees as being sanitized by chauvinist Malay and Muslim literati, there is a similar contestation of the religious censorship occurring in contemporary local filmmaking. In *Selubung*, for example, there is the magic realist scene of moths fluttering in the hospital room, healing the heroine, and *Ringgit Kasorrga*, *Amok*, and *Perempuan, Isteri Dan ...?* incorporate various scenes that involve sexual potency and charms.[40]

In addition to censorship of particular anti-Islamic practices, there are problems posed by language chauvinists. For example, in July 1998, the government-run television station, RTM (Radio Televisyen Malaysia), began to ban actors from using any English words in television dramas. The frequent "I" and "you" were not even allowed. An anonymous filmmaker I interviewed thinks that there has to be a line drawn between linguistics and entertainment. After all, visual art is not about speaking in Malay. Moreover, an enforced "proper" Malay has been attempted before, resulting in stiff and formal acting and boring and unrealistic Malay dramas. This idea of linguistic correctness revolves around the casual usage of "I" and "you" which is more comfortable and less rude than the informal Malay equivalents, *aku* and *kau*. There are several ways of saying "I" and "you" in Malay: the formal *saya* or the informal *aku*, which can sound rude depending on the context, and the formal *kamu* or the casual *engkau*, *kau* for short. To circumvent this problem of impoliteness, urban Malay speakers prefer to use the English equivalents. The debate about using too many English words in television dramas has been continuous, with the censorship board alternately relaxing and strengthening its rules over time: some filmmakers initially comply only to slowly break the same rule later. On a more positive note, progressive cultural producers keep up the resistance by continually pushing the limits, and popular television programs like *Pi Mai Pi Mai Tang Tu* push the linguistic envelope by sometimes featuring the use of English, Chinese, Tamil, and other regional Malay dialects. The use of dialects is usually prohibited by the Ministry of Information but it is permitted here because it plays against standardized Bahasa Malaysia (Thompson n.d.).

Although the censorship board purportedly considers the overall impact of a film on its audience, in practice, their concerns are focused obsessively on the superficial signifiers of decadent Westernization. One television producer voiced her frustration about the fact that an actor was not permitted to wear his trademark bandana for a television drama because bandanas are associated with the image of urban gangs. There was also a ban on showing men with long hair in film and television at some point, which nearly meant a ban on Shuhaimi Baba's film *Selubung* because Hattan, a local rock singer with long hair, appears in it. This ruling stems from the association of long-haired male youths with rock bands that are stereotyped as immoral, anti-establishment, and, at their worst, satanic. In this small postcolonial nation that is anxious to assert itself in the global arena but also fearful of cultural imperialism and First World domination, nationalism or chauvinism is fought on many levels, and television and film are merely two of many sites of contestation.

The failure to deal with the complexities of censorship causes Hatta to write off the themes in Malay cinema as trivial, the "issues and problems ... shallow, artificial and pretentious and the presentation is always glossy and glamorous" (1997, 200). As a result, he makes no attempt to conduct an in-depth class/race/gender analysis of some of the so-called commercial films. It is as if his overall pessimism clouds his ability to find the subversive and satirical moments in Malay cinema. For example, he argues that there has never been a film that focuses on corrupt police (ibid., 202), but this is partly because censorship forbids showing the police not performing their duty (Lent 1990, 197). So all films have to show the police apprehending the criminal by the film's conclusion. In fact, one of the reasons behind the ban on *Kaki Bakar* is that the murderer is not shown as being apprehended by the law (Al-Attas 1996, 15). As for the over-vigilant and incorruptible traffic officer in the comedy *Mekanik*, one should read the representation as replete with irony because of its very blatant denial that police corruption is rife. In one scene, the policeman refuses to back down from issuing a famous national soccer player a ticket for a traffic violation, despite having obtained his autograph. In reality, Malaysia's traffic police are notorious for soliciting bribes or "coffee money" and are not above privileging some lawbreakers over others.

Irony and parody are strategies for circumventing censorship. But by overlooking the use of irony as a potentially subversive and satirical tool in comedies, it is easy to miss the critique of class. Comedies featuring comedian A.R. Badul, such as *Si Badul* (1979), *Jejaka Perasan* (1986), and *Tuan Badul* (1979-80), usually champion the poor over the rich while criticizing the corruption and lechery of the wealthy. In *Tuan Badul*, he satirizes the New Malay or Melayu Baru. More broadly, many urban comedies may be slapstick, cheap productions but they feature the ordinary person from the lower class: mechanics, factory workers, *jagong* [corn] sellers, bus drivers, squatters. *Bas Konduktor* (1986), *Ragam Pemandu* (1989), *Penyamun Tarbus* (1981), *Sikit Punya Gila* (1982), *Setinggan* (1981), *Mekanik*, *Bujang Lapok Kembali Daa* (1986) and *Awang Spanar* (1989) are examples.

As for Hatta's remark about the "glossy and glamorous presentation," one can draw some conclusions about Malaysian class and gender instead of stopping short at this statement. Hishamuddin Rais characterizes 1990s Malay cinema as a celebration of "arriviste culture." More often than not, it showcases the nouveau riche culture of the New Bumis: "The constant backdrop is a display of material wealth which is vulgar, ostentatious, kitsch. It reflects the chaotic development and unevenness of modernity in Malaysia. Increasingly too there is a narrowing of themes and settings to the very urban and very middle class," away from rural locales and issues (22 June 1998, personal interview). A brief general analysis of films from 1979 to 1995 shows that while the locale of the films has changed, the issues still centre on domestic or family situations and romantic plots. The families are middle class or wealthy, industrialist or business types, in line with the NEP ideology of erasing the traditional representations of Malays as villagers, fishermen, and paddy farmers.

Underneath this veneer, though, lies a strong belief in traditional values perceived as being under siege by modernity (a siege mentality defining Malay cinema as Second Cinema). For example, some of the domestic urban dramas illustrate how corporate greed and corruption threaten the integrity of the family (e.g., *Matinya Seorang Patriot*, *Abang 92*, *Puteri*). Further, they display how the parents' politicking and business concerns adversely affect the children's education and well-being (e.g., *Interlud*). The films illustrate the breakdown of the nuclear family (through adultery, separation, and divorce) and its effects on the children as women abandon their traditional roles as caring mothers and loving wives in order to pursue glittering careers (*Bintang Pujaan* or Superstar).[41] They express a general unease towards modernity, and towards urban living and the pursuit of capital in particular, which threaten to destroy traditional values of social and family unity. Not surprisingly, women characters in these films symbolize the embodiment of traditional values and they are also the markers of modern changes. Moreover, it is their bodies, no longer under the control of domestic patriarchy, that cause a deep discomfort (see Chapter 6).

Nevertheless, the 1990s television sitcoms and soap-operas are more upbeat about modernity, presupposing, as do some of the 1990s films, that urbanization, globalization, or more precisely, Westernization, are a part of a desirable modern Malay identity.[42] And they had reason to be more upbeat: prior to the currency crisis that led to the economic recession in mid-1997, the Malaysian economy was doing extremely well, recording an average of over 8 percent annual growth. However, the focus on the urban middle class does tend to deny the unevenness of modernity and development throughout the whole nation, an unevenness that's especially apparent at the peripheries of the nation.

Aside from irony and parody, other strategies around censorship may include shooting extra scenes that are even more sensitive than the intended ones in order to distract the censors. Other filmmakers eschew representing the present by producing period films. *Jimi Asmara* is set in the 1950s and '60s, and *Sayang Salmah* takes place in pre-Independence Malaya. According to Hishamuddin Rais, these films are "pre-*dakwah*," set in "an age of innocence when the clear enemy is the white man" (22 June 1998, interview). Aesthetically beautiful, they nostalgically try to recapture the glorious heyday of Malay cinema during the 1950s, hoping to attract the vast numbers of viewers their predecessors did. At the same time, a film like *Sayang Salmah,* which is set in the past but reflects the current political turmoil within UMNO, becomes a clever political allegory whose message is clear even though it's distanced by history.

Even though censorship plays a major role in shaping Malay cinema into the Cinema of Denial, the LPFM is arbitrary in its choice of targets and uneven in carrying out its goals. Despite the implementation of the VHSC policy in 1995 (banning violence, horror, sex, and counterculture content in all media), films that contain some of these elements do get past the censors and are either shown in the cinema or sold as videos. One such example is the digital video *Gedebe* (2003), which is adapted from Shakespeare's *Julius Caesar* and set among the subcultural world of Malaysian punks and skinheads, which many read as a political allegory of the Anwar-Mahathir conflict.

REVIVING INTEREST IN FEMALE SEXUALITY

The Cinema of Denial acknowledges the commercial idea that sex sells and therefore does not censor the connotations of sex as heavily as one might expect. During the 1950s, there were two opposite images of women in Malay cinema that were dichotomized as "racun dan penawar" – poison and antidote: "The character and behaviour of women represented in Malay films were negative, the temptress, the source of marital breakups or the gold digger. In short, they were the poison of the world" (Hamzah 1997, 84, my translation). Taking Hamzah's remark as the foundation of their research, two female academics, Fuziah Kartini Hassan Basri and Faridah Ibrahim, wrote a paper analyzing the positive and negative images of female characters in the films from the so-called golden era. While the types of bad female characters were more diverse during the 1950s, encompassing the wicked stepmother and mother-in-law, the 1990s *racun* image of women tends to be focused on the sexualized and/or materialistic woman. As for the 1990s female *penawar*, she remains, as described by Fuziah and Faridah, the sweet-tempered, virginal, patient love interest or the loving, supportive, and sacrificing mother or wife (1998, 11-12).

Despite the pervasive impact of reformist or resurgent Islam on Malay society and culture since the 1970s, much of contemporary Malay cinema does not seem to reflect this religious conservatism, especially when its locus is the city. In fact, there has been ambivalence in the censors' approach towards the portrayal of sensuality and sexuality on screen. It is as if the early to mid-1990s promised not only a free-market economy but also a liberal atmosphere where issues such as sexuality could be raised for discussion. Malay writers and playwrights who had been educated abroad dared to feature topics such as gay and female sexuality in their works and were not censored.[43] When I met Soleha Ishak, a theatre professor at the National University of Malaysia (UKM) in 1998, she was collecting materials for a future publication tentatively entitled *Love and Sexuality on the Malaysian Stage: Stretching the Limits.*[44] Portraying gay men or female sexuality in a sympathetic light is a political statement not just from a queer feminist perspective but also because it challenges the boundaries policed by the Muslim religious authorities (and inadvertently forces the secular government to challenge the Muslim clergy). Religion and politics are deeply intertwined in the history of Malay political identity. And there were various attempts made by state religious leaders to challenge the federal authority and power of Mahathir's secularist government in 1997-98 with regard to questions of sexuality: fines were levied on two Malay female contestants for participating in a beauty pageant and being inadequately covered according to Muslim law (they were unceremoniously dragged off the stage by the religious officers); and a year later, a group of transvestites involved in a beauty contest were arrested in Alor Setar. In retrospect, making the argument that "the sexual is political" and, by extension, allowing films to be made that deal with sexuality may help to divert attention away from the real politicking occurring in the supposedly liberal and democratic centre. By targeting the Islamic periphery, the secular government poses as the more humane, liberal alternative, playing to the majority of educated, cosmopolitan Malay as well as non-Malay voters. However, this liberal disguise slipped when, in the wake of Anwar's arrest for charges of sodomy and corruption, a conservative group calling itself The People's Movement Against Homosexuality organized within the ranks of UMNO to rally behind the prime minister. Fortunately, the movement, lacking a leader, disbanded shortly after this, when the ruling elite acknowledged that support from such a conservative front would be politically detrimental.

My interest here is on some films that are suggestive of sexuality, but Malay films as a whole tend to avoid controversy by not showing, for example, characters experiencing sexual pleasure. Moreover, if and when they do, it usually involves the "immoral" woman or *racun* (poison). In this schema, there is a certain asexuality that is ascribed to the traditional positive female stereotype – the *penawar.* The fresh-faced actor Deanna Yusoff best exemplifies this image when she appears as the heroine in Shuhaimi Baba's films, *Selubung* and *Ringgit Kasorrga.* She is attractive and innocent compared to Tiara Jacquelina's character, Meera, a model/high-class prostitute. In *Ringgit Kasorrga,* both women vie for one man and, unsurprisingly, it is the prostitute, Meera, who dies, since sexualized women are punished for their moral and sexual transgressions in classical narratives. The sexually and morally transgressive male characters in the film, notably the married politician who was Meera's lover and whose thugs murdered her, literally get away with murder.[45]

Despite *dakwah* activism, diverse images linking sex and women abound in Malay cinema during the 1980s and 1990s: from the sexy distraught secretary, played by Yasmin Yusoff (former Miss Malaysia), who is chased around the office by her employer, to the entrance of the femme fatale, Susan Lankester, in *Mekanik.* Our first view of Lankester in *Mekanik* is from the ankles upwards, as the mechanic spies her legs from under the car he is fixing. Even though kissing (considered tame by Western standards) is not allowed on screen, there are other images that can be construed as erotic in Malaysian culture. Instead of explicit American-style sex scenes, we are given women in shower and bathing scenes, women in lingerie or wrapped only in a towel or sarong, women wearing tight-fitting and short dresses, clingy camera shots of women's bare legs, and facial expressions of wantonness or sexual pleasure.[46] Short scenes of lovers caressing are shown in *Ringgit Kasorrga* and *Panas* but they are conducted by or with women who are understood to be excessively sexualized.

There are differences between the portrayal of sexual desire among men and women: while criticized, women's sexuality or sensuality is visually exploited (expressed by their movements, gestures, and bodies) whereas men's sexual desires are expressed audibly and verbally. For example, Tapa, the simpleton in *Perempuan, Isteri Dan ...?* states unabashedly to Zaleha that "aku mahu" (I want). The high-profile politician Datok verbalizes his desires for Deanna Yusoff's character in *Ringgit Kasorrga* by caressing her hand and admiring its softness before suggesting they have sex. Lust-filled older men are portrayed as sleazy and animal-like by their moans or grunts (Paiman in *Panas* and the Thai-Malay pimp in *Perempuan, Isteri Dan ...?*). While lascivious men are unattractive looking, the sexualized women actors are usually young and physically attractive. Often, they play the role of prostitutes (Erma Fatima in *Hati Bukan Kristal* [Hearts Aren't Crystals] and *Bintang Malam*, Sofia Jane Hisham in *Perempuan, Isteri Dan ...?*, and Tiara Jacquelina in *Ringgit Kasorrga*) and Eurasian or Caucasian women (Susan Lankester in *Mekanik* and *Femina*, and Ramona Rahman in *Amok*).[47]

Films from the late 1990s such as *Panas* and *Lenjan* (1998) produced sexualized women of a different breed, who are both virgin and whore, *racun dan penawar*. However, in the case of *Lenjan*, its genre, based on the Hollywood serial-killer-on-the-loose theme but with a plot twist, explains why Nina Juren's character embodies both the virgin and whore roles (see Chapter 6 for an in-depth analysis of the film). True to Hollywood conventions, Nina Juren's character has to die because "the closure of the classical narrative (of which the Hollywood happy ending is a typical form) enacts the restoration of patriarchal order; the transgressing woman is either forgiven and subordinated to that order, or punished, usually by death" (Wood 1990, 343). However, in the domestic drama *Panas*, the young husband, Ariff, overlooks the protagonist Sofiah's sexual transgression with her ex-husband, the old Paiman, for the narrative's sake of perpetuating the yuppie image of the ideal compatible young couple. Incidentally, the pardon also occurs after Sofiah cures Ariff's sexual impotence by feeding him Chinese traditional medicine. Sofiah's sexual desires can now supposedly be fulfilled by her younger, more energetic, handsome, and wealthy husband. The happy ending is ironically unsatisfactory because there is no retribution: Paiman is not punished for acting upon his lustful desire; instead he is paid a large sum of money by Ariff to get out of their lives. Sofiah, for all her protests when Paiman says that he wants to have sex with her one last time, finally gives in to her own sexual needs (which the impotent Ariff could not fulfill) by driving him to her apartment to have sex. Here, Ariff discovers them together and a fight breaks out between the two men, ending with Paiman hitting Ariff in his groin. Yet the film ends with the young couple cycling happily on a lonely stretch of road, Ariff, healthy and in the lead, urging Sofiah to hurry up.

The problematic happy ending in *Panas* is probably not a conscious attempt on the part of the filmmaker to disrupt the classical patriarchal narrative. Rather, this cliché happy ending may be inherited from the filmmaking mores of past Malay cinema. Pak Hamzah notes that a film may evoke tears for more than an hour, but it is crucial to have a happy ending in the final few minutes if a producer wants to make a commercially viable film. This in a way explains why some conclusions in Malay films are both narratively implausible and rhythmically disjunctive.[48] Of course, the other explanation for the unevenness of the plot is the heavy-handed effect of the censors throughout the entire film, if not the poor directing and editing on the part of the first-time filmmaker, Nurhalim Haji Ismail. Gordon Gray explains that *Panas* was shown at FINAS as part of the Film Appreciation series and other directors who were present then were equally mystified by the plot of the film (e-mail, 24 October 1998). Alternatively, my dissatisfaction with the *Panas* ending may also stem from my rejection of the too-perfect fantasy of Sofiah's progress and growth: from a simple, inexperienced kampung girl to a sophisticated model and fashionable boutique owner accustomed to a Westernized yuppie lifestyle all within a year! The excess of fulfillment offered by the fairytale ending – that of upward class mobility, female sexual desires, romance, career, and artistic ambition – leads to the collapse of our suspension of disbelief. It simply demands too much of its viewers who, in retaliation, turn against the fantastical aspects of an otherwise realism-based narrative cinema.

A film like *Panas* suggests that, in line with government policy of Vision 2020, wealth, and subsequently happiness, is attainable if one has the looks, talent, and ambition.[49] More than that, the film takes for granted and even encourages its audience's aspirations to yuppiehood – signified by conspicuous consumption, a nice car, a nice condominium apartment, jewellery, make-up, and beautiful clothes, all decorating the body or surroundings of the desiring and desirous heroine.[50] Maila Stivens would consider the femininity of the new woman, Sofiah, as "sliding more easily into moral ambiguity" (1998, 94). For Stivens, the femininity of the new woman "is clouded with the eroticisation of the commodity inherent in neomodern/post-modern consumption in contemporary Malaysia" (ibid.). Taking a slightly different angle, Salecl suggests that "contemporary consumer society reli[es] upon changing, subversive identities in order to inspire people to develop ever new desires and to seek new modes of enjoyment" (1994, 3). Her question "Were not yuppies the subjects who constantly invented new forms of enjoyment, scrupulously producing new self-images, obsessively attentive to their bodies?" appropriately conveys how the focus on the self contributes to the expansion of consumer society in the ideology of late capitalism (ibid.). More important, Salecl warns that this ideology is politically motivated: "As long as people are concerned with their own performances, they pose no threat to the political system" (ibid., 4).

Sexuality has become a popular topic with current Malay filmmakers. It subverts and challenges narrow moral assumptions from certain quarters of Malay society while simultaneously promoting the agenda of the hegemonic centre. Salecl would say that we organize our enjoyment in response to the fantasy that the government or big Other must be getting more liberal if it allows discussion and representations of sexuality in film and literature. We forget that this is merely a diversionary strategy around the unsymbolizable trauma, whether the trauma is May 13, class disparity, or other discursively suppressed social antagonisms that the state finds threatening. Moreover, despite putative liberalism, state patriarchy ensures that all deviant views or explorations of female sexuality will, for the most part, be contained or subsumed into patriarchal bourgeois order by the closure of the narrative. Female characters who break out of the mould for nice girls (*penawar*) to become tomboys, (Sofia Jane Hisham in *Cinta Kita* [Our Love]), men in disguise (Dina becomes Don in *Sama Tak Serupa*), feminists (Erma Fatima in *Femina*), and women who work in jobs traditionally designed for men (Jacqueline Mitchell as a security guard in *Kepala Angin* [Crazy]) are anomalies who are "normalized" or tamed by the love of a good man in the overarching heterosexual scenario.

LAYAR LARA

The obsession with female sexuality in films is, to an extent, a discourse shaped by the gender experience of its producers. For women filmmakers like Shuhaimi Baba and Erma Fatima, the focus on the representation of modern female characters does not involve female sexual emancipation. Neither does modernity signify sexual licence for the female characters. Instead, the women characters embrace modernity and are comfortable with it without going overboard. They not only dress in Western-style clothing but are also progressive, independent, and strong-minded; they're articulate and speak a mixture of

Malay and English. Shuhaimi Baba and Erma Fatima's films in the 1990s imply that Malay women don't need to be reminded about their own "essential" pre-*dakwah* sexuality or to be freed from their own Islamicized sexual inhibitions and repressions.[51] Rather, the female characters' desires revolve around other crucial issues: career choices, emotional relationships with friends, family, and the potential romantic partner, and how to lead a productive, satisfactory life as a decent human being in a rapidly industrializing society.

In all of Shuhaimi's three films, there is evidence of the dynamic between rural and urban spaces, the juxtaposition of kampungs and urban skylines, people inhabiting the older, traditional slower pace of life and those who work and play in the big bad city. This is because for her, the reclamation of adat is not simply a question of searching for authenticity but a self-conscious attempt to find a balanced representation and a positive role for the Malay woman in modern times. It's a balance between her rural ethnic identity's resistance to homogeneous globalizing cultures, and, simultaneously, a desire to liberate herself from any kind of patriarchal constrictions – to be paradoxically an individual yet part of a community. Possessing or achieving a balance between modernity and tradition is a key theme for the heroines in her first two films (which I will discuss in more detail in the next chapter).In *Layar Lara*, it is precisely this equilibrium that the female protagonist, Ena, has lost and must regain in order to be successfully inculcated into an idealized Malaysian modern community – that is, the relocation of traditional ideas of community from the kampung to the city. She has to learn to adapt to the community around her, whether it is a village or urban community, by shedding her egocentric behaviour and cavalier attitude towards film acting (the film is about a film crew), and by showing more consideration for other people.

In the end, she learns (the hard way) how to get her priorities straight, choosing a serious career over her sexist rocker boyfriend and becoming just another film crew member instead of a prima donna on set. This position between individual and community resembles the gender bilaterality that is found in adat, which acknowledges gender hierarchies "but attempts to reduce their importance through reinforcing values of generosity, generalized reciprocity, co-operation and sharing" (Wazir 1992, 5). This idea of adat is very evident in *Layar Lara:* Ena gets a humiliating scolding from her superior, Malik, who almost hits her on the head because he is so frustrated with her. As the director, Malik controls the film production and also takes on the role of the disciplining father for the seemingly fatherless Ena. Yet he is also portrayed as vulnerable and reliant on his efficient female assistant, Zizie, as well as the cooperation of the rest of the crew members. Ultimately, it is the generosity of the film crew, to whom Malik also defers, that allows Ena back into the production. In the closing scene, when they meet at the coffee stall and he lets off his frustration by breaking a plastic chair, Ena is no longer frightened by this violent act, as she had been in a similar scene in the beginning of the film. And while before she had left hurriedly with her boyfriend to escape Malik's anger, this time Malik puts his arm around her shoulder and she leaves together with him and the others.

In addition to adat's gender bilaterality, the film also reclaims a different type of adat. Instead of focusing on the *wayang kulit* (shadow puppetry) and on black magic, *Layar Lara* pays tribute to the actors of another kind of *wayang*, the *wayang gambar* (movies/cinema), with the magic here evoked by the silver screen. It is a magic that is irresistible, that attracts actors (such as Erma Fatima and veteran Rosnani Jamil) to participate more fully in the art of visual storytelling by turning their hands to directing and producing. Unlike Mahadi J. Murat's nationalist *Sayang Salmah* and Erma Fatima's *Jimi Asmara*, which feature 1990s actors playing historical characters in Malaya during the 1950s and 1960s and are shot in a beautiful golden hue, Shuhaimi Baba features actual Malay veteran actors in her film, suturing a kind of bond and unified history between the past and present of Malay cinema. Nowhere is this suturing clearer than in the scene in which Ena role-plays with Auntie Zai, the two women coordinating their dance movements in an improvisatory choreography, reflecting a creative and imaginative space where the old and the younger generation of female Malay actors can meet and bond (Figure 4).

As a movie about filmmaking in Malaysia, *Layar Lara* captures the realities of the industry by showing the conflict between the desire of the director, Malik, to make an artistic film and the producer's desire to turn a profit. The producer suggests hiring Ena, a commercial artiste, for his latest film project and, when Malik looks unhappy, the producer reminds Malik that his previous film was a financial disaster. *Layar Lara* can also be defined by Hatta's notion of middle cinema because of its incorporation of popular singers such as Manbai into a visually artistic and layered narrative.

Ostensibly, the film is apolitical – revolving around the antics of a spoiled young female actor, Ena, and a group of old film veterans, led by Auntie Zai, who would like a part in the film her nephew is working on. But as the film approaches its conclusion, the parallels between the lives of the actors and their roles in the film within a film reinforce each other's meanings as fact and fiction coalesce. *Layar Lara* saves the best for last: while the film within a film has so far featured Ena, Malik, and Jan as the main characters, the most important role in it is given to Auntie Zai. We see her throughout most of *Layar Lara* as an aging, slightly senile, former actress whose dying wish is to appear on the big screen one last time, even if only as an extra. In this last role, in which she plays an old village woman, she stands as a symbol of the displaced Old Malay, or Melayu Lama, whose identification with the land is being rudely severed by the crass materialism and corporate greed of the new generation, the Melayu Baru: "Hey, kid," she says, "Come here. You think it's easy to get land these days? You! You take this land. Take it! Take it! but don't pull the wool over our eyes. We've all lived here for generations. This land is our flesh. You think money can buy heritage? There is no price worth our roots and heritage" (my translation). Her bit part crystallizes her moment in cinematic history that she had waited so long to recapture: she dies before the scene is shown. The poignancy is further achieved by inserting this climactic scene from the film within a film between scenes of Seniwati Zai's funeral and using slow motion and haunting music.

Layar Lara succeeds in reclaiming Malay cinematic history by reviving interest in Seniwati Zai as a famous and talented film veteran from the studio days. In the closing scene, Malik expresses a wish to hold a benefit in honour

Figure 4 Two generations of female actors (Azean Irdawaty and Ida Nerina) reclaim another form of adat, and together make Malay cinematic history in *Layar Lara* (The Sad Screen), with permission from Pesona Pictures

of Seniwati Zai and to make a film about her life. Moreover, as the scene closes and before the credits appear, there is a dedication in English to the real-life film veterans of Cathay Keris Studio. In addition to this dedication to film history, the film also projects a sense of disbelief in the big Other: in Mahathirism, censorship, and the whole symbolic network. Such disbelief is expressed by Auntie Zai's impassioned cry, "This land is our flesh," not as a critique or outright resistance to modernity. After all, one of Auntie Zai's other long-time wishes is to ascend a skyscraper, a symbol of modernity, to view the city from the top. Rather, the disbelief reflects a resistance to capitalism and its values rather than modernity per se. More than that, the metaphor reminds the viewers that the identity of the (old) Malays is autochthonous (especially in light of the modern political construction of Malay ethnic identity) and the struggle between the developers and the villagers for land begs the question about the existence and effectiveness of the Malay Land Reservation Act, which was formed to protect precisely this aspect of Malay identity.[52] *Layar Lara* shows the difference between the *Melayu Baru* (as portrayed both by Ena's spoiled, fake, sexually manipulative behaviour and her acting role as the real estate agent who has sex with a married male villager in order to obtain the land grant) and the *Melayu Lama* (embodied by the film veterans and Auntie Zai's role as a vocal villager). The contrast between these roles is meant to critique the *Melayu Baru* for their neglect of their past, their roots, their adat, and their respect for the experience of their elders. The final reference to censorship in the closing scene – Malik's film has been approved for exhibition by the authorities but incurred five cuts – portrays the stark reality of problems encountered in the film industry.

We can conclude that Malay cinema (or television for that matter) is a Cinema of Denial in several ways. Through self-censorship and the LPFM, it exercises state repression on the freedom to express Malaysian realities: it erases the "multi" from Malaysian multiculturalism, and it focuses largely on the wealthy urban Malay population even as it ironically caters to a Malay lower-income audience. As a cultural state apparatus, it functions directly and indirectly to propagate government capitalist ideology and patriarchal discourse. For all the government's ambitious rhetoric about becoming a truly Malaysian society as projected in Mahathir's Vision 2020 – "Establishing a united Malaysian nation with a sense of common and shared destiny ... at peace with itself ... (and) ... made up of one 'Bangsa Malaysia'" – the evidence of recent media cultural apparatuses structured along ethnic/nationalist/linguistic lines suggests otherwise. For example, Astro cablevision offered twenty channels grouped under the categories of ethnicity, nationality and language (Zaharom 1994, 180). Thus, all the programming on the Ria channel is Malay (except for a historical drama called *Mount Estate* set during the 1950s about an English woman doctor's experiences in communist-torn Malaya, played by Deanna Yusoff). Initially, there were two Chinese channels – AEC, which comes out from Taiwan (in Mandarin), and another from Hong Kong (in Cantonese). As for the linguistically and culturally diverse Indian community, they share one Indian channel that airs Tamil programs. The rest of the sixteen stations air American sports, MTV, news, and cable movies.[53] If the goal is to work towards a Malaysian race/nation ("bangsa Malaysia"), and Astro cable is only one of the newest media manifestations of Malaysia's development towards Vision 2020, then Malaysian society still has a long way to go to achieve an identity that is not split into three or four segregated ethnic enclaves. What the separate satellite channels imply is that the affluent are furnished with foreign models of global citizenship: Malaysian Cantonese speakers are encouraged to identify with Hong Kong fashion and sophistication via the satellite TV programs including soap operas, talk-shows, and Hong Kong pop, while Mandarin speakers can look outwards to the Taiwanese channel, which offers a "purer" Mandarin culture.[54] Hence, each language group ends up watching their own language channel rather than watching each other's culture or participating/performing in one another's culture within Malaysia. Would it be too much trouble to make an attempt to create a multi-ethnic national channel?[55] Given the fact that the 1998 street demonstrations called by Gerak Keadilan in Kuala Lumpur included Malaysians of all ethnicities and religions, perhaps it is becoming clear that while the ruling coalition, Barisan Nasional (the National Alliance), espouses a rhetoric of ethnic unity, its internal structure, consisting of mostly communal-based parties, continues to perpetuate the divide-and-rule policy for which they have blamed the British colonizers, but which they now adopt in order to preserve their own power and interests. Yet despite self and state censorship, films like *Layar Lara* show us that it is possible to read articulations of disbelief in, or points of resistance against, this aspect of the big Other in current Malay cinema.

But despite their moments of critical acumen, Malay films up to the late 1990s can still be generally situated within the Cinema of Denial. This judgment seems harsh: Malay cinema's ellipses and unfair representation of women and racialized minorities are after all, common practices in Hollywood and other screen traditions. Yet compared to other national cinemas (such as Iranian cinema) that undergo more drastic forms of repression than do ours, more levels of censorship, and more state bureaucratic barriers, most Malaysian filmmakers in the 1990s seemed content to keep within the boundaries, constructing and perpetuating hegemonic images that corresponded with the government's nationalist agenda of capitalist modernity. As for those who might make films that cannot be shown in local cinemas – banned for whatever reason – they would lose their financial backers, who had hoped to make a profit from their investment. This explains why the history of Malay cinema is filled with single attempts at producing and directing. An example is Patrick Yeoh's critically acclaimed gritty *Kami* (1982), which starred the popular singer of the time, Sudirman, as a street-wise homeless orphan. Hamzah Hussin attributes its financial failure to the notion that Sudirman fans expected their idol to be singing and dancing in his flashy Michael Jackson-like outfits, not playing a poor teenage kid in rags, digging in the trash for empty bottles to return for refund. Clearly then, mainstream Malaysian cinema is a Cinema of Denial fostered not only by the state but also by its audience, which is trained to desire nothing more than entertainment and fantasy rather than critical cinema.

A brief tantalizing word about Malaysian cinema beyond the millennium to end this chapter: the advent of digital video technology has allowed a parallel low-budget independent cinema to develop after 2000. This alternative cinema is changing Malaysian filmmaking and poses a serious challenge to the Cinema of Denial in style, content, genre, ethnic representation, and method of production. (It is mostly outside of the national film industry and without membership in the various film organizations that seek to legitimize its membership and serve as gatekeepers against upcoming filmmakers.) The "revolution" began with Amir Muhammad's *Lips to Lips* (2000), which was touted as Malaysia's first digital video feature. *Lips* was closely followed by James Lee's features *Snipers* (2001) and *Ah Beng Returns* (2001). Many other independent filmmakers subsequently appeared with their works.

These films are considered independent because the directors ignore the multiple barriers for inclusion into Malay cinema, opting instead to be self-produced, self-funded, low-budget, avant garde, or at least artistic films that may not be shown in local cinemas (and they therefore need not undergo censorship from the national censorship board). The presence of independent filmmaking introduces new terms to the field, thus making the Cinema of Denial "mainstream" Malay cinema and perhaps, reclaiming the pluralist, hybrid, multi-ethnic national term "Malaysian cinema" for itself. Many independent filmmakers are, for the first time, Malaysian Chinese (with a few Malaysian Indian directors as well), whose representations of themselves, as well as the stories they tell – whether in Malay, English, Mandarin, Hokkien, Cantonese, etc. – all challenge the negative ethnic stereotypes prevalent in the Cinema of Denial.[56] Out of this group of people, many of whom are from the post-1969 generation, it remains to be seen how many will be interested in reclaiming adat, and why. While definitive answers aren't possible, the landmarks of this new cinematic (and literary) terrain will likely be quite postmodern (or cosmopolitan) and instead of representing adat, which is probably regarded as too ethno-specific, these filmmakers are likely to represent elements shared by as many Malaysians as possible across ethnic groups. My tentative theory is that what is shared or common in Malaysia in the works of these independent filmmakers will be spatial rather than customary.

Perhaps in time to come, independent Malaysian cinema will become the genuinely representative national cinema and surpass mainstream Malay cinema, which remains mired in a formulaic and imitative mode, an example being *Cinta Kolestrol* (2003), which many have pointed out was influenced by *Shallow Hal.* As for the Malay New Wave filmmakers, those who have continued making art films in the new millennium include Adman Salleh (*Paloh* 2003), Shuhaimi Baba (*Pontianak Harum Sundal Malam* 2004), U-Wei (*Buai Laju-Laju* 2004), Mahadi J. Murad (*Putera Merdeka* 2001) and Erma Fatima (*Embun* 2002). Aziz M. Osman, who always had a more commercial streak in him than the others, continues to be the most prolific among them in directing feature-length comedies derived from popular TV sitcoms such as *Senario* and various romantic dramas catering to a younger audience.

5

Representations of the Modern Malay Woman of the 1990s

Issues such as resurgent Islam, polygamy, and even traditional healing have been raised by anthropologists studying the influence of modernity on gender and class in 1990s urban Malay society. Anthropologist Maila Stivens suggests that while contemporary Malaysian newspapers and other media may identify modernity with "Westernization," and may sometimes resist it for that very reason, perhaps we should understand Malaysian modernity somewhat differently (Stivens 1994, 81) as a hybridized or alternative modernity. By "alternative modernity," I mean an assertion of Malaysian self-confidence that challenges the fundamental assumption of Western cultural domination, though the term also problematically reinforces notions of self-Orientalization.[1] It all depends on who is looking at modernity, resurgent Islam, and polygamy. Stivens notes that various versions of resurgent Islam appeal to some sections of the contemporary Malay middle classes (including many women) and that "traditional" healers in urban areas are popular (1994, 81). Taken together with "the occurrence of polygamy among the very men who might be seen as particularly 'modern,' entertainers, academics and other members of the intelligentsia," such instances "in different ways begin to illustrate some of the specifics of modernity (and perhaps postmodernity) in the country" (ibid.).[2] Uncertain of the productiveness of the word "postmodern," she suggests "neo-modern" instead (1998, 111). The three issues she raises – modernity and neo/post-modernity, resurgent Islam, and polygamy – will be taken up in my reading of the literary and cinematic texts produced by the modern Malay middle class. While "traditional" healing, an element of adat, will be considered, the focus here is on resurgent Islam and polygamy. While this exploration of the modern Malay woman is inspired by Stivens's remark, my choice of texts indicates a different segment of the Malay middle class or bumigeois than the one she observes. I'm interested in those who are not as enthusiastic about the types of resurgent Islam Stivens mentions, though some of the men take advantage of its opportunities to be polygamous.

Anxieties related to modernity and tradition are often projected onto women. Deniz Kandiyoti suggests that we consider "the perils of a 'modernist' position on women and gender relations in many post-colonial societies," adding that "tensions between modernist and organicist, anti-modernist strands in nationalism found a natural focus around the personal status of 'modern' citizenry and, more particularly, around the place and conduct of women" (1994, 379). Focusing on Malaysian modernity and Malay women, Wazir Jahan Karim concludes that young women factory workers have been victimized by their participation in industrial development in the same way as other women have been victimized by their support of resurgent Islamic movements (1992, 228). Aihwa Ong, too, discusses "the ways in which competing state and Islamic resurgent discourses use women as symbols of motherhood, Malay vulnerability, and as boundary markers in their visions of Malaysian modernity" (1995, 163). In other words, women end up bearing the burden of nationalist, ethno-religious representation in the (male) politics of modernity, which usually places them at a socio-economic and political disadvantage. At a discursive level, "Women ... are deployed as metaphors for often conflicting aspects of modernity in popular, religious and official discourse" (Stivens 1998, 93). As examples, Stivens refers to the varied images of "the new woman" (the successful career woman) as well as the dangerously sexualized woman, as embodied by *Minah Karan* (literally, "Electric Minah") – the female factory worker, or the *boh sia* teenage girl who engages in sexual promiscuity (Stivens 2000, 2002).[3] To say the least, the prevalent ideology and feeling involving women and modernity is ambivalent.

For example, the dominant subtext of Malay women's magazines "is that Malaysian women are being centrally placed as producers of contemporary urban culture and middle classness" (Stivens 1998, 109). However, these magazine images are not monolithically uniform. They include a range of identifications such as *ibu muthali* (ideal motherhood), corporate women, working supermoms, "chaste, modern Muslim wives" who are "keepers of the family and Malay modernity," as well as glamorous cosmopolitan-looking models (ibid., 108). Under the umbrella term of cultural studies, and forging links between anthropology and literary and film studies, my concern is whether the range of images and issues is supported by the works of Malay writers and filmmakers like Karim Raslan, Dina Zaman, Shahnon Ahmad, and Shuhaimi Baba.

These four offer the perspectives of the Malay middle class or bumigeois in the urban areas (most of whom are either local or overseas university graduates). By virtue of their ethnic identity, Malays are complicit in and benefit from the nation's project of modernity whether they are pro-government, like Karim Raslan, or not, like Salleh Ben Joned. Within the bumigeois, there are distinct divisions along the lines of language and politics, which define various positions regarding resurgent Islam and polygamy: the progressives who believe in multiculturalism, bilingualism, and secularism such as Shuhaimi Baba, Karim Raslan, and Dina Zaman, whose works I will examine, and the religious conservatives like Shahnon Ahmad, who want a more rigid Islam to be the encompassing Malay way of life. I am using mainstream cultural products like Shuhaimi Baba's acclaimed films, Karim Raslan's and Dina Zaman's short fiction, and the work of the Malay literary pioneer and poet laureate, Shahnon Ahmad, to examine the country's current political and cultural tensions about gender and modernity. Dividing the bumigeois perspectives into two broad categories – the secularists who use English as their linguistic medium and the religious who write in the official language, Bahasa Malaysia (BM) – helps to question the notions of local/global. While the use of English is commonly regarded as global in today's modern world, resurgent Islam is a comparably globalizing phenomenon that threatens to "Arabicize" Malayness (Ong 1995, 177). Tensions occur between local adat and a more global Islam. But these tensions get even more complicated when, within these two factions, those who write in English (seen as pro-Western) nevertheless manage to incorporate elements of adat while an Islamic writer like Shahnon, who claims that he writes for the sake of Allah (Aveling 1996, 216), writes in the national language and incorporates the Kedah dialect rather than Arabic.

I have chosen Shuhaimi Baba's film *Selubung* (1992) because its central issue is resurgent Islam and the modern Malay woman. The film was also very popular artistically and commercially, winning the best story and best actress awards (as well as in other categories) at the Malaysian Film Festival that year. Shuhaimi's work presents a Malaysia that is secular, progressive, and liberal. The characters in *Selubung* as well as in *Ringgit Kasorrga*, her equally successful follow-up feature in 1993, are fluent in English and Malay. To that extent, her vision resembles the mainstream project of modernity that Mahathir articulates for the nation. In order to discuss polygamy and Malay sexuality or sensuality more broadly, Karim Raslan's short stories in *Heroes and Other Stories* (1996) are useful, as is Dina Zaman's *Night and Day* (1997). These three cultural producers reflect the rising Western-educated Malay middle class: children of the NEP, they are comfortable with English and their urban ethnic identity, and do not feel the need to cling to "tradition," which all too often signifies Islamic repression of adat. "Tradition" is a particularly dangerous arena because it can so easily be associated with "backward" modes of thinking and behaviour such as superstition. (While I seem to be constructing a Manichean binary out of adat and Islam by privileging one over the other and portraying adat as the more positive force, the line between the two is not clearly defined. Moreover, the rejection of "tradition" is complicated by other factors, not the least of which is a desire to be "modern.")

Filmmaker Shuhaimi Baba is in her late forties or early fifties, a graduate from the English department at the University of Malaya and a child of the NEP insofar as she was sent by the government to study abroad, as were so many others after 1971, in her case to the Beaconsfield Filmmaking and Television School, UK, from 1980 to 1983. Born in 1963, Karim Raslan is a practising lawyer whose work has included speaking in seminars in South Africa on the Malaysian model of equity through growth and the NEP. His conservative political journalism makes him the perfect mainstream candidate for Mahathir's modernist project, though writing fiction as opposed to journalistic essays allows Karim Raslan to be more subversive. The youngest writer in this discussion, Dina Zaman (b. 1969), has no political affiliations with the state ideology that I am aware of and this is very evident in her fiction.

Generally, the chosen medium of language defines a writer's political and cultural position in Malaysia. Thus, I contrast Karim Raslan and Dina Zaman with Shahnon Ahmad, a pioneer of Malay literature, a Malaysian poet laureate who has been writing since the 1960s and who embodies the extreme right religious position. Shahnon is most famous for creating the genre of the rural Malay novel. Needless to say, not all writers who write in Malay are as ethnocentric, religious, or conservative as Shahnon, even those of his generation.

As a theoretical framework, Stivens tentatively includes postmodernism to escape the Eurocentrism of the modern subject and to suggest non-European alterity and even Third World difference.[4] In her work on Malaysian modernity and the Malay middle classes, Stivens raises some interesting questions that can be fruitfully taken up to discuss local/global tensions: "Is the Malay Muslim embrace of re-emergent Islamic practices to be seen solely as a resistance to Western hegemony within terms set by the West, an expression of a number of ambivalences about Western-style modernity? Or should we also explore its place within the globalisation of Islam and the complex relationship of this globalisation to the Malaysian development of an alternative modernity?" (1998, 116). Stivens's nuanced perspective of the global as being heterogeneous, multidirectional, and complex is persuasive, though her tendency to pitch East against West by using words like "Westoxification" persists. To deal in more depth with the tensions fostered by local/global linkages and modernity, the combined theoretical aspects of Jürgen Habermas, Anthony Giddens, and Arjun Appadurai are more productive. Appadurai's theory of modernity as a system of cultural flows is especially pertinent to a rapidly developing postcolonial nation like Malaysia. These tensions include the ways Western theories of modernity have been adopted or rejected by Malaysian feminists in addressing the issues of resurgent Islam and polygamy. While the theoretical discussion of modernity takes up a large part of this chapter, the second section, which focuses on the representations of the modern Malay woman in Malaysian cultural texts, will provide some practical and contemporary discursive examples of local/global tensions.

MODERNITY

Modernity conjures up a range of different meanings for different people. If the Malaysian mass media tend to identify it with Westernization, it is because most theorists generally agree that modernity derives primarily from European Enlightenment rationalist philosophy with an emphasis on individual liberties, which were "the institutions and modes of behaviour established first of all in post-feudal Europe but which in the twentieth century increasingly have become world-historical in their impact" (Giddens 1991, 14-15).

One can see how this definition of modernity would appeal to both Malaysian feminists and Muslim secularists. Malaysian academic Maznah Mohamad argues that women in the Third World who are fighting for their individual rights do so at the level of basic human rights rather than on the grounds of gender difference (1994, 123). One of the strategies of Third World women confronted by "a monolithic male-empowered situation" is "the appeal to reason and rationality and a respect for free thought and expression" (ibid., 124). Maznah regards the anti-humanist paradigm of postmodernist feminisms (i.e., deconstruction) as unproductive for women's groups in Malaysia (ibid., 127) because deconstruction's tendency to collapse binary subject positions undermines the construction of an alternative unitary subject position for the oppressed.[5] Moreover, non-Western feminists "have to resist the non-white male, non-rationalist discourse [resurgent Islam] which is increasingly becoming the authoritative voice outside the Western hemisphere articulating the new meta-narrative of the anti-West movement" precisely because these "Islamic fundamentalists in non-Western societies also share the same sentiments [as Western deconstructionist feminists by] countering that same white, rationalist discourse" (ibid.).

This ideological tension between fundamentalist Islamic discourse and feminism is most apparent in the work of Sisters in Islam, an urban-based Muslim feminist organization whose membership consists of female professionals and academics. Sisters in Islam (SIS) holds that interpretations of the Quran and *hadith* need to be historically and culturally contextualized. For example, in her discussion of women's rights as human rights within Islam, Norani Othman, a key member of the group, illustrates the complexity of reconciling what has been generally considered a highly patriarchal religion, Islam, with feminist principles of gender equality (1997, 7-10). Norani would likely concur with Maznah that "Third World feminism is a *modernising* movement – a battle for the recognition of the humanist philosophy, through a legal-rational discourse and the realisation of individual human rights" (Maznah 1994, 122, emphasis mine). Maznah maintains that fundamentally, "much of the activism of Third World feminists is defined by the modern agenda, and modernisation as the unstated destiny" (ibid.).

Modernity is also "roughly equivalent to 'the industrialised world,' so long as it be recognised that industrialism is not its only institutional dimension" (Giddens 1991, 15). By "industrialism" Giddens means "the social relations implied in the widespread use of material power and machinery in production processes" (ibid.). This form of modernity does not really have a place for feminism, for reasons that will become apparent. In *The Consequences of Modernity*, Giddens describes four inter-related dimensions of globalization: world capitalist economy, the nation-state system, world military order, and the international division of labour. With the exception of "world military order," Malaysia is striving to become part of this global picture under the political leadership of Dr. Mahathir Mohamad. His modernist ambitions are reflected in his "Look East" policy, Vision 2020, and the Multimedia Super Corridor – all of which are meant to attract foreign investment and capital and develop Malaysia into a highly technological, industrial, and wealthy nation. Stivens finds that the "new" Malaysian "modernity" is positively regarded as "synonymous with 'progress,' with economic development, and negatively with encroaching, colonising 'Westernisation' or 'Westoxification'" (1994, 80-81).

What needs to be unpacked in her definition is the Habermasian division between social modernity – "the systematic imperatives of the state and the economy" – and cultural modernity (D'Entrèves 1997, 4). This too-easy dichotomization, propagated by Malaysian state ideology as well as by the neo-conservative mainstream, which accepts economic imperatives (capitalism) as "good" modernity and rejects its cultural effects (Westoxification) as "bad" modernity, makes it seem as if these two spheres are mutually exclusive of each other and not, as they are in reality, conjoined. For example, moralists decry the teenage pastime of loafing (*lepak*) in shopping malls, regarding it as a bad habit of cultural modernity without making connections to the state capitalist ideology of encouraging consumption and accumulation of wealth. The labelling of cultural modernity as "colonizing Westernization" or "Westoxification" indicates the reaction to what Giddens calls "the reflexivity of modernity," that which "turns out to confound the expectations of Enlightenment thought – although it is the very product of that thought" (1991, 21). Giddens explains:

> The original progenitors of modern science and philosophy believed themselves to be preparing the way for securely founded knowledge of the social and natural worlds: the claims of reason were due to overcome the dogmas of tradition, offering a sense of certitude in place of the arbitrary character of habit and custom. But the reflexivity of modernity actually undermines the certainty of knowledge, even in the core domains of natural science. Science depends, not on the inductive accumulation of proofs, but on the methodological principle of doubt. No matter how cherished, and apparently well established, a given scientific tenet might be, it is open to revision – or might have to be discarded altogether – in light of new ideas or findings. The integral relation between modernity and radical doubt is an issue which, once exposed to view, is not only disturbing to philosophers but is *existentially troubling* for ordinary individuals.[6] (ibid.)

It can be argued that resurgent Islam is a reaction against a "reflexive" modernity that destabilizes traditions while simultaneously offering no certainty or stability.[7] Modernity in the form of rapid industrialization and women in the workforce threatens the patriarchal status quo in Malaysia. While religious conservatives point to the excesses of capitalism – corruption, materialism – as viable reasons to return to a fundamentalist Muslim lifestyle, this lifestyle is inherently more patriarchal and sexist, which suggests that even though there is little conservatives can do about the uncertainties of modernity, they can at least retain patriarchal control over women. This is in fact what occurred in Iran when the fundamentalists overthrew Shah Pahlavi's secular government in 1979. Of course, the Ayatollah's coinage of the term "Westoxification" is also political and not just a reactionary response to "reflexive modernity": it comes from a tradition of militant anti-Western Muslim rhetoric that began (in this period of late modernity anyway) with the 1973 oil "shortage" that OPEC launched, the politics of which encompassed all of Giddens's four dimensions of globalization. In other words, revivalist Islam is a cultural effect stemming from radical doubt, which, however, does not place Islamic resurgence in the time of postmodernity.[8] Instead, Giddens's theory of reflexivity would locate such dialectical reactions within modernity itself.

As Habermas has noted, "It is quite true that cultural modernity also generates its own aporias ... [Those] who recommend a return to pre-modernity, or [who] radically repudiate modernity altogether, all appeal to these aporias" (1997, 44). A Malaysian example of this appeal to modernity's aporias is the now-disbanded Islamic group Al-Arqam which, by advocating economic self-sufficiency, opted out of a global economy and the aporias of Western cultural modernity.[9] As well as advocating veiling, the leader of Al-Arqam also actively encouraged polygamy. Other resurgent Islamic groups (ABIM and PAS), which are not economically self-sufficient, nevertheless still seek ways of preserving their "traditional" identity through regulating their female members' behaviour and appearance.

Returning to Stivens's hypothesis about the condition of modernity among some of the Malay middle class who find resurgent Islam appealing, her statement implies that modernity, like Westernizing globalism, is a linear inevitability. To this end, resurgent Islam and polygamy, signifiers of tradition and the pre-modern, may seem like grit in the wheels of "progress": they present the contradictions that local forms of modernity have thrown up (Stivens 1994, 83). But instead of it being inevitable, Giddens insists that modernity or globalization "has to be understood as a dialectical phenomenon, in which events at one pole of a distanciated relation often produce divergent or even contrary occurrences at another" (Giddens 1991, 22). So it is through accepting the dialectic of modernity that we can more easily see how the consequences of Malaysian modernity can lead to resurgent Islam. Malay anthropologist Wazir Jahan Karim supports the notion of dialectics too: "Social trends in religious revivalism or, alternatively, modernity and Westernization reflect the convergence of two trends of thought in contemporary life. The presence of two sets of ideological and social intrusions reflects the dialectical relationship between Westernization and fundamentalism" (1992, 24). However, Wazir's argument differs from mine; while I see Westernization or modernity as a means of reclaiming adat for writers and filmmakers, she sees adat playing a mediating role between Westernization and fundamentalism "in providing an intimate and intuitive mechanism for reordering relationships according to the requirements of culture" (ibid.). However, we share the same desire to find or recover an approach that is flexible and accepting of an ethnically diverse nation.

Stivens's examples of how we should look at Malaysian modernity differently – resurgent Islam, a return to traditional healing in urban areas, and polygamy – are actually outcomes of modernity's reflexivity rather than signifiers of an alternative (non-Western) modernity or even postmodernity. Such outcomes are unsurprising reactions to modernity that occur anywhere, even in the West. This reaction against modernity does not appear outside of modernity, but should be conceived as part of modernity's dialectic. Perhaps different resurgent Islamic groups in Malaysia can be compared to the Christian television evangelists and the pro-life or anti-abortionist groups in the West. The rationale for their existence may resemble the kind that reflects the general Western political climate of neo-conservatism. As for the interest in traditional healing in Malaysia, how does it differ from "the flourishing of New Age movements, the Greens, homeopathic medicine, the interest in Asian medicine in both the U.S. and in Western Europe" that C.J. Wan-Ling Wee considers "rebellions against modernity, especially in its ravaging positivist, rationalizing, and often, nation-statist form and expressions of desire for the archaic?" (1996, 215). While these movements may be hostile towards modernity (however they define "modernity"), unless they are Luddites, they are still very much implicated in modernity. For example, PAS, the Islamic opposition party that advocates gender segregation in its home state of Kelantan, set up a bilingual web version of its paper, *Harakah*, for Malaysians to have access to the latest information regarding Anwar Ibrahim's trial and *reformasi* in September 1998.

What Giddens's dialectic of the local and global may suggest is the need to redefine and reconsider modernity as not necessarily Western, but only, perhaps, as novel or contemporary. As for non-Westerners who react to modernity as Westernization or "Americanization," perhaps one should ask if they are not neo-Orientalizing themselves by the suggestion that Asia symbolizes "tradition."[10] Arjun Appadurai's discussion about global cultural flows suggests the possibility that the flows travel in more directions than one, "The United States is no longer the puppeteer of a world system of images but is only one node of a complex transnational construction of imaginary landscapes" (1996, 31). In the Malaysian case, modernity flows from the West as well as from the Middle East. For those women enthusiastic about resurgent Islam, wearing a *tudung* (head scarf) and attending religious classes became class markers as "*dakwah* clothing became a symbol of depeasantization, a process of class mobility whereby successful Malay women explored their gender identity in modern Islamic terms" (Ong 1995, 181). This "Arabicization" is a modern phenomenon in the sense that it is new and presently occurring; an outcome of the reflexivity of modernity, it is also a result of urbanization, new wealth, and tertiary education. In this sense, then, the reflexivity of modernity in Malaysia is similar to that in the West.

If Stivens has been cautious to highlight cultural difference without explicitly taking a feminist stand against polygamy or the more radical versions of resurgent Islam, it is because of her own unstable position as an outsider: she's a "Western" academic who faces strong criticism from defensive Malaysian academics about cultural appropriation and Eurocentric bias. She writes extensively about her epistemological and political problems doing research in Malaysia (see Stivens 1992, 1994). In her general discussion of gender and modernity in Malaysia, her argument is that, in the application of feminist theories and methodologies, one should always take into consideration the complex localized cultural and historical specificities. In the Malaysian case, there are multiple, varying positions on women, on resurgent Islam, and on modernity, even among Malaysian and Malay women themselves. It could be argued that in the wake of poststructuralist consciousness and the decentring of universalist theories, Stivens's endeavour is not to pose non-Western modernity against a hegemonic Western modernity (which is an almost inescapable binary), but to point out the existence of multiple, differentiated modernities that must always be fully contextualized.

However, as far as this context is concerned, her choice of polygamy as a way of viewing Malaysian modernity differently gestures towards some kind of alterity without exploring its complexities. Polygamy is an easy target for feminists: it is sanctioned by Islam and, in a sense, "institutionalizes" sexuality into a widely discursive and documented topic. It especially becomes the intriguing culturally different object of study for anthropologists who are accustomed to the monogamous norm of the West. What is, in fact, less written about but more prevalent in society (across cultures, both Western and Eastern) is adultery or the difficulty of fidelity in non-polygamous relationships, which is linked to the broader subject of Malay sexuality or sensuality. In Malaysia, polygamy for Muslims may be legal but adultery is not, but the topic of adultery seems less glamorous to academic researchers and Western feminists. To Stivens's credit, she acknowledges that the few cases of polygamy that achieved notoriety may have led to an exaggeration of their significance. In fact, the 1994 figures for Muslim polygamy is fairly low: between 1 and 3 percent of marriages are polygamous (Stivens 1994, 81). Moreover, Stivens adds that polygamy "has often been the preserve of better-off men located in the 'advanced' 'modern' economic sectors" (ibid., 81). She suggests that polygamy is a class issue when she warns that "we need to reject the association of religion [Islam] with 'tradition' [polygamy] in much commentary and conventional models of modernity" (ibid.). In other words, polygamy is tied up with socio-economic factors precipitated by rapid urbanization and an expanding capitalist market economy rather than by Islam alone. Rohana

Ariffin, a Malay sociologist and grassroots worker at the Women's Crisis Centre in Penang, would agree: "Many Malays (men) are enriching themselves after the New Economic Policy and these new rich seek local and foreign women as second (third and fourth) wives. The Menteri Besar of Selangor is an ardent follower and supporter. The personality of this man goes hand in hand with money, power and corruption."[11] However, the sexual expression of these men, who marry a second or third wife for socio-economic status, is supported by religion and by cultural discourses that allow them to rationalize their libidinal desires, their *nafsu* (lust or passion). Following this argument, the question of polygamy can be redirected to an analysis of Malay sexuality instead, as represented in the texts of Karim Raslan, Dina Zaman, and Shahnon Ahmad.

For a Muslim Malay writer such as Shahnon Ahmad, who is negotiating the global flow from the Middle East and that from the West, the equation of aspects of modernity (such as an open discourse on sexual relations and sexuality) with Westernization may be a way of dissociating himself from those very elements already present in the local culture (adat) that may contradict the more rigid tenets of a globalizing resurgent Islam. Thus, Shahnon's exposure to resurgent Islam enables him to recognize and then critique adat for compromising the practice of Islam in Malaysia. But for other writers, the Western discourse of sexuality – fostered by tertiary education in the "West," the increasingly advanced level and pace of modernity in Malaysian cities, and exposure to all things "Western" – paradoxically opens up discussion of the relation of sexuality to Malay adat.[12] Western discourse enables Malay writers to recover the sensuality, earthiness, and sexuality in adat that are being repressed by the new Islamic hegemony. One detects this preoccupation with sex even in writings that supposedly contain an Islamic fundamentalist morality.

In other words, modernity allows the conscious and unconscious recuperation of Malay adat, whether this reclamation means focusing on sexuality or returning to forms of the archaic such as magic or traditional healing. Wazir Jahan Karim's idea of adat is useful here. According to Wazir, adat encourages women's power and autonomy and continues to function in Malaysia as "a system of 'checks and balances' between incompatible or conflicting ideological systems [resurgent Islam and Westernization] which culturally determine the distribution of power and responsibility between the sexes" (1992, 230). The emphasis on sexuality of English-language mainstream writers and filmmakers alike in the 1990s is linked to the proliferation of ethical discourse on sexual conduct by the ideological state apparatus – the media – not to mention by political and religious leaders.[13] Prior to the economic slowdown in 1997, space for sexual as opposed to political discourse was permitted when the state carefully cultivated a liberal, cosmopolitan image in order to encourage foreign investment. Global trends like the discourses around AIDS prevention have also opened up issues of sexuality, especially when workers at Pink Triangle (an HIV and queer-friendly non-governmental organization) and the Malaysian AIDS Council in Kuala Lumpur set up awareness programs. But perhaps the most overt use of sexual discourse to silence political dissent is manifested in the charges of sodomy and adultery that were levelled at former deputy prime minister Anwar Ibrahim by Mahathir, a move many critics, including Anwar, see as a political manoeuvre to preserve Mahathir's authoritarian power by besmirching the moral image of his former deputy. The local government-controlled media has been largely responsible for perpetuating this sexual discourse, featuring words like "sodomy" and "intercourse" in the headlines, much to the disgust of parents forced to explain the birds and bees to their young children.

Modernity is full of contradictions: on the one hand, it attempts to delineate the boundary separating the public from the private realms (home and the world) but, on the other hand, modernity also breaches this boundary on its own terms. For example, the Domestic Violence Act allows the secular state to regulate the private lives of Muslim couples, undermining the jurisdiction of the Islamic *syariah* court. Another example comes from Mahathir's heavy-handed tactic of outmanoeuvring Anwar by launching a media onslaught and exposure of Anwar's alleged sexual exploits. This tactic spurred talk from ordinary Malays about how untraditional and unMalay it was: "Our leaders are coming out with so much filth in the papers. It shames his family and it shames our race." The speaker, a Malay woman standing outside the courthouse during Anwar's trial, went on to explain to other Malaysians around her that "we Malays don't usually treat people like this. *Maruah* (dignity) is very important to us" and that according to the *Sejarah Melayu,* even the guilty deserve dignity (Sabri 2000a, 39). In a way, this criticism of Mahathir's actions probably demonstrates the conflict between modernity and adat. Malays opposed to him also regard his actions as highly unIslamic, and they appeal to Muslim ideals of social justice and equality to counter corruption, cronyism, and nepotism.

GLOBAL/LOCAL TENSIONS: ISLAM/WESTERNIZATION AND ADAT

When adopted by local Islamic groups, the fundamentalist project of returning to live the Islamic way of life exposes the paradoxes and compromises of traditional Islamic practice in Malaysia because Islam came into the Malay Peninsula through a benevolent process – it was adopted by the Malay juridical system without totally undermining adat or customary laws (Maznah 1994,

127). Secularism is a product of modernization, but it is also aligned with aspects of Malay adat that are regarded as traditionally tolerant (though still patriarchal) and more open to sensual or sexual matters than resurgent Islam. The forms of adat or Malayness referred to in this chapter are the dichotomy of *nafsu* (passion) and *akal* (rationality), bilaterality in gender relations, an openness about sexuality and sensuality, and a non-Western understanding of power.

In *Selubung*, Brother Musa bases his polygamy on the missionary goal of saving the "weaker sex." His rationale coincides with the common, official Malay and Muslim rhetoric of linking *nafsu* (desire, lust, passion) with women, and *akal* (reason, intelligence, rationality) with men. Moreover, "gossiping, desiring material possessions, being especially (or overly) interested in sex" are attributed to "passion," which is associated with the devil and evil spirits who tempt people with sinful behaviour (Peletz 1995, 89). Because women are considered passionate (having "hot blood") and lacking in reason, they have to be saved from evil temptation. Due to its Arabic origins, according to anthropologist Michael Peletz, the *akal/nafsu* dichotomy is more central to Islamic discourse than to Malay adat as it was before the coming of Islam around the thirteenth century. Malay "villagers also contend that 'reason' and 'passion' forever struggle against one another within the individual, and that 'good behaviour' (*budi baik*) is evidence of the preponderance, however temporary or qualified, of 'reason' over 'passion,' just as 'bad behaviour' (*budi jahat*) reflects the dominance, however short-lived or partial, of 'passion' over 'reason'" (ibid., 91). In other words, passion and reason exist in both men and women in Malay adat. But more than that, "the *adat* emphasis on bilaterality" is being undermined by the Islamic resurgence that "increase[s] male control in the emerging Malay middle class" (Ong 1995, 164). The tension between Islam and adat is a big enough issue that it becomes Wazir Jahan Karim's central focus in her book *Women and Culture: Between Malay Adat and Islam* (1992).

Ample sociological and anthropological evidence has pointed to Malay society "as an example of a Muslim society that permitted relatively egalitarian relations between the sexes ... compared, say, with the rigid gender segregation found in Bangladesh" (Ong 1995, 163). This measure of gender equality extends to sexual relations because Malay adat expects that "husbands and wives will satisfy each other sexually" whereas Islam emphasizes the husband's sexual needs over the wife's (ibid., 189n17). Overall, Ong insists that the "Arabization of Malay society depended in large part on implementing a rigid separation between male public roles and female domestic ones, a concrete realization of the architecture of male rationality (*akal*) and female eroticism (*nafsu*) that went way beyond any arrangement found in indigenous village arrangements where *akal* and *nafsu* are found in both women and men" (ibid., 177). Ong also notes that "Malays acknowledge sexual drives and provide cultural means for their adequate satisfaction in daily life. Until recently, parents arranged early marriages for sons and daughters for the legitimate management of sexual needs (among other reasons)" (1990, 416). This means that sexuality is not repressed in Malay adat. In fact, adat recognizes female sexual pleasure: Ong mentions "*kampung* women [who] use different techniques and tonics (*jamu*) to condition their bodies for enhancing erotic pleasure" (1995, 188n5).

According to Benedict Anderson, the idea of power in traditional Javanese political thought differs from the Western notion of power. It is concrete, "an existential reality," something that is "intangible, mysterious, and divine energy which animates the universe" (Anderson 1972, 7). Manifested in every aspect of nature, power is "expressed quintessentially in the central mystery of life, the process of generation and regeneration" (ibid.). Shelly Errington calls this notion of power "spiritual potency" (1990, 42). Further, she cites O.W. Walters, who suggested that tapping the powers of the spirit realm (*alam ghaib*) and emerging as a leader with an entourage is a very ancient Southeast Asian form of politics and political structures. Walters "calls the leaders 'men of prowess,' and points out that their follower-worshippers believed that care of the leader and the potency he embodied would bring them prosperity and fertility" (ibid.). Errington's book focuses on the pre-colonial pre-Islamic cultures of island Southeast Asia; her discussion of power as manifested in the notion of spiritual potency may explain the linkage between socio-economic status (class) and sexuality in the discourse of modern-day polygamous practices in Malaysia.

A scene in Shuhaimi Baba's film *Ringgit Kasorrga* illustrates the juxtaposition of sexual and political powers. Datuk Shah is a crooked, licentious, married politician who goes to a traditional healer to garner this invisible potency and to enhance his political and sexual appeal. Here, he undergoes *susuk* or *tusuk*, which is a traditional process of inserting gold needles underneath one's facial skin to increase one's attractiveness. A practice Islam frowns on, its incorporation in the film is another way of asserting adat as part of Malay identity. After the *susuk* session, when Datuk Shah stands up, his Chinese henchman looks down at Datuk Shah's penis while holding out his sarong for him. The henchman then flatters Datuk Shah's sexual potency. After the *susuk* session, Datuk Shah stretches in front of the window, shirtless, a fulfilled expression on his face. The heroine, who passes by and sees him standing there, gives him a look of fearful recognition of his harnessed potency before she quickly scurries away. (Shortly before this, she had just rejected his sexual advances.)

SELUBUNG: RESURGENT ISLAM, MODERNITY, AND THE MALAY WOMAN

The local and global tensions involving Islam that are explored in Malay woman filmmaker Shuhaimi Baba's film *Selubung* (1992) reveal the film's strong proclivity towards secularism while showcasing an example of the *dakwah* movement. Historically, the *dakwah* movement grew on university campuses in the early 1970s and developed among the kampung-born and educated Malays who had emerged as a new social force under the NEP (Ong 1995, 174). Students who were sent abroad on scholarships were exposed to various strands of Islamic resurgence on foreign campuses. *Selubung* revolves around the Malay female protagonist Mastura and her Malaysian medical student friends. While at the University of Western Australia in Perth, Mastura's best friend, EJ, a scholarship student, gets involved with a fundamentalist Muslim group headed by Brother Musa, a non-Malaysian of indeterminate nationality or ethnicity. EJ decides to drop out of her final year to become Brother Musa's second wife in a polygamous marriage, much to the disappointment and frustration of her other Malaysian friends. But EJ tells Mastura (who tries to talk her out of her decision) that a treacherous wife is one who is more educated than her husband.[14] EJ's decision to forsake a career for her husband is treated as anti-modern and aberrant, for Hani, Brother Musa's first wife, also has a medical degree, though we do not see her practising medicine. In fact, except for EJ and her mother, all the women in the film have paid work outside the home.

In many ways, EJ is the foil for Mastura. (Mastura is the kampung girl who makes good in the city and with whom the audience identifies.) EJ wears a head scarf and the *baju kurung* – a long skirt and a loose, shapeless, long-sleeved blouse – whereas Mastura usually wears Western-style clothing except when she comes to see EJ after EJ's wedding and once when she attends Muja Semangat with her grandfather.[15] EJ is portrayed as naïve to accept Brother Musa's sexist dogma seriously when he proclaims that young women with "hot blood" who are exposed to the open social norms of the West (Australia) would be easily tempted unless they marry "those already on the righteous path" (i.e., himself). She skips tutorials to attend his lectures, looks at him with total admiration and a shy smile on her face during his lecture, and constantly quotes him to her friends. Brother Musa's words to Mastura, "I have saved her soul. It is a sin for women to expose their flesh and expose themselves to temptation," clearly demonstrates his patriarchal Muslim arrogance. He insults Mastura (Mas, for short) by suggesting that she too should get married in order to be saved, and that perhaps he could help find someone for her.

Despite the representations of Brother Musa and his Australian first wife, Hani, who cautions Mas not to be like Zek (the Malaysian woman student counsellor at the University of Western Australia), who is described as "overly friendly with men, uncovered ... people like her are Satan," Shuhaimi Baba's approach towards Islamic fundamentalism is tolerant. This tolerance is reflected in Zek's attitude towards Brother Musa and his flock. Although aware of the things they say about her, she reassures Mastura and Halim: "They're all good people. Though sometimes they go a little overboard" (my translation). Just after her wedding, EJ also reassures Mastura that she is fine. Again, she says that Brother Musa and Hani are good people; only their methods differ. Indeed, if anything, the film shows how different Islamic groups unite to work for the common good: although Brother Musa is wary of liberal secularists like Halim, he realizes they are working for the same cause and joins Halim and the other medical interns in Beirut to help the Palestinian refugees. This overtly humanist cause actually contains threads of anti-Zionism and echoes the government's official policy towards Israel.

The film's title refers to the cloth (*selubung*) used for covering one's body or head and may suggest elements of conservative Islam that are substantiated by Brother Musa's remarks about women and temptation. But "resurgent Islam" in the film is actually motivated by global political events, which are represented in the scene in which the Malaysian students watching Perth television see Israeli soldiers beating up Palestinians. The students' subsequent involvement with Rescaid (Rescue Aid – a relief organization that helps Palestinian women and children who are victims of the Arab-Israeli war) is set up in this scene as Mastura remarks, "I wish we could help them." However, the title word *Selubung* is also the foundation of the verb *menyelubungi* on the cover of the video and entails a broader reading: "Seruan hidup mereka dibelai harapan dan kasih halus, *menyelubungi* pengorbanan dan perjuangan" (Their lives' calling, fostered by hopes and refined love, *encompasses* sacrifice and struggle [my translation and emphasis]). Like the transformation of the verb into the noun, and the movement from the title to the poster and video cover blurb, the film moves from its focus on Brother Musa's proselytizing activities around the Perth university campus to Mastura's later involvement with Rescaid in Kuala Lumpur and her aggressive campaign there to raise money for the children and women of Palestine. At the same time, "their lives' calling" is not so much a religious call for the young Malaysians as it is a humanitarian one. For example, Mastura and Kamal are dedicated to Rescaid but, unlike Dr. Sardar, they are neither particularly religious nor traditional.

They go out on dates (*berdating*) and do not observe the strict Islamic code of gender segregation that is normally upheld in the traditional setting of the kampung, or by the urban Islamic resurgents. Moreover, Vincent, Dr. Sardar's assistant, informs Mastura that the objectives of Rescaid are humanitarian rather than religious; Rescaid is a charity organization that helps out women and children everywhere. It is only this year that its project happens to be in the Middle East.

The film conveys a positive sense of globalism and modernity in its links to the Islamic world community (*umma*), as these are signified by what Appadurai calls the "five dimensions of global cultural flows" – ethnoscapes, mediascapes, technoscapes, financescapes, and ideoscapes (Appadurai 1996, 33). The Muslim Rescaid workers, Dr. Sardar (Jordanian) and Alwi (Palestinian), who are based in Kuala Lumpur, and Halim and the other Malaysian medical graduates who are interns in a refugee camp in Beirut, function as an ethnoscape: "the landscape of persons who constitute the shifting world in which we live: tourists, immigrants, refugees, exiles, guest workers, and other moving groups and individuals constitute an essential feature of the world and appear to affect the politics of (and between) nations to a hitherto unprecedented degree" (ibid.). References to the mediascape and technoscape occur throughout *Selubung:* just as the students watch events from the Middle East on Perth television, so too does Dr. Sardar as she later sits gloomily in front of the television, her eyes glued to the smoke-filled screen with the voices of children penetrating the thick smoke. There are newspaper headlines from Sydney, Kuala Lumpur, and London, and the constant flow of images and sounds of the Middle East war haunts the imaginations of the characters in the film. Shuhaimi Baba also employs the simple technique of a radio deejay to introduce the different landscapes: the section set in Perth opens with a view of the city and an Australian woman deejay's voice announcing the time of day and the name of her radio station. The film's subsequent transition to Kuala Lumpur is then mediated by the smooth, relaxed voice of a male deejay speaking in Malay as the camera focuses on the Rescaid office. The deejay voices help not only to contextualize and locate the viewers within the different cultural zones but they also simultaneously suture the seams of two geographically disparate places, using a by-now familiar global phenomenon – the spinning of pop music on radio waves. The fact that these various "scapes" interface is clear in the closing scene when a radio announcement states that the Malaysian government is officially sending donations to the Middle East in aid of the Palestinians. Through efforts involving the use of various media and technological tools, the Rescaid workers (the ethnoscape) have indeed succeeded in affecting international political relations. Audiovisual technological details such as faxes, courier, cellular phones, satellite pictures, and computers establish Malaysia's status as part of the technoscape, by which Appadurai means "the global configuration, also ever fluid, of technology ... [where] technology, both high and low, both mechanical and informational, now moves at high speeds across various kinds of previously impervious boundaries" (1996, 34).

This is all to say that Shuhaimi Baba perceives Islam in Malaysian modernity as part of a larger global cultural religious economy rather than as a localized fundamentalist movement confined by the borders of the nation-state and isolated from the Islamic world at large. In this sense, Appadurai's general theory of modernity as an interactive system of global flows functions to locate postcolonial Malaysia within the global scheme. Shuhaimi's portrayal of a young galvanized Malaysian community volunteering to work under war-time conditions in Beirut (Halim and Wn Ng die during a bomb blast at the clinic) and raising money for the dislocated Palestinians (with the sponsorship of the ubiquitous multinational McDonald's) is rather idealizing in light of the sacrifices made (Mastura herself is injured when a bomb goes off in the Rescaid building). But perhaps the film is Shuhaimi's response to the negative images of Islam emerging from the West.

The portrayal of fundamentalist Islam is tempered by several factors: the fact that the Muslim clique in the Australian university is headed not by a Malay but a foreigner shows that the hegemonic Malaysian brand of Islam is moderate and liberal; it perceives religious fundamentalism as an outside threat to Malayness, which is symbolized by the traditional vulnerable virgin (*anak dara*), EJ. Shuhaimi Baba's critique of fundamentalist Islam taking over adat's more flexible interpretation of Islam, most notably bilaterality, supports Wazir J. Karim's point about adat acknowledging gender hierarchies yet reducing their relative importance (1992, 5). As for tolerance, while Brother Musa seems unfriendly towards EJ's Malaysian friends and wants to keep her away from them, the non-Muslim society seems even less tolerant: following unrest in the Middle East, "Arabs go home" is spray-painted across the walls of a mosque in the Sydney suburbs by an arsonist.[16] Moreover, the bombing of Rescaid headquarters in London and Kuala Lumpur reverses the association of violence with Islamic fundamentalists that is all too common in the Western media.[17] Islamic fundamentalism is personalized in the characters of Brother Musa, Hani, and the impressionable EJ. While the background history of Brother Musa is somewhat unclear (i.e., why he converted), and he remains rather two-dimensional, it is perhaps easier to account for Hani's extreme actions: her mental distraction and jealousy of EJ stem from her traumatic experience of delivering a stillborn child. To compensate for her failure to be a mother or a productive, dutiful wife, she becomes a rigid enforcer of her husband's beliefs. Rather than being a picture of demonized Islam, Hani unfortunately presents a case of demonized gender (overwrought by jealousy and insanity, she suffocates EJ's baby). But even then, Shuhaimi Baba's humanism shows Hani as a woman to be pitied as she is bundled away to a mental hospital.

Other than EJ, who represents the traditional submissive Muslim woman, *Selubung* mostly presents a benign secularist version of Islam where women can hold positions of power. Dr. Sardar, a Jordanian who has lost family and friends in the PLO-Israeli struggle, heads the Rescaid office in Kuala Lumpur. She first appears in the film holding an antique sword that "could have belonged to a great Ottoman soldier." Explaining the significance of the sword to her young assistant, Vincent, she declares that she wishes she were one of the soldiers who fought to defend God's truth: "What I'd give to be one of them, but women don't go to war," she says, eyes shining, both hands gripping the handle of the sword. "Allahu Allahaq, Allahu Allahaq, Waljannah!" she exclaims, waving the symbol of masculine and religious power around the room and pointing it at Vincent's neck. "You go to war, Vincent?" she asks playfully and he replies, bending backwards, "Not against you."

Using figures of female agency like Dr. Sardar and Mastura, Shuhaimi Baba demonstrates that Islam can co-exist with Western modernity. In fact, the spirit of Islam that Dr. Sardar first assumes is dead is revived through Mastura via the tools of Western modernity. For example, it is Mastura who proposes a more aggressive campaign to raise money after explaining that merely sending out letters of appeal to potential sponsors is not nearly effective enough. Instead, Rescaid needs to network with and woo corporate sponsors as well as publicize their goals through the media (newspapers, radio). Their campaign includes a charity dinner, a benefit music recording (à la "Live Aid"), and an outdoor concert. Utilizing her physical and social charm along with her intelligence, enthusiasm, and business sense, Mastura succeeds. When she finds a sponsor for the air freight, Dr. Sardar turns to the silent Alwi and says wryly in English, "She has the spirit, this one!" It is clear that by the end of the film, Dr. Sardar will return to Jordan and Mastura will take charge of the operations at KL Rescaid. The spirit of Islam is resuscitated by the five dimensions of global cultural flows that characterize modernity, which is embodied in Mastura, the modern Malay woman.

As for the question of polygamy, it is evident from *Selubung* and, perhaps, if we generalize, from the perspective of a modern secularist Malay woman like Shuhaimi, that the modern ideal relationship is monogamous and heterosexual: Mastura refuses to see Kamal once she discovers that he is married and agrees to continue the relationship only when he tells her he is already divorced. As for the polygamous relationship between Brother Musa and his wives, EJ and the unstable Hani, jealousy and insanity occur when EJ has a baby and the new addition to the family causes Musa to neglect Hani. Consequently, Hani attacks and kills the baby when Musa and EJ are out of the house one day. Shuhaimi's female protagonists, both played by Deanna Yusoff, force their male love interest to choose and to be monogamous: in *Ringgit Kasorrga*, where initially it looked as though Khal was involved with two women, the worldly sophisticate Meera and the younger heroine Nina, Khal finally confides in Nina that he and Meera are only friends and business partners. Monogamy becomes the only choice when Meera, the female competitor for Khal's affections, is murdered. As for adultery, the social escort Meera is reduced to shame by the heroine Nina's goodness and genuine high expectations for Meera's dance studio, Blaze (a front for the social escort service).

Shuhaimi Baba's ideal modern Malay woman, as embodied by her filmic heroines (played by Deanna Yusoff), feels equally at home in the city and in the kampung. She easily crosses and re-crosses rural and urban boundaries, straddling both Western and uniquely Malay cultures without fear of one subsuming the other. In *Selubung*, Mastura's fashion sense is a blend of East and West: at her kampung back in Trengganu, she wears batik, but batik cut in a Western casual playsuit of matching sleeveless top and pants, suggesting a tradition that is hybrid. At other times, her wardrobe ranges from jeans and long-sleeved shirts to three-piece office suits. In touch with her roots, she plays the *rebana*, a traditional drum.[18] Injured in the bomb blast, she is healed by both Western and traditional "medicine": while lying unconscious in a KL hospital, she is revived by the collective chanting/prayer of her grandfather's villagers, which in turn invokes the magical lucky butterflies that flutter and perch on her scarred face, healing her.[19]

Despite 1990s modernity, Shuhaimi Baba's heroines continue to retain some of the female traits noted by Ungku Maimunah in her essay on modern Malay women's literature, "Perceptions of the Ideal Malay Woman." Writing about Adibah Amin's 1968 novel, *Seroja Masih di Kolam*, Ungku Maimunah claims that, "by and large, the gentleness of the Malay heroine, her natural beauty, graceful and winsome ways, held up as Malay, Eastern and Islamic values, are often favourably compared to the harsh and artificial beauty of the Western-influenced [one] who is often presented as crass, strident and pushy" (1994, 16). Mastura can certainly be described as gentle and possessing natural beauty and graceful, winsome ways, though they do not compromise her "Western-influenced" values. But Ungku Maimunah's uncritical approach to these texts is problematic: her description of the "ideal Malay woman" (whose ideal?) reassures the patriarchal ego and reinforces the traditional social hierarchy. Such a mutually exclusive polarity makes "Malay, Eastern, and Islamic values" seem impermeable to modernity or Westernization when Malaysian women have in fact already subscribed to the Western "beauty myth." For example, a woman has to look good or she may be blamed for her husband's philandering or polygamous desire. EJ suggests that the reason Kamal is no longer interested in his first wife is that she may be sick, have short legs, or look ugly – all rather shallow reasons that might just reflect EJ's shallow nature, but which nevertheless illustrate Malaysian society's objectification of women. There is a hint that the beauty myth's oppressive influence, which Maznah Mohamad associates with women in the West (1994, 129), is also at work in *Selubung* – unfortunately, it's one of the effects of a cultural and consumerist globalization. For example, when Kamal invites Mastura out for lunch and she declines, he asks whether she is on a diet. Naomi Wolf's book *The Beauty Myth* describes "a condition in Western cultures, which women's liberation notwithstanding, still constrains women" (quoted in Maznah 1994, 129). Women "become their own subject-agents sustaining male privilege while circumscribing their own autonomy" (ibid.). Without men telling them how they should look, they regulate their own appearance and behaviour to create the perfect image; this self-enterprise includes a strict regime of diets, exercise, plastic surgery, etc. (ibid., 130).

Let us return to Stivens's questions that opened this discussion: "Is the Malay Muslim embrace of re-emergent Islamic practices to be seen solely as a resistance to Western hegemony within terms set by the West, an expression of a number of ambivalences about Western-style modernity? Or should we also explore its place within the globalisation of Islam and the complex relationship of this globalisation to the Malaysian development of an alternative modernity?" (1998, 116). Brother Musa's Muslim group is portrayed as resisting Australian racism in Perth, not to mention a more general sense of resisting Western hegemony and modernity. But *Selubung* also exemplifies the Malaysian role within Islamic globalization by featuring Malay Muslims working together with Muslims from Jordan and Palestine in the development of a uniquely Malaysian modernity.

MALAY SEXUALITY/SENSUALITY IN THE WORK OF KARIM RASLAN, SHAHNON AHMAD, AND DINA ZAMAN

Karim Raslan's representation of polygamy confirms Stivens's notion of a class link. Polygamy and the more common topic of adultery appear in all the stories that revolve around the bumigeois in urban KL, with the exception of the title story in Karim Raslan's *Heroes and Other Stories*. For example, in "A New

Year's Lunch at Jalan Kia Peng" there are three characters who are either polygamous or adulterous – Mahani's husband, her ambitious architect brother, Kam, and Fat Chew, Kam's Chinese father-in-law, who has "a propensity for mistresses and concubines (he had had five on his deathbed)" (1996b, 59). The thematic recurrence of adultery and polygamy suggests the predominance of sexuality in the lives of the modern urbanized characters. Mahmud, the erring husband of the wealthy and successful Mahani, has recently acquired a second wife with the excuse: "to save me from committing *zina* [adultery]" (ibid., 58). By this, Karim shows how easily the Islamic sanction of polygamy can be used hypocritically to legitimate adultery among the decadent, wealthy, and non-practising Muslim Malays. Mahmud's roguish comment partly demonstrates his self-awareness that men will stray and that an opportunistic take on Islam will sanction this "natural" male behaviour rather than force him to change.[20] In a paradoxical way, the story reflects the disparity between the official and practical representations of Malay gender. Although women are officially supposed to be more passionate and less rational than men, Mahmud's confession acknowledges male passion, which has to be brought under control for religious reasons. Moreover, while Islam may concede men's "unbridled lust" when it suits Muslim men (i.e., in order to encourage polygyny, polygamy for men), women, who are supposed to have more *nafsu* according to Islam, are not allowed to practise polyandry, polygamy for women.

In the urban, materialist landscape, second (or third or fourth) wives and mistresses are objects of material and social value to the professional men and politicians who acquire them. In "Sara and the Wedding," Sara's aunt, Mak Cik Khatijah, informs her that men remarry because "if they have money, like your uncle before, they want to show off the size of their balls. If the second wife is young and hot, then they are hot, too" (ibid., 97). Socio-economic and political power are thus linked to sexual prowess and male virility.

For conservative Malays, "the city [has] meant chaos and moral bankruptcy, inundated as it was with aliens [this includes Asian immigrants and Westerners] whose life-style revolved around gambling, illicit sex, alcohol and the like, all of which were proscribed by Islam" (Ungku Maimunah 1994, 13). "All things 'Western'" include television and movies, "regarded as the major vehicles for transmitting undesirable foreign values" (Ong 1990, 411). Shahnon Ahmad's novel *Tivi* (1995) is a didactic and rather two-dimensional account of the corrupting influences of television on a simple-minded poor peasant couple. Addicted to television, the rural couple begins to imitate what they see on screen to the point of neglecting their daily chores. Their sex life is activated by Mat Isa's uncontrolled libido, leading to his committing incest with his two daughters. Such scenes are portrayed without any resistance on the part of the women characters who are all passive and willing participants. Shahnon's techno-paranoia reflects the dislocation of people caught between an agricultural tradition and the too-rapid processes of modernization, unable to defend themselves against the onslaught of suggestively sexual media images. The increase and expansion of satellite systems that offer more and more television channels showing American programs in the 1990s adds to the fear of religious conservatives like Shahnon Ahmad. However, some of Shahnon's earlier work in *The Third Notch and Other Stories* (1980) already features an obsession with sexuality in its graphic misogynistic images of rape: for example, in "Igau" (written in 1971), the implication is that women who do not cover up their bodies provoke male sexual violence and deserve to be raped. The Malay male protagonist sees a woman in a miniskirt in Australia and he imagines tearing her clothes off and raping her. His fantasy is interspersed with his homesick images of celebrating Hari Raya in his kampung surrounded by family and friends.[21]

In *Tivi*, the urban, working daughter Chah is a typical Minah Karan who brings home the television set; it is her tight-fitting sleeveless clothes and seductive modern sexuality that eventually lead her father to incest. In fact, the power of modernity or "progress and development" is signified by Chah. Her sexual emancipation is very much Western: she teaches her younger sister how to dress in a modern way and to pay attention to her body, buying her hair dyes and a powder to enhance her bustline. Moreover, Shahnon seems to delight in reminding the readers that Chah works in a factory producing screws, hoping we will catch the sexual pun. Shahnon's work was often described as "earthy" prior to his "rather dramatic conversion to a fundamentalist form of Islam of the Al-Arqam movement in the mid-70s" (Aveling 1996, 217). Although Shahnon may be critiquing the shallowness of the couple's faith in Islam by showing how quickly they give up the prayer corner of their small dwelling to house the television, the obsessive emphasis on sexuality, sexual organs, and the female body's contours in the story suggest that beneath the moral didacticism lies a conflicted subject trying to deal with the inconsistencies of his identity as a Muslim Malay, with adat resurfacing to challenge the purity of the Islam he now seeks. In order to create a unified and purified Muslim subject, Shahnon has to disavow elements of his adat, such as an openness about sexuality/sensuality, and treat them as Western and therefore, Other. Indeed, in an interview after the publication of his controversial political satire *Shit* (1999), he attributes the earthy/offensive language to his "split personality": "People look at me and see a pious man, but there's a repressed side which comes out in my writing. That's when I don't censor myself. I let it all out" (Amir Muhammad 1999, 41).

On the liberal end of the political spectrum, Karim Raslan, too, reiterates the construction of the city as a place of moral decadence and sensuality in his tribute to Malaysia's capital, beginning with an image of a feminized Kuala Lumpur: "KL, KL ... or why I love the slut that straddles the steaming rice-pot that is the Klang Valley" (1996a, 112). However, the difference between his approach and Shahnon's is that Karim celebrates the sensual aspects of Malay identity rather than the global neo-Islamic elements. Nevertheless, his idea of sensuality can also be construed as sexist and misogynist. The act of a woman straddling a rice-pot derives from adat rather than Islam, signifying a reassertion of feminine sexual power over her erring husband to whom she will serve the rice. For Karim, the urban space of KL is defined by sexual and power relations, mapped not only by delicious cuisine but also by a chain of gossip about who is or is not sleeping with whom: "From the songstress who slept with the politician who slept with the pretty TV journalist ... who slept with the gangster who slept with the call girl who slept with the record producer who slept with the songstress – and so it went on. KL, KL. I love you" (113-14). This outlook is precisely what is under attack by *dakwah* leaders who rail "against the decadent lifestyle of nouveaux-riches Malays, with their pursuit of glittering acquisitions and sensual pleasures, and their blithe disregard of Islam" (Ong 1995, 175). He may be critiquing a *dakwah* point of view, but in Karim's tribute to the city is an erotic embracing of urban Malay sensual identity.

Karim Raslan's texts on sexuality follow a tradition of local popular constructions of Malay sensuality. For example, as I suggested in Chapter 2, Salleh Ben Joned concludes from his analysis of the contents of the traditional *pantun* (Malay rhymed quatrain) that the Malay race "cannot be a stranger to sexual hedonism" (1994, 161). Censorship has not deterred Malay male filmmaker U-Wei Saari from portraying the potent sexuality of a Malay woman in his controversial 1994 film *Perempuan, Isteri Dan ...?* (Woman, Wife, and Whore).[22] Neither has Islamic modesty stopped Malay male writers from portraying Malay women as sexual objects: from A. Samad Said's sympathetic portrait of a prostitute, *Salina* (1961), in 1950s Singapore to sexy Pinky, the dance hostess at a cabaret, whose rear end is constantly admired by the male characters in the same writer's more recent play *Lantai Di Pinky* (Pinky's Dancefloor, 1996).[23] So the male reinscription of adat on the body of the sexualized woman is problematic: it signals the Foucauldian idea that the modern discourse of sexual liberation "is always a prelude to a new insertion into another model of power" (Yang 1997, 311). The Anwar sex scandal coverage in the Malaysian media gives a clear case of how liberal sexual discourse can be strategically deployed for the political purpose of preserving hegemonic power. More generally, whether unconsciously or not, the struggles and tensions in the realms of literature, film, and politics between men who are clothed in a strongly masculine rhetoric (of "virility"), despite the frequent construction of women as the gender of modernity, expose the true patriarchal nature of modernity in the discourses of the nation-state. That is, we live in a masculinist modernity.

Karim Raslan's collection contains not only numerous cases of polygamy and adultery but also two stories about homosexuality. And Dina Zaman, too, features a story about a homosexual affair in "Two Men." This triggers several questions: has sexuality become increasingly central because of modernization and urbanization? If it has, should we subscribe to the belief that "the West [is] obsessed with issues of sexuality," and that in the process of modernization and Westernization, "sexuality has become the truth of our [Malaysian] being" (Stivens 1994, 83)? The idea that sexual issues dominate the feminist agenda has been an accusation by non-Western feminists against Western feminism.[24] Non-Western feminists however prefer to think that their own concerns revolve around the "political" in a more public sense.

While women filmmakers do not focus on female sexuality, their peers in the field of literature have been less shy about broaching this topic in recent times. But then again, they are not faced with such strict state censorship as are filmmakers. For example, woman novelist Raja Azmi's well-received Malay novel, *Black Widow*, contains graphic sexual scenes in which the lead character masturbates as well as dreams of making love to a spider. However, when she turned her novel into a film, scenes like this could not be depicted on the screen (S. Bissme 1999, 29). The sexual *is* political in Dina Zaman's writing. She courageously takes on issues such as abortion ("Philippa"), incest ("Her Son Is Her Lover"), women's rape fantasies ("The Passenger"), and sadomasochistic sex ("Night and Day"), which would seem merely sensationalist were it not for its critique of Islamic repression and hypocrisy. In "The Passenger" the young woman in a taxi reads the Ministry of Health's Safe Sex poster on a bus – "Stay Away from Adultery" (my translation of "Jangan Hampiri Zina") and observes, "Surrounding the propaganda were young and impressionable faces, all swearing off pre-marital sex. Wait 'til they give in to lust or loneliness. Stupid poster" (1997, 32). The protagonist regards the state ideology's attempts to deny sexual desires, which she considers an integral part of one's identity, as vain and impractical. Rather than writing about the subject of sex for its own sake, Dina explains that she uses sex as a metaphor for human drama to illustrate the loneliness we all endure and the ways in which the degenerates of society try to find some magic or relief in their lives through sexual contact (e-mail, 28 June 98). She feels that these are issues we should address, because Malaysians, who are "no saints," are "rather inhibited about sexuality," and will deny having sexual desires or thoughts. She surmises that perhaps the reason people are uncomfortable about sexuality is that "it makes them discover truths [about themselves]" (ibid.).

Sexuality has always been an important issue for Malays but it's seldom discussed openly, especially by women, because of Islam and the social modesty prescribed for their gender. Marina Mahathir suggests that perhaps it is also the failure to implement proper sex education in schools and the inability to deal openly with sexual discourse cross-generationally and across genders that have given rise to the number of cases in the media about abandoned fetuses and babies, and incest (1997, 122, 127-30). A scene in Dina Zaman's short story "Ani" illustrates this point. Ani, a young, innocent housemaid, an *anak dara* or virgin new to the urban area, is horrified by the other maids' talk of sex. She considers Midah's decision to sleep with her married employer "a holy sin" but Midah explains, "Ani, I'm forty-five and an old maid. I'm human and I need sex. I also like what I see" (1997, 26). Midah's calm answer is accompanied by her "gestures to her groin" (ibid.). The other women's unrepressed attitudes towards sex challenge Ani's social modesty and religious morality. Letchumi tells her, "*Adei, dara,* we're not prostitutes. We just like good lays" (ibid.).

Most of Dina's stories reflect earthiness or bawdiness and the characters' constant self-awareness of female libidinal desires, as women refer to their breasts (Ani's "papaya breasts") and their genitalia: the *kacang puteh* and *assam* lady's "beneath will tug and tug and tug.[25] Her wet comes out. Her nipples, flat from lack of attention, become hard and erect" (ibid., 11-12). The use of specific Malay words demonstrates that her focus on sexual themes is not merely a Western influence but is more localized – the nuances are somehow different and untranslatable. The *kacang puteh* lady uses a common obscenity, *pukimak,* that refers to one's mother's vagina (ibid., 10), as does the fat woman who "knew she could swear any man out of his sarong. She could '*puki*' this, '*pantat*' that, she could 'asshole' any man, woman, child or animal out of his, her or its asshole" (ibid., 54). The old fat woman's power to curse parallels her former sexual feminine power as the "Virgin Killer": "She took all the boys in the neighbourhood to her room and slept with them" (ibid., 57). While female agency is tied to the exercise of female sexuality, the women characters are torn by moral guilt: the woman who picks up a male prostitute in "Night and Day" tells herself "tonight i will be a man and have a bit of rough myself" (ibid., 45) but then later questions her actions, "why am i doing this stop it stop it no more thoughts i am not committing a sin" (ibid., 48). The story ends after the night of consensual S and M tails off into more gentle lovemaking as the lovers comfort each other and nurse each other's wounds. The fact that the story focuses more on the woman's perspective and her agency, yet ends with a contented sense of heterosexual bilaterality, brings home my point that the writer is referring to adat, which emphasizes bilaterality and recognizes female libidinal desires.[26] Dina Zaman's confrontational writing style is a calculated move against Islamic repression of sexual discourse and the clampdown on female (and gay) sexualities.

Sexuality is more complicated for Karim Raslan, whose stories are characterized by a strong sense of morality that does not so much judge sexual and social practices as it confronts the issue of truth and self-awareness in a materialist environment where self-knowledge is increasingly hard to achieve. For example, in "Neighbours," when a middle-aged, neglected, wealthy, busybody housewife, Datin Sarina, spies on her handsome neighbour only to discover that he is gay, the onus falls on her rather than on him: "It was a rare moment, a moment of shocking clarity. She could see herself as she was – the pretence and the falsity of how she lived her life had slipped away ... She had nothing herself: she was nothing herself" (1996b, 131). In "Go East!" the closeted male protagonist's denial of his homosexual identity after he forces himself to have sexual intercourse with a thirteen-year-old girl turns him into the kind of hypermasculine closed-minded loser that his colleagues represent: "I had learnt something that had freed me from all my problems. I laughed again and took my shower, safe in the certainty that I knew, I knew. I, too, no longer had need for any more questions" (ibid., 118). The quest for self-truth, however, betrays Karim's "Western" preoccupation with the individual rather than the group, most clearly reflected in the liberal individual interpretation of Islam voiced by the characters Encik Kassim and Mus in "Neighbours." Mus comments that "There are many ways of serving Allah and it is important to allow each individual his right to choose his own way, and his own time within the dictates, as you say, of the Koran and the Hadiths" (ibid., 123). Encik Kassim's own liberal interpretation and concurrence with Mus's words assume added significance when later, Mus's wife, Sarina, spies on Kassim and his "spouse" from her verandah and discovers that he is having sex with a man. As a gay Malay man leading a double life (he informs Datin Sarina that his wife is related to her), unable to escape the religious identity of the Malays, his only recourse is to modify or liberalize, if only in his own mind and for himself, the tenets of the religion he has to live with. Mus's philosophy, on the other hand, reflects his background as part of the older liberal Malay elite, those who had come to power under British tutelage.

Karim Raslan's fiction privileges female sexual desires. For example, now that her husband has taken a second wife, Mahani likes to relive her first kiss because it makes her "feel young, invigorated and desired again" (ibid., 58). As for the forty-five-year-old neighbour Datin Sarina, her voyeurism is motivated by her sexual attraction to Encik Kassim, her latent sexual desires reinvigorated by what she sees. She is reminded of "similar fleeting encounters with Mus, and the men before Mus, meetings that had been snatched in between dances and dinners, baby-sitting and badminton. Those were the days when sex had been something exciting for her and Mus" (ibid., 128). If anything, Karim Raslan represents modern Malay women as strong, independent, and imbued with desires they are in charge of fulfilling, whether they are career women or mistresses.[27] The mistresses he portrays (Zeraphina in "The Mistress" and Jamilah Jamboo in "A New Year's Lunch") are self-possessed, self-determining, sexual subjects who benefit materially and financially from their wealthy lovers. These women have learned to operate within what Maznah Mohamad has called "the rules of the male privileging system" (1994, 135). As the male protagonist of "The Mistress" notes about his father's mistress, "She had outmanoeuvred me" (Karim 1996b, 85). The customary bilaterality of the sexes provokes the notion too that if men were polygamous, women could then be adulterous: Mak Cik Khatijah's advice to Sara is to "take a man and treat him like he'd treat you. *Buat dulu* [Do it first], only with the handsome one and then you get rid of them: Kelantanese style" (ibid., 98).[28]

Perhaps the most sensitive portrayal of the modern Malay woman appears in "Sara and the Wedding." Sara, a "plump and homely" successful, single lawyer in her mid-thirties, attends her younger sister's wedding only to be reminded by her insinuating relatives that she looks unhappy because of her unmarried state (ibid., 88). Unlike the Malay women's novels discussed by Ungku Maimunah, the story explores not just the emotional inner life of the heroine but also her sexual desires, which have been put aside for far too long. Her sense of inferiority about her physical appearance, which is reflected in her inner thoughts about herself as "the ungainly, unfashionable sister" (ibid., 93), is overcome by her decision to entertain the sexual advances of her married second cousin, Ramli. Their attraction to each other is characterized by mutual surveillance, but she is the watcher first, subjecting him to her gaze "all evening, observing the way he scratched his belly after the *makan* [meal]" (ibid., 99). When she realizes that she too is being watched, she revels under Ramli's gaze, which "filled her with a delicious sense of being desired. She knew what it was like to be wanted" (ibid., 100). Her brief sexual encounter in the garden with him may fall short of her earlier hopes of a romantic, fantasy-like male partner, "brighter, more charming and less arrogant" than her attractive and young new brother-in-law, Azman (ibid., 93). But in terms of fulfilling her sexual needs and pleasures, she "had achieved all she wanted" (ibid., 101). When Ramli asks her urgently when they can meet again, she replies, "Never" for "now it was her turn to assert herself" (ibid., 101). By this, she means to "prove everything to her family," to "prove her true desirability, her power" (ibid., 101). The story ends with her screaming, "Rape, rape!"

Applying ideas of Enlightenment and human rights to feminism, and combining them with a non-Muslim, Malay, open attitude towards sexual and gender relations, Karim's feminist sympathies ensure that Sara winds up having the upper hand: now she would be regarded not only as the "clever, hard-working" and responsible daughter who supported her family after her father's death (ibid., 95) but also as a sexually desirable woman. Her episode with Ramli fulfills one other political dimension of her gendered, social, and familial identity. (Of course, one might as easily make the case that her cry of rape shows she is still susceptible to social stigma, or that it is misogynist in the sense that it feeds into the sexist notion that rape victims lie or "ask for it.")

As far as gender politics are concerned, sexism has certainly been the reception for many writers who attempt to represent women's active sexuality. Dina Zaman talks about the negative reception of her work from the Malay male literati who have reduced her to "a sex maniac heathen." Moreover, she adds,

> A friend of mine, Faridah Manaf, who writes in BM [Malay] faces the same problem too. It's a case of sexism and paranoia. Which makes me wonder – it is true *dulu-dulu perempuan semua ni diam belaka* (in the past all these women were quiet) but look at our heroines who were vocal, and fought for our lands! So Malay women aren't passive after all. And if you look at literature in the '50s and '60s, (and before that) there were women writers, and they were encouraged as part of the nationalist movement (if I remember my history correctly). But now, I feel the Malay literati has turned extremely conservative and [are] not encouraging at all. Suddenly there's this moralistic edge Malay academics have in them, as if they are the morals police and that the country depends on their intellectual thoughts so Malaysia would function. (e-mail, 24 April 1997)[29]

The paranoia of the Malay literati Dina mentions stems from their anticolonial nationalist sentiments, expressed through an alignment with global Islamic interests in response to secularist forces within the government. Therefore, competing state ideologies of resurgent Islam and Western liberal attitudes react with and interpenetrate each other. On the one hand, the secularist forces "want Malaysians, especially Malays, to be seen as urban-based and progressive" to the point of eliding from advertising campaigns rural or kampung scenes that can potentially be perceived as nostalgic (Rastam 1995). "It is very difficult for an advertisement showing a rural scene to be passed ...

The Government believes they will cause people to look back and not forward," says Lillian Tan, creative director of Saatchi and Saatchi Advertising (ibid., 7). On the other hand, there are the Malay academics from the national university (Universiti Kebangsaan Malaysia) and the government-supported Dewan Bahasa dan Pustaka (DBP), the Language and Literature Board, which stamps the state approval on what it considers serious national (i.e., Malay) literature. The DBP's protectionist, ethnic, and language-based stance acts as a guardian of so-called national culture against non-BM writing in English, Mandarin, or Tamil, usually by non-bumiputera Malaysians – the Chinese and Indians.

Because those writing in English are isolated by the Malay literati, who consider writing in the English medium at best "Malaysian literature" as opposed to "national literature" and at worst, "minority literature," Dina Zaman's work is probably more easily dismissed by Malay academics than her friend and academic Nor Faridah Manaf's work which, because it's written in Malay, is more heavily policed. However, just as in the colonial past, when English was the "passport to the 'modernisation' process which could secure entry to the world of professions, politics, administration and the like" (Ungku 1994, 12), today, English has become "the world's lingua franca and most convenient means to economic and technological competitiveness" (Salleh 1994, 65). For example, the fact that most of the characters in *Selubung* are fluent in English and interject English words into their conversations in Malay demonstrates their middle-class modernness, urbanity, and Western education. Similarly, Dina Zaman and Karim Raslan's choice to write in English, not to mention their unflinching approach to sexual themes, projects the image of Malays as urban and progressive. This is in full accord with Mahathir's secularism and his drive to achieve a Malaysian modernity on a par with that of the West. As early as 1993, Mahathir had announced that there would be greater emphasis on English as the medium of instruction in Malaysian universities to fuel his pet project, Vision 2020 (Salleh 1994, 63).

Just as the *dakwah* movement is a reaction against Westernization and urbanization, Malay writers writing in English may be responding to the narrowing of their cultural boundaries that is advocated by resurgent Islamic groups. The world of English, too, is no longer the sole claim of the British; its neutrality and creative and imaginative spaciousness allow Malay writers to preserve or revive, reclaim and re-imagine their adat and to reconstruct a new secular identity for themselves. While it retains a hint of colonialism for some Malays, the non-association of the English language with a particular ethnic group and its internationalism today makes it neutral space in multiethnic Malaysia.[30] As Salleh Ben Joned explains, "It's our English; along with

BM it expresses our 'soul,' with all its contradictions and confusions, as much as our social and material needs" (1994, 65). One should bear in mind that bumi (rather than non-bumi) writers like Karim Raslan and Rehman Rashid are more likely to get away with critiquing sensitive racial and religious issues. For example, Rehman's self-published political novel sold very well and was into its fourth printing in 1996. His success as a bumi writer writing in English might have made the larger publication houses (Times International, for example) more open to other Malay writers writing in English. And though he's not as critical as Rehman, a savvy young writer like Karim Raslan, whose political journalism is conservative enough, is published by Times Books International (Singapore), whereas the more radical Salleh Ben Joned gets published by small presses such as Skoob Books, which was started by a Malaysian based in London, Pustaka Cipta, which issued a remixed version of his earlier poetry collection *Sajak-Sajak Saleh: Poems Sacred and Profane* (2002), and Maya Press, which brought out his collection of essays and columns, *Nothing Is Sacred* (2003). Dina Zaman's book was published by Rhino Press, a small, new, ambitious (and short-lived) publisher hoping to showcase new Malaysian writers writing in English. Prior to the economic recession and the Anwar scandal, the 1990s political climate seemed liberal because Mahathir Incorporated strove to put Operation Lallang behind it in order to encourage foreign investment and capital. Despite the economic downturn after 1997, the ISA political detention of various activists in 2001, and long-time Prime Minister Mahathir's retirement at the end of October 2003, those in the culture industry will likely continue to test the limits of liberalism, whether by consciously or unconsciously reclaiming adat or by dealing with sexual matters openly in literary and cinematic discourses.

So to return to Stivens's question about those "sections of the contemporary Malay middle classes (including many women)" who are enthusiastic "for various versions of resurgent Islam," we have seen quite different views of modernity, with the exception of Shahnon Ahmad, among the writers and filmmaker discussed here. These secularists in the 1990s provide yet another dialectical response to the Islamic resurgents' reflexivity concerning modernity. Similarly, Sisters in Islam, in seeking "to articulate women's rights within Islam by emphasizing the need to interpret the Quran and hadith in their proper historical and cultural contexts," provides another reaction to its more submissive female peers who have succumbed to the dogmas of other fundamentalist movements (Ong 1995, 185). Concerning polygamy, SIS asks men who practise it "to seek Islamic guidance to change their promiscuous attitude to 'one of self-discipline and respect for the opposite sex'" (ibid.).

It is imperative to uncover the various ideological bases behind positions taken with regard to modernity, alternative modernity, or postmodernity. For example, the arrest of three Malay beauty contestants by the Selangor Religious Department for being "indecently dressed in public" was interpreted by the prime minister as an exercise of power by the clergy: "The Quran never said that Islam must be different in each state. But there are people who want to show their power. This is the problem."[31] In the week before, the *Southeast Asia Post* had linked the reassertion of Islamic authority throughout the peninsula (and in other states as well) by the top clergy to Mahathir's scolding them in 1996 and their failure to block the introduction of the Domestic Violence Act, which they had opposed "on the grounds that it encroached on their authority to deal with family matters."[32]

Nevertheless, the prime minister's daughter, Marina Mahathir, had other reasons for disapproving of the arrest. Her rhetoric expresses and addresses feminist concerns, favouring a liberal, Western-style modernity: "We should all be alarmed ... [that the laws in Selangor place more emphasis on women's dress than men's] because it means that there are people out there to repress women in our country. They want us to be at home having babies endlessly and covered head to toe because they think that that's what good women do ... Otherwise we are out there to tempt weak, sex-crazed men." She goes on to point out that relative to issues like incest, child abuse, wife-battering, drug abuse, and corruption, "whether you're dressed right or wrong according to someone's arbitrary values should rank pretty low in the scale of the concerns of our times." She questions the motives of the religious zealots: "Marina noted that the authorities who arrested the contestants said nothing at all about protecting the rights of the women from being exploited."[33] They are hypocritical for banning participation in but not the viewing of beauty contests, or, for that matter, the commodification of female bodies on television: "What is the use of banning [them] when you can always go home and watch *Baywatch*?"

Her father's discourse, on the other hand, reflects a recognition of the nation's dispersal of "power and authority on religious matters" and, perhaps, a need to consolidate this power. In calling for all the states to practise a uniform Islam, he says, "We definitely want to standardise the laws, but the power is not with us" (ibid.). In fact, this power lies in the hands of the Malay rulers. Mahathir's statement brings to mind his failed parliamentary attempt to remove the rulers' legal immunity in late 1992. While he was prime minister, he certainly posed an ever-present threat to their already much-diminished public roles as heads of religion in their respective states and the symbolic representation of Malays' identity and power as the original and dominant people of the country (Nagata 1994, 81).

Whether religious matters are in his jurisdiction or not, an authoritarian leader needs little excuse to consolidate his power if religion interferes with his economic project of modernity. Thus, we can still read Mahathir's position regarding women and resurgent Islam as privileging industrialized modernity – which Giddens defines as "the social relations implied in the widespread use of material power and machinery in production processes" (1991, 15) – above the interests of women. Matilda Gabrielpillai suggests that Mahathir does not broach the event from a feminist perspective because of his difficult position as leader attempting to balance resurgent Islam and secular governance. If he favoured the feminist approach, he would appear unIslamic; yet with his immense political power and influence, he has not prevented his outspoken daughter from voicing what are possibly his own thoughts about the situation. However, this point about Mahathir's differing approach to the event should not undercut the power of Marina's words nor her autonomy as one of the most vocal feminists in Malaysia today. My point is that the religious department's arrest of the beauty queen contestants exemplifies a typical situation in which a power struggle between secular and religious forces, between modernity and "tradition"/alternative modernity or postmodernity, takes place over the bodies of women.

6

What Is It to Be a Man? Violence in the Time of Modernity

Before we move onto cinematic representations of masculinity, it is productive to explore the perception of feminism in Malaysia through a brief analysis of the film *Femina* (1993) because this will help to explain why so-called authentic masculinity is under threat. Feminism is often represented as an anomalous import obstructing and redefining Malaysian gender relations. New Wave filmmaker Aziz M. Osman's work *Femina* centres on Tina (played by Erma Fatima), a radical feminist who works for a women's magazine of the same name. By the end of the film, she is forced to modify her hostility towards men through her initially reluctant romance with a minibus company owner, Pyan, who, despite his sexist views, brings a young runaway girl to Tina to escape her pimp. Pyan is played by Eman Manan, who represents "authentic Malay masculinity."

The response to the film by Malay film critic, Hamzah Hussin, is interesting. He argues that the film is not representative of Malaysian culture.[1] Moreover, he believes that the script was probably based on a pre-existing Western script, as are most Malay television dramas and films. This remark precludes any discussion of the film's content, because feminism, being conceived as Western, has no real influence on local gender relations and therefore merits no serious analysis. I interviewed Pak Hamzah on his views about feminism two years later (8 July 1998). Although he seems to believe in gender equality and sympathizes with women, his understanding of feminism is somewhat reductive, because the definitions he gives for the term – gender exclusivism and women wanting to be better than men – arguably pertain to a common misreading of radical feminism. The representations of Tina and her boss Anita Daley, played by Susan Lankester, support this reductive definition.

A power struggle revolving around ideological differences and varying interpretations of feminism ensues between the two women, with Anita being the antagonist. However, Anita is an antagonist only because she is power hungry, manipulative, hypocritical, and does not do things the Malay way, which is to maintain a non-confrontational position in polite speech. Her words are provocative but not ultra-radical: she points out that husbands abandon their spouses and families, and this has nothing to do with Western influences. She also states that it is difficult for men like Pyan to accept that women can be fathers but there are very few men capable of being mothers. Pyan's wrongly conceived sense of Anita is that she is totally against men and heterosexual family values. (Viewers know he is wrong because Tina catches Anita in bed with a man in a scene prior to this.) Pyan insinuates that Anita's feminist concepts cannot possibly shape a future generation. He asks if she wants to return them to the period of "Arab Jahilia" when children were buried alive, except that this time, boys would be the victims. His patriarchal hyperbole spawns passionate anger from male members of the audience for the film within the film, who stand up and cheer him on during their public debate. Despite his leap of logic in twisting Anita's arguments to conform with his biologically essentialist and conservative view, it is clear that Pyan (or Aziz M. Osman, the filmmaker and scriptwriter) does not stand alone in the act of demonizing feminism in Malaysian popular discourse. Pyan's intention is to suggest that Western feminism will upset gender relations in Malaysia and bring back the chaos and savagery of the pre-civilized past. But it is perhaps doubly ironic that the temporal results of contemporary women's emancipation, introduced via Western modernity (represented by the Eurasian actor, Susan Lankester), are conceived as similar to the conditions found in what Muslim feminists like Nawal El Saadawi and Fatima Mernissi would regard as a less patriarchal era, the pre-Islamic "Arab Jahilia."

As for Tina, she loses her militant edge when she breaks the rule of non-association (*kaitan*) with men that she had set for members and employees of *Femina* via her involvement with Pyan. As the point of spectatorial identification for Malay viewers, Tina's character must ultimately be resocialized into heterosexual Malayness. In the climactic scene, she makes a speech during a televised public forum on women's rights in Malaysia. Taking an opposite stance from Anita, she announces rather paradoxically that women want civil rights (*hak saksama*), not equality (*persamaan*): "We don't want to be men. All we want is to be treated equally. And with respect. We Malaysian citizens are very lucky because we're given the opportunity to learn from the mistakes of those in the West before reaching disastrous levels." Then, looking up at Pyan, she continues, "We live according to tradition. A written tradition. Men are entrusted to defend and support women. And responsibility is laid on the shoulders of 'tuan' towards his wife, mother, children, and younger siblings and all women who need looking after. Give-and-take needs to exist between the sexes. We women really need men to defend and support us. We are women. For tradition. A good tradition needs to be fostered. For us and for the future generation" (my translation).[2] In drawing a distinction between Malay and Western cultures, Tina resorts to an essentialist mode, ironically the same one that Pyan employs before Tina's speech when he accuses Anita of wanting to construct a women's force to take over a world she feels is controlled by men. Hence, a supposedly feminist film that begins quite promisingly ends by "ensuring the continuance of the patriarchal order through the reconstitution of the family or the couple" (Wood 1990, 344). This is evident in the camera's slow pan of photographs on a shelf, one of Tina and Pyan's wedding, which is then replaced by another family picture of them with, presumably, *their* brood of four children.

Several reading positions are offered by the ending: if one were to perceive Anita's point of view as liberal feminist rather than radical feminist, and to therefore side with her, one cannot help but establish that the conclusive arguments put forth by Pyan are illogical and spurious, and that Tina's speech is a retreat from feminism. On the other hand, Anita's defeat by Pyan's Quranic reference to "Arab Jahilia" and Tina's point about the unsuitability of feminism in Malaysia are localized expressions of difference in a globalizing urban environment. Inherently, the rather ambiguous ending implies that the Malaysian audience and public are not ready or willing to accept more egalitarian concepts of feminism just yet.

"AUTHENTIC MASCULINITY"

If the emancipatory ideals of modernity for women that are found in feminism make them transgress traditional boundaries of gender (the way Anita is shown transgressing), we see how these same emancipatory ideals, when taking the form of uncontrolled female libidinal desires, threaten "authentic" masculinity. There are four physical types of masculinity on screen: the putative authentic masculinity, the teen heartthrob, the pop singer, and the hard body.

The Freudian notion of the libido as sexual drive, uninfluenced by conscious (social and moral) thought, strongly inflects my definition of "female libidinal desires" but this is not the full extent of its usage and meaning. In *Perempuan, Isteri Dan ...?* (Woman, Wife, and Whore), "female libidinal desires" incorporate Zaleha's desires to please or pleasure all of her senses and to fulfill her needs – and her senses and needs, material or sexual, are interconnected. For example, her material need for clothing is complicated by her aesthetic sense for beautiful and fashionable designs which, in turn, serve to enhance her sex appeal. Engaging in conspicuous consumption of fashion and beauty products to improve one's self-image is conventionally treated as a modern feminine preoccupation, encouraged not only by increasing affluence among the rather broad-ranging Malaysian middle class but also because women are now often financially independent (Ong 1995, 171-72). As Rita Felski notes, "the discourse of consumerism is to a large extent the discourse of female desire" (1995, 65). She claims that "women's desire for commodities could be publicly acknowledged as a legitimate, if often trivialized, form of wanting" during the period of modernity in late nineteenth-century Europe (ibid). Her analysis of "the gender of modernity" in the European context bears a remarkable resemblance to the male projections of the effects of modernity on women in 1990s Malaysian literary and cinematic discourse:

> The addressing of middle-class women as consumers leads to a new prominence of icons of femininity in the public domain, and a concomitant emphasis on sensuousness, luxury, and emotional gratification as features of modern life. Such a feminization of the public sphere was clearly threatening to bourgeois men, whose psychic and social identity had been formed through an ethos of self-restraint and a repudiation of womanly feelings and whose professional status was based on an at-best ambivalent relationship to the marketplace. Thus fears of an uncontrollable female desire converge with a pessimistic view of the hedonistic excess engendered by capitalist expansion to create a dystopian vision of the all-consuming woman. (Felski 1995, 90)

In the Malaysian case, the Islamic discourse that women are more passionate and have less self-control than men adds to the concept of rampant female desires, even though life experiences of men and women in Malay kampungs actually disprove and contradict this ideology (see Peletz 1995, 93).[3]

The putative authentic male, when faced by his inability to control the all-consuming woman, lashes out in physical violence in a gesture of hypermasculinity in order to reassert his masculinity. According to Mosher's and Tompkins's research on hypermasculine socialization and enculturation, which Hans Toch draws upon in his discussion on hypermasculinities and prison violence: "Like any warrior, [the macho man] assumes power, pride, and glory" over the vanquished who "reap the fear, distress, and shame that once was [sic] his" (Mosher and Tompkins 1988, 69). Commenting on the macho man's motives for assaulting his fearful opponent, Hans Toch employs the language of gender that describes the assault victim's fear as "demeaning 'femininity,'" from which the macho man tries to distance himself (1998, 173).

Hypermasculinity or violence is the overacting or highly dramatic performance of authentic masculinity in crisis. Frequently, the performance of hypermasculinity is a disguise, or disavowal, of lack or inadequacy, a lack often gendered as feminine, emasculating, or effeminate. Judith Butler in her book *Gender Trouble* refers to Joan Rivière's 1929 essay "Womanliness As a Masquerade," which posits how masculinity is "taken on by the male homosexual who, presumably, seeks to hide – not from others, but from himself – an ostensible femininity" (1990, 51). I am not suggesting that the authentic masculine figure is a closeted homosexual, but I do think that the underlying homophobia and misogyny that structure this fear of women's desire and initiate the "performativity" of hypermasculinity must be acknowledged. Butler theorizes that, rather than being grounded in ontological truth, gender is a fantasy construct inscribed on the surface of bodies. For her, gender trouble describes the condition whereby "acts, gestures, and desire produce the effect of an internal core or substance, but produce this *on the surface* of the body, through the play of signifying absences that suggest, but never reveal, the organizing principle of identity as a cause. Such acts, gestures, enactments, are generally *performative* in the sense that the essence or identity that they otherwise purport to express are *fabrications* manufactured and sustained through corporeal signs and other discursive means" (1990, 136).

Butler's concept of gender as performance leads to gender panic (as reflected in the Malay films selected here) which, in turn, leads back to a reinscription of highly gendered performative acts, that is, hypermasculinity. By "gender panic," I mean the panic among men whose traditional roles of power are being eroded by forces of modernity that are sometimes conceived as Western, such as female emancipation and feminism. According to George Mosse, a precedent was set for this in modern European history when first- and second-wave feminism challenged normative masculinity: "Women who wanted to be emancipated posed a threat that was even more powerful in its impact than that posed by the ever more visible countertype [i.e., gypsies and Jews]" (Mosse 1996, 103). In Malaysian discourse, the feminist is the ultimate Other, which is made evident in *Femina* by the representation of unswerving feminism in the foreigner, Anita Daley.

If feminism's emancipation of women is threatening to men, men's engagement in gay bashing is a hypermasculine activity triggered by comparable feelings of emasculation or homophobia. Earlier, in Chapter 2, I referred to Eve Kosofsky Sedgwick's theory of homosociality, which holds that male-to-male desire is triangulated through a woman in order to socially "legitimize" that desire in a deeply homophobic environment. Due to the complex network of issues in Fatimah Busu's Hang Tuah story, which includes the possible notion of a fluid sexuality that hints at decadent feudalism, I was reluctant to concede that there was underlying homophobia beneath the friendship between the sultan and Hang Tuah. But here the notion of masculinity, especially in the extremely binary way it is constructed in the films selected, is so powerful that to feel emasculated by a woman is equivalent to having one's heterosexual male identity undone. It is equivalent to being gay, or being a *pondan* (transvestite who may possibly be gay), as the "authentic" male is labelled in the film *Amok* (1994). In this sense, it is analogous to George Mosse's suggestion that "the [European] ideal of masculinity and what it represented were challenged by ... the increased assertiveness of unmanly men and unwomanly women" (1996, 86). According to Mosse's schema, from the mid-1700s onwards, outsiders like the gypsies and Jews, as well as homosexuals and women, were lumped in the category of what he calls "the countertype" when they threatened the European ideal image of a man. In fact, the construction of modern masculinity defined itself in contrast to these ethnic, sexual, and gendered Others. The films reviewed here are set in contemporary Malaysia and are therefore also informed by some of the theories, notions, and discourses of modernity that went into the construction of ideal European masculinity in the last two centuries. Mosse paraphrases Johann Gottlieb Fichte, who in 1796 wrote that there had to be a clear division between the sexes because if they were in constant flux, it would mean an eternal becoming and the inability to settle upon a determinate mental and bodily form (Mosse 1996, 54). In the process of conceiving this ideal, the female was placed a step below the male. In addition, "Man once again was said to incorporate all of humanity; divine unity was no longer exemplified, as it had been, by the androgyne – part man and part woman – but had been co-opted by man alone" (ibid., 55).

The assertion of a putative authentic masculinity in Malaysian cinematic texts befits the transition from a more egalitarian sense of gender identification, in which the idea of the androgyne prevails, to a more modern, contemporary, patriarchal sense of masculinity that is more in line with the bourgeois colonial notion of masculinity described by Mosse.[4] Mosse defines the ideal image of man as athletic, strong, handsome, courageous, manly, and capable of exercising restraint. In addition, masculinity also "symbolized the moral universe of the middle classes with its emphasis upon chastity, earnestness, and self-control" (ibid., 79). The modern bourgeois man as the sole breadwinner and head of the household emerges most clearly during the Industrial Revolution. Because aspects of this ideal masculinity were probably carried down through British colonial administration, education, and the Boy Scout movement in Malay(si)a, they inevitably inform modern Malay notions of masculinity.

The Boy Scout movement in Malaya began as early as 1910. According to the former national chief commissioner of Malaysia, Mohamed Yusof bin Ahmad, scouting turned boys into moral "citizens, healthy, active, well-mannered, and useful so as to be able to fulfill the Scout Promise" (Tan and Wan 2002, 59). Scouting ideals emphasized loyalty to God, king, and country, unquestioning obedience to one's parents and scouting superiors, brotherhood/equality, service to others, optimism, courtesy, kindness, thrift and purity in "thought, word, and deed." While these principles functioned to discipline and create colonial subjects who were loyal to the British Empire, they were also easily adapted to the ideals of postcolonial nationhood.

Although some versions of these masculine qualities were clearly colonial imports, the same values that structure ideal Malay moral masculinity *always already* existed in adat. For example, some of the rules and taboos (*pantang-larang*) observed in rituals inside and outside the Malay martial arts arena (*gelanggang silat*) resemble the scouting ideals. These include sexual abstinence before coming for *silat*, unquestioning obedience to and respect for the *silat* master, and refraining from disrespectful or vulgar types of behaviour such as spitting, smoking, or idling around the ring, which contravene "the basic tenets of *adat*" (Razha 1990, 69). In this parallel, it becomes difficult to sort out the threads of modernity from those of adat, but it can certainly be argued that "authentic Malay masculinity" embodies certain traits from both ideal colonial masculinity as well as some uniquely localized characteristics.

Just as Mosse explains that he is dealing predominantly with stereotypes of masculinity rather than trying to describe reality, the term "authentic masculinity" here is also used as a stereotype to refer to a film's male protagonist, who functions as the Malay traditional Everyman or archetype. In Malay films, ethnicity is the basis of authenticity. The authentic male is therefore distinguished by a Malay physical appearance as opposed to a pan-Asian (Eurasian) look. He has a dark complexion, moustache, facial features that are not particularly striking or handsome, and a medium to lean build – he is perhaps even scrawny. The authentic male could be any Malay man walking down the street. But in film, he is distinguished from the ordinary man by his use of symbols of traditional Malayness. Authentic masculinity is performed or staged not only through the actor's actions; it is also aided by bodily accessories or props that signify his Malay maleness. That is, he is armed or "manned" with traditional weapons like the *badik* and *keris*. For example, in Adman Salleh's films, two actors who typify authentic masculinity, Eman Manan in *Bintang Malam* and Nasir Bilal Khan in *Amok*, carry these weapons and use them on their enemies as a phallic assertion of traditional Malay identity.[5] If this last point of identity seems rather flimsy, it is precisely because such an ethnic and gendered subjectivity is fragile and needs to be constantly reinforced through "performativity" in order to fulfill its ideological function.

Additionally, the authentic male has a *pendekar*, or warrior-like image – he has knowledge of or skill in the Malay martial arts, *silat*. He expresses his authenticity by practising, upholding, and preserving adat through *silat* or more extremely, by running amok. According to Razha Rashid, there is a deep connection between the *pendekar silat* and the *pengamuk* (the person who runs amok): the two "represent a double-edged blade of violence – both may be used for defending emotions of group or personal honour, except that *silat* violence is an emotional mirror of the Malay as saviour and aggressor. It brings out the heroism in persons or groups but unlike amok is restorative rather than disruptive to culture and society" (1990, 93). In other words, amok redeems or recuperates lost or vanquished honour at the expense of life and reason, whereas *silat* upholds and increases honour through defending life within reason (ibid., 67-68). Thus, it is no surprise that Eman Manan was cast in *Femina* as "the reasonable man," a type that coheres with authentic masculinity in the sense that both are crucial aspects of Malay masculinity (Gray 2002, 175).

The authentic Malay man's toned (rather than overly muscular) physique, a result of disciplined martial arts training and practice in the *gelanggang silat*, not to mention his graceful or purposeful comportment, all testify to this warrior-like image. Befitting the way he is addressed as "abang" (literally, "big brother" and a term of respect for one's husband), he plays the traditional role of protector of his female relatives, wife, and younger sister, and by extension, of his community, nationality, and race.[6] Being the *abang*, the authentic male is responsible for the family when his father passes away, and in the capacity of husband he is of course already in charge. In fact, the ties between family and nation are mediated through the image of the warrior. After all, "the warrior story genre" from Malay folk tales basically functions "to inculcate *semangat kebangsaan* or national spirit particularly amongst children" (Kueh 1997, 11), gradually moulding them into good citizens much like the Boy Scout movement does. And as we saw earlier, warriors like Hang Tuah and Hang Jebat will also always incorporate the concept of their loyalty and duties to the nation.

The two actors who embody authentic masculinity, Eman Manan and

Nasir Bilal Khan, have been nominated or have won best actor awards for their hypermasculine roles. The films examined in this chapter, whether coincidentally or not, seem to be loosely grouped under the different image of Malay masculinity that each man personifies. Physically, both are slim, tall men. Eman usually plays suave, sophisticated, articulate heroes while Nasir projects an inarticulate, troubled, and troubling (i.e., causing trouble) younger working-class Malay masculinity that is unable to cope with female sexuality, female sexual betrayal, and the rapid changes that modernity and globalization have brought to village life and relationships between women and men. In *Perempuan, Isteri Dan ...* and *Amok*, he responds with explosive violence, but in the television drama written and produced by woman filmmaker Erma Fatima, he conforms to female domestic desire by playing the part of the jealous reformed husband that his wife (and scriptwriter) sets up for him.[7] There are also several other representations of masculinity in the films of the 1990s that I will briefly highlight because they show men performing hypermasculine acts or they contest the legitimate standing of the authentic male. While it is usually men who are violent in the films, women with guns (and other weapons) do appear. In fact, they constitute some of the threat that puts authentic masculinity in crisis.

Admittedly, my focus on masculinity centers on Malay masculinity alone, but this is more a result of the racialized nature of the national film industry, which produces only Malay heroes, than of a bias on my part. As Chapter 4 explained, the majority of Malaysian actors appearing in Malay films are Malay rather than Chinese or Indian, with some Eurasians proving the exception. While film portrays masculinity visually and has the ability to transform hypermasculinity into a spectacle, one literary example, "Go East!" also raises the unquestioned given of the authentic male's heterosexual "normativity" in the films. By blurring the lines between homosexual panic and gender panic, this short story crucially interrogates and destabilizes the meanings of Malay masculinity.

HARD BODIES

Violence has increased on the Malaysian screen and television due to what Appadurai calls the "mediascape" that characterizes modernity: the commercial success of Hollywood and Hong Kong action films in Malaysia sets up the expectation for more action in Malay cinema itself. Malaysian film critics have noted how the traditional martial arts form, *silat*, shown in the historical action television dramas of the 1990s, now incorporates the faster, more spectacular *kung fu* style because the production companies and directors of these serials are likely to come from Hong Kong or are influenced by

Cantonese video and television serial makers. Not only do foreign blockbuster action films change the pace of Malay films but they also change the look of desirable male bodies to conform to what Susan Jeffords calls the "hard bodies" of Hollywood masculinity during the Reagan era: for example, Rambo, Robocop, or Schwarzenegger. Jeffords makes the connection between the well-built, muscular heroes of Hollywood action films and the conservative politics and discourse of Reaganism that emphasize a more aggressive foreign policy than President Carter's "soft" approach.

The hard body in Malay films does not convey the same political and military aggression that has characterized American films and society. Some of the Malaysian examples include the sexy but boyish Shaharuddin Thamby in *Bintang Malam* and *Pemburu Bayang*, the dumb muscleman Ong Soo Han in *Red-Haired Tumbler di Malaya*, the human killing-machine Razman Razak in *OPS: Belantara*, and the latest hard-body figure, a pumped-up sex-crazed Rosyam Nor in *Lenjan*. Due to the entertainment-oriented mentality of Malaysian audiences, the introduction of the hard body into Malaysian films is largely a commercial ploy. While Chris Berry notes that American macho figures like Sylvester Stallone appeal to mainland Chinese audiences because they signify a freedom from authority (1994, 108), in Malay cinema, a hard body does not a hero make.[8] These "tough guys" – the kind of genre they act in, the roles they play, and the aura they emit – do not usually take a central place in the hearts and minds of Malay viewers.

Instead, hard bodies make better secondary characters (or at least get second billing in the credits) and are brought in literally as action fillers in the narrative gaps of the romance or love story, which is the most popular genre of Malay film.[9] Hence, much like commercial Indian cinema, the romance genre remains the buttress of Malay cinema, though filmmakers and producers aiming to widen the market may resort to combining romance with the action film to attract even more male viewers.[10] For filmmaker Yusof Haslam, who churns out one box-office hit after another, the formula of his financial success stems from the combination of a love story – supplied by two popular young Malay rock stars turned actors – with an action-filled subplot, *Pemburu Bayang* (1993) and *Sembilu* (1994) being two such examples. In *Pemburu Bayang* (Shadow Hunter), Shaharuddin Thamby plays the ex-convict brother of the popular rock singer Awie, the romantic lead. Needless to say, Shaharuddin's character provides most of the film's action. Again, in *Bintang Malam* (Night Star), Shaharuddin plays Eman Manan's playful, wild sailor buddy, who gets shot halfway through the film, allowing the authentic male, Eman, to take full control of the action sequences at the end of the film.

Even though the old Johnny Weismuller Tarzan movies have been around in Malaysian culture for a long time, and are still evident in Lat's cartoons, beefy bodies have never really caught on as a definition of ideal Malay masculinity. The guest-starring appearances of Malay bodybuilders like Malek Noor in films such as *Pemburu Bayang* (where he plays a police inspector) in the 1990s is possibly a phenomenon triggered by the influx and monopoly of American action heroes with musculature like that of Arnold Schwarzenegger and Bruce Willis in the 1980s.

The crucial cultural difference between the hard body and the toned authentic male body emerges from the individual versus social dichotomy that is associated with the two body types. For example, the hard body trains alone on the machines in the gym, narcissistically focusing on adding bulk to his own body. He may have a trainer to help him but his time there differs from the more social experience of the authentic male who practises *silat* in the *gelanggang silat*, usually outdoors, with other *silat* learners, practitioners, and their teacher. *Silat* is also a spiritual art: the teacher will begin the lesson with a prayer/chant/invocation to the spirits. Moreover, unlike the "bigger is better" mentality, Malay folklore supports the notion of the small but cunning hero who triumphs over his much larger, more dangerous opponents. The famous story of the trickster mousedeer, Sang Kancil, who outwitted the predatory crocodiles in the river, comes to mind. Generally, hard bodies in Malay cinema function quite simply as brawny support to the male leads of the narrative: Ong Soo Han plays strongman Tet Tang in *Red-Haired Tumbler* (shown breaking some bricks over his chest in his first scene) but he occupies the lowest echelon of the hierarchy of evil and comic characters in the film.

Things may be changing for the hunky category of masculinity, however, particularly for those who are also talented, handsome, and have sex appeal. One such actor is Shaharuddin Thamby who, after establishing himself as a capable supporting actor in *Bintang Malam*, has reached new heights, getting nominated for best actor in *Pemburu Bayang* and later taking top billing above Nasir Bilal Khan in *Pesona Cinta* (Spellbound, 1995).[11] While *Pesona Cinta* might not have been a box-office hit, the image of a hard-bodied Malay actor with sex appeal seems to be shown more and more on screen of late. Following this trend, Rosyam Nor, better known in the role of Jimi Asmara's clean-cut (i.e., desexualized) best friend, who takes the bullet meant for Jimi in *Jimi Asmara* (1995), recently starred in Malaysia's first serial killer thriller, *Lenjan* (Deceit, 1998), as a bearded, long-haired, leather-clad, virile psychopath.

OTHER MASCULINE TYPES: TEEN HEARTTHROBS AND POP SINGERS

Hard bodies coexist with other more common Malaysian forms of cinematic masculinity. Overall, for commercial, cultural, moral, and ideological reasons,

1990s Malay cinema offers four types of physical masculinities in dramatic roles.[12] In addition to the "authentic" Malay and the hard body, there is also the teenage heartthrob: a handsome boyish-looking actor ranging in age from the late teens to the early thirties, usually clean-shaven, sweet, and sensitive. Examples include Hans Isaac, Hani Mohsin, and Azhar Sulaiman, who are clean-shaven (depending on current fashion trends) and play romantic leads. There is also the pop or rock singer who does not necessarily have any acting talents but sings during the course of the film. There will obviously be overlaps among the four categories. Sometimes the third and fourth types merge, for example, in the form of the three young members of the rap group KRU – Norman, Edry, and Yusri in the film *Awas* – or with singer Awie in *Sembilu*. Awie's female fans want to see him as the object of desire on the big screen while young male viewers identify with him as rock star.[13] Giving leading roles to the teenage heartthrob or pop singer attracts more young audiences to the cinemas. Arguably, this may be one way of "shaping young minds" and prescribing certain behaviour but this depends on the politics and personalities of the "stars" themselves, who may not be interested in becoming good role models for their fans. Such features, usually romances or comedies or a blend of both, have young male (and female) leads and are set in colleges or revolve around college-aged characters. There is little evidence to make a general statement that the singer or the teen heartthrob represents a certain type of traditional masculinity. If anything, they often signify modern masculinity.

These four types of physical masculinity are not unique to the 1990s. In fact, to feature a famous pop singer in the leading role goes all the way back to the studio system of the 1950s in Malaya. At one time or another in his career and depending on the genre of the film, P. Ramlee, a film director but also an acclaimed singer and musician, embodied at least three of the physical male types: the teen heartthrob, the pop singer, and the authentic male. For example, he played the traditional hero or "authentic male," Hang Tuah, in the 1956 version of *Hang Tuah*. However, these four physical types of masculinity are neither stable categories nor are they impermeable to each other. With the exception of the hard body, which is a 1990s phenomenon, they have consistently appeared in Malay cinema since the mid-1950s but the contexts for such images of masculinity are quite different.[14] Current cinema reflects the social conditions of a Malaysia that has undergone twenty years of the NEP and industrialization – which has given rise to fears of the impact of modernity on gender. The rest of this chapter will examine the portrayals of authentic masculinity in crisis as exemplified by actors Eman Manan and Nasir Bilal Khan.

EMAN MANAN: *SILAT* MASCULINITY

> A pendekar, his character on film, is always serious or detached but he protects and saves his woman and community. A little like Hang Tuah perhaps. Observing Malay culture and values, he would fight against injustice to his last drop of blood.
>
> —NOR FARIDAH ABDUL MANAF

Four films in which Eman Manan starred feature a display of this actor's actual *silat* skills: *Matinya Seorang Patriot* (1984), *Bintang Malam* (1992), *OPS: Belantara* (1993), and *Lenjan* (1998).[15] *OPS* and *Lenjan* in particular show how the emasculating female figure that appears in both these films is deeply implicated in the crisis of authentic masculinity.

Eman won best actor for his role as the conflicted son forced to choose between his brothers (and a consequent path of violence) and his girlfriend in *Matinya Seorang Patriot* (Death of a Patriot). This film established his image as a *pendekar* or warrior who defends women and upholds justice.[16] Unlike his four hypermasculine brothers who avenge their father's death and their mother's honour by murdering their father's enemies, he does not misuse his *silat* skills, thereby proving to be the more honourable son after all. The parallel drawn between Eman's character and Hang Tuah is especially pertinent when Saiful (Eman) disputes his eldest brother Safuan's plans to carry out a vendetta, claiming Safuan and the other brothers are *gila* (mad) to do so. But Safuan distinguishes between *gila* and amok, claiming that what the nationalists Mat Kilau and Hang Jebat did was amok, not *gila,* and that he and the other brothers are only following a nationalist tradition of justice, which is their rightful duty as warriors (see Chapter 2 for more on Hang Jebat and the concept of amok).[17] To echo this tradition further, they number five brothers altogether, similar to Hang Tuah and his four childhood friends in classical Malay myth.

His decision not to exact revenge on his father's murderers does not undermine his loyalty to his mother or challenge his warrior/nationalist stature, for Eman as Saiful is indeed a nationalist in *Matinya.* In one scene, he champions national culture over foreign culture, or at least argues that Malaysian culture is as good/universal as other international cultures. He even makes an indirect snipe at Mahathir's "Look East" policy that was first proclaimed in late 1981 (Khoo B.T. 1995, 69), and there's an anti-neo-imperialist position in the following statement by Saiful: "When it comes to costumes (*pakaian*) perhaps we would have to wear a cowboy hat, Japanese slippers, or an African loincloth like Tarzan. Maybe then it can be universal."[18] This pronouncement is accompanied by his gesture of removing his jacket, girding it around his loins, and doing the Tarzan call, which evokes laughter from his love interest, Hanis. His parody of Tarzan is a critique levelled at Malaysians who still symbolically desire a white father, albeit one who has gone native. Also evident in his comic mimicry of Tarzan's naked vulnerability is a rejection of the Western macho image of masculinity. Ever the nationalist, he reminds us, "Sometimes people are blind, we aren't aware of our own [cultural] values."

The values or authenticity he embodies in *Matinya* carry over into his other films. *Bintang Malam* (1992) reinforces his image as a *pendekar*. He plays Razif, a sailor who discovers that his sister was raped by their stepfather and then brought to the city to become a prostitute while his mother died of a broken heart. Again, his *silat* talents are fully employed in this action drama. His sister getting shot triggers his amok and he goes on a spree of violence, killing all the human incarnations of immorality in the narrative, such as the pimp, the drug dealers, and their thugs. (This plot resonates with the Charles Bronson figures of the 1980s and the vigilante justice they popularize, so it comes as no surprise that *Bintang Malam*, according to Hamzah Hussin, may be based on an American or British film.) In the world of these films, hypermasculinity or male violence stems from the threat to family and female honour, for the underlying factor in the brothers' violent vendetta in *Matinya* is the misguided attempt to cover up their mother's past sin and regain the honour she has lost for the family.[19] Again, the final scene in *Bintang Malam* reiterates the importance of family ties when his sister, who survived the shooting, receives his *badik* (a small traditional knife) in her tin box of childhood photographs, signalling that he is alive and reconnecting with her but simultaneously unable to fulfill his role as protective brother any longer.[20] By handing over the signifier of his authentic masculinity, the *badik*, he surrenders his protectorship and relinquishes his phallic power to her. Family is important to the warrior who upholds the sacredness of family. The warrior defends the "weak," who usually turn out to be female characters, either by taking his mother's side and adopting his girlfriend's pacifist ideals in *Matinya* or by defending his sister's honour in *Bintang Malam*. In other words, the family is the nation.

Eman's qualities as a *pendekar* stem not only from his *silat* prowess but from his physical form, his lanky body, and moustache, as well as his theatricality. The measured posing and control over his movements and the constant modulating of his tone of voice, his "theatricality," sometimes seem anachronistic in films with contemporary settings. These are better served in a film set in an early Malay court where the required acting and dialogue is more formal (though amazingly enough, Eman Manan won the best actor award in the 1992 Malaysian Film Festival for his role as Razif in *Bintang Malam*). In the action-adventure film *OPS: Belantara* (1993), this theatricality works when he plays a villain among a cast of other equally flat cardboard characters. But in *Lenjan* (1998), the theatricality that has become an integral part of his style makes the character unconvincing and out of place. Compared to the other actors, Eman seems to be overacting. In his character's conversations with his wife, he appears so patronizing that the action thriller scenes in the second half of the film, which agitate his calm and smooth exterior, come as a welcome relief to the viewers. It is as if there were no place for *pendekars,* with their fifteenth-century ideals and melodramatic acting style, in the contemporary Malaysian cinematic world.

Eman's overacting hovers close to male hysteria, especially when the traditional masculinity he embodies is brought into direct conflict with modernity and the new hard bodies, which signify the emergence of the action genre and the potential destabilization of traditional Malay masculinity. In *OPS*, he becomes hysterical when explosions occur in his campsite and his diabolical plans are on the verge of failing. He shrieks out orders to his men, the muscles in his body wound tight only to be loosened by his fight with Kapten Zack. Male hysteria, a sign of masculinity in crisis, is intricately connected to hypermasculinity: in this case, male hysteria leads to violence.[21] If hysteria is defined as an inability to function as one's normal rational self, an inability to move beyond uncontrollable laughter or weeping, hypermasculinity or physical violence is the ultimate release from this state. Hypermasculinity can be construed as overcompensating for male hysteria, which is a condition usually associated with women or female behaviour. Performing hypermasculinity thus disavows masculinity in the crisis of potential feminization (or emasculation). For example, in *Bintang Malam*, Razif's spate of cruel violence is not only precipitated by the thought of his sister dying in his arms; it is actually a culmination of self-blame, guilt, and helplessness. When he left his kampung because he could not get along with his stepfather, he unknowingly left his younger sister open to the sexual advances of their stepfather.[22] In short, his hypermasculine actions seek to compensate for his failure to protect his sister and to prevent his mother's death. He does not even take responsibility for his hypermasculine actions when Pak Oleh, a village elder who accompanies him to the city in search of his sister, stops him from going too far (killing the men) and bids him escape when they hear the police sirens. Pak Oleh, the surrogate father, then takes full responsibility by pretending to be amok as the police cars arrive.

STATE HYPERMASCULINITY AS A STRATEGY TO DISAVOW "LACK"

In *OPS: Belantara* (Operation Jungle Storm), Eman Manan is Master Johan, a martial arts expert and the criminal mastermind behind an international conspiracy to destroy Malaysia's tropical forest.[23] It is significant that he plays a villain in this film collaboration between Chinese Malaysian producer Sunny Lim and an Australian director/actor, Toby Russell. The fact that it is a joint venture plays a large role in determining the style and content of the film, with its hopes and plans for future distribution in the overseas video market. But the collaboration proves problematic in many ways: culturally, the film follows a very Hollywood narrative formula and concept in its nationalist adoption of state militarism and violence. There is no sense of reclaimed adat in this pro-hypermasculine vehicle. Eman's character, Johan, lacks a family and thereby does not fully represent Malayness. In fact, the closest thing to family ties comes from the state "buddyhood" or camaraderie that Mejar JJ and her team symbolize, reinforcing the family as equivalent to the nation. Having an international cast of actors who do not speak Malay and Malay actors who do not speak English stretches credibility in the cross-cultural exchange between the characters. In casting Eman as a villain, the non-Malay filmmakers do not fully exploit what he symbolizes on screen for Malay audiences. Though he is miscast in this role, there is some compromise in maintaining Eman's status as unchallenged *silat* expert. As Johan, Eman evokes ambiguous feelings in audiences used to seeing him play only positive and heroic roles that emphasize his authentic masculinity. Are they supposed to identify with him and to cheer him on in *OPS*?

As villain, Eman's status as authentic masculinity is challenged by two characters, the hard body and the woman with a gun. When his plans are foiled by the special task force headed by a female agent, Mejar JJ (Oggy Ahmad Daud), he tries to escape but is forced to fight with Kapten Zack, the second-in-command. Newcomer Razman Razak plays Zack, the official hard body in *OPS*, who can do almost anything, from hand-to-hand combat and martial arts to shooting guns and arrows and flying a surveillance plane. In the fight between Zack and Johan, both men seem equal in skill and strength, despite the contrast between Eman's lightweight leanness and Razman's stocky firmness. The battle ends when Johan throws Zack off a bridge and a long stick penetrates Zack's thigh, disabling him. The evil Johan flees to the waiting helicopter but Mejar JJ appears. Zack quickly urges her to blow up the helicopter, which she does, using a bazooka, killing Johan and his cohorts, one of whom was a terrorist who eluded her grasp in the film's opening scene. In this film, proving whether a hard body or "authentic" ethnic masculinity makes the better man can be conveniently deferred by the disruptive entrance of a third party: the woman with a gun.

The woman with a gun is a gendered metaphor for modernity. She possesses the same power as men through wielding the most obvious phallic symbol in film, the gun. The woman with a gun is a misogynist concession to the progress charted by the women's liberation movement in the West. It simultaneously gives a nod to the feminist movement while subtly undermining the gains made by women. To illustrate the point in *OPS: Belantara*, in a cast of countless men, there are two women who can fight. Halfway through the narrative, Mejar JJ, who is herself a skilful martial arts fighter, is overpowered by Johan's many thugs, including a female martial arts student whom we see undergoing Johan's training in the beginning of the film. Mejar JJ refuses to divulge any information, even at the risk of being tortured and stung by a poisonous scorpion. Finally, Johan, defeated, gives her over to his beefy American right-hand man, Scorpio, to be sexually humiliated. The scorpion is obviously a phallic metaphor: the image of the live scorpion that carries its poison at the tip of its tail is reinforced by her rapist, a man named Scorpio. Whereas before she had remained silent and contemptuous of all attempts to beat the truth out of her, she finally voices her protest as she is untied from a wheel and Scorpio carries her struggling body over his shoulder into the night. The film does not show the rape scene. In fact, nothing is mentioned about it again, although the next we see of her proves that she is a woman after all, underneath her performance of masculinity and her badge and rank.

The next morning, she is shown caged with the Mendali men, the indigenous people who have been manipulated by Johan's man, Thomas (Toby Russell), a white "environmentalist" who incited them to resist the government and fight for their land. The Mendalis are portrayed as passive victims whose emasculation is complete when Thomas poisons their resistant and wary leader, using a live scorpion, and then puts them in a refugee camp surrounded by armed men. "Emasculation" is appropriate here as the Mendalis portrayed in the film are all men; there is no hint of a real Mendali community that includes women and children. This is the lowest point in the film for Mejar JJ. As the raped Malay woman who has been performing or masquerading masculinity, she has fallen to the level of the subaltern men on the social hierarchy, a hierarchy that situates the Malay male at the apex and the subaltern men at the base. Although Oggy Ahmad Daud gets top billing and is the heroine of the film, playing the female leader of the special task force who finally gets her man (though she takes her orders from a male superior), this low point in the film for her character illustrates that a woman's superior position is never stable. Ostensibly, she can climb the social ladder and have a career that is traditionally masculine because of her abilities, but ultimately her gender difference or lack will show once her mask is wrenched from her.

As for Johan's female martial arts student, she puts up a good fight and manages to disable a few soldiers, but Leftenan Eddie, third in command, defeats her. On beating her, he also does something to her that he does not do to his male opponents: he reminds her of her femininity by yanking her ponytail and making her cry out in pain before he leaves. Her difference and vulnerability as a woman have to be pointed out when she threatens to destabilize the meanings of masculinity, blurring the once-clear definitions of gender. The rape of Mejar JJ and the yank of the ponytail signify instances where men, by highlighting women's feminine vulnerabilities, remind women of their "rightful" place (below men) and force them to submit to male power.

Mejar JJ regains her composure the minute her team comes to her rescue, freeing her and the Mendalis from the cage and putting a machine gun in her hand. Her "phallus" restored, she leads the Mendalis to safety, killing five mercenaries who get in her way. In the last scene, she lays down the machine gun, picks up an even larger phallic symbol, the bazooka, and blasts the helicopter with it, saving the day. Her men give her the thumbs up sign and the film ends with a shot of her doing the same while grinning and winking at them. Such a gesture of male buddyhood glosses over the moments when the film betrays women and gender equality, leaving the viewers with an image of a woman who can be "just as good as the guys."

The imagined community that this film tries to evoke is one without sexual discrimination, where state hegemony represented by the Malay woman or man can rule over the indigenous people in a paternalistic manner.[24] Earlier, the resistant Mendali leader accuses Thomas of being the troublemaker and outsider. He says the Mendalis have no quarrel with the government and that the land does not belong only to them but to all permanent residents of the country.[25] This speech indicates the desire of the Chinese Malaysian filmmaker and producers to be considered part of the imagined community by echoing the government's ideology against people like Swiss environmentalist Bruno Manser, who became the spokesman and leader of the Penans in Sarawak during the 1980s.[26]

OPS differs from the other films starring Eman Manan because here, his authentic masculinity is totally invested in hypermasculinity. In fact, hypermasculinity marks everyone in the film except the Mendalis. If hypermasculinity is a disavowal of lack, one may ask what the lack is in *OPS*. To answer this question, it is necessary to redirect the focus from the subject or individual to the hypermasculinity of the nation-state. Just as the warrior is supposed to defend his family and nation through hypermasculine acts when his masculinity is questioned, the nation-state sanctions and performs hypermasculinity to disguise its lack (of power). The keen emphasis on localizing the global and globalizing the local points to this lack: Malaysia's relatively minor role and status in the international arena. For example, the choice of the environmental issue as a modern concern concurs with the aspirations of Vision 2020 in showing how Malaysia fits into the global or international framework of things: it is a borderless world and Malaysia is part of numerous global networks. The terrorist Farouk has contacts with "international" syndicates and is "blacklisted by Interpol and the CIA"; Mejar JJ gets her information from an undercover CIA agent working for "an Asian magazine" in Malaysia who tells her about the conspiracy involving top American politicians, large corporations, and even top-level CIA officials. Agent Alvin Hudson informs her that "your government and mine are very concerned about these so-called environmentalists," suggesting some kind of solidarity or, at the very least, drawing a parity between the superpower and the developing nation that aspires to be a fully developed nation in 2020. To add to this picture of a borderless world, the people who work for Johan are of various nationalities: American, Australian, Middle Eastern (Farouk), as well as Malaysian. The courier who smuggles in the deadly virus is a professional American wrestler named Lord Little Brook.

The film as an ideological state apparatus disavows the nation's lack (its Third World/developing nation status) by reflecting the Malaysian government's competition with a global superpower and the need to assert national military or hypermasculine might. What distinguishes *OPS* from costly Hollywood action films is that, in this instance, both the protagonist and antagonist are Malaysians and the secondary characters are Western small-time actors. This reverses the stereotypical Eurocentric paradigm in Hollywood films that almost always feature white American actors as central characters. For instance, the CIA informant is assassinated early in the film and it is up to Mejar JJ's Malaysian task force to save the rainforest. Alvin's advice to her before he dies (about how to handle Johan) is, "You can do it the official way [but it's] too slow ... too much red tape. I'd just blow his head off," which she literally does at the film's conclusion.

It appears that violence is justifiable if it's carried out by the "moral" state, which of course assumes that the nation-state knows best how to protect its citizenry. Amid all the kung fu fighting, explosions, and flying bodies, one scene seems particularly violent since it is perpetrated by the moral force: Kapten Zack has to eliminate the mercenaries silently in order not to arouse suspicion that he and his troops are attacking Johan's camp. Following several scenes of him disabling unsuspecting opponents, there is one where he loops a rope around an opponent's neck, choking him before quickly circling a tree with the rope and stringing up the struggling man by his neck. Zack does this with complete efficiency and without showing any emotion. He is in this sense the perfect embodiment of the compassionless state in the actions he carries out on behalf of the state.

The nation-state's lack is disguised through the need to reclaim nationalist agency over one's own terrain in an increasingly globalizing (and neo-imperialist) era. However, saving the rainforest is in the sole interest of the state – a case of localizing the global instead of globalizing the local. For example, the rainforest is regarded as a precious national commodity rather than part of a larger biosphere shared with other nations. In the dialogue between Mejar JJ and Alvin, the potential destruction of Malaysian timber is reduced to the simple economics of supply and demand: if certain interests in the United States destroy the Southeast Asian forests, beginning with Malaysian timber, they will turn the global economy upside down and drive the price of timber up, thereby gaining more profits from the timber in their storehouses. At no time does the issue of ecology and conservation appear.[27] In other words, the film is not as interested in taking a pro-environment stance as it is in presenting a militarist nationalist and anti-Western position. Thus, the potential threat of environmentalist violence posed by extra-national forces can justifiably be countered with the heavy battery of explosions, military hardware, and weapons (helicopters clearly lent by the Malaysian government, hand grenades, machine guns, and other older, clunky-looking guns) and manpower from the nation-state. At the end, Mejar JJ's thumbs-up sign can be read ideologically as another instance of "Malaysia Boleh!" ("Malaysia Can!" a slogan that was regularly broadcast over Radio and Television Malaysia or RTM.)

The hard bodies in *OPS* are men of few words recruited predominantly to be action figures. Even though Scorpio supposedly rapes Mejar JJ, hard bodies in this film are not sexualized. However, the association between sex, masculinity, and violence is blatant in the opening scene of *Lenjan* as Rosyam struts, exposing his muscular arms and chest when he preys on women. We see him following women, approaching them, flirting with them, and then violently killing them during the anticipated love scene. At one point, he leaps on the bed and behaves like a wild animal, relishing the struggle his victim puts up. While this kind of masculinity poses the biggest threat to women and ethnic minorities (he kills several women and an old Indian man who gets in his way), he does not triumph over the moral force and authentic masculinity of Eman Manan. Two major fighting scenes occur between them.

The first ends with Eman seemingly killed (he falls into a rushing river) but he returns for another confrontation wherein his wife, who has conspired with Zarin (Rosyam) to kill him all along, points a sword at him but accidentally stabs and kills Rosyam's character instead. It is as if there is a reluctance in the unconscious of the filmmaker to have to prove which masculinity is the better one. Of course, being the star attraction, Eman plays characters who are seldom defeated in physical battle, even when he acts the villain in *OPS*. In this Westernized film that shows off technology and an array of weapons to aid the heroes and heroine battle the villain, the popularity of Eman must not be diminished by allowing his character to be defeated in a one-on-one combat, not if the producers want to profit from the film.[28]

AUTHENTIC MASCULINITY GONE SOFT

After we meet the killer Zarin (Rosyam) in the opening scene of *Lenjan*, we are introduced to Eman Manan, who plays a super-rich, super-suave industrialist, Amir, who derives his authentic masculinity from being the embodiment of the NEP Malay entrepreneur (that is, his masculinity is sanctioned by state ideology).[29] As Maila Stivens affirms, "In much commentary, then, the new middle-class Malay is undeniably a male citizen subject, whose wife and children are addenda, inhabiting a private space outside of politics" (1998, 92-93). We see Amir at his office, in control, professional, successful, and supremely confident. He enjoys being a patronizing, loving, and protective husband who lavishes his young wife with attention and luxury, especially during their first wedding anniversary.

As Amir's attractive wife, Zita, Nina Juren plays another woman with a weapon (a sword, actually) but she offers a different image than Oggy's Mejar JJ. She is a fairly new actress who was a model before starring in television dramas in the 1990s, whereas Oggy has had a long acting career and is an established actress. In a way, Nina is a cross between the woman with a gun/weapon and the figure of uncontrollable female desires that threaten the authentic male. In the first half of the film, Nina performs femininity to an extreme, playing a childish, helpless, saccharine-sweet "pretty young thing" whose idle home life revolves around her daydreams about her billionaire husband. She calls him on his cellphone to exchange empty sweet words while waiting for him to finish work so that they can spend time together. Amir treats her like a child. Or rather, considering that authentic masculinity is more than just a body – he is expected to fulfill his traditional social role as *abang*, or "elder brother," which is also the word used by wives to address husbands – Amir may be merely treating his wife properly, as a younger sibling. At one point, when a man comes to take their orders in a coffee shop,

Zita does not directly address the waiter. Instead, as if she is incapable of ordering her own food, Amir asks her what she wants and then relays her desires to the waiter. This may be construed as old-fashioned polite manners for men in the company of women, but her childish helplessness in this scene heightens the disparity in their relationship.

Earlier on, Amir had dismissed his best friend and lawyer's warning about not trusting his new wife and had drawn up a will, leaving a vast sum of money to her. Then the couple leaves the city for a weekend getaway in the jungle. Here Amir rescues an injured Zarin (Rosyam Nor), who has been trailing the couple, and brings him back to their isolated cabin. The film viewers empathize with a frightened Zita when Amir belittles her instincts that tell her that Zarin is a threat. In fact, this performance of her womanly fears turns out to be a ruse. And nothing prepares the viewers or Amir for Zita's betrayal except, in retrospect, her exaggerated femininity and the too-perfect image of couplehood that they project.[30]

After Zarin thinks he has killed Amir in the jungle, he returns to the cabin for Zita, whom he has been lasciviously eyeing since having met the couple. In a scene that hearkens back to the violent rape scenes in *Lenjan*'s opening, he and Zita "struggle" on the floor and roll under the bed in a wild bout of passion and the viewers realize that the lusty duo has been conspiring all along to kill Amir for his money. Suddenly, the earlier love scenes when she entices her husband and they engage in playful pursuit around the house seem less wholesome in comparison. No longer the innocent, passive, or coy wife, she becomes (in the eyes of the audience) an adulterous femme fatale whose sexual passion matches that of the crazed serial killer, whom the viewer recognizes from the film's opening scenes. Or even more likely, her unbridled passion and lust has led her to betray her lover by having sexual intercourse with their intended victim, Amir, as the suspicious and jealous Zarin suggests once their collusion is revealed. Viewers realize that if Zarin could have those women he seduces and then kills in the opening scenes, why could Zita not initiate sex with her husband? Thus, she represents the modern woman who wants it all and is not afraid to take it all: to have sex with both men for pleasure and ultimately as a means of achieving her materialistic goals. Her masquerade of femininity slips even further when she aims a sword at the struggling men and accidentally kills Zarin instead of Amir. Her husband is shocked to see his usually timid, helpless wife holding a sword and saving his life.[31] But he is even more devastated when he discovers her betrayal.

Symbolically, she constitutes a far bigger threat to the figure of "authentic" masculinity than does the hard body, not just because of her sexual betrayal and her uncontrolled female libidinal desires but because she wants his wealth (the crux of his authenticity as a New Malay), not him.[32] Notable in this instance is the easy divestiture of authentic masculinity that recalls Butler's theory of gender as an unstable construct. Amir's masculinity is based on his New Bumi wealth and status more than on anything intrinsic or traditional. Therefore, his wife and her lover, who covet his wealth and are willing to kill him for it, can easily divest him of his masculinity (more on this later). Like many female characters from Malay film history, Nina Juren's character represents the ill effects of modernity, which is constantly gendered as female: somehow, adat has determined that women are too weak/passionate to handle wealth without succumbing to greed and passion.[33] Zita's rejection of Amir's body only to appropriate his wealth subtly indicates the precarious and ephemeral nature of Amir's new "authentic" masculine identity. He is perfectly urban and urbane, at home in a tuxedo while having a candlelight dinner for two with his wife. Unlike the example of *Bintang Malam*, where Eman Manan's authenticity is linked with a symbol of Malay tradition, the *badik*, a small knife he carries for protection, in *Lenjan*, there is no hint of tradition or roots at all underneath the bumi, yuppified façade. The film may unconsciously be making this very point: that there is something missing, something not-quite-right in this supposedly "authentic" modern image of Malay masculinity that the Cinema of Denial has constructed.

Missing are the traditional cultural values instilled by the extended family and Malay society that are present in most other Malay films. In *Lenjan*, neither Amir nor Zita have parents, grandparents, or siblings; they rely solely on each other in the Western sense of romantic couplehood. Although there is Amir's childhood friend, their relationship is marked by business because the friend is also his lawyer. Amir's sense of isolated modernity is reinforced in the final scene when he returns to the city after the deaths of Zarin and his wife, only to be greeted by his best friend on a helicopter landing pad at the top of a skyscraper. The choice of location, with the KL Twin Towers as an immediate backdrop, brings to mind the clichés "it's lonely at the top," and "once you've reached the pinnacle of success there's no other way to go except down." Implicitly, the height of the building also suggests the instability of bumi yuppiehood and wealth as markers of the authentic Malay male. Uncannily, this final image foreshadows the nation's sudden economic and political crisis in the months to come: even as Malaysia boasted of having the world's tallest building dominating the Kuala Lumpur skyline, a popular image broadcast around the world during the Commonwealth Games in September 1998, its economy continued to be in recession and the state of its democracy came once more under siege with the arrest of the former deputy prime minister, Anwar Ibrahim, under the Internal Security Act. Moreover, the ease with which Nina's character hopes to appropriate her husband's wealth (a year of marriage to win his trust before disposing of him) and to transfer his "authenticity" to her hard-bodied lover, Zarin, I think, suggests that bumi yuppiehood is indeed transferable (or divestible).

A scene that clearly illustrates this occurs when Amir catches Zarin trying on his shirt in the couple's bedroom. Actually, Zarin covets not only the industrialist's shirt but also his impressive motorbike and beautiful wife, who with Amir forms a couple looking straight out of a Gap ad (Figure 5).[34] Unlike Amir, Zarin's long hair and beard, his singlet, leather jacket, and cowboy boots identify him as a working-class Malay. Zarin's covetous desires undoubtedly illustrate his aspirations to bumi yuppiehood, an aspiration that Prime Minister Mahathir encourages: "'Someone may be the son of a taxi-driver but there is nothing to prevent him from becoming the head of a corporation'" (Khoo B.T. 1995, 126). The insistence that wealth can so easily be transferred or obtained is fostered by the NEP itself, whose "restructuring appeared to have removed the racial imbalances only in form because in reality the NEP had fostered a 'dole,' 'subsidy,' or 'get-rich-quick' mentality among the Malays" (ibid., 127).

Figure 5 Eman Manan and Nina Juren as the loving new Malay yuppie couple in *Lenjan* (Deceit), with permission from Berjaya Film Production, Sdn Bhd.

Zita's ideal image of masculinity – to combine the dangerous animal sexuality (that is one aspect) of the hard body with the legitimacy of NEP bumi wealth – literally threatens the body of the authentic Malay male by substituting her husband with her lover. She is excessive in daring to transgress gender and class norms. The woman with the sword in *Lenjan* overturns Eman Manan's frequent cinematic image as a serious, detached *pendekar* or warrior-like figure who defends his woman and saves his community up to the last drop of his blood. Instead he plays the unknowing victim who is unintentionally rescued by his wife. In the end, the only person he has saved is himself, which does not say much for heroic authentic masculinity. (As symbols of rampant *nafsu* – uncontrollable and uncontrolled libidinal desires – both Rosyam's and Nina's characters must ultimately be killed off within the repressive moral design of the film in order to guarantee the survival of the visibly shaken icon of authentic Malay masculinity.) In fact, unlike the example of *OPS: Belantara* where his wealth does not seem to emasculate him (there he is still a martial arts expert), in *Lenjan*, Eman's NEP wealth softens him and he is reduced by the aspirations of the working class and by uncontrollable female libidinal desires. He slides from his position as the smirking confident boss in the city to the scared and hunted man in the jungle. Yet this is not so much an assault on capitalism as it is an indication of discomfort with the resultant new image of Malay masculinity formed under the NEP's get-rich-quick philosophy and political expediency.

Mahathir himself had foreseen this unease in the pre-NEP days during Tunku Abdul Rahman's government, when he wrote, in *The Malay Dilemma:* "Politics [in the post-war years] provided a shortcut to everything. It made possible the attainment of positions of immense power. It brought about laws and policies that placed some Malays in a position to acquire great wealth, or at least a good livelihood without trying too hard ... politics created for the Malays a *soft* environment which removed all challenge to their survival and progress" (1970, 31, emphasis mine). In fact, he predicted that the Malays "will become softer and less able to overcome difficulties on their own," again seeming to undermine his own later goals of constructing a new form of Malay masculinity – via economic might – when he becomes prime minister (ibid.).

If masculinity has been shaken, the woman with a gun has another role to play. *OPS: Belantara* suggests that the woman with a gun is the moral force in the film because she succeeds where the men have failed in killing the enemies. It would not be incorrect to imagine that Nina Juren's character, when she stabs Zarin, acts as the moral force avenging (albeit by accident) the deaths of his female victims and ensuring an end to the serial killings. Three-quarters of the way into the film, the moment she kills her lover instead of her husband provides the fleeting possibility of restoring the fantasy of ideal couplehood in the film's conclusion. And maintaining this fantasy is important for Malay audiences: an anonymous filmmaker explains that in a survey her production company conducted, filmgoers preferred that the couple reconcile even if the male character had abused the female character during the course of the film. This desire for reconciliation is compounded by the fact that women are generally still portrayed as peace-loving, as is the passive mother of the five warriors in *Matinya Seorang Patriot* who had never approved of her husband teaching her sons *silat.* She did not want them to become aggressive and cruel, as they undoubtedly proved to be. Women are driven to use violence for the sole purpose of restoring social order and bringing an end to violence: for example, in Jong Chian Lai's novel, *Gugurnya Langit Hijau Nanga Tiga* (End of Green Skies over Nanga Tiga), Jabau's mother Mina shoots him after he commits murder and is about to kill the chief in front of their community.

In *Lenjan*, Zarin's anarchic violence is difficult to explain because the film does not provide any clues about whether the serial killing is a red herring meant to divert the viewers' attention from the plot to kill Amir for his money, or whether Zita is inexplicably attracted to a psychotic killer. Rosyam's character, Zarin (Figure 6), serves as a foil for Eman's authentic masculinity, providing highly libidinized, uncontrolled sexuality (he can have sex any time he wants and with anyone) in contrast to the yuppie who works late in the office and badly needs a vacation or some special occasion to have sex with his wife. The strong contrast between sanctioned and unsanctioned sexual practices is intended. Sex within the heterosexual marriage is good sexuality as associated with Eman's character; it is *nafsu* socially and properly channelled. But unorthodox (i.e., violent and perverted) sexual practices outside of marriage are condemned, as is portrayed in the extreme character of Rosyam.

NASIR BILAL KHAN: WORKING-CLASS MASCULINITY

> You think I'm trash (*sampah*)? Trash that can be discarded any time?
>
> —NASIR BILAL KHAN playing Amir, the cuckolded husband in *Perempuan, Isteri Dan ...?*

If Eman Manan represents masculinity gone soft from wealth, Nasir Bilal Khan gives us another version of the Malay man, this time working class. In three films, beginning *with Perempuan, Isteri Dan ...?* (1993), then *Amok* (1995), and finally, *Ku Kejar Kau Lari* (1998), a teledrama, Nasir Bilal Khan generally looks like a drug addict: he has a sullen expression, a thin and lanky body, sometimes a droopy moustache or lank hair, and an overall sense of low self-esteem that has to be displaced onto women. Working-class, rural characters seem to be his forte. Neither attractive nor charming in the style of Eman Manan, his screen personality is even more high-strung, cold, and detached than Eman's. Nasir is a low-key, serious actor who is not a likely candidate for comedies or musicals (Figure 7).

In *Perempuan, Isteri Dan ...?* (Woman, Wife, and Whore), Nasir plays another Amir, a man who arrives at his bride's house on his wedding day only to discover that she has run away. He suffers a tremendous loss of face. Shame dogs him throughout the film as he tracks down Zaleha, who has eloped with another man to Golok, Thailand. He shoots her husband in cold blood, rapes her, and then lends her to a Thai pimp for six months before returning to torture her further. Despite his terrible treatment of her, Zaleha tricks him into marrying her and taking her back to his village where she initially hopes to be a good wife. However, full of contempt, hatred, and vengeance, Amir spurns her wifely ministrations and does not return for dinner, going away to run his business for days without telling her. When he comes home, it

Figure 6 Rosyam Nor as the working-class Malay hard body in *Lenjan*, with permission from Berjaya Film Production, Sdn Bhd.

seems she can do nothing right because he continues to inflict verbal and physical abuse on her. At the end of the film when he again discovers she has cuckolded him, he demands to know why she left him at the altar the first time around. He taunts her with "I wasn't good enough for you!" only to have her turn around to face him in a deliberate manner and to admit with equal malice, "Yes, you were so-so" (*macam tu aja*). To have her confirm his lack, which he suspected all along, is the final blow. Unable to deal with the truth and the dishonour, the only form of disavowal left for his bruised authentic masculinity is the ultimate face-saving act of killing her.

One would think that it would be difficult for male viewers to identify with the excesses of the uncouth, surly, and violent character of Amir.[35] Even before the jilting, when he comes to the *kenduri* (ritual feast) all dressed up for the wedding, his ungraceful gestures and shrill, grating voice mark him as unrefined and probably someone with a low level of education.[36] But it's likely that male spectators can identify with Amir insofar as they understand and fear the consequences of unleashing female sexuality and giving free reign to feminine libidinal desires as they are projected on screen by Sofia Jane's

Figure 7 The authentic Malay male (Nasil Bilal Khan) under the spell of Zaleha (Sofia Jane Hisham) in *Perempuan, Isteri Dan ...?* (Woman, Wife, and Whore), with permission from Berjaya Film Production, Sdn Bhd.

character, Zaleha.[37] The film attracted viewers, not because of their identification with Amir's character or Nasir's great acting, but because of the controversy over the titillating title.

The film demonstrates the consequences of unleashing female sexuality and feminine libidinal desires on the community. Zaleha encourages conspicuous consumption among the women when she goes to Asiah, the local seamstress, to order some new clothes. Her trendy fashion sense infects the village women and, soon, Asiah is sewing full time and neglecting her cooking chores as she tries to cope with new orders. This incurs the wrath of her husband, who demands to know why his wife has not prepared his dinner. But Asiah is not easily cowed like Maria, Zaleha's neighbour, who gets slapped by her husband in an earlier scene where he, too, wants to know why she has not prepared his dinner. Asiah confronts her husband in front of the other women and produces the money she has earned from taking in sewing. She tells him in Malay, "I've worked non-stop with my hands from this morning, do you know that? Here, here [she pulls out the dollar notes from her neckline], who do you think all this is for? Have you ever asked me where I get the money for the children's education? From this, this [she flings the money at him]! You don't realize anything!" (my translation). Her husband is stunned into a shamed silence. Although Zaleha herself does not have the skills to earn any income in a legitimate way and is forced to rely totally on her husband for money, she has created business for Asiah, unintentionally demonstrating that the only way for women in the village to earn any respect and power from the men is to become wage earners themselves.

Zaleha continually challenges the boundaries of the village mindset and thereby exposes the repressive limits on women in the kampung. She persuades her neighbour Maria to accept an invitation from the truck driver and his friend to go to the cinema. She convinces her that they should not give up the opportunity, especially considering that women are usually cooped up in the house.[38] While her complaint is uttered out of boredom it also highlights that kampung women are restricted in terms of social and spatial mobility. It seems women are denied any interlude for recreation or levity; just as Zaleha succeeds in persuading a group of women who were washing clothes by the river to join her for a swim or to play some kind of girlish game in the water, a male passerby orders the women back to work.

Representing female sexuality and femininity, Zaleha exudes and projects this on the social gaze that defines her as "perempuan" (woman) and "isteri Amir" (Amir's wife). Her sexuality figures largely in the diegesis (i.e., the fictional world) of the film. One hot night, she sits on a low stool in the kitchen facing an electric fan, her top shirt button undone. Using a metal plate, she fans into her sarong (Figure 8). The camera then cuts to a close-up of her uplifted face with eyes closed, a slight smile gripping her cigarette, looking either aroused or relieved from the heat. Meanwhile, the audience is aware of the presence of a peeping Tom, Tapa, spying at her through a hole in the outer wall of the house. Next, she levels her look straight into the camera as if she is aware of being stared at by Tapa (and the cinema spectator), still fanning herself and smoking. Contextually, this voyeurism reinforces the viewer's sense of forbidden pleasure and encourages us to suspect an underlying sexual meaning in her facial expression.

Zaleha is perfectly aware of herself as the object of the male gaze when she states candidly, "Kita orang perempuan, orang suka tengok cantik" (We are women and people like to look at attractive women). She even encourages the other women to be proud of their bodies, "Kalau kita dah ada, kita tunjukkanlah" (which loosely translates into "if you've got it, flaunt it"). These occasions of boosting female pride occur at the seamstress's house, demonstrating that Zaleha's clothing expenses are utilized to accessorize and enhance

Figure 8 Zaleha exudes female sexuality in U-Wei's *Perempuan, Isteri Dan ...?* (Woman, Wife, and Whore), with permission from Berjaya Film Production, Sdn Bhd.

her sexual appeal. Although in most instances it might be conceived as disempowering to cater to the male gaze, in Zaleha's case, her sexual image is her only weapon of power. This is evident in the sway of her hips while walking, her eye contact with men, and her flirtatious gestures. She attracts the attention of male onlookers without even trying. Totally comfortable with her body and sexuality, she immodestly speaks to the cloth merchant when she is dressed only with a sarong tied around her midriff (*berkemban)*, exposing areas of her body such as her shoulders and arms that are considered *haram* (forbidden) under Islamic law.

While most women represented in the film do not wear the *tudung*, or head scarf, they are also not shown *berkemban* (with an upper-body cloth wrap) either, except when they are bathing and washing clothes at the river. Zaleha is different. She does not hesitate to carry out her heart's desires, whether it is eloping with her first husband, a town dandy, or having a secret tryst in the rubber estate with Tapa during a stormy afternoon. In her relationship with Tapa, she has complete autonomy and power in deciding when they meet. Unsurprisingly then, she encourages a young village girl, Mina, to respond to the attentions of Bakri, a young man who has been following the girl. She tells Mina to be direct and as a result, Mina willingly meets Bakri in secret for a sexual tryst. Unfortunately, the pair is caught by the villagers and punished. Thus, Zaleha triggers conflict among the villagers with her lack of concern for social propriety.

One cannot help but feel that it is Amir who has transformed the naïve village girl – who believed she was eloping with a man who truly loved her – into a whore and that it is prostitution that unleashes her sexuality, shaping all her consequent actions in the plot. Malay male filmmakers of the 1990s are possibly reclaiming adat and recognizing the latent power of female sexuality in Malay culture as a response to perceived Islamic pressures that suppress female sexuality, even if this "unleashed" sexuality is still patriarchally defined. By the time Amir returns to collect her from the pimp, she has become a true *jalang*, wearing a short Western dress and chain-smoking.[39] Amir, as the one responsible for releasing Zaleha's female sexuality, is now unable to keep it in check. A conversation Zaleha has with her neighbour, Kak Maria, is telling. She describes how she feels after flirting with a truck driver in a restaurant: "Don't you feel our blood rise? This feeling is difficult to imagine. How shall I say it? Surrender. I like it. It makes my blood hot. Can you feel it? Not knowing what will happen next, left to the circumstance at hand. Don't you?" Kak Mariah hesitantly asks, "Isn't that dangerous?" to which Zaleha admits, "Precisely" (my translation). These are the words of a woman who courts danger when exercising her libidinal power.

If Amir has indeed unleashed Zaleha's feminine libidinal desires by forcing her into prostitution, he is totally at a loss as to how to control her except through the threat of physical violence. But she is not subject to his control. She manipulates him without utilizing violence or her sexuality because she knows full well that she is no match for his physical strength and hypermasculinity (having witnessed his cold-blooded murder of her first husband) and she understands that he is immune to her physical attractions.[40] Her manipulation begins when he collects her from the pimp and humiliates her: he makes her sleep on the floor and refuses to let her share his bed, saying it is reserved for his wife and that she is only a prostitute. In response to his cruelty and in an attempt to regain some social standing, she tricks him into marrying her when they get "caught" for *khalwat* (close proximity) in the hotel in Golok, a border town infamous for its brothels and hasty marriages. Unknown to him, she tips off the religious office that there is an unmarried couple in their hotel room and the religious officers appear at their door. After the married couple returns to Amir's village, her attempts to be a good wife fail when he refuses to play his part as a caring husband. Finally, when she has had enough of his abuse and finds another man who can satisfy her sexual desires (Tapa), she puts a spell or charm on Amir. This controversial scene, what is known as the *nasi kangkang* (lit. straddled rice) scene, was censored because it was considered unIslamic. It is an adat undertaken by women to gain control over straying husbands. Standing with her legs apart over his rice bowl, she allows the rising steam from the hot rice to stimulate vaginal fluids to drop into the rice (Figure 9). This symbolizes the assertion of female power and dominance over the man who eats this charmed rice.

As a result of her spell, he becomes more generous and caring. For example, he gives a whole pack of cigarettes instead of just one to an Orang Asli man and also gives his brother a generous bunch of fresh *buah petai* (a type of tree bean) for his family the day after he has been hexed. The spell weakens his constitution and he suffers from a headache, fatigue, pallor, and sweating the following day. There is also heavy rain, which does not bode well, as a man tells Amir: "Hujan macam ini, tak elok pula." As if to confirm these words, when he starts his truck in the downpour, he punctures a tire. The crosscutting between scenes of Amir changing the tire in the rain and Zaleha's seduction of Tapa among the rubber trees juxtaposes emasculation and cuckoldry. To carry the metaphor of emasculation further, there is even a scene where a male villager slaughtering a calf teases the young uncircumcised boys about splitting a boy's penis into four if he, the villager, were blind. Zaleha's hex domesticates Amir and he even returns home early to look for his wife, intending to spend more time with her. Another day, he decides to go home early to rest when he spies Zaleha outside the meeting hall. And then he does something completely out of character: he hurries to the passenger side of the car and holds the door open for her to get in, smiling at her.

This kind of deference towards his wife does not go unnoticed by his friends, who are equally misogynistic in their treatment of women; thus far in the film, erring wives are slapped or reprimanded. For instance, Maria is slapped in public for returning late at night in a truck with two male strangers and, Halim, Amir's older brother, does not intervene to prevent Amir from forcing the soup bowl to Zaleha's mouth and spilling soup all over her. Careful to preserve his younger brother's "face," his advice about letting bygones be bygones and being a better husband comes only when both their wives are out of earshot. Halim is also the man who yells at the women to return to their work of washing clothes when he sees them having fun and playing in the river. If we include the close homosocial rapport Amir evidently has with the men in the village and their treatment of women, it would seem that Amir

Figure 9 The controversial *nasi kangkang* scene in *Perempuan, Isteri Dan ...?* (Woman, Wife, and Whore), with permission from Berjaya Film Production, Sdn Bhd.

signifies the typical kampung male who outlines and prescribes the gender mores and conduct for women.

Zaleha's hex is so effective that she is able to safely reject Amir's sexual advances with the excuse that she does not feel well. The dialogue between the two here hints of irony and role reversal when he asks her to approach, "Mai sini" (Come here). She is standing at the entrance of the bedroom and answers in an incredulous tone, "Who? Me? You want me?" (my translation). Suddenly finding herself in charge, she seizes the opportunity for vengeance and denies him his spousal "rights" to her body. After all, he has not performed his social role as a husband by caring for her, providing adequately for her, or fulfilling her sexual needs. For example, when she first arrived at his village, she had no other dresses or clothes of her own apart from what she was wearing. Consequently, she gets into debt with the cloth merchant because Amir has not given her any money for clothing. As a further conjugal failure, they have not been having any sexual relations as husband and wife, which is a valid argument that Malay Muslim men would be likely to make. That is, men might claim that had Amir kept her sexually gratified, Zaleha would not have turned to Tapa, even though her reasons might have more to do with Tapa's kindness and simplicity than his sexual prowess.

Female sexuality or libidinal desires seem to be a popular theme in Malay 1990s cinema because, while being sensationalist in attracting audiences, they also reflect modernity and the liberal challenges posed by changing gender configurations. Of course, these are male projections; women filmmakers seem more interested in exploring the fuller sense of female subjectivity, representing needs and desires for a career, romance, and a social and familial identity (see Chapter 4). In U-Wei Haji Saari's vision, as woman, wife, and whore, Zaleha symbolizes modernity and capitalism. Her cigarette-smoking alone, which encodes the contagion of urban modernity, marks her as rebellious, independent, and transgressive. In short, she epitomizes female sexual autonomy and sexual liberation, which is good for some men, but not for others. In this world, female sexual activity has to be regulated by the patriarchy, as illustrated in hypermasculine acts of violence on intruding male strangers in the village such as the truck driver and his friend, and the itinerant cloth merchant, Si Majeet, who is killed by Tapa. In both instances, the male villagers act aggressively and violently before giving their victims any opportunity for explanation. The adulterous Tapa, in turn, is slain by Amir. But most of all, it is Zaleha's presumption that she has liberties that enrages and emasculates Amir. Zaleha also spends a lot of her husband's money – money that she does not have – on consumer goods and she is able to create a high demand for Majeet's goods as well as Asiah's skills. One of the women comments that ever since Zaleha's arrival, the cloth merchant's trips to their village have become more frequent. In keeping with the capitalist fashion industry, she advocates the modern and the *en vogue*, telling Kak Maria that "if you make a modern baju kurung, it would suit your skin" (my translation).

Deeply resilient and ever resourceful, Zaleha employs whatever talents and skills she has to survive. Her assets being her sexual charms and body, she uses both to full advantage by flirting with and seducing men to get what she wants. Yet her desires for material things seem to undermine a story that may be trying to deal sympathetically with the alienation and oppression of women. Her desires are for beautiful fashionable clothes, jewellery, and high-heeled shoes – essentially the trappings of femininity that cater to her vanity and self-image. Even though some sense of female bonding develops around shared interests in fashion and femininity, the issues are too shallow to guarantee any strong female solidarity in the village. For example, feeling as though their presence is intruding on a domestic argument, the women make their excuses and start leaving after Asiah's confrontation with her husband. Moreover, Zaleha's decision to try to make the best of the volatile situation that is her marriage is problematic. She may have tricked her husband into marrying her to gain some social respectability, to ensure that her past profession stays a secret, and to get back at Amir (who has to marry a woman he has forced into prostitution). But there is a streak of recklessness in her, too, for wanting to marry Amir despite having witnessed his cruelty and egoism. Assuming she has no family or is too proud or ashamed to return to them, why should she try to make her marriage to a cold-blooded murderer work? And to dispute with those viewers who might actually want it to work, why should she want any kind of sexual attention from him after all the abuse she has suffered at his hands? For a film that purports to represent the power of unleashed female sexuality, it seems all too eager to co-opt its heroine into the bourgeois fantasy of heterosexual marriage. Zaleha actually plays wife to Amir by preparing him dinner and, in front of the neighbours, she tells Maria that they will go shopping together once he gets back from work. (However, she ends up going to the store alone when he intentionally stays out till late at night.)

By killing her, Amir destroys the dominant symbol of female libidinal desires in the village. When she dies, the spirit of female autonomy, libidinal agency, and feminine consumerism die with her because she has been the agent of change, the symbol of the gender of modernity, all dolled up with no place to run to within the oppressive patriarchal structures of the kampung. She becomes an example to the other women that testing patriarchal boundaries will not be tolerated; and neither will emasculating female libidinal desires. In fact, these will be punished severely by hypermasculinity that empowers men to re-establish their hegemonic control.

AUTHENTIC MASCULINITY LASHES BACK: AMOK

Amok is the most frequent manifestation of hypermasculinity in Malay films. For instance, Pak Oleh pretends to be the *pengamok* (man who runs amok) to account for the deaths in the wake of Razif's violence in *Bintang Malam* (1992). Filmmaker Adman Salleh explores the connections between hypermasculine violence and amok in greater depth in his later film, *Amok* (1995). In *Amok*, Adman attempts to rationalize or offer a psychoanalytical explanation of the incidence of amok – of the unaccountable and anarchic. The film begins with the by-now-tired quotation from Mahathir Mohamad's *The Malay Dilemma* written in Jawi (Malay written in Arabic) script: "Amok represents the external physical expression of the conflict within the Malay which his perpetual observance of the rules and regulations of his life causes in him" (1970, 118). Because the *pengamok* is gendered as male, it is safe to conclude that amok expresses the resurfacing of repressed masculinity. It is gender specific because it is usually men who go amok. Women, according to Aihwa Ong, respond to repression through other behaviours such as spirit possession, and *latah*, "during which the victim breaks into obscene language and compulsively imitative behavior" (1990, 389).[41]

For the film to begin with a quotation from a book that so strongly reflects and defines Malay nationalist sentiments is to colour the whole film as extremely nationalist. While *The Malay Dilemma*, first published in 1970, was originally written in English and only later translated into Malay, the filmmaker has chosen to represent the message in Jawi as if it contains some kind of Islamic message or some kind of ancient historical truth. This historical if fictional appeal to tradition is deliberately intensified with the background music of a traditional Malay oboe-like instrument, the *serunai*. Together, the audio and visual effects signify a very traditional Malay identity. To have Mahathir's message in English would undermine the anti-Westernism of the film, which relies heavily on extreme representations. Therefore, Jawi script is even more effective than the romanized Bahasa Malaysia that appears as subtitles below the script.

The film's anti-Western message echoes Mahathir's sentiments in his later book of essays called *The Challenge*, which gives as examples of the decline of the West, stereotypes of licentiousness such as "acceptance of nudity in public" (1986, 91), "smoking marijuana" (ibid., 92), and "homosexual liaisons" (ibid., 101). Likewise, Adman features some of these stereotypical traits in *Amok:* Natalie, Wan Man's American girlfriend, often sunbathes on the beach in just a batik sarong. The expatriate culture the film represents involves hippies who gather at a bar to drink, dance, sing, and generally have a good time. The narrative takes place during the 1970s on the east coast of Malaysia and its cultural references coincide with some of Mahathir's stereotypical notions about Western decadence. The choice of hippie subculture to represent Western decadence in the 1970s is interesting: why not a critique of the yuppie lifestyle of the 1990s, with its conspicuous consumption and excessive materialism? Adman's critique of Malay mimicry is reminiscent of Mahathir's. This is how Khoo Boo Teik sums up Mahathir's concerns: "The Malays – for whom 'the wild ways of the West are quickly assimilated, but not the values and norms which have given strength to the West' – had not fully awakened to the seeping danger of indiscriminately copying the 'forms rather than the substance of Western civilization.' Now 'as the value changes in the West are more towards bad than good, and as it is easier to copy the bad, Malay society is showing definite signs of changing for the worse'" (Khoo B.T. 1995, 45).

Adman may have imbibed more Mahathirism than he ever acknowledges, for like Mahathir's targeting hippies (with their "wild ways" and their rejection of capitalist norms) rather than yuppies, Adman's Malay nationalist fervour does not critique capitalism but tries to deal mainly with cultural neo-imperialism.[42] If Mahathir's occidentalism is monolithic and lacks complexity, Adman's portrayal of the West, as embodied in the American girlfriend, Natalie, is equally naïve in its occidentalism. It comes as no surprise, then, that when the film was to be banned for its "unIslamic" content, Prime Minister Mahathir himself intervened and allowed it to be shown. The problem with *Amok* is that, like Mahathir's anti-Western rhetoric, it is too simplistic and reduces everything to this Manichean dichotomy. Concurring with the ideology of Malay nationalism and the goals of the cultural policy, the film suggests that there is no place for "foreigners" (which indirectly refers to non-Malay Malaysians) who do not assimilate culturally to Malayness. For example, during his amok, Wan comes upon but spares Pak Malah, the converted Caucasian who told Natalie earlier on that he had become like the Malays, with the exception of his skin colour.

As in all nationalist discourse, the "authentic" Malay masculinity has a major role to play. In the opening scene, the American woman, Natalie, tells her lover Rem (played by teen heartthrob Hans Isaac) to keep their sexual relationship a secret from her boyfriend and Rem's best friend, Wan Man. Natalie assures Rem that Wan Man is altogether quite different from Rem. He's "authentic," she says in English, unlike Rem, who is "a decadent Melayu." Wan's authenticity lies in his dark complexion and flat features, his strait-laced ways and beliefs in Malay tradition and superstition. Nasir Bilal Khan, who plays

Wan, is clean shaven and has longish hair in this film. He carries the same kind of tension as did his character, Amir, in *Perempuan* except that here this tension is more noticeable in his constantly exposed toned body and in the strain of his muscles as his condition progressively worsens and he goes amok. The only sign of his hippie ways is that he wears his polyester long-sleeved shirts unbuttoned. His lanky, toned body gives the impression of a sleek panther or a warrior, especially when he is running or acting the *pengamok*. For example, when Natalie sees him poised on a rock looking down at her on the beach, she goads him on with, "Well come my hero, my warrior, jump!" Wan is trained in *silat* so Nasir's role here approximates Eman Manan's *pendekar* image. But although Wan appears so toned and "authentic," he is a beaten man, shuffling with his head downcast and his shoulders slouched; and he usually stands slack-kneed, unlike the supremely confident characters Eman plays.

Wan's foil is his friend Rem. Natalie knows that the sensitive and strait-laced Wan would not be able to tolerate her promiscuity whereas Rem prefers women who are not looking for commitment. Rem jokes with Wan that "silat di katil" – *silat* in bed – is good enough for him. In contrast to the simply dressed Wan, Rem, who plays guitar and sings with a band, sports fashionable tie-dyed T-shirts, a waistcoat, a peace sign pendant hanging round his neck, and sometimes a bandana around his head and sun glasses. While Wan works as a waiter at the hippie bar and restaurant, he is not as outgoing as Rem. He still has family obligations to his mother, who is pressuring him to return to his home village to marry his fiancée because his father passed away and left his mother all alone. Rem, on the other hand, does not seem to have any family and does not want to have anything to do with them, which is best exemplified when he says that he is glad not to receive any telegrams while at Kampung Kayu Api (where the tourists and hippies stay). The authentic Wan knows more about Malay culture and tradition than Rem does. He tells Natalie that her *keris* is more than just a souvenir: "I feel this *keris* is old, it has history. This *keris* has eaten [killed] people before."[43] Moreover, he abides by certain superstitions and wears a *tangkal* or talisman around his waist. Although a talisman usually keeps one safe from evil spirits, his seems meant to bring him back to his own village (unbeknown to him but desired by his mother, since she is the one who makes him wear it).

Wan, the authentic Malay male, is emasculated by his American girlfriend in innumerable ways. First, she makes him the subject of her doctoral research on the Malay psyche. As she tells her roommate, he is part of her practical work that has become "too absorbing." When she accuses him of not even taking off his *tangkal* when they make love towards the end of the film, he hurls it at her and says she can make it her souvenir, just like she has made him her souvenir. Her acquisition of the *tangkal* follows after another acquisition, the Javanese *keris*, which she calls her "good luck charm" and carries everywhere with her. She puts on his *tangkal* without realizing that it would not work for her because charms are custom-made. Her haste in putting it on shows her careless disregard for the culture she is supposed to be studying and for the feelings of Wan, with whom she is having a relationship. Wan is not wrong to accuse her of turning him into another useless object (and sexual conquest). If the *keris* and *tangkal* once held historical and cultural meaning, they are now trivialized by her appropriation and neo-colonial arrogance.

By the same token, Wan, too, is trivialized: he is more an object than an autonomous person. Natalie's arrogance appears in her defiant "Oh yeah?" when Wan adds that she might as well make the book she is reading a souvenir, too ("Dan buku yang kau tengah baca itu!"), and warns her not to fool around with his *tangkal* ("Kau jangan main-main dengan benda itu!"). The book presumably focuses on Malay traditions and customs because she has just found something in it that explains why Wan usually removes his *tangkal* before sex. His warning comes from someone who feels his masculine and cultural identity slowly being eroded by an overbearing American woman who seems to think she knows more about his culture than he does. Thus, he screams after her, "Kau ni dah melampau!" (You're too much!). "Melampau" connotes the idea of extremism and transgressing boundaries. Hence, symbolically Wan keeps the *tangkal* on in the later scene to prevent her from further draining whatever little power and potency he has left. Without it, he is vulnerable to her libidinal desires. (In an earlier scene he ends up, much to his regret and self-hatred, making love to her after slapping her, which only aroused her passion further.) She also emasculates him by asking him to cook for her. When she successfully gets his job back for him after he fails, he is jealous and suspects she used her sexual charms on his employer. He is unhappy with her answer that, as long as he has his job, her methods should not matter.

When he loses his job yet again, he becomes demoralized and knows that without a job, he cannot support a wife, whether it is the young village fiancée his mother has arranged for him to marry, or Natalie. He explains to Rem: "Even if I wanted [to marry Natalie], she wouldn't. You've already said that she doesn't like being tied down. Not like our women. Even if she wanted to, I don't even have a job. It's not as if I want to be a kept man" (my translation). His poverty is highlighted by the fact that he has no house of his own, no rented room, and no form of transportation. If he does not live at his mother's house, he is seen at Natalie's shared house or her chalet. Once, he even moves in with Rem. He does not have a car like Natalie or a motorbike like Rem. Instead, he has to take the public bus or be driven around by Natalie in her flashy red sports car, yet another sign of her boldness. "Aku bukan aku lagi. Kadang-kadang aku sumpah Natalie," he tells Rem (I'm not me any more. Sometimes I curse Natalie).

Not only does he rely on her for transportation and accommodation, he also depends on her emotionally, even though she humiliates him in front of her roommate for this dependence. For example, the camera focuses on the roommate who, while walking away from the patio, eavesdrops on their conversation. As Natalie complains loudly that she is tired of Wan following her around, that he is "crowding" her, and yells at him to leave, the roommate grins as if enjoying his humiliation. It is as if there is an unwitting white female conspiracy to emasculate the authentic Malay male (unwitting because Natalie does not know that her roommate is envious of her relationship with Wan, though the viewer knows). Throughout this bizarrely shot scene, we do not hear his voice at all, only Natalie's screaming at him. Afterwards, he leaves in a taxi but tells himself that he is to blame for her burst of anger. He is so clearly smitten with her that he accepts her callousness towards him. It is therefore surprising when Tok Lah, the *silat* teacher and magic practitioner, assures Wan's mother, Mak Wan, that he has seen the two of them together and knows that there is nothing between them. (We shall return to Tok Lah's motives and reasons later.) Mak Wan is not convinced and she accuses Natalie of perhaps putting a spell on her son, "Mak tahu betina kafir tu yang buat kau macam ini" (Your mother knows that female heathen has made you like this) she declares to Wan. Here, Mak Wan is referring to the emasculated condition of her son, an emasculation she rightly believes stems from Natalie. Mak Wan disapproves of the sinful acts ("buat maksiat") committed each time Natalie comes to visit Wan.[44]

Natalie epitomizes the uncontrollable female libidinal desires that put authentic masculinity in crisis. She teaches Tennessee Williams's texts in her literature course at the college – the choice of author aptly encapsulating the film's themes of repression, emasculation, and masculinity in crisis. Her openness and friendliness, her casual attitude towards sex, and her freedom of movement and dress invite the sexually deprived and desperate male gaze of three men in the village who hold stereotypical notions of the Western woman. Although young, single, rural Malay women are not supposed to go out unaccompanied or unchaperoned, this rule does not apply to non-Malay women, but it is still something that influences Malay minds when they look at women. In fact, Natalie's bodily gestures would be considered unfeminine, coarse, and rude by Malay standards: for example, she picks up a rambutan fruit from the box in the grocery shop and bites into it in one huge bite instead of peeling it with her fingers as a Malay woman would do. The stereotype is that a woman who exposes parts of her body by wearing revealing clothes, such as Western women do, must intentionally be inviting the sexual attentions of men. One of the men claims that Caucasian women ("perempuan Mat Salleh") practise "free sex," and his friend replies that "they are attracted to our race" ("Ha, orang tau, dia tu shokkan bangsa kita").

Given that Wan is her boyfriend, his inability to restrict Natalie's mobility or protect her honour from other men frustrates him even more, as these three often refer to him as "Si Pondan," the transvestite/homosexual. The derogatory term is meant to put him down but it inevitably reflects the three men's own lack. Because they do not succeed in bedding any of the white women they approach, all three, despite their boasting, are incompetent in attracting white women, unlike Wan, the "authentic" Malay male. But for Wan, the nickname "Si Pondan" resonates with pain because he feels feminized and powerless, which motivates him to describe himself to Rem as a "kept man" ("lelaki simpanan"), thereby reversing the traditional gender and power relations of man and kept mistress. Natalie's description of her desire for the Malay male body conveys a similar effect to that of the nickname "Si Pondan": "The best thing about Malay boys, apart from the witty bum [sic], is the fact that they have lady body hair. My boy didn't have any, not a single hair on his chest." Note the orientalist undertone as she infantilizes Wan as a "boy" and feminizes him, equating his body with that of a woman – "lady body hair." To further his feminization, Wan cannot make Natalie an honest woman as she rejects his marriage proposal, laughing at him jeeringly, "Oh God, you're funny!" When he sees Rem and her falling on the ground together in a secluded spot away from the dancing crowd, it is the last straw. He leaves without seeing that they did not have sex after all, not this time anyway. But instead of confronting them verbally about the incident, he becomes even more withdrawn.

While there is sufficient reason to believe that Wan's amok stems from Natalie emasculating him, there are also subtle suggestions that imply other forces at work. The film begins with his ailing father, who has the same nightmare as Wan, except that it is the father who is led to the mount for his execution and stabbed with a *keris*. Meanwhile, Wan, the only child of Wan Setia and his wife, lives with the thought of his dying father hanging over him. His father's passing will mean that Wan, as the son and only heir, must take over as the head of the household and become a responsible adult male. Wan is unprepared to take up this role, which explains his involvement with the hippie subculture, a culture represented as rebellious, anti-establishment, anti-tradition, and anti-family. He is embarrassed when his mother comes to visit him at Kampung Kayu Api and he quickly puts her on the next taxi out. Yet ineluctably, he does indeed become his father's heir by having the same nightmare that foreshadows his own fate.

In his dream, he sees two Wans – the shirtless one standing on the mount gets stabbed with a *keris*, and the other Wan, dressed in a polyester shirt, is running from a crowd that cries, "Pengamok! Pengamok!" The second dream shows the shirtless Wan holding out his hand towards the contemporary Wan as if pleading for help before the angry mob with blackened faces, looking like demons, drag him down and stab him repeatedly with pitchforks ("amok catchers"). Unprepared to be a man, he still needs a father and a strong male role model. The film implies that the mother's desires overruled his sickly father's when the father was alive. In the scene where Wan's father wakes up after his dream, he is lying face down on the floor, grunting for help after having rolled off the mat. Paralyzed, he needs Wan's mother to help him back into the bed. She urges that he strengthen his spirit. They have a conversation about their son but it is obvious that she is the one who arranged Wan's engagement. Hardly able to speak, his garbled words when interpreted by her reflect that all Wan's father cares about is his son's own wishes. He asks whether she has written to Wan (to which she replies in the affirmative but complains that Wan has not replied), and later, with much difficulty, he suggests waiting for Wan to make up his own mind. Mak Wan will not accept this and asks, "Until when [do we have to wait till he comes around]?" ("Sampai bila?") This is her perennial impatient line about her wayward son. In fact, she utters this line four times throughout the film, twice in this particular conversation, and twice when Tok Lah advises her to be patient with Wan.

Wan lacks direction without his father, as we see later when he ends up praying at his father's grave after the amok. Once, he actually tells Rem that he does not know what to do, what with his mother forcing him to get married and his father dead. His mother's reason for forcing him into marriage is to get him back to his own village to be closer to her. She asks Tok Lah to make a "tangkal penyejuk" for her son so that he will happily settle back in their village, which Tok Lah obliges after a slight hesitation; and she returns Wan his old *tangkal*, presumably with the new charm on it. Next, she goes further by asking Tok Lah to make Natalie forget her son, but the old man tells her it is unnecessary. Actually, he has already put things in motion to make sure Wan returns to the village. He says mysteriously that he feels there is something that wants to resurface (my loose interpretation of "ada sesuatu yang bermahu tebus kembali"). Then he reassures her that he will try his best and that she should continue doing her part by carrying out his earlier orders: "Mak Wan kena amalkan apa yang saya telah bagi itu, ya?" We see crosscutting between Tok Lah inviting a spirit into his house one stormy night and the scene of conflict and passion between Wan and Natalie, which ends with Wan running out of the chalet in despair and crying in the sand. Finally, when a villager, Sani, brings the message of Wan's amok to Tok Lah, Tok Lah lets out a "hah!" showing a toothy grin before grunting, as if to hide the fact that he has some prior knowledge of the event. Even Sani looks a bit puzzled by his reaction. Tok Lah then tells Sani to inform the others to gather at his compound, certain that Wan will return to the village in his state of amok. As Tok Lah watches Sani's departing figure, a slow smile appears on his face.

If, as Mahathir has argued, "amok represents the external physical expression of the conflict within the Malay which his perpetual observance of the rules and regulations of his life causes in him," perhaps the conflict in Wan is that of a youth torn between tradition and modernity, between his mother and Natalie (Mahathir 1970, 118). Should he bow to the rules and regulations of his mother, who keeps insisting that he is his father's only heir, or should he be allowed to find himself in the modern alternative? His conflict is not made easier by the fact that the modern option held out by Natalie as the signifier of Western hippie culture poses as much of a challenge to the authentic Malay male psyche as the traditional culture does.

In the end, his inner conflict erupts in a bloody display of hypermasculinity. Throughout, the film is filled with ironic hints that anticipate this hypermasculinity: the dreams and the proverbs that befit the Malays, as voiced by Natalie and her roommate about Malay men, "Tiny and harmless-looking but how they sting" and "Soft, soft as dynamite." Even the choice of the song "Ikan Todak," which tells the myth of Bukit Merah (Red Hill) in Singapore, includes references to sharp dangerous weapons (the *ikan todak* or swordfish) and blood. In the gory finale, Wan runs amok and stabs Natalie, ironically with her "good luck charm," her *keris.* He also stabs Rem the "decadent Melayu," the three male loafers who have long provoked him, his Chinese employer (who runs the hippie bar and restaurant), and two Caucasian women who happen to be at the restaurant. Although these two women are innocent, having just arrived at the village, Wan sees them only as female symbols of his emasculation by Western culture, its free-flowing sexuality blatant not only on the bodies of the Caucasian tourists but also in their popular music (James Brown's "I Feel Good" and "Feel Like Being a Sex Machine" are played at Rem's party).

Wan's amok can be read as the surfacing of hostile resistance to Western cultural neo-imperialism, but it is interesting that this "clash of civilizations" is constructed through the discourse of gender – through a seemingly passive Malay man emasculated by a sexually promiscuous, uncontrollable, independent American woman. In short, the continuing postcolonial struggle is still constructed in the language of masculinity and the film, in detailing the psychological journey to Wan's amok, makes the effort to reclaim authentic Malay masculinity. Its reclamation of masculinity cannot be overemphasized in light of the reversed gender power dynamics between Wan's parents (a domineering nagging mother and a passive, weak father), because Wan's psychological and social emasculation mirrors his father's physical state of paralysis. In other words, authentic masculinity within the traditional familial structure is already in crisis. Of course this conclusion about the traditional family in crisis is located within the particular, localized circumstances offered by the film. It is not an attempt to generalize on the dynamics within the traditional Malay 1970s family.

DOMESTICATING THE AUTHENTIC MALE: ERMA FATIMA'S *KU KEJAR KAU LARI*

In the television drama *Ku Kejar, Kau Lari* (I Pursue, You Flee), Nasir Bilal Khan reprises the role of authentic masculinity in crisis except that, this time, the root of his problem is not a conflict between two women who embody opposing forces of tradition and modernity. The conflict he faces comes from his wife and personal manager, Nita. As a modern Malay woman, she balances the roles of career woman and caregiver (including cook, lover, etc.). Yet at some point in the narrative, he accuses her of being a nag (just like the mother in *Amok*). The script, conceived by female actor and director Erma Fatima, offers a different perspective on authentic masculinity in crisis. The man does not lapse into acts of hypermasculine violence, presumably by virtue of its writer's gender and its genre, the domestic TV drama. It is a female fantasy of domesticating the authentic masculinity.

The fantasy element manifests itself in the form of the ideal Harlequin romance man, Eddie (Hans Isaac), an ex-boyfriend who returns, determined to win the married but unhappy Nita (Erma Fatima) back. Like the romance novel archetype, Eddie is wealthy and well-dressed, charming, handsome, sensitive, confident, and assertive. He is able to sweep her off her feet and will not take "no" for an answer because he knows, in that intuitive, presumptuous manner that romantic heroes have, that she still loves him. As a contrast, Nasir's character, Nafique, is quiet – an introvert who prefers to stay home and talk to his collection of cacti instead of accompanying Nita to a disco. A dedicated cameraman, he is also a workaholic who neglects his wife, takes her for granted, forgets their wedding anniversary, and has a "take me as I am or not at all" attitude. Celebrating one's wedding anniversary is certainly "Western" and goes to show Nita's "modern" desires. What adds to the fantasy of this television drama is that, due to her initiatives, Nafique overcomes his passivity as a husband in order to win her back from Eddie's arms. Nita's ploy includes getting a male stranger to phone Nafique after their quarrel. The man claims that if Nafique really cares about his wife, he should come to the quay before she leaves with Eddie. In the tradition of happy endings, Nafique shows up and the couple is reunited. Nita is able to domesticate or at least educate her husband about her expectations as a modern urban Malay wife. The heroine of this soap opera has practical expectations. She rejects the Harlequin hero in order to make her eight-year-old marriage to Nafique, the authentic man (read: realistic, macho) work, hoping that he will be more considerate and loving.

"I don't understand, what else do you want?" This bewildered response to his wife's simple demands highlights the authentic male's inability to cope with modern life: urban living, cellular phones, and juggling a hectic career with his role as a caring, expressive husband. All she really wants is for them to spend more time together and for him not to take on so many shooting assignments. She even buys him a cellphone so that he will not have an excuse to be uncommunicative when away on assignment for days, but he does not use it. When she finally forces him to confront the fact that their marriage may be falling apart, and she articulates her feelings (of being neglected, uncared for), he replies that he feels as if she cannot be satisfied. The idea of the authentic male threatened by uncontrollable female desires is apparent here: these desires and demands are unending, excessive, and impossible to satisfy. Forced into a corner, he proclaims that he loves her only to have her answer, "Love is not enough!" She wants him to show he cares and, in her attempt to settle their problems through discussion, she needs him to verbalize his feelings: "Talk to me!" she begs. Nasir's screen personality of the introverted silent man has already cropped up in *Amok* when Natalie slaps his shoulder in her attempt to elicit a reply, "Hey! I'm talking to you! Damn!" The female characters resort to physical violence when faced with a wall of male silence. In *Ku Kejar*, it is Nita who is physically violent, tugging at Nafique's shirt, punching his shoulder, and slapping him as she tries to get through to him the extremity of her frustration and emotion.

There is an ambivalence about his passivity in the drama: it is good because he never once hits her back or pushes her away, but bad when he does not try hard enough to save their relationship. His only violent gesture is throwing his cactus on the floor after she says that he pays them more attention than he pays her. The cactus has phallic connotations (in shape and in its hardy and prickly nature), as does his preoccupation as "one of the best cameramen in town," symbolizing his unspoken, quiet, but ever-present masculinity. This unassuming nature, the man of few words unable to articulate his strong feelings, encapsulates a female version of authentic masculinity that does not necessarily have a specific ethnic reference, although, intertextually, Malay film audiences would be familiar with Nasir's past roles. In fact, with so much English in the dialogue, the drama can appeal to non-Malay female viewers as well. For example, while watching the drama with my mother, I could see her relating to the Malay heroine's modern expectations of marriage and concerns about male egoistic attitudes within marriage.

As envisioned in this domestic drama, women accept and desire some of the basic, positive qualities of the authentic male (Nafique does not drink, gamble, or respond to other women's sexual advances), on condition that he catch up with modernity by modifying some of his more sexist and selfish attitudes and behaviour. If women seem to have adapted more quickly to modernity, it is because they have generally undergone more drastic social changes than men have since Independence (i.e., compulsory education for girls, joining the workforce and civil service, geographical and social mobility, etc.) and they have found, too, that they have more to gain from modernity.

Erma Fatima's approach to the authentic masculinity in crisis provides an alternative path to resolution, which swerves away from hyper-masculinity. Nafique's destruction of the cactus is highly symbolic: the cacti contained in glass boxes all around their apartment signify the fragility of his male ego. For him to smash one of them reflects how he has channelled Nita's anger inward, on himself instead of at her. This is a complete reversal of Nasir's past roles as the authentic masculine figure besieged by uncontrollable feminine libidinal desires, who lashes out at others, specifically the woman responsible, rather than inflicting (symbolic) violence on himself. It remains to be seen whether this alternative to hypermasculinity will be taken up in future films by male filmmakers. After all, the title of this drama, *Ku Kejar Kau Lari* (I Pursue, You Flee) blatantly indicates the female principle at work: the "Ku," as the female active voice expressing desire and the masculine "Kau" as the passive object of her pursuit. The medium of the domestic television drama also plays a part in this alternative vision of authentic masculinity in crisis because it caters to female spectatorial desire. The relatively cheap and fast production of television drama means less energy needs to be concentrated on visual spectacle and artistic editing, and more energy can perhaps be spent on acting, resulting, consciously or not, in the emotionally raw performances by Erma and Nasir in the long single take of their confrontation.

Malay cinema offers several versions of what it takes to be a man in modern times, but I have concentrated on the enduring image of the "authentic" masculinity whose dominance in cinema is undergoing some challenges from social realities and changes in Malaysia. It is difficult to be an authentic man living in the boom times of the 1980s and '90s, whether in the city or the kampung: he has to fulfill his traditional male roles as son, husband, elder brother (fatherhood is not broached at all), and warrior, able to protect mothers, wives, girlfriends, and sisters.

He faces the challenges of modernity that prescribe a faster pace of life, migration, and separation from family – all of which make familial obligations harder to fulfill. These modern challenges include aspects of Western culture that contradict his own Malay roots, aspects such as becoming focused on his selfish desires and coveting material goods instead of fulfilling family obligations. To complicate his life further, the modern women around him expect him to be a 1990s man who will be sensitive and expressive, who will believe in gender equality but respect their difference, and still maintain some semblance of his traditional social roles. To further complicate his life, ideas about gender equality and women's liberation have produced the male fantasy figure of the transgressive woman – the woman with a gun or weapon and the woman whose libidinal desires are beyond the control of patriarchy.

Altogether, these forces of change that are part of the flux of modernity are seen as emasculating or effeminizing, thereby revealing the authentic man's masculinity in crisis. Feeling besieged on all sides, the Malay man is liable to retaliate violently through hypermasculinity. Amok is thus constructed as an extreme, localized form of hypermasculinity that rids the culture of the impure, corrupt, decadent forces brought about by the rapid drive for urban development and material success. It is a wholesale purifying reaction of authentic masculinity under siege. The authentic male figures represented by Nasir Bilal Khan and the *pendekar* image of Eman Manan have their traditional roots in the kampung and thereby allow the male audience (who will most likely have kampung roots themselves) to identify with them in the cinematic fantasy.

Yet as money politics and cronyism increase in Malaysia among the elites, and the economic and political gap between the ruling elite and the masses widens, we can read in these films a growing distrust of modernity and of state ideology that calls for development and modernization. Thus, the cinematic investment of authenticity in the figure of the NEP bumi yuppie is unconsciously treated with suspicious caution in the way the film is shot and in the slightly anachronistic acting style of the male hero. Eman's authenticity comes under attack in *Lenjan* once he moves away from his *pendekar* image, once the definitions of authenticity shift to include an urban, yuppie,

Westernized identity emasculated by feminine libidinal desires, and he is unable to respond in his characteristic *silat* ways. Assuming the audience consists mostly of rural Malays and those who have migrated to urban areas, filmmakers keen to at least break even at the box office must still provide a figure whose authenticity reflects the audience's own tradition, culture, and class.

There is continuity in tradition between Eman Manan and Nasir Bilal Khan that supports the theory that Nasir has replaced Eman as the new authentic masculinity. In *Femina* (1993), Eman plays the sexist male hero who turns the two feminist women, Erma Fatima and Susan Lankester, against each other. The script is conceived by male filmmaker Aziz M. Osman. On the other hand, with the rise of Erma Fatima as a director, script writer, and producer, a TV drama including the same two women actors and Nasir can have a more progressive portrayal of masculinity in crisis (the man learns from women rather than teaching or reforming them) and maintain female agency without repressing feminist desires. Nasir's more naturalistic acting style, his unassuming passive presence, and rough-edged film persona that immediately classifies him as the underdog or working-class man may define his authentic masculinity as one that post-boom Malaysian viewers identify with as they grapple with their own struggles with changing gender roles and expectations. The progressively cosmopolitan climate of the mid-1990s and the rise of female filmmakers such as Shuhaimi Baba and Erma Fatima also downplay, domesticate, or diffuse the virulent hypermasculine images portrayed by male filmmakers like Adman Salleh and U-Wei Haji Shaari.

The medium of film itself, its historical function as a form of entertainment rather than as an artistic and intellectual form in Malaysia, does not encourage filmmakers to discuss issues critically. For example, while the *silat* and fighting sequences in the films seem stagey or theatrical, film viewers suspend disbelief in order to follow the plot, not questioning the very performativity of hypermasculine actions. To obtain a critique of hypermasculinity that destablizes the notion of gender and sexuality, one must look to literature.

In Karim Raslan's short story "Go East!" the protagonist's hypermasculinity emerges as a disavowal of his homosexuality; when the frightened naked Filipina girl ends up on Mahmud's lap, he kicks and hits her so hard that she is "knocked halfway across the floor" (1996b, 117). He attributes his hypermasculine violence as a reaction to his fear of female sexuality. He openly admits his "impotence" and masculinity in crisis when he says, "I felt as if she was trying to trap me and pin me down ... and all I could think of was how to escape" (ibid., 116). In contrast, homosexuality is an issue that cannot be dealt with in a realistic manner in the Cinema of Denial: the gay man in

Awas (1995) is frightened into heterosexuality at the film's conclusion when his sexual partner contracts AIDS. Karim Raslan's story is subversive in its ambiguous ending: Mahmud finally passes the ritual test of male hetero-normative adulthood he sets himself by having sex with a female prostitute. When Mahmud is described laughing, feeling relieved, and saying "I knew everything I needed to know" (1996b, 118) the narrator suggests that he is in homophobic denial rather than "cured."

The evidence of his repressed homosexual identity is staggering: he chooses the youngest prostitute they have, aged thirteen, because her pubescent body facilitates his fantasy that he is with Anton, the man to whom he is deeply attracted. Then, after his heterosexual performance, the last three paragraphs of the short story strongly imply that he is hysterical. The word "laughed" appears four times and he "sang," in his own words, "like a mad man" (ibid., 118). His hysteria here needs to be distinguished from his earlier hysteria when he kicks the Filipina. There, the close proximity of her womanliness reminded him of his inability to respond favourably to women. This masculinity in crisis manifests itself as male hysteria whose only recourse is hypermasculinity: "I too kicked at her, releasing my fear as I did" (ibid., 116). But Mahmud's hysteria at the conclusion hints of something more subversive: that a homosexual man finds it "so simple, so clear" (ibid., 118) to "perform" sexually with a woman (or, in this case, a girl), demonstrates that heterosexuality itself is an act, a "performance" that is not at all "natural." Like the other men who had no need for questions, only confirmations (ibid., 103), Mahmud learns that he is able to disavow his lack, here constituted as his homosexual desires, through a performance of heterosexual masculinity. To disguise his homosexuality further, he behaves in a macho manner, exercising violence or hypermasculinity. His intention to continue with his charade of heterosexuality that makes a man a "man" calls into question the so-called stability and innateness of heterosexuality. In raising the question of repressed homosexual desires, Karim Raslan's short story destabilizes the nature of what it is to be a man that the films take for granted: a heterosexual identity.

Appendix A: Cultural Representations of Hang Tuah and Hang Jebat

Author or director and title	*Year and genre*	*Summary*
Phani Majumdar, *Hang Tuah*	1956 realist film	Pro-Hang Tuah
Kassim Ahmad, *Hikayat Hang Tuah* (The Story of Hang Tuah)	1959 thesis, first edition published 1964	Pro-Hang Jebat as Malay socialist hero
Ali Aziz, *Hang Jebat Menderhaka* (The Betrayal of Hang Jebat)	Realist drama, staged 1958, published 1960	Hang Jebat as hero
Hussain Haniff, *Hang Jebat*	1961 film based on Ali Aziz's script	Pro-Jebat, sadistic portrayal of violence and misogyny
Usman Awang, *Matinya Seorang Pahlawan, Jebat* (Death of a Warrior, Jebat)	1961 musical drama, combining traditional music and dance, published 1992	Jebat as a sensitive, artistic hero
Syed Alwi al-Hady, *Hang Tuah, atau, Pahlawan Melayu* (Hang Tuah, or, Malay Warrior)	1963 realist drama	Uses Tuah as a nationalist (anti-Japanese) figure
Dinsman, *Jebat*	1973 absurdist drama, published 1979	Jebat is stabbed but then stands up and reads a Chairil Anwar poem
Johan Jaaffar, *Kotaku Oh Kotaku* (My City, Oh My City)	1975 modern drama, published 1983	Jebat dies of "air pollution" (Napiah 199); physical heroism is insufficient in an urban environment and society

Appendix A: *continued*

Author or director and title	*Year and genre*	*Summary*
Hatta Azad Khan, *Jebat*	1982 drama, published 1984	Jebat as a modern-day Robin Hood, ultimately tricked into accepting a bribe from the sultan (downfall)
Fatimah Busu, "Al-Isra" (Dark Night of the Soul)	1985 absurdist mythical short story	Jebat as the voice of truth, incorporates Sisyphus
Rehman Rashid, *A Malaysian Journey*	1992 journalistic novel	Author asks which is the hero, Tuah or Jebat
Karim Raslan, "Heroes"	1996 short story	Protagonist emulates Tuah

Note: Consult Abdul Rahman Napiah, *Tuah-Jebat Dalam Drama Melayu: Satu Kajian Intertekstualiti* for an analysis of the plays mentioned here.

Appendix B: Primary Filmography

Plot summaries are provided only for the films that were discussed in some detail but for which plot summaries were not made evident in the chapters. Dates for the films vary according to occasionally contradictory information in FINAS publications such as the *Daftar Filem Melayu* (1993) and the *Filem Malaysia 1975-1999* guide (1999).

Bintang Malam (Night Star). Directed by Adman Salleh. With Eman Manan, Shaharuddin Thamby, Fauziah Ahmad Daud, Erma Fatima. Nizarman Productions, 1992.

Two sailors, Yazid (Eman Manan) and Johari (Shaharuddin Thamby), dock in a city en route to their hometowns. They check in at a hotel. The next morning, Johari finds the prostitute he took to his room last night, dead in the bathtub. Panicked, he moves to another hotel where the same prostitution racket is based. He tries to help another prostitute Aishah escape from her pimp because she wants to return to her village, thinking her brother (Yazid) is already back. Eventually, Yazid meets up with Johari and discovers that Aishah is Yazid's sister, who was brought by their stepfather to the city after their mother's death. The brother and sister are reunited briefly before being pursued by her pimp, drug dealers, and thugs. Fighting occurs, Johari is shot, and Aishah is wounded. Yazid goes berserk and kills all his opponents. The police arrive and Pak Oleh, a village elder who has accompanied Yazid on this trip, takes the rap for Yazid, who flees. Pak Oleh goes to prison, Yazid returns to the life of a sailor, and Aishah recovers in hospital.

Femina. Directed by Aziz M. Osman. With Eman Manan, Erma Fatima, and Susan Lankester. SV Productions, Sendirian Berhad, 1993.

Tina (Erma Fatima) and Anita (Susan Lankester) are best friends who publish a monthly magazine *Femina* representing the voices of women seeking equal rights for women. While their struggle is the same, their motives and goals differ. Tina's reasons are mainly defensive because she is bitter about her irresponsible father who abandoned the family and forced her mother to raise her alone in financial difficulties. Anita, on the other hand, is more interested in championing women's rights. The two women's ideology is resisted strongly by some men but they courageously plough on. However, everything changes when Pyan, a minibus driver and the owner of the bus company, subtly succeeds in tempering Tina's radical edge, giving Anita the opportunity to become the sole champion of women's rights. Anita, hoping to oust Tina from the magazine, encourages a younger worker to undermine Tina's credibility. Consequently, Tina is accused of being a traitor, and her special privileges at the magazine are revoked. Confronted with pressure at work and on the social front, Tina is forced to choose. Should she sacrifice her struggle for women's rights or her feelings for Pyan? (from Malaysian Film Festival guide)

Layar Lara (The Sad Screen). Directed by Shuhaimi Baba. With Man Bai, Ida Nerina, and Azean Irdawaty. Pesona Pictures, 1997.

The film opens with Daud (Man Bai) and the mostly old kampung men and women asking veteran actress, Seniwati Zai (Azean Irdawaty) to describe her experience at the Malaysian Film Festival awards dinner the night before. She jokes about being ignored by the media and people present. Attention had been focused on Ena (Ida Nerina), an up-and-coming young actress who received the best actress award. Two years later, Daud, the nephew of Zai, gets a job as a "gopher" on a film set. The ailing, slightly senile Zai and the other film veterans want a final opportunity to be on the big screen and they urge Daud to make their request known to the director, Malik. Malik is forced by his producer to hire Ena, the prima donna actress, for commercial reasons. Ena does as she pleases on set, manipulating people, flirting with Daud and Malik, fighting with the other actresses, and calling in sick whenever she feels like spending time with her boyfriend instead. Finally, Malik fires her and she realizes how much acting means to her. She dumps her boyfriend Shak and proceeds to make amends. Seniwati Zai and friends eventually get to play extras in the film and Ena and Zai become friends. After various setbacks to the production, the crew receives word that Seniwati Zai has passed away. They all attend her funeral. The film is completed when the actors and director decide to reshoot without pay when their funding runs out. *Layar Lara* closes when Malik learns that their film has been approved by the censorship board with five cuts.

Lenjan (Deceit). Directed by Ismail Yaacob. With Eman Manan, Nina Juren, and Rosyam Nor. Berjaya Film Production, 1998.

The film begins by trailing Zarin (Rosyam Nor), a serial rapist and killer who uses his looks and charm to trap his victims before viciously killing them. In an unrelated storyline, we are introduced to Amir (Eman Manan), a successful industrialist happily married to Zita (Nina Juren). For their first wedding anniversary, the young couple vacation in a house in the woods. Zarin trails them on a motorcycle. When his bike breaks down, he is saved and brought back to the house by Amir. Zita is uncomfortable with Zarin's presence. When the husband and wife believe their lives are threatened by this stranger, they try to escape. Zarin tracks them down and gets into a struggle with Amir, who falls. Zita runs back to the house in fear and Zarin follows. Will Zita be able to save herself and avenge her husband's death? (from VCD jacket)

Matinya Seorang Patriot (Death of a Patriot). Directed by Rahim Razali. With Eman Manan and Noor Kumalasari. Zsa Holdings, 1984.

A series of mysterious murders occur. They are actually carried out by four of the five sons of Haji Shahban, who died of a heart attack when he received pictures of his wife posing nude for her British employer when she was young. The photos were meant to prevent him from exposing the four directors of his company for using company money for political gains. Eman Manan plays the uncooperative brother. Noor Kumalasari plays the innocent daughter of one of these men.

OPS: Belantara (Operation Jungle Storm). Directed by Rodzee A. Razak. With Fauziah Ahmad Daud, Eman Manan, and Razman Razak. Showcase Communication and Sunny Film, 1993.

A syndicate headed by a few American timber industrialists plans to destroy the logging industry in Southeast Asia. This sabotage is meant to strengthen their control in the world of timber. They send their man Thomas, a so-called environmentalist, to live with the indigenous Mendalis in order to obtain their cooperation. Their evil plan is set in motion when they succeed in inventing a viral chemical "VX2000" to destroy the quality of timber. Johan (Eman Manan) is the Malay racketeer who will carry out the syndicate's plans to spray the tropical forest with VX2000. Oggy heads a Malaysian special task force formed specially to stop the syndicate from achieving their evil intentions. (from Malaysian Film Festival guide)

Panas (Heat). Directed by Nurhalim Haji Ismail. With Aleeza Kasim, Yusuf Mohammad, and Eizlan Yusuf. Take One Production and Nur TV Production, 1998.

Sofiah, a beautiful young village girl, is forced to agree to marry her stepfather, Paiman, at her mother's deathbed but she never agrees to willingly surrender her body to him. However, Paiman's heat (passion?) arouses Sofiah.

When Paiman's jealousy of the younger men in the village gets him into trouble, the mismatched couple moves to the outskirts of Kuala Lumpur. There, Sofiah attempts to forge a more meaningful life for herself by working as a batik designer in a factory while Paiman works selling traditional medicine and love potions on the sidewalk. She meets Ariff, her boss, a young man of wealth and status whose sincere love fulfills her dreams. Sofiah and Ariff's affair arouses Paiman's jealousy; enraged one night, he tries to kill them at a dance. Paiman goes to prison. Sofiah and Ariff get married but because Ariff is impotent, Sofiah's life is not complete. When Paiman is released, he returns to try to get the now-sophisticated Sofiah to spend at least one night with him. At first, she snubs him but in the end, Paiman cuts a deal with Ariff to cure his impotence if the younger man would allow him one last tryst with Sofiah.

Appendix C: Secondary Filmography

Abang 92 (Elder Brother '92). Directed by Rahim Razali. With Deanna Yusoff, Azhar Sulaiman, and Rahim Razali. ASA XX, 1993.

Ah Beng Returns. Directed by James Lee. With Loh Bok Lai, Amy Len Siew Mee, Lee Swee Keong, Ee Chee Wei, Tan Eng Heng, and Kiew Suet Kim. Produced by Vernon Adrian Emuang and Sylvia Tan, 2001.

Amok. Directed by Adman Salleh. With Nasir Bilal Khan, Ramona Rahman, and Hans Isaac. Nizarman Productions, 1995.

Anak Sarawak (Child of Sarawak). Directed by Rahim Razali. With Yusof Wahab, Alice Voon, and Ahmad Yatim. ASA XX, 1989.

Antara Dua Darjat (Between Two Classes). Directed by P. Ramlee. With P. Ramlee and Saadiah. Malay Film Productions, 1960.

Awang Spanar. Directed by Z. Lokman. With Imuda. Produced by V.N. Raj, 1989.

Awas (Caution). Directed by Abdul Aziz Razak. Starring KRU members Norman, Yusri, and Edry. Produced by Anita Rafar, 1995.

Bas Konduktor. Directed by Z. Lokman. With Maidin and Dayang Ku Intan. Produced by Zahari, 1986.

Big Durian, The. Directed by Amir Muhammad. With Bernice Chauly, Nam Ron, Farish A. Noor, Jo Kukathas, Rashid Salleh, and Patrick Teoh. Produced by James Lee, 2003.

Bintang Pujaan (Superstar). Directed by Shahrom M. Dom. With Latif Ibrahim and Sharifah Aini. Syed Kechik Production, 1981.

Buai Laju-Laju (Swing My Swing High, My Darling). Directed by U-Wei Haji Saari. With Khalid Salleh, Betty Banafe, and Eman Manan. Produced by Julia Fraser, 2004.

Bujang Lapok Kembali Daa (The Return of the Broke Bachelors). Directed by Aziz Sattar. With S. Shamsuddin and Nasir P. Ramlee. Produced by A.A. Sattar, 1986.

Bukit Kepong (Kepong Hill). Directed by Jins Shamsuddin. With Jins and Jamaliah Arshad. Jins Shamsuddin Production, 1982.

Buluh Perindu. Directed by B.S. Rajhans. With Rosini, Shariff Medan, Bakarudin, and M. Amin. Cathay-Keris, 1953.

Cinta Kita (Our Love). Directed by A. Razak Mohaideen. Story/screenplay by Kamal Ishak. With Sofia Jane Hisham and Aman Graseka. Produced by Pansha, 1995.

Cinta Kolestrol (Cholesterol Love). Directed by A. Razak Mohaideen. With Erra Fazira and Yusry (KRU). Metrowealth Productions, 2003.

Cucu Datuk Merah. Directed by M. Amin. With Nordin Ahmad and Latifah Omar. Cathay-Keris, 1963.

Dari Jemapoh ke Manchestee (From Jemapoh to Manchester). Directed by Hishamuddin Rais. With Acui Zul Karnian, Indra Syahril, Arista Akma, and Fariza Azlina. Produced by Halim Sabir, 1998.

Embun. Directed by Erma Fatima. With Umie Aida, Aqasha, Dato Rahim Razali, and Hani Mohsin. Filem Negara Malaysia and FINAS, 2002.

Fantasia. Aziz M. Osman. With Erma Fatima, Faizal Hussain, and Melisa Saila. Teletrade, 1991 (released in 1993 as *Fantasi*).

Fenomena. Aziz M. Osman. With M. Nasir, Ramona Rahman, and Search. Teletrade, 1989 (released in 1990).

Gedebe (Gangster). Nam Ron. With Zul Huzaimy Marzuki, Md. Ezendy Aziz, Abdul Galil, and Mohammad Hariry. Cipta Films, 2003.

Hang Jebat. Directed by Hussain Haniff. With Nordin Ahmad, Latifah Omar, M. Amin, and Siput Sarawak. Cathay-Keris, 1961.

Hang Tuah. Directed by Phani Majumdar. With P. Ramlee, Saadiah, Ahmad Mahmud, and Zaiton. Malay Film Productions, 1956.

Hati Bukan Kristal. Directed by Raja Alauddin. With Erma Fatima, Ridzwan Hashim, and Julia Rais. Director's Team, 1990.

Interlud. Directed by Othman Zainuddin. With Azhar Sulaiman and Sofia Jane Hisham. United Kodilla, 1992.

Istana Berdarah (Palace of Blood). Directed by Hussain Haniff. With Yusof Latiff, Salleh Melan, and Fatimah Ahmad. Cathay-Keris, 1964.

Jasmin. Directed by Jamil Sulong. With Noraini Jane, Rosnani Jamil, and Johari. Kay Film Productions, 1984.

Jejaka Perasan (Unbashful Youth). Directed by A.R. Badol. With A.R. Badol, Liza Abdullah, and N.D. Lala. Produced by Shah, 1986.

Jimi Asmara. Directed by Erma Fatima. With Hani Mohsin, Rosyam Noor, and Maizurah Hamzah. BNE Studio, 1995.

Jogho (Champion). Directed by U-Wei Haji Saari. With Khalid Salleh. Produced by U-Wei and NHK Japan, 1998-99.

Kaki Bakar (The Arsonist). Directed by U-Wei Haji Saari. With Khalid Salleh. Produced by U-Wei and Tini Arshad. 1995.

Kalong Kenangan (Necklace of Memory). Directed by Hussain Haniff. With Tony Kassim, Nordin Ahmad, and Latifah Omar. Cathay-Keris, 1964.

Kami (Us). Directed by Patrick Yeoh. With Sudirman, Haji Arshad, and Ho Kwee Ling. Indra Filem, 1982.

Keluarga Si Comat (Si Comat's Family). Directed by Aziz Sattar. With Aziz Sattar, Deddy Borhan, and Junaidah M. Amin. Sabah Filem, 1975.

Kepala Angin (Crazy). Directed by Azmil Mustapha. With Azmil Mustapha and Jacqueline Mitchell. Amircom, 1987.

Ku Kejar Kau Lari (I Pursue, You Flee). Directed by Rashid Sibir. With Erma Fatima, Nasir Bilal Khan, and Hans Isaac. Produced by Erma Fatima and BNE Studio Ltd., 1998.

Laila Majnun. Directed by B.S. Rajhans. With M. Suki, Fatimah Jasmin, and Syed Ali Mansoor Al Attas. Motilal Chemical, 1933.

Lips to Lips. Directed by Amir Muhammad. With Anitha Abdul Hamid, James Lee, and Ernie Chen. Produced by Dhojee, 2000.

Mahsuri. Directed by B.N. Rao. With Kasma Booty, Nordin Ahmad, and Roomai Noor. Cathay-Keris, 1958.

Mawar Merah (Red Rose). Directed by Rosnani Jamil. With Raja Ema and Mustaffa Noor. RJ Filem, 1987.

May 13. Directed by Ahmad Mahmud. With A. Rahman, A. Din, and Norezan. Ahmad Mahmud Production, 1984.

Mekanik. Directed by Othman Hafsham. With Azmil Mustapha, Julie Faridah, and Susan Lankester. Syed Kechik Production, 1983.

Paloh. Directed by Adman Salleh. With Janet Khoo, Nam Ron, Gibran Agi, Ellie Suriaty, and Hasnul Rahmat. Filem Negara Malaysia and FINAS, 2003.

Pemburu Bayang (Shadow Hunter). Directed by Yusof Haslam. With Awie, Ella, Shaharuddin Thamby, and Erma Fatima. Skop Productions, 1993.

Pendekar Bujang Lapok (Broke Bachelor Warriors). Directed by P. Ramlee. With P. Ramlee, Aziz Sattar, and S. Shamsuddin. Malay Film Productions, 1959.

Penyamun Tarbus. Directed by Aziz Sattar. With Aziz Sattar and Aznah Hamid. Indra Film Productions, 1981.

Perempuan, Isteri Dan ...? (Woman, Wife, and Whore). Directed by U-Wei Haji Saari. With Sofia Jane Hisham and Nasir Bilal Khan. Berjaya Film Productions, 1993.

Perempuan Melayu Terakhir. (The Last Malay Woman.) Directed by Erma Fatima. With Vanida Imran, Eizlan Yusof, and Ahmad Yatim. Grand Brilliance, 1999.

Pesona Cinta (Charmed Love). Directed by Arief Karmahani. With Shaharuddin Thamby, Ida Nerina, and Nasir Bilal Khan. Medan Mas, 1995.

Pontianak Harum Sundal Malam. Directed by Shuhaimi Baba. With Maya Karin, Azri Iskandar, Eizlan Yusof, Kavita Sidhu, Sahronizam, and Ida Nerina. Pesona Pictures, 2004.

Putera Merdeka (Prince of Freedom). Directed by Mahadi J. Murat. With Jalil

Hamid, Sidi Oraza, Shaharuddin Thamby, Naa Murad, and Janet Khoo. Karya Impian, 2001.

Puteri (Princess). Directed by Rahim Razali. With Eman Manan and Fauziah Ahmad Daud. ASA XX Film Productions, 1987.

Ragam Pemandu (The Way of Drivers). Directed by Raja Ismail. With Hamid Gurkha, Aznah Hamid, Latiff Ibrahim, Bibi Yem, and Azmi Suhaimi (Tam). Solid Gold Studio, 1989.

Ranjau Sepanjang Jalan (No Harvest but a Thorn). Directed by Jamil Sulong. With Ahmad Mahmud and Sarimah. Kay-Sarimah Filem, 1983.

Red-Haired Tumbler di Malaya (Red-Haired Tumbler in Malaya). Directed by Eddie Pak. With Ahmad Fauzie, Os, Wilson Tin, Elaine Kang, Shima, and Ong Soo Hoon. 2020 Productions, 1994.

Ringgit Kasorrga (Dollar to Heaven). Directed by Shuhaimi Baba. With Deanna Yusoff, Tiara Jacquelina, Hans Isaac, and Zaidi Omar. Pesona Pictures, 1995.

Rozana Cinta '87 (Rozana Love '87). Directed by Nasir Jani. With Hilmi Hussain and Bibiana Loyola. Amircom, 1987.

Sama Tak Serupa (No Difference). Directed by Yuzwan Wahid. With Sasha Mohd. Saidin, Muzaffar Shah Baharin. Daya Pentas, 1995.

Sayang Salmah (For the Love of Salmah). Directed by Mahadi J. Murat. With Azhar Sulaiman, Sidi Oraza, Fauziah Nawawi, Norish Karman, and Sofia Jane Hisham. Grand Brilliance and Perkasa Filem, 1995.

Selamat Tinggal Kekasihku (Goodbye My Love). Directed by L. Krishnan. With Roomai Noor, Molly Lim, and Chang Lai Lai. Cathay-Keris, 1955.

Selubung (Covering). Directed by Shuhaimi Baba. With Deanna Yusoff, M. Nasir and Ida Nerina. Identity Entertainers, 1992.

Sembilu (Bamboo Splinter). Directed by Yusof Haslam. With Awie, Erra Fazira, Khairil Anwar, Mustapha Kamal, Ziana Zain, and Noraini Hashim. Skop Productions, 1994.

Senario the Movie. Directed by Aziz M. Osman. With Wahid, Azlee, Mazlan, and Saiful Apek. Paradigm Film and Grand Brilliance, 1999.

Sergeant Hassan. Directed by Alberto Avellana. With P. Ramlee, Salleh Kamil, Jins Shamsuddin, and Saadiah. Malay Film Productions, 1958.

Setinggan (Squatters). Directed by Aziz Sattar. With S. Shamsuddin and Yusni Jaafar. Indra Filem, 1981.

Si Badul. Directed by Aziz Sattar. With A.R. Badul. Sabah Film Productions, 1979.

Sikit Punya Gila (A Little Crazy). Directed by R. Ismail. With Dharma A. Rashid and Hamid Gurkha. Indra Filem, 1982.

6horts. Directed and produced by Amir Muhammad, 2002.

Snipers. Directed and produced by James Lee. With Tan Eng Heng, Pang Khee Teik, Huzir Sulaiman, Sue Ann Gooi, and Merissa Teh. Doghouse73 Pictures, 2001.

Spinning Gasing. Directed by Teck Tan. With Ellie Suriaty Omar, Craig Fong, Corrine Adri, Hani Mohsin, Edwin Sumun, and Sanjeet Jarnail. Produced by Dominique Hee and Teck Tan, 2000.

Tsu Feh Sofia. Directed by Rahim Razali. Rahim Razali and Jacqueline Mitchell. ASA XX, 1986.

Tuan Badul (Mr. Badul). Directed by Jamil Sulong. With A.R. Badul. Varia Film Productions, 1979/80.

Tun Fatimah. Directed by Salleh Ghani. With Yusof Latiff, Nordin Ahmad, and Maria Menado. Cathay-Keris, 1962.

Wanita Bertudung Hitam (Black-Scarfed Woman). Directed by Mahadi J. Murat. With Ramona Rahman, Imuda, and Jalil Hamid. Teknik Suria, 1992.

XX Ray. Directed by Aziz M. Osman. With Aziz M. Osman, Vianney Anastasia Lee, and Faizal Hussein. Nizarman Film Productions, 1992.

Yassin. Directed by Kamarul Ariffin. With Eman Manan and Uji Rashid. Kay Filem, 1988.

Notes

CHAPTER 1: RECLAIMING ADAT

1 For full details about Vision 2020, refer to Mahathir (1991, 2-4).

2 "Reality shows that what constitute [sic] *adat* and Islam actually varies according to time and place. A practice that was regarded as Islamic in the seventeenth century, such as saint worship, for instance, in the 1960s, was classified as part of local adat. Similarly, what was thought of as an adat practice, such as the *kenduri selamat* or communal feast, might incorporate Islamic elements" (Sharifah Zaleha 2000, 24).

3 Indeed Amir Muhammad's film *Lips to Lips* (2000) is an irreverent, almost schoolboyish, exploration of sex, food, and accidental deaths. The focus on sexuality and magic here has less to do with adat than with Western-style modernity.

4 Judith Nagata writes that Malaysian Islam too is constantly being reinterpreted and "reinvented" as the state leaders try to appear appropriately Islamic both to conservative PAS supporters and to more "secular" or "progressive" Muslims and overseas investors (Nagata 1997, 99).

5 Virginia Hooker's book *Writing a New Society: Social Change through the Novel in Malay* (2000) covers Malay novels up to 1980 only. See Gray (2002).

6 For the sake of argument, one might even characterize IT as a mark of postmodernity in the era of late capitalism. Rita Felski, in her discussion of gender in Western modernity, describes modernity as an epochal term that includes modernization ("the complex constellation of socioeconomic phenomena which originated in the context of Western development but which have since manifested themselves around the globe in various forms"), the artistic movement of modernism that arose in Europe and America about a century ago, and the French term *modernité*. Like modernism, French *modernité*, "while also concerned with a distinctively modern sense of dislocation and ambiguity, locates it in the more general experience of the aestheticization of everyday life, as exemplified in the ephemeral and transitory qualities of an urban culture shaped by the imperatives of fashion, consumerism, and constant innovation" (1995, 13). I would characterize Malaysian modernity as being quite close to Felski's definitions of Western modernity. Chapter 5 takes up the way in which resurgent Islam becomes one such "imperative" that defines, for example, the fashion and trend of modernity.

7 It was superseded by another building in Taipei in 2004.

8 The currency crisis began in mid-1997. By mid-1998, Malaysia had descended into a full economic recession. Prime Minister Mahathir's anti-George Soros rhetoric did little to stabilize the flailing stock market and Malaysians were filled with ambivalence over his nationalist and anti-Western position. Moreover, Malaysians worried whether the service at the newly opened KLIA was going to be efficient after initial problems with the operating systems, baggage transport, etc. during the first few weeks of its opening in July 1998. At the time of the Commonwealth Games, too, a political crisis arose within the Malay ruling party, UMNO, after the sacking of Deputy Prime Minister Anwar Ibrahim, who was leading street marches and speaking out about the corruption of the then government at large illegal rallies. Pro-Anwar street demonstrations led to heavy security measures when Queen Elizabeth attended the Games. There was also some speculation about a slump in the economy immediately after the Commonwealth Games, when the facilities, housing, hotels, etc. built especially for the event would be left largely unoccupied.

9 "Race" is a colonial construct/category but a ubiquitous category in Malaysian social discourse. I will substitute the word "ethnicity" where possible and appropriate.

10 Roughly, the ethnic percentages of the population of Malaysia today are: Malays (55 percent), Chinese (30 percent), Indians (9 percent), and others (6 percent). These official racialized categories conveniently

homogenize the dialect, linguistic, regional, and cultural differences within each "racial" category. For example, Indian Malaysians may include Tamils, Sikhs, Parsi, Indian Muslims originally from Kerala, and Sinhalese, etc.

11 An earlier precedent (1800-50) to the tension between modernity and feudal loyalties is provided by Malay scribe Munshi Abdullah's use of liberal European discourse to critique the Malay rulers. See Milner (1994).

12 Also see Rema Nambiar 1995; and Samy Vellu Meets Indian Gangsters 1997.

13 The bumiputera category includes all Malays (e.g., Bajau, Minangkabau) and the "indigenous" groups of East Malaysia as well as the Orang Asli in Peninsula Malaysia. However, despite the extension of the term *bumiputera* to encompass the "indigenous" peoples, the Orang Asli are not accorded the special privileges given to those other bumiputera in the constitution.

14 "The [DBP] was established in 1957 following the recommendation made by the Abdul Razak Committee on Education in the Federation of Malaya, 1956. Despite this, it is only since 1970 that literature in the Malay language (then retitled 'Bahasa Malaysia') has been more actively supported by the Malay political elites" (Tham 1981, 217-18).

15 In the new millennium, the government has made an attempt to rectify its neglect of English-language Malaysian literature in the form of the IRPA research grant. This effort has produced a few anthologies of essays and creative writing, such as *Petals of Hibiscus* (2003) edited by Mohammad A. Quayum.

16 Here, Mandal refers to Mahathir Mohamad's controversial book *The Malay Dilemma* (1970) as well as that of his former deputy prime minister, Anwar Ibrahim, *The Asian Renaissance* (1996).

17 For an in-depth comprehensive account of anglophone writing in Malaysia by women, see Nor Faridah Abdul Manaf and Mohammad A. Quayum (2001); for Malay-language novels, see Virginia Hooker (2000) and Banks (1987). All three touch on social themes. Judging from Hooker and Banks, the issue of social change affecting Malay ethnic identity and culture is common in Malay novels.

18 The national film industry is dominated by Malays and their culture. Because it's played by Malay actors and largely caters to a Malay audience, the dialogue is in Malay.

19 In *Colonialism and Nationalism in Asian Cinema*, Wimal Dissanayake expands on Benedict Anderson's idea of reading the nation through novels by applying it to film, suggesting that cinema functions even better as a popular tool for the formation of national identity and the creation of an imagined community (1994, xiv).

20 Gabrielpillai's doctoral thesis combines Foucauldian discourse analysis with Žižek's theory of ideology to investigate 1980s developments in Singapore's discourse of national identity. It speaks for my use of Žižek too: "Žižek's approach to political critique is especially useful in moving beyond the historical/Western constraints of discourse analysis by working into its perspective the difference of post-colonial subjectivity, and post-colonial identifications, not to mention its potential for beginning an inquiry into the post-colonial unconscious as a cultural and material determinant" (1997, 20). Lim applies Žižek's theory of subjectivity to the literary work of Malaysian writer K.S. Maniam and concomitant issues of ethnicity and national belonging. Yao, a cultural anthropologist, cites Žižek in discussing ethnic othering and power relations in Mahathir's *Malay Dilemma* as it relates to his ethnographic study of food, alterity, and the "pleasure of Chineseness" in contemporary Malaysia (Yao 2000, 74-75).

21 For a similar methodology, see Alan Dundes, where he suggests subjecting texture, text, and context to structural analysis, and where he discusses psychoanalytical projection in folklore (1980, 20-32, 33-61).

22 The Internal Security Act (ISA), a remnant of British colonial administration, today allows for indefinite detention without trial.

23 A Malay filmmaker I interviewed in 1998 who would like to be able to see more Malay movies with a Malaysian sentiment felt that representing ethnic diversity was the last barrier in the film industry. Sumit Mandal (2000) also makes the case that English-language theatre, performance arts, and literature have more successfully articulated the multi-ethnic, hybrid character of Malaysian society.

24 Here I am confining my analysis to literary works and excluding comic books, women's magazines, and other mass media that may put new humorous twists on the Hang Tuah/Hang Jebat myth.

25 For a brief summary of Third Cinema, Third Worldist films, and the critics, filmmakers, and theorists involved, see Michael T. Martin (1997, 20-21).

26 Personal interview, 8 July 1998.

CHAPTER 2: MALAY MYTH AND CHANGING ATTITUDES TOWARDS NATIONALISM

1 *Amok* comes from the Malay word *mengamok.* It is often described as a murderous uncontrollable frenzy and is supposedly unique to Indonesia and Malaysia. However, recent studies have opened new perspectives on this phenomenon. See, for example, Badriyah Hj. Salleh (1993) and John Clark Spores (1988).

2 The *hadith* is a report or narrative about the Prophet Muhammad's words and acts. *Hadiths* confirm, extend, elaborate, explain, and complement the revelations in the Quran (Denny 1985, 175). In Malaysia, Kassim Ahmad's book *The Hadith: A Re-Evaluation* (1986) spurred debates over reliance on the *hadith* instead of the Quran (Salleh Ben Joned 1994, 30-36).

3 The "Look East" policy was spurred by Mahathir's admiration of the so-called economic miracles of Japan and South Korea. The underlying elements of these economic transformations were, he believed, "their moral and cultural pillars: a strong work ethic, worthy Eastern values, a capacity for learning, courage to compete, self-reliance, and national pride" (Khoo Boo Teik 1995, 68).

4 For an in-depth analysis of the fundamental differences in the two men's leadership styles and on what issues they had conflicting opinions, see Anwar's letter from prison "From the Halls of Power to the Labyrinths of Incarceration" (1998a). For a more neutral academic account, see Khoo Boo Teik's *Paradoxes of Mahathirism* (1995) and Jomo (1998).

5 Such an allegation appeared in the book by Khalid Jafri Bakar Shah, *50 Dalil Mengapa Anwar Tidak Boleh Menjadi PM* (50 Reasons Why Anwar Cannot Be PM) (Selangor, Malaysia: Media Pulau Lagenda, 1998), which Anwar believed was circulated by his political enemies.

6 Filmmaker Hishamuddin Rais also lived through a similar situation but at a different historical period (Stothard 2001).

7 My analysis is based on Aveling's translation which, for the most part, captures the essence of the short story accurately. It is difficult to describe Fatimah Busu's readership or compare her work to that of the play versions of the Hang Tuah/Hang Jebat myth because too many factors are involved. Her short story genre makes for a different kind of "audience," mainly readers. As a woman writer, she appeals to a predominantly female readership, and as someone who is published by Dewan Bahasa dan Pustaka (DBP), which publishes literary textbooks, her books are made available to students. I should add that because DBP also publishes plays that have been staged, those plays would also be made available to readers, not only to playgoers.

8 Rafidah Aziz, the woman who is currently the minister of International Trade and Industry, would never hold a powerful position such as the Minister of Finance, or Education, positions held by previous PMs and Deputy PMs. Moreover, the Ministry of Women and Family Development and also the Ministry of Social Welfare, now renamed the Ministry of National Unity and Social Development, are, unsurprisingly, headed by women.

9 "Bahasa, agama dan raja" or language/Malay, religion/Islam, and royalty/sultan-chiefs constitute the three pillars of Malay identity (Shamsul 1999, 94).

10 Certain topics pertaining to race are deemed so sensitive that those caught publicly discussing them are subject to imprisonment. This includes citizenship rights, Malay special rights, the status and powers of the Malay rulers, the status of Islam, and of Malay as the sole national language. Censorship and self-censorship since 1971 are therefore very common. Anti-democratic government rhetoric insists that, in a multi-ethnic society liable to ethnic strife, individual liberties must be sacrificed to preserve peace and order.

11 Western universalism in this case presupposes that forms of nationalism in developing or formerly colonized countries will be no different from the forms of nationalism that began in the West. Oriental exceptionalism would therefore be the unique, anticolonial nationalism emerging from the East that would challenge the hegemonic notion of Western universalism.

12 See Van der Heide (2002) for an analysis of *Hang Tuah.*

13 Official nationalism is "a conscious, self-protective policy, intimately linked to the preservation of imperial-dynastic interests." It emanates from the state and serves the interests of the state first and foremost (Anderson 1991, 159). As examples, Anderson discusses the People's Republic of China, Socialist Republic of Vietnam, Democratic Kampuchea, and Thailand.

14 It is unclear whether the misquotation is the fault of the publisher or the writer.

15 "What was once the moral responsibility of the rulers, protection now became the primary mobilizing force of UMNO which perceived itself as the premier protector of the Malays and Islam." Shome believes that the transfer of trust from the monarchy to UMNO was perhaps a reaction against the carelessness with which the sultans had signed their consent to the Malayan Union accord (Shome 2002, 62).

16 Sabri Zain (2000b) notes that at the root of cronyism is feudal loyalty or specifically, political loyalty to the ruling elite; it is not economics.

17 Patricia Sloane's study of the anxieties around networking practices among Malay entrepreneurs in Kuala Lumpur during the early to mid-1990s arguably reflects an urban modern form of Umnoputraism. Sabri Zain (2000b) believed that the root of cronyism lay in feudal loyalty to the ruling elite but that more Malaysians were questioning that loyalty, for example, when Chinese associations under the Suqiu lobby group renewed a call for a review of the NEP in August 2000.

18 "With political power in UMNO's hands, government licences, contracts, finances, and other concessions could easily be awarded in the party's interest or to individuals aligned to it" (Gomez 1990, vii-viii).

19 One of the major opposition parties is PAS, which controls the state of Kelantan. See Rehman Rashid's analysis (1993, 258). For a Kelantanese perspective, see Che Husna Azhari's *Melor in perspective:* "Another important factor that has contributed to Kelantan's isolation is its strong political will; its isolation has been self-imposed. Time and time again, Kelantan proved to be troublesome to the central government when it chose to elect the Opposition, the post-Independence state elections of 1959 being a milestone ... Economic hardship, poverty, high infant mortality rates, and indifferent public services did not break the collective will of this stubborn people. It was as if they all endured the hardship together as a necessary penance for being of a different race, but perhaps more importantly, of having a different ideology and ethos towards life" (1993, 3-4).

20 A curious discrepancy occurs here in the translation. In Malay it reads, "sifat taat setia yang tidak seharusnya diberikan kepada seorang manusia yang cuma dijadikan oleh Tuhan untuk hidup sementara di dunia ini, bukan untuk hidup abadi" (loyalty that should not actually be given to a human being, who is merely created by God to live temporarily on earth, not to live forever – my translation).

21 One can also make the argument that for every Hang Tuah there must be a Hang Jebat, if one supports the idea of the dialectical Malay psyche. This would then facilitate the presence of resistance and rebellion in the face of authoritarianism.

22 To be fair, in the post-Anwar period, Karim Raslan's newer book of essays, *Journeys through Southeast Asia: Ceritalah2* (2002) is more pessimistic of Malaysia's democratic potential.

23 See "Conference in Chaos" (1996), from the *Aliran Monthly.*

24 Karim illustrates the tension in the new Malay who is still "expected to conform to certain set norms – many of which were quasi-feudal in their emphasis on loyalty, obedience and blind devotion to authority" (1996a, 15).

25 *Puteri Gunung Ledang,* a costly historical film released in 2004, portrays the princess (played by Tiara Jacquelina) of the film's title falling in love with the dutiful Hang Tuah (played by M. Nasir). Here,

Hang Tuah is caught between loyalty to the king and to the woman he loves. When away from the politics of the court in pursuit of the princess, he is unsure who he is and too weak to envision a future for himself that does not revolve around the king. This is literally demonstrated in a scene in which Hang Tuah, emotionally impoverished and powerless as an individual, is reduced to grovelling in the mud.

26 For the history and background of resurgent Islamic movements in Malaysia since the late 1960s, see Jomo and Shabery Cheek (1992); Nagata (1994); Shamsul (1995 and 1997); and Syed Ahmad (2002).

27 *Hamba* literally means "slave" or "unpaid servant" but is also used as a first person pronoun in friendly but not familiar terms (Wilkinson 1959). For conciseness in the rest of the chapter, I prefer the Malay word *hamba* to its English translation.

28 There is a symbolic connection between the sultan's decadence (the dictionary yields synonyms such as "period of decline," "putrification," "deterioration," and "self-indulgence") and the moral judgment imposed on social relationships that people perceive as perverse, such as homosexuality (see Edelman 1992, 270).

29 By sexual betrayal, I do not mean that the sultan felt betrayed by his concubine – he cannot because women are objects, not subjects. Rather, he felt betrayed by another member of this homosocial society, Hang Tuah, whom he believed had encroached on his sexual ownership of the woman slave/concubine.

30 One might argue here for the relevance of Sedgwick's theory that a deep homophobia underlies the theory of homosocial relations because the king, as if out of homophobic panic, vomits after eating Hang Tuah (Fatimah 1991, 262-63). But I doubt this is the ideal reading. His Highness's vomiting more likely indicates his greed, decadence, and guilt for betraying and oppressing his loyal *hamba*.

31 Sedgwick suggests that Lacan's elaborate meditation on introjection and incorporation forms the link between desire and identification (1985, 24).

32 The film revolves around a singer and bandleader whose failing career is saved by a woman's love (and her money) but whose life is preserved ultimately by his most loyal male friend and band member who jumps between him and a fatal bullet. Moreover, throughout the film, Jimi's band members and friends keep reinforcing the misogynist idea that women are not worth the emotional pain. The film ends with a poetic statement that no one ever dies because of love – people die because of *poisoned* love, but most of all, a love that is pure requires sacrifice.

33 *Kapok* looks like cotton and grows on trees.

34 Malay queens sometimes ruled in the absence of their husbands. A series of queens once ruled in their own right in the Malay kingdom of Patani from 1584 to about 1688 (Teeuw and Wyatt 1970).

35 Malayan independence was gained by an ethnic coalition of male leaders. Very few women, with the exception of Khatijah Sidek, known as Ibu UMNO, mother of UMNO, participated in politics then. Some believed she was forced out of the party when she became a feminist threat to the first PM, Tunku Abdul Rahman.

36 Hassan Karim (2000) notes that the results of the Lunas elections in 2000 meant that the citizens (*rakyat*) of Lunas broke the social contract with the Barisan Nasional, much like Jebat had, in the past, openly challenged the social contract between Demang Lebar Daun and Sang Sapurba.

37 In the Dantean landscape of hell, before meeting Sisyphus, Hang Jebat meets a man who keeps cutting off his lips with a pair of scissors every time they grow back; a group of people who eat rotting flesh, vomit it out, and then eat their vomit; a frail old man who overburdens his back with a large load of wood; a farmer who cuts down green plants before replanting them; and a man in pain who claws his skin until he bleeds but cannot stop. All of them cannot answer for their illogical actions. Instead, they tell Hang Jebat to ask Sisyphus.

38 Ahmad Faiz's revisionary account of the Tuah/Jebat duel in light of the Anwar case is interesting. Here loyalty to friendship makes a compromise with Tuah's loyalty to the king. Tuah feigns killing Jebat and, in reply to the king's concubine, who said that he would live but his good name would be

tarnished forever, states: "Someday, our descendants will understand. They will know the truth. And with that knowledge and understanding – who knows? – maybe they will find another way" (Ahmad Faiz 1998).

CHAPTER 3: DISSEMINATION OF MALAY/SIA

1 The quotation can be found at Wira (2003).

2 This chapter was first written as an essay in the mid-1990s. The currency crisis and the post-Anwar events have affected the outlook of some of these writers: some became more pessimistic, some went into retreat, and others, like Amir Muhammad, became even more active in critical discourse through filmmaking and internet journalism (see Karim Raslan 2002, 14-17; and Khoo Boo Teik 2002, on the effects of *reformasi* in Amir Muhammad's *New Straits Times* column "Perforated Sheets" from 2 September 1998 to 3 February 1999).

3 Donna Amoroso points to Cheah's work *Malaysia: The Making of a Nation* (2002), which indicates that there was a lack of common political discourse between the Malay and English languages. "Malayan" was regarded as a colonial construct and Malay leaders, when addressing an all-Malay audience, would refer to *Persekutuan Melayu* instead of Malaya. "Malayan" functioned as a rival root word to Malay or Melayu and symbolized to Malays the Malayan Union's erasure of their sovereignty and elevation of non-Malays at their expense (Amoroso 2003, 6-7).

4 Pluralism here does not refer to a multi-ethnic population. Bhabha is referring to Benedict Anderson's "sociological solidity" fixed in a "succession of *plurals*" – this being hospitals, prisons, and remote villages where the social space is clearly bounded by objects that represent a naturalistic, national horizon (1994, 305).

5 Amir Muhammad's newspaper articles are collected together with those of two other writers, Kam Raslan and Sheryll Stothard, in *Generation: A Collection of Contemporary Malaysian Ideas* (1997). I have chosen to focus on Amir Muhammad's work rather than that of the other two as he is a bumiputera unrelated to Karim Raslan, and I find his work the most interesting among the three.

6 Francis Loh's theory (2002) that there was a discursive shift away from exclusivist ethnic issues and inter-ethnic competition to a discourse of developmentalism in the 1990s among the Malaysian business and middle classes as well as ruling coalition politicians does not, however, negate the very real ethnicized debates that occurred in academic circles and were publicized in these newspaper columns. For example, Loh points to the Mahathir government's move back to using English for teaching mathematics and science but Amir Muhammad regards this as an ineffective attempt to beef up English proficiency and only as a short-term political strategy (see S. Tan 2002).

7 Salleh informs us that in Tagalog, a cousin of Malay, "malaya" means freedom or consciousness (1994, 50).

8 Translation "As Malays, we should ..."

9 Indeed, this is the point all three writers, Amir Muhammad, Sheryll Stothard, and Kam Raslan, wanted to emphasize in their collection *Generation*. However, their optimism about media freedom was somewhat short lived when their articles were "spiked" (not published) when it came to the second Asia Pacific Conference on East Timor (APCET II) in 1996.

10 See the production notes for *Friday* at <http://6horts.tripod.com>.

11 *Mat Salleh* is a nickname for Europeans or Caucasians. The Malay word *salih* means strange.

12 Mandal (2001) asserts that a newer attitude towards race/ethnicity has emerged from members of the NEP Generation. This newer form of pluralism, compared to the old model where ethnic groups were less likely to intermingle, signals a newer, more fluid, cross-ethnic hybrid form of pluralism. But downplaying ethnic differences while encouraging new economic, social, and ethno-religious realignments as part of the strategies or results of developmentalism also ensures that such ethnic solidarities occur only within the same class (Embong 2001) and do not threaten the political status quo (Loh 2001, 201-2). The hegemony, lure, and enjoyment of the big Other continues and will most likely continue

under Mahathir's successor, Abdullah Badawi, who has promised to perpetuate policies begun by his predecessor, albeit on a smaller scale.

13 Amir Muhammad also took his short films on a campus tour: "More shows should be done this way ... travel around, bring them to the students" (Al-Attas 2002). The filmmaker talked about educating Malaysians about the short film and its usefulness as an experimental form, but I suspect the contents of the films are just as, if not even more, important to be circulated and discussed openly by Malaysians. In fact, six months later, when asked how he thought a young Malaysian would view race and religion, Amir replied that he could not speak on behalf of the younger generation any more as someone turning thirty: "That's why it was important for me to screen the works to students and to get their reaction. There have been more reviews on *6horts* from the internet blogs of students than from the mainstream media" (S. Tan 2002).

14 Literal translations: sweet blackness and yellow-white.

15 Shaharuddin Maaruf takes a hard look at the problem of leadership and "some attitudes of the Malay elite which have bearing on the social, economic, cultural and political development of the Malays" in his book *Concept of a Hero in Malay Society* (1984, 1). He also discusses the thinking and values represented by Hang Tuah and Hang Jebat. It should be noted that his research concentrated on UMNO leadership before Dr. Mahathir became prime minister. But despite the changes from an aristocratic line of prime ministers to a leadership led by a commoner (Dr. Mahathir), there is some continuity in the present form of rule that relies on feudal values and a patronage system to preserve the material interests of the political elite. For example, Shaharuddin claims that "the ruling elite which promotes feudal heroes is also responsible for the promotion of well-known capitalists as heroes to be also emulated by the Malays" (ibid., 92). Shaharuddin describes the emulation of millionaires like Ford and Rockefeller in a collection of essays, *Revolusi Mental*, written by the Malay elite in 1971 – there's a trajectory from this mentality to the subsequent Asian values debate that formed around the Asian economic miracle in the late 1980s and early 1990s.

16 Amir seems to be a man of action compared to his peer, Kam Raslan, who frequently mentions in his columns that he is a filmmaker who, apart from some television directing work, has yet to make any films of his own since his return to Malaysia in the mid-1990s.

17 For the sake of argument, there are other theories of the mirror stage that do cross gender. For example, Erin Soros (1998) theorizes the identification of the child with the mother that s/he sees in the mirror, rather than merely with his/her own reflection as whole.

18 The pun is intended to show that in Malay/sian tradition, there are more male than female writers. Moreover, it is mostly male writers who have been celebrated poet laureates and literary award winners in Malay literature, which is to say that Malay women's writing was not considered "serious" literature, until Zaharah Nawawi's heavy tome *Anugerah* (1995) won the best Malay novel award.

19 According to Maila Stivens, "the masculinity of the new (middle-class) Muslim Malay represented as inhabiting such global spaces is not directly problematic for his moral and business identity" but "the femininity of a new woman slides more easily into moral ambiguity" (1998, 94).

CHAPTER 4: MALAY/SIAN FILMS

1 Krishna Sen's *Indonesian Cinema: Framing the New Order* (1994), particularly her argument that Indonesian cinema "frames" the New Order government of Suharto, has stimulated my giving name to the Cinema of Denial. Sen illustrates the intimate connections between Indonesian politics, media ownership, the role of the military, state policies, and the kinds of films made and shown in the country from the late 1960s to the early 1980s. While the Indonesian socio-political situation differs from its Malaysian counterpart, Sen's book, especially her feminist position with regard to the oppositional cinematic representations of women outside of the conventional roles of wife, mother, or prostitute, partially inspires my discussion of gender representations in Malaysian cinema.

2 Hatta's book was withdrawn from the shelves shortly after its publication, ostensibly due to extensive

typographical errors. But according to Hamzah Hussin, the book contains some factual errors as well. While dated, the book remains the first comprehensive published book on the history of Malay cinema.

3 In her book, *Primitive Passions* (1995), Rey Chow notes a similar representation of the sexualized female body in Zhang Yimou's films. There, female sexuality is made into an aesthetic ethnographic spectacle that "embodies" the Chinese archaic.

4 This book covers films only up to 1999. Erma Fatima's later film, *Embun* (2002) is problematic in numerous ways, not least of which is her use of precisely this image of the *perempuan berkemban,* an image that does not appear in the original script *Titisan Air Mata Embun* (The Teardrops of Embun) by Rohiman Haroon. That the filmmaker felt the need to reclaim such an idyllic image more likely from the Golden Era of Malay cinema than perhaps reality itself points to the (re)constructedness of adat.

5 Shamsul Amri Baharuddin (1995) also uses May 13, 1969 as a crucial point of awareness for *dakwah* activism in Malaysia.

6 I would like to thank Daniel Goh of the Department of Sociology at the National University of Singapore for reading through this chapter and providing his valuable insights on Lacan, Žižek, and Laclau and Mouffe.

7 "Class" is the implied antagonism of the 1969 race riots, acknowledged by one of the tenets of the NEP, which called for the eradication of poverty across all ethnic groups.

8 The catalyst that sparked the riots was the victory procession that the opposition party (a predominantly Chinese party) held in the streets of Kuala Lumpur after elections. The common view is that the cockiness of the Chinese during the procession provoked the Malays who were Alliance supporters. Chinese Malaysians believe that the race riots were instigated by Malay "ultras," Malay politicians who were anti-Chinese/pro-Malay in their outlook. Mahathir blamed Tunku's government for not having the foresight and political acumen to withhold the permit for the procession. This followed after two conceivably racially and politically motivated murders – a UMNO publicity officer was battered to death in Penang and a Labour Party member shot during the protracted electoral campaign (Mahathir 1970, 14).

9 See the National Operations Council report (1969), Gagliano (1970, 16-17), Goh (1971), Parker (1979), and Ee (1980), some of which critique the unreliability of foreign media reports.

10 The Malaysian People's Justice Movement, or Gerak Keadilan, is a group made up of opposition parties, NGOs, prominent citizens, church groups, etc. calling for the repeal of the Internal Security Act. Led by Wan Azizah, it is not to be confused with Dr. Lim's Gerakan Party, which comes under the Barisan Nasional. To run for the 1999 elections, Wan Azizah's party became Parti Keadilan Nasional (the National Justice Party).

11 See Chandra Muzaffar's *Challenges and Choices in Malaysian Politics and Society,* which details the gradual moves to undermine democratic institutions in Malaysia, including the media and the judiciary (1989).

12 Hishamuddin Rais and Amir Muhammad, personal interview, 22 June 1998.

13 In fact, Amir Muhammad explained that a television drama entitled *Amy Anuar,* which was supposed to celebrate World AIDS day, displayed a "condescending or patronizing attitude" towards non-heterosexuals. It details a man who picks up a *Mak Nyah* (the preferred term for transsexuals) in a back alley and then tries to reform her. The narrative concludes with her dying of AIDS, and the moral implications are supposedly clear: those who stray from hetero-normative behaviour will be justly punished.

14 For a more detailed history of Malay cinema, refer to Hatta Azad Khan's *The Malay Cinema* (1997) and *Memoir Hamzah Hussin: Dari Keris Film ke Studio Merdeka* (1997). Gordon Gray's dissertation (Chapter 2) is a careful, well-researched, and up-to-date work on Malay cinematic history (2002). Gray's analysis complements my own because he is interested in modernity and its effects on Malay society of the 1990s. For a summary of its multi-ethnic beginnings, see William Van der Heide (1996).

Suraya Al-Attas (1996) gives an overview of the 1990s' filmmakers, A. Wahab Hamzah (1998) talks about cineplexes implanting a new culture on Malaysians and the privatization of FINAS is addressed by Mohd. Yusman Awang (1998, 5-19). See also Fuziah Kartini and Raja Ahmad Alauddin's 1995 essay, which features a brief introduction to three 1990s Malay filmmakers and talks about the role of the film censorship board, the LPFM. Unfortunately, the essay does not discuss censorship pertaining to each of these filmmakers as the title implies. See Hassan Muthalib and Wong Tuck Cheong (2002), which covers Malaysian animation and documentaries, among many other issues.

15 The ones I know of include Shuhaimi Baba, Adman Salleh, Kamal Mustaffa, Othman Shamsuddin (better known as Hafsham), Nasir Jani, Meor Hashim Aziz Razak, Isa Abdullah, Aida Buyong, Aziz M. Osman, and U-Wei, who had gone to the United States to study engineering but ended up with a degree in filmmaking.

16 In 2004, FINAS came under the Ministry of Culture, Arts, and Heritage.

17 The FINAS website is http://www.finas.gov.my/objectives.shtml

18 Although the first Malay film in colour, *Buluh Perindu*, appeared in 1953, colour films were expensive to make because there were no colour film laboratories to process the films within Malaysia. Black and white films continued to be made until 1975.

19 Al-Attas claims this film dared to include lesbianism but because I have not seen it, I cannot comment on the treatment of this issue.

20 Ironically, in a newspaper article about the problem with piracy, the journalists raised the question of how piracy of American video and music products jeopardizes trade relations between the United States and Malaysia, undermining the national MSC project, which requires the cooperation and technological know-how of the Americans. See Goh and Patrick (1999). The two also report that "the recession is spurring the public to look for pirated products" and that while music piracy has increased from 15 percent in 1997 to 40 percent in 1999, video and film piracy is estimated to have increased to 90 percent, an all-time high.

21 The government station, RTM or Radio Televisyen Malaysia, has direct control of two channels. RTM 1 features programs in the Malay language and RTM 2 is a combination of English/Chinese and Indian programs. The other stations are privately owned but the supposed political "independence" of TV3, the first private station to provide an alternative to RTM, is questioned by Zaharom Nain in "Commercialization and Control in a 'Caring Society': Malaysian Media." According to Zaharom, TV3 is "under the control of Realmild Sdn. Bhd., a private limited company that is in turn fully owned by a publicly listed company, Malaysian Resources Corporation Sdn. Bhd. (MRCB). MRCB is effectively controlled by four individuals widely recognized as close associates of Anwar Ibrahim, the [former] Deputy Prime Minister" (1994, 183). In fact, when Dr. Mahathir forced Anwar out of power, Mahathir accused TV3 of providing biased news and of being sympathetic to Anwar. Subsequently, the head of TV3 was forced to resign.

22 One filmmaker was given a used car. Before the recession, the foreign-made car would have had a high resale value.

23 Yingjin Zhang (1994) refers to Jameson's essay, "World Literature in an Age of Multinational Capitalism," and applies the idea of Third World film as a national allegory to the Chinese film, *Red Sorghum*. Jameson himself applies this political reading to the Taiwanese film *The Terroriser*.

24 See Dissanayake's introduction (Zhang 1994, x).

25 One of the critiques Julianne Burton makes of Gabriel is that "his commitment to presenting Third Cinema as a unified and unitary signifying practice [over the course of thirty years] thus leads him to ignore or suppress contradictions within the texts themselves and within and between the film movements which produce these texts" (1985, 9). Burton suggests that, in order to circumscribe problems of categorizing what exactly the term "Third Cinema" includes, we should adopt the terms "marginal" and "oppositional" cinema instead (ibid., 10). See her essay "Marginal Cinemas and Mainstream Critical Theory" (1985).

26 For an updated account of the debates about Third Cinema, see the introduction to Guneratne and Dissanayake's *Rethinking Third Cinema* (2003, 1-28).

27 I would not, as William Van Der Heide does in his book *Malaysian Cinema, Asian Film* (2002), go so far as to say that all Malay films, even as late as U-Wei Haji Saari's *Perempuan, Isteri Dan ...?* (1994), can be traced back to Hindu cultural roots without seriously grappling with what indigenous Malay culture, beyond the mere narrative of Hang Tuah-Hang Jebat, may offer on its own terms.

28 Lent states that political themes glorifying communism are banned (1990, 197).

29 According to Hamzah, an earlier Indonesian version *of Oedipus Rex, Sangkuriang,* was used to test the sensitivities of Malays towards the subject of incest. "If the number of spectators can be used to measure this, the film directed by Hussin Haniff had a moderate reception. As for the aspects of 'haram' [illegal by Muslim law] and sin, there was no feedback from viewers, critics or cultural and religious leaders" (1997, 55, my translation).

30 See *Tun Fatimah* (1962), *Hang Jebat* (1961), *Hang Tuah* (1956), and *Mahsuri* (1958). With the exception of Mahsuri, the protagonists were warriors before the colonial era in Malaya. The legend of Mahsuri, a chaste woman unjustly punished for adultery, is the foundation myth of the island of Langkawi.

31 The people I interviewed with this casual question include film critics, filmmakers, and generally those in the industry (see also Hassan and Wong 2002, 316).

32 *Merriam Webster's Collegiate Dictionary*, 10th ed., s.v. "Pluralism."

33 For example, although the Chinese are allowed to practise their religions, Buddhist associations and churches wanting to build their places of worship were not given permits to construct free-standing temples and churches. Neither were new churches allowed to have a large cross on the front of the building. This information cropped up when I saw a curious phenomenon in Petaling Jaya, a suburb of Kuala Lumpur: a Buddhist temple stuck in the middle of a row of terrace-houses. It was a home that had been converted into a temple. Obviously, the authorities, while building more and more ostentatious mosques, were also simultaneously playing down the visibility of other religions in the country. Several years ago when the Kek Lok Si temple in Ayer Itam, Penang, was being renovated and there were plans to construct a gigantic statue of the Goddess of Mercy on the hill, the size of the statue had to be scaled down in order not to shadow the Penang State Mosque.

34 Many intellectuals have pointed to the multi-ethnic street demonstrations in Kuala Lumpur after the arrest of former deputy prime minister, Anwar Ibrahim, as a dramatic consequence of this long repression through various state apparatuses such as the Internal Security Act and the Official Secrets Act (1972). Amendments in 1988 made to the Publication Act (threatening the freedom of expression), to the Police Act (striking at the freedom of assembly), and to the Societies Act (jeopardizing the freedom of association) further reduced individual rights in Malaysia (Chandra 1989, 182).

35 Daniel Goh notes that the contemporary cinematic pairing of Malay men with Chinese women reverses the historical reality of earlier centuries in which Indian and Chinese male migrants who came to seek work in Malaya married Malay women. This reversal means that the female ethnic Other (who constitutes and supposedly preserves her tradition) is assimilated to hegemonic (and patriarchal) Malayness in the postcolonial era.

36 Zawawi Ibrahim (2003) regards U-Wei's trilogy of films as an exploration of peripheral Malay cultures, featuring the regional dialect and culture of the Kelantanese, the Javanese immigrants, and oppressed women in the rural village. All these provide counternarrations to the hegemonic urban national Malay identity. The issue of representing Bahasa Malaysia, the standardized national language, on screen is also problematized by the diverse range of regional (not to mention "rural") dialects. The regional dialects are brought out clearly in *Jogho* (Kelantanese) and *Dari Jemapoh Ke Mancestee* (Negeri Sembilan). See also Khoo (2002b).

37 Hatta recalls that the film was "one good film which did not manage to capture the interest of Malaysian audiences simply because they found the film too heavily laden with social and political references to Malaysia" (1997, 135). In addition, he mentions that *Matinya* "was a dismal failure at the

box office despite having won five awards at the Fifth Malaysian Film Festival in December 1984." The full extent of his analysis of the film was that it "was about the power struggle and dirty tactics in a big business organization" (ibid.).

38 In Malaysia, the prime minister simultaneously holds the position of Minister of Home Affairs, probably to ensure that he maintains knowledge and control over his political allies and enemies since the capacity of the Home Affairs minister includes heading the Special Branch police. In the aftermath of the police brutality towards Anwar Ibrahim, Dr. Mahathir handed this position over to his newly appointed deputy PM, Abdullah Ahmad Badawi.

39 This refers to Meera's funeral scene.

40 Incidentally, the film *Amok* derives from Salleh Ben Joned's novel, *The Amok of Wan Man.*

41 Adapted from the Barbra Streisand/Kris Kristofferson movie *A Star Is Born* (1976).

42 Examples include programs like *Identiti, The City of the Rich* (a kind of Malay *Dallas* in the English language), and *Tiara Point* (about the dwellers in a condominium).

43 See Karim Raslan's short stories "Go East!" and "Sara and the Wedding" in *Heroes and Other Short Stories,* and Jit Murad's 1993 play *Goldrain and Hailstones,* which was so popular that it had a second run in July 1998.

44 While these plays may feature the topic of sexuality, they are not allowed to be graphically erotic. Professor Soleha referred to Ramona Rahman being banned from the stage for two years because of what local theatre-folk called "the kiss," a scene where she locked lips with a man in *A Streetcar Named Desire.* Yet Ramona's return to stage continued a trend of risqué sexy performances as she starred in a one-act play written by Sabera Shaik where, according to Soleha, she made love (masturbated?) to a tree on stage.

45 This reflects the filmmaker's cynicism about the influence of money and power over the judiciary system in Malaysia. While it may be purely coincidental, at the time the film came out there was a case of statutory rape where the young victim was penalized for her sexual history and the chief minister involved, Thamby Cik, got off lightly. In *Ringgit Kasorrga,* Deanna's character together with the male love interest, Hans Isaac, attempt to expose Meera's murderer but the politician appeals to Deanna not to shame his family by turning in the videotapes of his and other high-powered men's sexual affairs. In the end, Deanna decides to destroy the taped evidence because she does not believe it would incriminate the politician. Instead, she considers that the families of those models/prostitutes would be humiliated. This ending would be considered evasive if it had not reflected Malaysian reality so accurately.

46 Sexual pleasure is conveyed in the scene in which Sofia Jane is fanning air into her sarong; she seems to be playing to the male peeping tom, Tapa, and to the voyeuristic film spectators. There's also the scene of Ramona Rahman having what appears to be an orgasm in *Amok.*

47 A 1990 feature written by a woman writer and journalist, Adibah Amin. I have translated *hati* as heart but it literally means liver, the seat of Malay passion.

48 Another example is the widely acclaimed film *Sayang Salmah.* Salmah, the young, materialistic, vain wife of Salleh, rejects Salleh's older schizophrenic brother, Hassan. When she neglects to feed him one day, he breaks out of his cage and enters the house. She provokes him by beating him and, frightened, he pushes her away, knocking her out. As a result, Salleh sends him away to Tanjung Rambutan, a mental institution. In the last five minutes of the film, Salleh narrates in a voice-over that Salmah has finally accepted Hassan, eight years later. There is a family reunion as Salleh brings his wife and daughter to visit Hassan and Salmah feeds her brother-in-law. In between the scene where Hassan is taken away and the reunion scene lies a huge temporal and psychological gap that is left unexplained. Salmah's sudden change of heart is questionable, given the fact that she has been portrayed negatively throughout the narrative.

49 The ninth challenge facing the nation in the attempt to attain fully developed status as outlined by Mahathir is: "Establishing a prosperous society, with an economy that is fully competitive, dynamic, robust and resilient" (Zaharom 1994, 180).

50 At one point, Sofiah displays anger towards her husband/stepfather's possessiveness by lashing out at him for holding her back. She complains of being fed up with living in a broken-down, smelly shack with him after having been exposed to Ariff's wealthy surroundings.

51 Erma Fatima's desire to promote women as strong, independent, courageous, and as nationalist if not more nationalist than her male peers in *Embun* (2002) is problematic in its rewriting of national history. In highlighting the oppression of the Malay woman during the Japanese occupation (Embun is gang-raped by Japanese soldiers), she also minimizes and erases the worse and real suffering experienced by the ethnic Chinese at the hands of the Japanese, none of which is reflected in her film. In fact, the original scriptwriter, Rohiman Haroon, informed me that in his research, he never found any rapes committed by the Japanese against Malay women during that time (personal interview, Taman Jaya, 13 October 2003). Erma also places her heroine Embun in harm's way by setting up an impossibly idyllic scene where Embun and the other young women are bathing by a stream, an activity that most critics claimed would not have occurred during the brutal Japanese occupation. Perhaps this film of Erma testifies clearly that reclaiming adat is a gesture still trapped within the Cinema of Denial, a fantasy that she seems unable to traverse.

52 The Malay Land Act was part of British colonial policy in their strategy of dividing and conquering the various races and it was meant to keep land in the hands of the Malays. What *Layar Lara* suggests is that under the present government, which inherited and kept the act, it is Malay capitalists rather than other ethnic groups who are oppressing (*menganiayai*) fellow Malays by trying to buy off their heritage and uprooting them. The word *akar umbi*, which roughly translates as "roots," is used in the dialogue.

53 The number of Astro channels has since increased.

54 The initial instalment of Astro vision costs more than RM$1,000. The monthly bill is quite high too. At least this is my opinion after speaking to two women watching a Hong Kong serial on Astro. They believed that the Hong Kong actress had "better makeup" compared to the Malaysian actress in the locally shot Cantonese serial. One of the women thought that the Hong Kong actress was also more talented. Not being a Cantonese speaker, I asked them if they could identify any differences between the two actresses when they spoke Cantonese, to which they replied that Hong Kongers spoke a purer Cantonese. From this, I assume that Mandarin speakers would also consider Taiwanese Mandarin as somehow more pure.

55 Iranian filmmakers face five levels of censorship throughout the entire process, from script approval, shooting, and editing to exhibition. Moreover, all female actors can only be shown wearing the *hejab*, or headscarf.

56 Independent filmmaker Yasmin Ahmad's interracial teen romance *Sepet* (2004) sparked comments in Parliament. Member of Parliament Dr. Wan Hasim Wan Teh was quoted as saying that "the love story between a Chinese boy and a Malay girl is 'nothing great' and does not reflect the national identity." Moreover, he objected to the multilingual script, calling it "rojak language" (31 March 2005, http://www.memyselfnchris.blogspot.com/). This goes to show that the issue of Malay/sian ethnic/national identity continues to play a role in the local film industry.

CHAPTER 5: REPRESENTATIONS OF THE MODERN MALAY WOMAN OF THE 1990S

1 I am indebted to Aihwa Ong's definitions of Asian alternative modernity in her essay "Chinese Modernities: Narratives of Nation and of Capitalism" (1997, 194-96).

2 Stivens uses "postmodernity" to suggest non-European alterity but I am more interested in Jürgen Habermas's idea that the project of modernity is unfinished; therefore, I want to extend the term "modernity" to encompass postmodernity as well. In addition, Anthony Giddens's notion of "the reflexivity of modernity" – its accounting for radical doubt and the tendency towards self-deconstruction – factors postmodernity into modernity, which is the space wherein I wish to dwell for this discussion.

3 Between 1994 and 1995, *boh sia* was given substantial media coverage. Literally meaning "no noise" in Hokkien, it refers to teenage girls silently soliciting sex from male strangers outside shopping complexes and casually exchanging minor sexual favours for money or thrills. *Boh sia* is not race-specific. The girls are generally believed to be motivated by thrills and possibly by peer pressure. Most of the articles written about *boh sia* speculated and moralized about parenting, sex education, and the general state of social morass in modern Malaysian society. In an interview with some sixteen-year-old girls, journalist Marina Mahathir was told by one of them that her friend did it not for fun but out of "revenge" because she had been raped by her own father (Marina 1997, 129).

4 The term *postmodern* can of course be readily applied to any cosmopolitan city in the developing world in this period of late capitalism because it captures the mixture of old and new, and East and West in its combination of cultures, diverse ethnic migrants, and populations, as well as in its architecture. But as I am drawing from Stivens's hypothetical statement about how resurgent Islam operates on gender, producing either a kind of non-European modernity or postmodernity, I shall keep to her definitions and limits of postmodernity. As for "neo-modernity," Stivens conceptualizes the first wave of modernity in Malaysia as occurring during the British colonial period. Therefore, the NEP, its processes, and results in a new Malay middle class in the 1980s, is, for her, a neo-modern phase (1998, 111, 117).

5 When Malaysian feminist theorists use the term *postmodern*, they generally mean poststructuralism or, more specifically, deconstruction. This is not to say that Maznah is ignorant of the fact that Western feminism emerged out of a specifically *male*, universalist, and humanist discourse that had excluded women in the past.

6 If the inclusion of radical doubt makes this sound like a description of postmodernity, it would more closely resemble the Lyotardian concept of postmodernity where the "post-" means reflecting, analyzing, and remembering the more avant-garde and critical aspects of modernity. I do not intend to move into a discussion of postmodernity but merely to demonstrate the expansive and incorporationist dimensions of Giddens's and Habermas's theories of modernity.

7 Resurgent Islam is usually construed as fundamentalist and therefore, "anti-modernist, anti-secularist" (Baykan 1990, 136) and "premodern" (Maznah 1994, 122). Although Islam, especially in its fundamentalist forms, contains irrational elements that make it "anti-modernist," its resurgence or revival in Malaysia is a contemporary or modern occurrence and therefore considered to be part of the dialectics of modernity. To explore the many forms and various ideological positions resurgent Islamic groups have taken in Malaysia, see Jomo and Ahmad, "Malaysia's Islamic Movements" (1992) and Judith Nagata, "How to Be Islamic without Being an Islamic State" (1994).

8 Shamsul Amri Baharuddin also mentions that the *dakwah* (proselytizing) movement in Malaysia is "an attempt to resolve how to live in a world of radical doubt" (1995, 113).

9 Giddens's model of the four dimensions of globalization seems limiting. By assuming that nation-states are "actors jealous of their territorial rights, concerned with the fostering of national cultures" (1994, 186), he makes nation-states into whole and unified subjects. He glides over the fact that there are cultural schisms within national boundaries that prove the national subject is not unified. Moreover, although Giddens mentions that "cultural globalization" is a fundamental aspect of globalization lying behind the four dimensions he discusses, he focuses mostly on the political and economic impact rather than the cultural (though in *Modernity and Self-Identity*, he focuses more on the psychology of the individual coping with marriage, divorce, etc.). This is why I have incorporated Habermas's notion of "cultural modernity," though I am aware that it has come under fire from poststructuralists who accuse him of not recognizing the split subject and for ignoring non-European alterity.

10 C.J. Wan-Ling Wee accuses Samuel Huntingdon of neo-orientalism in his dichotomy of West and non-West, which suggests that Asian cultures are unchanging: "A so-called throwback to religious 'medievalism,' as we know in Singapore and Malaysia, with the reinscription of Malay-Muslim culture, is itself a *modern* reaction to the rapidity of change that thirty-odd years of post-independence

development have wrought, a reaction that may be similar to the interest in the primitive and the archaic we see in parts of the West" (1996, 216).

11 E-mail communication, 7 August 1997. Stivens mentions polygamy in her 1994 essay but downplays it. Rohana, writing in response to my queries only three years later, claims that polygamy is "quite common and the state religious department is trying to make it easier [to be practised]." While the actual polygamy rate for Muslim marriages is only 1-3 percent (Stivens 1994), the threat of male polygamy is constantly present in the Malay woman's mind (Stivens 1998, 102; 2000, 27). Rohana's work at the Women's Crisis Centre in Penang with "common" Muslim women such as factory workers and housewives whose husbands neglect them and their children at the expense of their second wives, or violently abuse them because they will not agree to the men's taking a second wife, seems to contradict the deceptively small figure. Wazir Jahan Karim explains that the Muslim Family and Marriage Bill for the Federal Territory of Kuala Lumpur, passed in February 1984, attempts to integrate polygamy with Islamic fundamentalism by removing the requirement of written consent from the first wife. It also "suggests that economic wealth should be the deciding factor for polygyny, subject to validation from the Syariah Court. In urban areas it can only succeed in becoming an added prestige item for successful bureaucrats and entrepreneurs, creating a parallel situation of polygyny amongst rural elites" (Wazir 1992, 25n1). Wazir uses the term "polygyny" instead of polygamy to emphasize the patriarchal bias of Islam that encourages men, and not women, to be polygamous.

12 Karim Raslan was educated at Cambridge and Dina Zaman at Western Michigan University. But many of those who follow some resurgent Islamic group or another, whether it is ABIM (Islamic Youth Movement of Malaysia) or Darul Arqam, have also been educated overseas or are graduates from local universities. For example, Shahnon Ahmad, a Malay writer whose works have become more religious over the years, and who was a member of Al Arqam, worked and studied at the Australian National University in Canberra from 1968 to 1972.

13 A sign of mainstream success and acceptability is to be published by Times Books International, a major publisher of local talents writing in English. In addition, many of the first set of books published by Rhino Press in English also deal with questions of female sexuality.

14 "Isteri yang derhaka adalah isteri yang lebih tinggi pelajarannya dari suaminya."

15 "Muja Semangat" is her grandfather's name for what I think is the spirit-cleansing ritual in Trengganu called "Puja Pantai." Wazir cites *puja pantai* as one of the many examples of adat (1992, 23).

16 It is difficult to guess the man's ethnicity or nationality. He was wearing a black leather jacket and jeans and had dark hair, but one might assume he is a Zionist.

17 Although, as Jacqueline Levitin points out, individual acts of terrorism are more likely to be employed by the oppressed group than by the hegemonic power, the Israelis. The portrayal of the ever-present anti-Palestinian threat in the film suggests an anti-Zionist reading of the text, which potentially troubles Shuhaimi Baba's moderate progressive position on fundamentalism of all types. Thus, even the secular Islam that is represented by the Malaysian "modern" community in *Selubung* is compromised by Israeli-bashing, which is a mere reversal of the Manichean binary.

18 Shuhaimi's choice of adat signifiers are rather superficial: "Compared to U-Wei, Shuhaimi's depiction of Malay culture is thought to be a little 'touristy' while U-Wei indulges in it more deeply" (Fuziah and Raja Ahmad 1995, 68). In personal communication, film critic Hassan Muthalib also articulated this point, stating that U-Wei's films reflect his deep knowledge of Malay culture, whereas Shuhaimi Baba's portrayal of kampung culture or adat is rather superficial. This is unsurprising if her portrayal is based on her own urban perceptions of the kampung (Kuala Lampur, 2003).

19 In a personal interview on 31 July 1998, Shuhaimi Baba explained that the idea of the lucky flying moths was not derived from any specific local belief. She discovered this existing superstition that moths were lucky only after she had written the scenes. Hence, it is entirely possible that the process of reclaiming adat entails the construction of new myths along the way, even as it taps into something more archetypal or atavistic.

20 It is "natural" in the eyes of patriarchal Islam, which sees polygamy as the answer to "men's allegedly unbridled lust" (Ong 1995, 185). Ungku Maimunah's essay on the ideal modern Malay woman shows how the woman adapts to modernity while retaining certain traditional patriarchal notions of Eastern femininity. There is no mention, however, of Malay men adapting to modernity or whether and how modernity has affected their gendered social roles. See Chapter 6 for Erma Fatima's perspective on modern male roles in the teledrama *Ku Kejar Kau Lari.*

21 Hari Raya is a national holiday in Malaysia celebrated by Muslims (and their non-Muslim friends) after the month of Ramadan. The semantics of the *baju kurung*, the appropriate apparel for Muslim women in Malaysia, suggests that blaming the West and Western lifestyles reveals the male fear of female sexuality and independence that threatens the traditional gender hierarchy in Muslim societies.

The verb *kurung* means "to imprison" or "to cage" but unlike the more tight-fitting *baju kebaya*, which is what the *baju kurung* replaced by the time of the Islamic resurgence, the *baju kurung* affords more physical movement and inspires less self-consciousness about one's body. Therefore, what the *baju kurung* cages or hampers is not the woman's physical movement but her sexuality, which the *baju kebaya* emphasizes by hugging her contours. On that note, it would seem that even the naming of the *baju kurung* is consistent with patriarchal bias!

22 The original title of the film was *Perempuan, Isteri dan Jalang* but the last word, *jalang*, was cut from the title when feminists complained about the negative stereotyping of women. The scene from the film showing the woman squatting over her husband's bowl of rice (a magic charm to ensure her husband's fidelity) is also cut from the final version because it was deemed unIslamic (another example of official Islamic discourse repressing adat).

23 Incidentally, A. Samad Said is one of those high-profile polygamous writers to whom Stivens might be referring. Wong Soak Koon (1996, 53)has criticized his portrayal of the title character in *Salina* for lacking inner life and perpetuating the stereotyped nurturing woman.

24 The Fourth World Conference on Women in Beijing faced similar tensions between Western and non-Western women. In the following statement, the binary is couched as "North vs. South": "Some Southern governments are concerned that certain values that have recently become part of Western culture might be promoted as universal values or rights in the final official document." The most serious contention was over sexual preference and lesbian rights (Khor 1995, 23).

25 To retain the local flavour of the Malay language, Dina has not translated some of the words that have nothing to do with sex. The *Kacang puteh* and *assam* woman sells roasted nuts and tamarind, among other candied fruits.

26 I specify "heterosexual" because the story includes the figure of a *pondan* or transvestite who is literally left out in the rain when the woman picks up the male prostitute. This indicates the recognition of alternative sexualities within Malay society, which are, nonetheless, marginalized.

27 Both Alissa in "The Beloved" and Sara in "Sara and the Wedding" are lawyers. Of course, there is the possibility of reading these all-too-perfect female figures as male fantasies, but their strength and capabilities are heightened by the weaknesses of the men surrounding them, perhaps implying a subtle critique of Malay masculinity.

28 It is widely believed that in traditional Kelantanese society, women have more financial power and are more independent. This can be seen in the fact that it is mostly women who conduct business at the outdoor markets. However, the gradual Islamicization of the state of Kelantan may have reduced women's power somewhat.

29 Dina Zaman, e-mail, 24 April 1997. Wazir Jahan Karim discusses Malay women's political role in the early nationalist movement in Chapter 4 of her book.

30 Arguably there are Eurasians and other ethnic groups whose main if not sole language may be English but they are small minorities that do not threaten Malay cultural hegemony. If anything, Malayness is more often positioned against Chineseness than against any other ethnicity.

31 The prime minister's criticism appeared in "Dr. M and Daughter Slam Muslim Hypocrites," *Southeast Asia Post*, 23 July-6 August 1997, 5.

32 The earlier article was "Anwar Calls for Moderation in Muslim Mayhem," *Southeast Asia Post*, 10-23 July 1997, 5.

33 Her comments appeared in the same article as her father's criticism, "Dr. M and Daughter Slam Muslim Hypocrites," 5.

CHAPTER 6: WHAT IS IT TO BE A MAN?

1 Personal interviews at FINAS office, Malaysia, July and August 1996.

2 "Kami tidak mahu jadi lelaki. Apa yang kami mahukan ialah dilayan sama rata. Dan dihormati. Kita rakyat Malaysia amat beruntung kerana diberi peluang untul belajar dari kesilapan mereka di barat sebelum sampai peringkat yang boleh merosakkan." Then, deferring to Pyan, she says, "Kita hidup melandaskan tradisi. Tradisi tertulis. Lelaki diamanahkan untuk membela dan menampung wanita. Dan tanggungjawab itu terletak di atas bahu tuan terhadap isteri, ibu, anak, adik serta sekalian wanita yang perlu perhatian. Tolak ansur perlu wujud antara kita. Kami amat perlukan para lelaki untuk membela dan menampung. Kami wanita. Untuk tradisi. Tradisi yang baik perlu dipupuk. Untuk kita dan generasi akan datang." What has to be clarified is her deference to Pyan when she calls him "tuan" which is a term of address/respect, meaning "sir" or "master" and conveys hierarchical difference.

3 Though I do not discuss the figure of the female shopper in Malaysian literature in this chapter, there are clear examples of a critique of women as conspicuous consumers in Karim Raslan's short stories "Neighbours" and "Sara and the Wedding." For more anthropological information on Malay middle-class women and consumerism, see Stivens (1998).

4 Malaysian anthropologist Shanti Thambiah notes that modernity has brought patriarchal values to more egalitarian societies like the indigenous Iban in Sarawak. She explains their belief that because both male and female principles are embodied in the effeminate man or *pondan*, he makes a powerful shaman (religious and cultural leader) in the community (personal interview, 24 June 1998). This is in line with the widely held idea that traditionally, Southeast Asian societies are more tolerant of sexually and gender-transgressive behaviours than Western societies.

5 The *keris* is symbolic of male honour and manhood and has anthropomorphic qualities (Razha 1990, 81). It is also explicitly phallic (Kenny 1990, 135).

6 This patriarchal notion is compounded in the film *Femina* by Tina's definitive pronouncements as she looks at Pyan, Eman Manan's character.

7 While I am aware of the problems in comparing two different types of medium (film and television), I find the comparison justified in the interest of exploring the discursive possibilities of modern gender configurations as played by Nasir Bilal Khan. The film industry is so small and unprofitable that most professional actors find more consistent employment in television. Moreover, many Malaysian viewers also assume that the films will eventually air on television and therefore do not go to cinemas to watch Malay films. Nasir has received awards for best male television drama actor (Anugerah Bintang Popular of 1996 and 1997/98).

8 Berry mentions how the kind of "macho" character appearing in mainland Chinese films like *Red Sorghum* had already been prefigured in popular genres like *kung fu* and crime movies since the early 1980s.

9 A 1995 study of trends of Malaysian cinema goers concludes that the most popular genres are romances and comedies, with love being the major theme. The study also shows that audiences are attracted to action films, which presumably include scenes of violence, though the researchers say that the Malaysian films are less violent than those from Hollywood or Hong Kong (Bukhory, Amelia, and Ch'ng 1995).

10 Bukhory, Amelia, and Ch'ng also conclude that men frequent the cinemas more than women (1995, 103). This was confirmed by personal observation during research in June-July 1998. Because the local film industry is by and large a male domain, viewers should keep in mind that the representation of femininity and the conception of the film plots are mostly male projections.

11 It's interesting to read the *Pemburu Bayang* poster semiotically. The two rock stars Awie and Ella stand back-to-back in the centre, their hands locked together. As the main attraction, their names do not even appear on the poster because they are so well-known to Malaysian audiences. As secondary characters, Shaharuddin's name and the name of the actress who plays his wife, Erma Fatima, appear at the top left-hand corner. His face and Erma's seem to jut out from Ella and Awie's central position in the poster, as if proving visually that their roles are tangential to the central plot.

12 I am specifically excluding comic, child, and veteran actors.

13 Shuhaimi Baba tells an anecdote about a young man auditioning for her film *Layar Lara* in which he fully impersonates Awie's role in *Sembilu* to the extent of recreating the echoes and other sound effects. Most of the young men who came to audition chose to play Awie. Cashing in on Awie's popularity, *Sembilu*'s plot was loosely based on Awie's real-life romance and Awie basically played himself, rather than a genuinely fictitious character.

14 For example, in the 1980s, teen heartthrobs and pop singers Jamal Abdillah and Sudirman also appeared in films, Jamal being the more successful.

15 Refer to filmography for plot outlines.

16 When he refuses to kill the daughter of one of his father's enemies, having fallen in love with her, his eldest brother Safuan challenges him to fight to defend his new loyalty to her, a challenge that he accepts.

17 Mat Kilau rebelled against the British during the British colonial period. Razha Rashid explains how cases of amok/hypermasculinity may be justified: "In the Malay Archipelago, eruptions of violence through the *silat* form in persons or groups as in amok, *perang sabil*, and riots ... are manifested when underlying sentiments of honour, social justice, patriotism, and ethnicity become visibly threatened or disrupted. In these situations, the emotive relationship of a man with his keris (dagger) is dramatically reinforced through anthropomorphisms of *silat* weaponry. At this level, violence is explained in terms of involuntary acts of aggression upon the enemy and consequently is justified" (1990, 64).

18 My translation. The reference to the Japanese slippers is filled with irony as Malaysians equate the term "Japanese slippers" with cheap rubber thongs rather than the slippers worn during Japanese cultural performances. This scene also makes an intertextual reference to a Hindi film.

19 Haji Shahban, their father and patriot, was the head of Melati Holdings. He found out that the other four directors of the board were involved in money politics. He threatened to report them to the prime minister but was blackmailed with nude photographs of his wife taken many years ago when she was working as a nanny and regular model for a British colonial whose hobby was photography. Haji Shahban died from a heart attack after seeing the photos.

20 He is on the run from the police and is on a ship sailing away. The gift of the *badik* signifies their close relationship (one of loyalty and constant attention) where the *badik* becomes a phallic substitute for him (see Razha 1990, 81).

21 I am unable to make a definitive statement about what other potential acts male hysteria could lead to. My assumption is that one could either be stuck in male hysteria and be functionless in this schema, or one could respond in violence. This is formulated against an ideal "ordinary" and "stable" form of masculinity that would presumably not lapse into hysteria or violence.

22 In Malay culture, the responsibility for an unmarried woman falls on her father and on her brother if the father is not around.

23 Names of the authentic masculine figure are significant. Here, Johan means champion. Later, both Eman and Nasir Bilal Khan play men named Amir, which means ruler.

24 The representation comes from a Chinese Malaysian male perspective which, in line with a moderate pro-multiracial policy, supports the central position Malays occupy in state politics and power. At the same time, the patriarchal bias inherent in the concept of nationalism remains intact, regardless of the ethnicized point of view.

25 "Bumi ini bukan milik kami sahaja bahkan milik semua penduduk tetap di negara ini."

26 Bruno Manser championed the rights of the Penans against government logging of the rainforest in Sarawak, pointing out that aside from destroying the group's way of life, the benefits of logging went into the pockets of politicians and their Chinese timber merchant connections rather than going into the coffers of the state. The Penans blocked logging roads, and Manser brought international media attention to their plight. The Malaysian government employed an anti-Western, Third World rhetoric and painted all environmentalists as tools of envious Western powers who were hostile towards Third World development and the potential competition they offer to the already wealthy, decadent West. While it is tempting to draw racial similarities between the scriptwriter and the timber merchants, the more pertinent observation is that Malay films written, conceived, or financed by Chinese Malaysians tend to emphasize racial harmony among the ethnic groups in Malaysia. There is usually a plea for inclusion of non-Malays and an attempt to demonstrate that they have a place within the imagined community, as long as they're not challenging Malay hegemony. Sometimes this desire to be included manifests itself in the form of glossing over oppressions against other minorities in the nation. To this end, oppression is channelled against the foreign national or colonizer, whose outsider status reinforces the insiderness of the non-Malay. See also *Red-Haired Tumbler,* which stars Mandarin singer Elaine Kang, whose character marries a kind Malay rubber merchant. Together, they expose Patrick, the greedy American capitalist.

27 Their plan is to spray a chemical virus (VX2000) that can destroy the quality of the wood without showing any signs on the trees.

28 Judging by the Anugerah Bintang Popular (Popular Star Award) poll conducted by the Malay daily newspaper *Berita Harian*, Eman's popularity as a film and television actor peaked between 1992 and 1993. The mid-1990s popularity polls were dominated by the likes of music-turned-film stars like Awie, the KRU boys, etc. Since 1997, Rosyam Nor's name has appeared almost annually in the Anugerah Bintang Popular. Unlike Eman and Nasir Bilal Khan, he has continued to get leading male roles, though none as "hard-bodied" as *Lenjan*'s Zarin.

29 Since I am dealing only with physical body types the figure of the NEP Malay entrepreneur is not considered another physical body type.

30 Nearly all the sentences in their dialogue with each other begin or end with the endearment "sayang" or "love," making the first hour of the film insipid and saccharine.

31 The cultural origin of the sword is unknown. We see it hanging on the wall as a potential weapon only.

32 Her libidinal desires here are sexual, materialistic, and uncontrolled and uncontrollable by men.

33 *Sayang Salmah* and *Perempuan, Isteri Dan ...?* being a few contemporary examples. According to Malay custom, while "passion" and "reason" are present in all humans, "'passion' is present in greater concentrations (or is more pronounced) among women, whereas 'reason' is less so. These latter contentions, which are part of the official discourse on gender, and which are clearly hegemonic (in Raymond Williams's sense of the term), focus on the culturally elaborated perception that women are less controlled and restrained than men insofar as they are more prone to gossiping *and desiring material possessions*, and are otherwise more closely tied to the 'baser' things in life" (Peletz 1995, 93, emphasis mine). Yet in everyday practice, Malay women manage household budgets and even family finances.

34 The Gap, an American retail-clothing store, carries yuppie casuals such as khakis and blue denim shirts. The couple also sports high-top hiking boots, which are in vogue for the outdoorsy elite in Malaysia. There are Gap stores in Malaysia and their items, though not exactly designer wear, are considered prestige items among the younger middle-class crowd.

35 He consistently points at her with his index finger instead of his thumb, a rude gesture in polite Malay society.

36 This is not a discriminatory comment about his class. Rather, I am pointing out that he is an anomaly in a culture usually considered to be polite, gracious, gentle, and non-confrontational.

37 Sofia Jane is fair complexioned and of mixed parentage, but this is not significant because female physical types found in film are usually fair-skinned, slim, young, and attractive.

38 "Ini kita perempuan asyik duduk di rumah saja."

39 Malay cinema usually encodes a woman who smokes as a prostitute or, at least, as someone aspiring to have the same privileges as men.

40 He warns her after they get married that despite her official status as legal wife, it does not change his feelings towards her: "Although we are married, you are still dirty and don't think you are now clean" (my translation). His murder of her first husband is treated as almost incidental – the murder scene does not recur in flashbacks and there is no discussion or internal reflection about it by any of the characters.

41 For more about latah and gender, see Winzeler (1995).

42 Khoo Boo Teik explains: "Mahathir's anti-Westernism did not derive from earlier radical critiques of the capitalist origins, impulses, and structures of Western imperialism and the global pattern of dominance and dependence. He was not an anti-capitalist but a capitalist" (1995, 64).

43 A constant phrase that highlights the anthropomorphism of the *keris* (Razha 1990, 81).

44 *Maksiat* implies acts of sexual transgression such as adultery, premarital sex, and prostitution.

References

Note: Out of respect for preferred Malay cultural norms, most Malay names are ordered by given name first followed by surname. For easy reference, Malay names listed below will follow the first name given in the chapter references.

A. Bakar Hamid, ed. 1979. *Peristiwa-peristiwa dari hikayat Hang Tuah* (Events from the epic of Hang Tuah). Kuala Lumpur: Dewan Bahasa dan Pustaka.

Abdul Rahman Napiah. 1994. *Tuah-Jebat dalam drama Melayu: Satu kajian intertekstualiti* (Tuah-Jebat in Malay drama: An intertextual analysis). Kuala Lumpur: Dewan Bahasa dan Pustaka.

Abdul Samad Said. 1961. *Salina.* Kuala Lumpur: Dewan Bahasa dan Pustaka.

Abrams, Meyer Howard. 1988. *A glossary of literary terms.* 5th ed. New York: Harcourt Brace Jovanovich.

Ahmad Faiz bin Abdul Rahman. 1998. Rethinking Jebat. *Afaiz Column,* 29 October. http://ireland.iol.ie/~afifi/BICNews/Afaiz/afaiz34.htm/.

Ahmad Fauzi. 1999. Millennium memoirs – The end of Malay film's golden era. *New Straits Times,* 25 November, lifestyle section, 4-5.

Alatas, Syed Hussein. 1972. *Modernization and social change: Studies in modernization, religion, social change and development in south-east Asia.* Sydney: Angus and Robinson.

Al-Attas, Suraya. 1996. Malay films make their mark again. *New Straits Times,* 31 August, sec. 2, 15.

—. 2002. Amir gives his best shorts. *New Straits Times* 13 July. http://6horts.tripod.com/.

Ali Aziz. 1960. *Hang Jebat Menderhaka (Satu lakonan tiga babak)* (The betrayal of Hang Jebat [A play in three acts]). Singapore: Malaya Publishing.

Althusser, Louis. 1994. Ideology and ideological state apparatuses (Notes towards an investigation). In *Mapping Ideology,* ed. Slavoj Žižek, 100-40. London: Verso.

Amir Muhammad. 1999. Raising a stink. *Asiaweek,* 7 May. http://www.asiaweek.com/asiaweek/99/0507/feat1.html/.

Amir Muhammad, Kam Raslan, and Sheryll Stothard. 1998. *Generation: A collection of contemporary Malaysian ideas.* Kuala Lumpur: Hikayat.

Amoroso, Donna J. 2003. Making sense of Malaysia. *Kyoto Review of Southeast Asia* 1, 3 (March). http://kyotoreview.cseas.kyoto-u.ac.jp/issue/issueo/index.html.

Anderson, Benedict. 1972. The idea of power in Javanese culture. In *Culture and politics in Indonesia,* ed. Claire Holt, Benedict Anderson, and James Siegel, 1-70. Ithaca: Cornell UP.

—. 1991. *Imagined communities.* London: Verso.

Anwar Ibrahim. 1996. *The Asian renaissance.* Singapore: Times Books International.

—. 1998a. From the halls of power to the labyrinths of incarceration. http://www.freeanwar.net/news/labyrinths_incarceration.html.

—. 1998b. The real business for APEC. *The Asian Wall Street Journal,* 18 November.

Appadurai, Arjun. 1996. *Modernity at large: Cultural dimensions of globalization.* Minneapolis: University of Minnesota Press.

Aveling, Harry. 1996. Claiming Islam: The religious dimensions of Shahnon Ahmad's novel *Al-Syiqaq.* In *Crossing cultures: Essays on literature and culture of the Asia-Pacific,* ed. Bruce Bennett, Jeff Doyle, and Satendra Nandan, 215-24. London: Skoob.

Azmi, Raja. 1992. *Black widow.* Kuala Lumpur: Creative Enterprise, 1992.

Badriyah Haji Salleh. 1993. Amuk: Implikasinya dalam masyarakat Melayu tradisional (Amuk: Its implications in traditional Malay society). In *Kekerasan dalam sejarah* (Violence in History), ed. Qasim Ahmad, 19-36. Kuala Lumpur: Dewan Bahasa dan Pustaka.

Baharudin Latif. 1983. *Krisis filem Melayu* (Malay film crisis). Kuala Lumpur: Insular.

Banks, David J. 1987. *From class to culture: Social conscience in Malay novels since independence.* New Haven, CT: Yale University Southeast Asia Studies.

Baykan, Aysegul. 1990. Women between fundamentalism and modernity. In *Theories of modernity and postmodernity*, ed. Bryan S. Turner, 136-46. London: Sage.

Benjamin, Walter. 1970. The storyteller. In *Illuminations*, trans. Harry Zohn, 83-109. London: Cape.

Berry, Chris. 1994. Neither one thing nor another: Towards a study of the viewing subject and Chinese cinema in the 1980s. In *New Chinese cinemas*, ed. Vivian Sobchack, Nick Browne, Paul Pickovicz, and Esther Yau, 88-113. Cambridge: Cambridge University Press.

Bhabha, Homi. 1994. DissemiNation: Time, narrative, and the margins of the modern nation. In *Nation and narration*, ed. Homi Bhabha, 291-322. London: Routledge.

—. 1995. *The location of culture.* New York: Routledge.

Bukhory Haji Ismail, Amelia Abd. Aziz, and Monica Ch'ng. 1995. *Trend penontonan filem di Malaysia* (Trends of Malaysian film audiences). Kuala Lumpur: FINAS and ITM.

Burton, Julianne. 1985. Marginal cinemas and mainstream critical theory. *Screen* 26, 3-4: 2-21.

Butler, Judith. 1990. *Gender trouble: Feminism and the subversion of identity.* New York: Routledge.

Camus, Albert. 1955. *The myth of Sisyphus and other essays.* Trans. Justin O'Brien. London: Hamish Hamilton.

Chandra Muzaffar. 1979. *Protector? An analysis of the concept and practice of loyalty in leader-led relationships within Malay society.* Penang, Malaysia: Aliran.

—. 1989. *Challenges and choices in Malaysian politics and society.* Penang: Aliran.

Chatterjee, Partha. 1996. Whose imagined community? In *Mapping the nation*, ed. Gopal Balakrishnan, 214-25. London: Verso and New Left Review.

Cheah, Boon Kheng. 2002. *Malaysia: The making of a nation.* Singapore: ISEAS.

Cheah, Pheng, and Bruce Robbins, eds. 1998. *Cosmopolitics: Thinking and feeling beyond the nation.* Minneapolis: University of Minnesota Press.

Chelvi, K.T. 1996. Lights, camera but little action. *Sun Megazine,* 23 May: 3.

Chow, Rey. 1995. *Primitive passions: Visuality, sexuality, ethnography, and contemporary Chinese cinema.* New York: Columbia University Press.

Conference in Chaos. 1996. *Aliran Monthly* 16, 9: 14.

Crouch, Harold. 1992. Authoritarian trends, the UMNO split and the limits to state power. In *Fragmented vision*, ed. Joel Kahn and Francis Loh Kok Wah, 21-43. Honolulu: University of Hawaii Press.

Denny, Frederick Mathewson. 1985. *An introduction to Islam.* New York: Macmillan.

Dentan, Robert Knox, Kirk Endicott, Alberto G. Gomes, and M.B. Hooker. 1997. *Malaysia and the original people: A case study of the impact of development on indigeneous peoples.* Toronto: Allyn and Bacon.

D'Entrèves, Maurizio Passerin. 1997. Introduction to *Habermas and the unfinished project of modernity*, ed. Maurizio P. d'Entrèves and Seyla Benhabib, 1-37. Cambridge, MA: MIT Press.

Dina Zaman. 1997. *Night and day.* Petaling Jaya, Malaysia: Rhino Press.

Dinsman. 1979. *Jebat.* In *Bukan bunuh diri* (Not suicide), 27-65. Kuala Lumpur: Dewan Bahasa Dan Pustaka.

Dissanayake, Wimal, ed. 1980. *Colonialism and nationalism in Asian cinema.* Bloomington: Indiana University Press.

Dundes, Alan. 1980. *Interpreting folklore.* Bloomington: Indiana University Press.

Edelman, Lee. 1992. Tearooms and sympathy, or, the epistemology of the water closet. In *Nationalisms and sexualities*, ed. Andrew Parker, Mary Russo, Doris Sommer, and Patricia Yaeger, 263-84. New York: Routledge.

Ee, Richard Cheng Hock. 1980. May 13th riots: An analysis of the causes. BA thesis, National University of Singapore.

Embong, Abdul Rahman. 2001. The culture and practice of pluralism in postcolonial Malaysia. In *The politics of multiculturalism: Pluralism and citizenship in Malaysia, Singapore and Indonesia*, ed. Robert W. Hefner, 59-85. Honolulu: University of Hawaii Press.

Errington, Shelly. 1990. Recasting sex, gender, and theory. In *Power and difference: Gender in island southeast Asia*, ed. Jane M. Atkinson and Shelly Errington, 1-58. Stanford: Stanford University Press.

Esslin, Martin. 1971. *The theatre of the absurd.* Oxford: Oxford University Press.

Fanon, Frantz. 1963. *The wretched of the earth.* New York: Grove.

Fatimah Busu. 1991. Dark night of the soul. In *Fables of Eve*, trans. Harry Aveling, 247-82. Kuala Lumpur: Dewan Bahasa Dan Pustaka.

Felski, Rita. 1995. *The gender of modernity.* Cambridge, MA: Harvard University Press.

FINAS. 1999. *Filem Malaysia 1975-1999* (A Collection of 25 Years' Film Synopses and Production Details). Kuala Lumpur, Malaysia: FINAS.

Fuziah Kartini, and Faridah Ibrahim. 1998. Racun dan penawar: Pertentangan citra wanita dalam filem-filem Melayu 50-an (Poison and antidote: Contrasting images of women in 1950s Malay films). Working paper, Position, images and identity of Malay women during the colonial era seminar, Institute of Malay Civilisation Studies or ATMA, UKM, Bangi, July.

Fuziah Kartini, Hassan Basri, and Raja Ahmad Alauddin. 1995. The search for a Malaysian cinema: Between U-Wei, Shuhaimi, Yusof and LPFM. *Asian Cinema* 7, 2: 58-73.

Gabriel, Teshome. 1982. *Third cinema in the third world.* Ann Arbor, MI: UMI Research Press.

—. 1989. Towards a critical theory of third world films. In *Questions of third cinema*, ed. Jim Pines and Paul Willemen, 30-52. London: British Film Institute Publishing.

Gabrielpillai, Matilda. 1997. Orientalizing Singapore: Psychoanalyzing the discourse of "non-western modernity." PhD diss., University of British Columbia.

Gagliano, Felix V. 1970. *Communal violence in Malaysia 1969: The political aftermath.* Athens, OH: Center for International Studies, Ohio University Press.

Giddens, Anthony. 1991. *Modernity and self-identity: Self and society in the late modern age.* Cambridge: Polity Press.

—. 1994. The consequences of modernity. Excerpt. In *Colonial discourse and post-colonial theory*, ed. Patrick Williams and Laura Chrisman, 181-89. New York: Columbia University Press.

Goh, Cheng Teik. 1971. *The May thirteenth incident and democracy in Malaysia.* Kuala Lumpur: Oxford University Press.

Goh, Daryl, and Steven Patrick. 1999. Mending a broken rice bowl. *The Star* (Malaysia), 22 January, sec. 2.

Gomes, Alberto, ed. 1994. *Modernity and identity: Asian illustrations.* Bundoora, Australia: La Trobe University Press.

Gomez, Edmund Terence. 1990. *Politics in business: UMNO's corporate investments.* Kuala Lumpur: Forum.

—. 1995. The Bakun business: Political rivalry and privatised patronage. *Aliran Monthly* 15, 7: 2-9.

Gray, Gordon T. 2002. Malaysian cinema and negotiations with modernity: Film and anthropology. PhD diss., Napier University.

Guneratne, Anthony R., and Wimal Dissanayake, eds. 2003. *Rethinking third cinema.* New York: Routledge.

Habermas, Jürgen. 1997. Modernity: An unfinished project. In *Habermas and the unfinished project of modernity: Critical essays on the philosophical discourse of modernity*, ed. Maurizio Passerin d'Entrèves and Seyla Benhabib, 38-55. Cambridge, MA: MIT Press.

Hamzah Hussin. 1997. *Memoir Hamzah Hussin. Dari Keris Film ke Studio Merdeka* (Memoir Hamzah Hussin: From Keris Film to Merdeka Studio). Bangi, Selangor, Malaysia: UKM Press.

Hang Nadim. 1998. Umno nazak sedang ditalqinkan (UMNO sounding the death knell). *Harakah*, 26 October. www2.jaring.my/pas.

Hassan Karim. 2000. Apa itu kontrak sosial (What is a social contract). 20 December. http://pemantau.tripod.com/artikel/20Dec_Prm.html/.

Hassan Muthalib, and Wong Tuck Cheong. 2002. Malaysia gentle winds of change. In *Being and becoming: The cinemas of Asia*, ed. Aruna Vasudev, Latika Padgaonkar, Rashmi Doraiswamy, 301-28. New Delhi: Macmillan India.

Hatta Azad Khan. 1984. *Jebat*. In *Drama Tiga Zaman* (Drama from three periods), ed. Zakaria Ariffin, 199-217. Kuala Lumpur: Dewan Bahasa dan Pustaka.

—. 1997. *The Malay cinema*. Bangi, Selangor, Malaysia: UKM Press.

Hooker, Virginia Matheson. 2000. *Writing a new society: Social change through the novel in Malay*. Crows Nest, NSW: Allen and Unwin and University of Hawaii Press.

—. 2003. *A short history of Malaysia: Linking east and west*. Crows Nest, NSW: Allen and Unwin.

Husna Azhari, Che. 1993. *Melor in perspective*. Bangi, Selangor, Malaysia: Furada.

Hussin Mutalib. 1990. *Islam and ethnicity in Malay politics*. Oxford: Oxford University Press.

Jameson, Fredric. 1986. Third world literature in the era of multinational capital. *Social Text* Fall: 65-88.

Jamil Sulong, Hamzah Hussein, and Abdul Malik Mokhtar, eds. 1993. *Daftar filem Melayu (1933-1993)* (Listed Malay films, 1933-1993). Ampang, Selangor: FINAS.

Jayasankaran, S. 1995. Malaysia: Balancing act. *Far Eastern Economic Review*, 21 December, 24-26.

Jeffords, Susan. 1994. *Hard bodies: Hollywood masculinity in the Reagan era*. New Brunswick, NJ: Rutgers University Press.

Jihad Siber. n.d. Hikmah disebalik pemenjaraan DSAI [Anwar Ibrahim]. UMNO dan Islam (The motivation behind the imprisonment of Deputy PM Anwar Ibrahim). http://www.geocities.com/jihadsiber/dsai.htm (link expired).

Jit Murad. 1993. Goldrain and Hailstones. Unpublished. Staged at the Actors Studio, Kuala Lumpur, Malaysia.

Johan Jaafar. 1992. *My city, oh my city*. 1983. In *Protest (Modern Malaysian drama)*, trans. Solehah Ishak, ed. Solehah Ishak, 80-125. Kuala Lumpur: Dewan Bahasa dan Pustaka.

Jomo, Kwame Sundaram. 1986. *A question of class: Capital, the state, and uneven development in Malaya*. New York: Oxford University Press.

—. 1998. Malaysia props up crony capitalism. *Asian Wall Street Journal*, 21 December, 10.

Jomo, K.S., and Ahmad Shabery Cheek. 1992. Malaysia's Islamic movements. In *Fragmented vision*, ed. Joel Kahn and Francis Loh, 79-106. Honolulu: University of Hawaii Press.

Jong, Chian Lai. 1986. Gugurnya langit hijau Nanga Tiga. Kuala Lumpur: Dewan Bahasa dan Pustaka.

Kahn, Joel. 2003. Islam, modernity, and the popular in Malaysia. In *Malaysia: Islam, society and politics*, ed. Virginia Hooker and Norani Othman, 147-66. Singapore: ISEAS.

Kahn, Joel S., and Francis Loh Kok Wah, eds. 1992. *Fragmented vision: Culture and politics in contemporary Malaysia*. Honolulu: University of Hawaii Press.

Kandiyoti, Deniz. 1994. Identity and its discontents: Women and the nation. In *Colonial discourse and post-colonial theory*, ed. Patrick Williams and Laura Chrisman, 376-91. New York: Columbia University Press.

Karim Raslan. 1996a. *Ceritalah: Malaysia in transition*. Singapore: Times Books International.

—. 1996b. *Heroes and other stories*. Singapore: Times Books International.

—. 2002. *Journeys through southeast Asia: Ceritalah2*. Singapore: Times Books International.

Kassim Ahmad. 1967. Dailog. In *Kemarau di lembah* (Drought in the valley), 48. Penang: Sinaran.

—, ed. 1964. *Hikayat Hang Tuah*. Kuala Lumpur: Dewan Bahasa dan Pustaka.

Kee, Thuan Chye. 1987. *1984 here and now*. Including reviews. Petaling Jaya: K. Das Ink.

Kenny, Michael G. 1990. "Latah": The logic of fear. In *Emotions of culture: A Malay perspective*, ed. Wazir Jahan Karim, 123-41. Singapore: Oxford University Press.

Kessler, Clive S. 1992. Archaism and modernity: Contemporary Malay political culture. In *Fragmented vision*, ed. Joel Kahn and Francis Loh Kok Wah, 133-57. Honolulu: University of Hawai'i Press.

Khoo, Boo Teik. 1995. *The paradoxes of Mahathirism: An intellectual biography of Mahathir Mohamad.* Kuala Lumpur: Oxford University Press.

—. 2002. Writing reformasi. *Kyoto Review of Southeast Asia* 1, 1 (March). http://kyotoreview.cseas.kyoto-u.ac.jp/issue/issueo/article_33.html/.

Khoo, Gaik Cheng. 2000. What is it to be a man? Hypermasculinity in contemporary Malaysian cinema. *West Coast Line* 32: 43-60.

—. 2001. Nationalism and homoeroticism: A feminist reading of the Hang Tuah and Hang Jebat debate. In *Risking Malaysia: Culture, Politics, and Identity,* ed. Maznah Mohamad and Wong Soak Koon, 45-72. Bangi, Selangor, Malaysia: UKM Press.

—. 2002a. Shuhaimi Baba and the Malaysian new wave: Negotiating the recuperation of Malay custom/adat. In *Women filmmakers: Refocussing,* ed. Judith Plessis, Jacqueline Levitin, and Valerie Raoul, 229-39. Vancouver: UBC Press.

—. 2002b. Strangers within the (imagined) community: A study of modern Malay identity in U-Wei Haji Saari's *Jogho* and Sabri Zain's *Face Off. RIMA* 36, 2: 81-114.

Khoo, Kay Jin. 1992. The grand vision: Mahathir and modernisation. In *Fragmented vision*, ed. Joel Kahn and Francis Loh Kok Wah, 44-76. Honolulu: University of Hawaii Press.

Khor, Martin. 1995. North-south issues emerge at talks. *The Star* (Malaysia), 5 September, 23.

Kristeva, Julia. 1992. *Powers of horror: An essay on abjection.* Trans. Leon Roudiez. New York: Columbia University Press.

Kueh Siaw Hui, Adeline. 1997. The filmic representations of Malayan women: An analysis of Malayan films from the 1950s and 1960s. MA thesis, Murdoch University.

Laclau, Ernesto, and Chantal Mouffe. 1985. *Hegemony and socialist strategy: Towards a radical democratic politics.* London: Verso.

Lai, Suat Yan. 2003. The women's movement in peninsular Malaysia, 1900-99: A historical analysis. In *Social movements in Malaysia: From moral communities to NGOs,* ed. Meredith L. Weiss and Salisa Hassan, 45-74. London; New York: RoutledgeCurzon.

Lent, John A. 1990. *The Asian film industry.* Austin: University of Texas Press.

Lim, Chong Lim. 2005. The infinite longing for home: Desire and the nation in selected writings of Ben Okri and K.S. Maniam. Amsterdam and New York: Rodopi.

Loh Kok Wah, Francis. 2001. Where has (ethnic) politics gone? The case of the BN non-making politicians and political parties. In *The politics of multiculturalism: Pluralism and citizenship in Malaysia, Singapore, and Indonesia,* ed. Robert W. Hefner, 183-203. Honolulu: University of Hawaii Press.

—. 2002. Developmentalism and the limits of democratic discourse. In *Democracy in Malaysia: Discourses and practices,* ed. Francis Loh Kok Wah and Khoo Boo Teik, 19-50. Richmond, UK: Curzon Press.

Loh Kok Wah, Francis, and Khoo Boo Teik, eds. 2002. *Democracy in Malaysia: Discourses and Practices.* Richmond, UK: Curzon Press, 2002.

Mahathir Mohamad. 1970. *The Malay dilemma.* Singapore: Times Books International, 1994.

—. 1986. *The Challenge.* Petaling Jaya: Pelanduk Publications.

—. 1991. *Malaysia: The way forward.* Kuala Lumpur, Malaysia: Malaysian Business Council.

Malhi, Amrita. 2003. The PAS-BN conflict in the 1990s: Islamism and modernity. In *Malaysia: Islam, society and politics,* ed. Virginia Hooker and Norani Othman, 236-68. Singapore: ISEAS.

Mandal, Sumit K. 1998. Bahasa Inggeris dan keperibadian nasional (English language and national matters). *Pemikir* 13: 59-86.

—. 2000. Reconsidering cultural globalization: The English language in Malaysia. *Third World Quarterly* 21, 6: 1001-12.

—. 2001. Boundaries and beyond: Whither the cultural bases of political community in Malaysia? In

The politics of multiculturalism: Pluralism and citizenship in Malaysia, Singapore, and Indonesia, ed. Robert W. Hefner, 141-64. Honolulu: University of Hawaii Press.

Marina Mahathir. 1997. *In liberal doses.* Singapore: Star Publications and Archipelago Press.

Martin, Michael T., ed. 1997. *Theory, practices, and transcontinental articulations.* Vol. 1 of *New Latin American cinema.* Detroit: Wayne State University Press.

Mauzy, Diane. 1993. Malaysia: Malay political hegemony and "coercive consociationalism." In *The politics of ethnic conflict regulation,* ed. John McGarry and Brendan O'Leary, 106-27. London: Routledge.

Maznah Mohamad. 1994. Poststructuralism, power and third world feminism. *Kajian Malaysia* 12, 1-2: 119-43.

Maznah Mohamad, and Wong Soak Koon, eds. 2001. *Risking Malaysia: Culture, politics, and identity.* Bangi, Selangor, Malaysia: UKM Press.

Milner, Anthony. 1994. *The invention of politics in colonial Malaya: Contesting nationalism and the expansion of the public sphere.* Cambridge: Cambridge University Press.

Mohammad A. Quayum. 2003. *Petals of hibiscus.* Petaling Jaya, Selangor, Malaysia: Pearson.

Mohd. Raman Daud. n.d. Isu Anwar: Adakah sejarah Tuah-Jebat berulang lagi? (Is the Tuah-Jebat history being repeated?) *Berita Reformasi.* http://www.geocities.com/Tokyo/Flats/3797/bm1022g.htm (link expired).

Mohd. Yuswan Awang. 1998. Penswastaan FINAS: Karyawan filem hilang hak? (The privatization of FINAS: Filmmakers lose rights?). *Massa,* 11 July, 12-17.

Mosher, Donald L., and Silvan S. Tomkins. 1988. Scripting the macho man: Hypermasculine socialization and enculturation. *Journal of Sex Research* 25: 60-84.

Mosse, George L. 1985. *Nationalism and sexuality: Middle-class morality and sexual norms in modern Europe.* Madison: University of Wisconsin Press.

—. 1996. *The image of man: The creation of modern masculinity.* New York: Oxford University Press.

Muhammad Haji Salleh. 1991. *Yang empunya cerita* (The mind of the Malay author). Kuala Lumpur: Dewan Bahasa dan Pustaka.

Nagata, Judith. 1986. The impact of the Islamic revival (dakwah) on the religious culture of Malaysia. In *Religion, values and development in southeast Asia,* ed. Bruce Matthews and Judith Nagata, 37-50. Singapore: ISEAS.

—. 1994. How to be Islamic without being an Islamic state: Contested models of development in Malaysia. In *Islam, globalization and postmodernity,* ed. Akbar Ahmed and Hastings Donnan, 63-90. London: Routledge.

—. 1997. Religious correctness and the place of Islam in Malaysia's economic politics. In *Culture and economy: The shaping of capitalism in eastern Asia,* ed. Timothy Brook and Hy V. Luong, 79-101. Ann Arbor: University of Michigan Press.

Naim Haji Ahmad. 1995. *Filem sebagai alat dan bahan kajian* (Film as a tool and object of research). Malaysia: Penerbit Universiti Pertanian Malaysia.

National Operations Council. 1969. *The May 13 tragedy: A report.* Kuala Lumpur, 9 October.

Nawawi, Zaharah. 1995. *Anugerah.* Kuala Lumpur: DBP.

Ng, Boon Hooi. 1999. Newspaper "ordered" to axe popular column. *Malaysiakini,* 8 December. Malaysiakini.com.

Ngugi, Wa Thiong'o. 1993. *Moving the centre: The struggle for cultural freedoms.* London: J. Currey; Portsmouth, NH: Heinemann.

Nor Faridah Abdul Manaf, and Mohammad A. Quayum. 2001. *Colonial to global: Malaysian women's writing in English 1940s-1990s.* Kuala Lumpur: International Islamic University Malaysia.

Norani Othman. 1997. *Shari'a and the citizenship rights of women in a modern nation-state: Grounding human rights arguments in non-western cultural terms.* IKMAS working paper 10. Bangi, Malaysia: Institute of Malaysian and International Studies.

Ong, Aihwa. 1987. *Spirits of resistance and capitalist discipline: Factory women in Malaysia.* Albany, New York: Suny University Press.

—. 1990. Japanese factories, Malay workers: Class and sexual metaphors in west Malaysia. In *Power and difference: Gender in island southeast Asia,* ed. Jane Monnig Atkinson and Shelly Errington, 385-422. Stanford: Stanford University Press.

—. 1995. State versus Islam: Malay families, women's bodies, and the body politic in Malaysia. In *Bewitching women, pious men: Gender and body politics in southeast Asia,* ed. Aihwa Ong and Michael Peletz, 159-94. Berkeley: University of California Press.

—. 1997. Chinese modernities: Narratives of nation and of capitalism. In *Ungrounded empires: The cultural politics of modern Chinese transnationalism,* ed. Aihwa Ong and Donald Nonini, 171-202. New York: Routledge.

Parker, William C. 1979. *Communication and the May 13th crisis: A psychocultural interpretation.* Kuala Lumpur: Penerbit Universiti Malaya.

Peletz, Michael. 1995. Neither reasonable nor responsible: Contrasting representations of masculinity in a Malay society. In *Bewitching women, pious men,* ed. Aihwa Ong and Michael Peletz, 76-123. Berkeley: University of California.

PKK. 1998. Barisan leaders should mind their words. *Harakah,* 26 October, English sec., 17.

Plato. 1989. *Symposium.* Trans. Alexander Nehamas and Paul Woodruff. Indianapolis and Cambridge: Hackett.

Rastam, Alina. 1995. Letting culture evolve naturally. *New Straits Times,* 4 November, sec. 2, 7.

Razha Rashid. 1990. Martial arts and the Malay superman. In *Emotions of culture: A Malay perspective,* ed. Wazir Jahan Karim, 64-95. Singapore: Oxford University Press.

Rehman Rashid. 1993. *A Malaysian journey.* Petaling Jaya: Rehman Rashid.

Rema Nambiar. 1995. Social ills. *Sun Megazine* (Malaysia), special issue, 28 December: 5-6.

Renan, Ernest. 1990. What is a nation? In *Nation and narration,* ed. Homi Bhabha, 8-22. New York: Routledge.

Rushdie, Salman. 1991. *Midnight's children.* New York: Penguin.

S., Bissme. 1999. Screen dreams. *The Sun Megazine* (Malaysia), 5 February, 28-30.

Saadawi, Nawal El. 1997. *The Nawal El Saadawi reader.* London: Zed Books.

Sabri Zain. 1998. Siapa betul – Aku ke Jebat? (Who's right – Me or Jebat?). *Reformasi Diary,* 15 September. www.reformasi.fsnet.co.uk/diary/jebat.htm/.

—. 2000a. *Face off: A Malaysian reformasi diary (1998-99).* Singapore: BigO Books.

—. 2000b. Questioning our feudal loyalty. *Asiaweek,* 3 November. http://www.asiaweek.com/asiaweek/magazine/2000/1103/cs.reform_malay.html

Salecl, Renata. 1994. *The spoils of freedom: Psychoanalysis and feminism after the fall of socialism.* New York: Routledge.

—. 1998. Do we still believe in authorities? Transcript of speech presented at UBC conference, The Role of the University, 26 October.

Salleh Ben Joned. 1994. *As I please: Selected writings 1975-1994.* London: Skoob.

—. 2002. *Sajak-sajak Saleh: Poems sacred and profane.* Kuala Lumpur: Silverfish Books.

—. 2003. *Nothing is sacred.* Petaling Jaya, Malaysia: Maya Press.

Samy Vellu meets Indian gangsters. 1997. *Southeast Asia Post* (Vancouver), 23 July-6 August, 6.

Sedgwick, Eve Kosofsky. 1985. *Between men: English literature and male homosocial desire.* New York: Columbia University Press.

Sen, Krishna. 1994. *Indonesian cinema: Framing the new order.* London: Zed Books.

Shaharuddin Maaruf. 1984. *Concept of a hero in Malay society.* Singapore: Eastern Universities P.

—. 1992. Some theoretical problems concerning tradition and modernization among the Malays of southeast Asia. In *Asian traditions and modernization: Perspectives from Singapore,* ed. Yong Mun Cheong, 241-65. Singapore: Times Academic Press.

Shahnon Ahmad. 1980. *The third notch and other stories.* Trans. Harry Aveling. Kuala Lumpur: Heinemann Educational.

—. 1995. *Tivi.* Kuala Lumpur: Dewan Bahasa Dan Pustaka.

—. 1999. *Shit.* Kubang Kerian, Kelantan: Pustaka Reka.

Shamsul Amri Baharuddin. 1995. Inventing certainties: The *dakwah* persona in Malaysia. In *The pursuit of certainty: Religious and cultural formulations*, ed. Wendy James, 112-33. London: Routledge.

—. 1997. Identity construction, nation formation, and Islamic revivalism in Malaysia. In *Islam in an era of nation states: Politics and religious renewal in Muslim southeast Asia,* ed. Robert W. Hefner and Patricia Horvatich, 207-27. Honolulu: University of Hawaii Press.

—. 1999. From orang kaya baru to Melayu baru: Cultural construction of the Malay "new rich." In *Culture and privilege in capitalist Asia*, ed. Michael Pinches, 86-110. London: Routledge.

Sharifah Maznah Syed Omar. 1993. *Myths and the Malay ruling class.* Singapore: Times Academic Press.

Sharifah Zaleha Syed Hassan. 2000. A fresh look at Islam and adat in Malay society. *Sari* 18: 23-32.

Shome, Anthony S.K. 2002. *Malay political leadership.* London: RoutledgeCurzon.

Sia, Andrew. 1996. Liberty or dignity? *The Star* (Malaysia), 29 November, sec. 2, 3.

Sloane, Patricia. 1999. *Islam, modernity and entrepreneurship among the Malays.* London: Macmillan; New York: St. Martin's Press.

Smith, Anthony D. 1991. *National identity.* Reno: University of Nevada Press.

Solanas, Fernando and Octavio Getino. 1970-71. Toward a third cinema. *Cinéaste* 4, 3: 1-10.

Soros, Erin. 1998. Mother may I: Specular embodiment excerpt. In *Views from the Edge – Six,* vol. 7, 3. Occasional working papers, 6th annual graduate student symposium in women's studies and gender relations, University of British Columbia.

Spores, John Clark 1988. *Running amok: An historical inquiry.* Ohio University Monograph in International Studies 82. Athens, OH: Ohio University Center for International Studies, Center for Southeast Asian Studies.

Stivens, Maila. 1992. Perspectives on gender: Problems in writing about women in Malaysia. In *Fragmented vision*, ed. Joel Kahn and Francis Loh Kok Wah, 202-24. Honolulu: University of Hawaii Press.

—. 1994. Gender and modernity in Malaysia. In *Modernity and identity: Asian illustrations*, ed. Alberto Gomes, 66-95. Bundoora, Australia: La Trobe University Press.

—. 1996. *Matriliny and modernity: Sexual politics and social change in rural Malaysia.* Victoria, Australia: Allen and Unwin.

—. 1998. Sex, gender and the making of the new Malay middle classes. In *Gender and power in affluent Asia*, ed. Krishna Sen and Maila Stivens, 87-126. New York: Routledge.

—. 2000. Becoming modern in Malaysia: Women at the end of the twentieth century. In *Women in Asia: Tradition, modernity and globalisation*, ed. Louise Edwards and Mina Roces, 16-38. St Leonards, NSW: Allen and Unwin.

—. 2002. The hope of the nation: Moral panics and the construction of teenagerhood in contemporary Malaysia. In *Coming of age in south and southeast Asia: Youth, courtship and sexuality*, ed. Lenore Manderson and Pranee Liamputtong, 188-206. Richmond, UK: Curzon.

Stivens, Maila, Cecilia Ng, Jomo K.S., and Jaharah Bee. 1994. *Malay peasant women and the land.* London: Atlantic Highlands; NJ: Zed Books.

Stothard, Sheryll. 2001. TAG SP 176:B5: Pengalaman seorang wiramarhaen yang bergaya. Forum KM2A1. Translated from English. Isham Rais: Adventures of a trendy rebel, Part 5. Malaysiakini. 20 June. http://lamankm2b.tripod.com/cgi-bin/m/KM2A1/4777.html.

Suh, Sangwon, and Arjuna Ranawana. 2000. A woman of grace. *Asiaweek online*, 25, 52. http://www.asiaweek.com/asiaweek/magazine/99/1231/year.azizah.html

Syed Ahmad Hussein. 2002. Muslim politics and the discourse on democracy. In *Democracy in Malaysia:*

Discourse and practices, ed. Francis Loh Kok Wah and Khoo Boo Teik, 74-107. Richmond, UK: Curzon.

Syed Alwi al-Hady. 1963. *Hang Tuah, atau, Pahlawan Melayu* (Hang Tuah, or, Malay Warrior). Singapore: Eastern Universities Press.

Tan, C.K. 2000. Reformasi: Berani sahaja tidak berguna (Reformasi: Courage alone is useless). *Detik Daily*, September. http://detik.daily.tripod.com/sept/b21septe.htm

Tan, Kevin Y.L., and Wan Meng Hao. 2002. *Scouting in Singapore 1910-2000*. Singapore: Singapore Scouts Association and National Archives of Singapore.

Tan, Stephen. 2002. Shooting from the hip: Amir Muhammad and his 6horts VCD. *BigO*. December. http://bigo.com.sg.

Teeuw, Andries, and David K. Wyatt. 1970. *Hikayat Patani, the story of Patani*. The Hague: Martinus Nijhoff.

Tham, Seong Chee. 1981. The politics of literary development in Malaysia. In *Essays on literature and society in southeast Asia: Political and sociological perspectives*, ed. Tham Seong Chee, 216-52. Singapore: Singapore University Press.

Thompson, Eric C. n.d. Unsettling absences: Place, migration, and urbanism in rural Malaysia. MS under review with Singapore University Press.

Toch, Hans. 1998. Hypermasculinity and prison violence. In *Masculinities and violence*, ed. Lee H. Bowker, 168-78. Thousand Oaks, CA: Sage.

Toh, S.B. 1998. Flushing and fleshing out absurdities. *The Star* (Malaysia), Weekender, 25 July, 3-5.

Ungku Maimunah Mohd. Tahir. 1994. Perceptions of the ideal Malay woman in the works of selected Malaysian women novelists. In *Gender and culture in literature and film east and west*, ed. Nitaya Masavisut, George Simson, and Larry E. Smith, 9-18. Honolulu, HI: University of Hawaii and the East-West Center.

Usman Awang. 1992. *Matinya Seorang Pahlawan, Jebat* (Death of a Warrior, Jebat). 1961; Kuala Lumpur: DBP, 1992.

U-Wei bin Haji Saari. 1995. Interview: Teller of tales. By Philip Cheah and Aruna Vasudev. *Cinemaya* 30: 14-17.

Van der Heide, William. 1996. Malaysian movies: The Shaw brothers meet the Pandava brothers in the land below the wind. In *Crossing cultures: Essays on literature and culture of the Asia-Pacific*, ed. Bruce Bennett, Jeff Doyle, and Satendra Nandan, 101-10. London: Skoob.

—. 2002. *Malaysian cinema, Asian film: Border crossings and national cultures*. Amsterdam: Amsterdam University Press.

Vickers, Adrian. 1997. "Malay identity": Modernity, invented tradition, and forms of knowledge. *RIMA* 31, 1: 173-211.

Wahab Hamzah, A. 1998. Cineplex mencambahkan budaya baru? (Cineplexes develop a new culture?). *Dewan Budaya* May: 28-29.

Wazir Jahan Karim. 1992. *Women and culture: Between Malay adat and Islam*. Boulder, CO: Westview.

Wee, Christopher Justin Wan-Ling. 1996. The "clash" of civilizations? Or an emerging "east Asian modernity"? *Sojourn* 11, 2: 211-30.

Wilkinson, R.J. 1959. *A Malay-English Dictionary*. London: Macmillan.

Willemen, Paul. 1989. The third cinema question: Notes and reflections. In *Questions of third cinema*, ed. Jim Pines and Paul Willemen, 1-29. London: BFI.

Winstedt, Richard O. 1961. *The Malays: A cultural history*. London: Routledge and Kegan Paul.

Winzeler, Robert L. 1995. *Latah in southeast Asia: The history and ethnography of a culture-bound syndrome*. Cambridge: Cambridge University Press.

Wira Md. Razak. 2003. Shorts and all. SuaraAnum.com (Voice of Youth). 1 January. http://www.freewebs.com/suaraanum/0101a03.htm/.

Wong, Soak Koon. 1996. Feminist literary criticism: Issues of positionality. *Tenggara* 38: 42-57.

Wood, Robin. 1990. Images and women. In *Issues in feminist film criticism*, ed. Patricia Erens, 337-52. Bloomington: Indiana University Press.

Wright Jr., Jerry W. 1997. Masculine allusion and the structure of satire in early 'Abbasid poetry. In *Homoeroticism in classical Arabic literature*, ed. Jerry W. Wright Jr. and Everett K. Rowson, 1-23. New York: Columbia University Press.

Yang, Mei-hui, Mayfair. 1997. Mass media and transnational subjectivity in Shanghai: Notes on (re)-cosmopolitanism in a Chinese metropolis. In *Ungrounded empires*, ed. Aihwa Ong and Donald Nonini, 287-319. New York: Routledge.

Yao, Souchou. 2000. Xiao Ye: Food, alterity and the pleasure of Chineseness in Malaysia. *New Formations* 40 (Spring): 64-79.

Yap, Brian. 2003. Bearing fruit in Singapore. *KLUE* 35 22 May-4 June. http://thebigdurian.tripod.com/media/klue.html/.

Yeap, Joo Kim. 1992. *Of comb, powder and rouge*. Singapore: Lee Teng Lay.

Yuval-Davis, Nira. 1997. *Gender and nation*. London: Sage.

Zaharom Nain. 1994. Commercialization and control in a "caring society": Malaysian media "towards 2020." *SOJOURN: Journal of Social Issues in Southeast Asia* 9, 2: 178-99.

Zawawi Ibrahim. 2003. The search for a "new cinema" in post-colonial Malaysia: The films of U-Wei bin Haji Saari as counter-narrations of national identity. *Inter-Asia Cultural Studies* 4, 1: 145-54.

Zhang, Yingjin. 1994. Ideology of the body in *Red Sorghum*: National allegory, national roots, and third cinema. In *Colonialism and nationalism in Asian cinema*, ed. Wimal Dissanayake, 30-41. Bloomington: Indiana University Press.

Index

Printed and bound in Canada by Friesens
Set in Minion, Meta, and Machine
Text design: Neil and Brenda West, BN Typographics West
Copy editor: Jacqueline Larson
Proofreader: Dianne Tiefensee